BIRTH *and*
the IRISH:
a miscellany

Salvador Ryan (ed.)

Word*well*

First published 2021
Wordwell Ltd
Unit 9
78 Furze Road
Sandyford Industrial Estate
Dublin 18
www.wordwellbooks.com

Vol. 3 in the series entitled: Birth, Marriage and Death Among the Irish.

ISBN: 978-1-913934-61-3 (Paperback)
ISBN: 978-1-913934-68-2 (Ebook)

British Library Cataloguing-in-Publication Data.
A catalogue record for this book is available from the British Library.

This publication has received support from the Scholastic Trust, St Patrick's College, Maynooth.

Typeset in Ireland by Wordwell Ltd

Copy-editor: Heidi Houlihan

Book design: Nick Maxwell

Cover design: Ger Garland

Printed by: SprintPrint, Dublin

BIRTH *and* *the* IRISH:
a miscellany

Contents

Acknowledgments

This is the third volume in the series Birth, Marriage and Death among the Irish. As in previous volumes, it covers a broad sweep of Irish history, in this instance from an entry in the Annals of Ulster from the year 657CE to the release of the report of the Mother and Baby Home Commission in early 2021.

I am often asked why I originally chose to publish the volumes in reverse order, beginning with death and ending with birth, and whether there was a special reason for doing so. Much as I would like to claim that it was part of a grand plan from the beginning, the truth is rather more mundane. The first volume, *Death and the Irish*, was originally conceived of as a stand-alone volume, and it was only towards the end of editing the collection – and when I discovered just how rich the contributions were – that I floated the idea of a series that would cover all three life events. I am very glad I did.

A work such as this incurs a number of debts. I am deeply grateful, first and foremost, to those who were enthused about the project from the outset; those who were willing to share the Call for Contributions across social media, and to spread the word to their colleagues, members of their research networks and their graduate students. I also greatly appreciated those who got in touch with me to propose individuals who should be invited to contribute, or who made suggestions regarding possible topics; the generosity of your responses has played an important part in making this book what it has turned out to be.

This volume could not exist without the contributors themselves. I wish to thank each person who has taken time out of their busy schedules to write a short article for the collection. The contributions might be short but, like small tiles in an impressive mosaic, each has played an invaluable part in creating what you are about to read. The enthusiasm conveyed in the contributors' responses has made my role as editor very easy indeed. While there is always a risk in naming individuals, when I mention 'enthusiasm', I cannot help but think of Clodagh Tait, who has been an enormous support to me over the last three volumes and who has authored a number of contributions in this collection. In fact, at one point, I was hearing from Clodagh every few weeks when she would propose yet another topic that she thought would be a good fit. And each one, in turn, was so interesting that I made sure it found a home here.

I would also like to specially acknowledge the important contribution that Georgina Laragy has made to the book. Over the past couple of years, as this volume was being prepared, the Commission of Inquiry into Mother and Baby Homes in Ireland was engaged in its work. It would publish its report on 12 January 2021. While I was very anxious that the topic be covered in the volume, I also wanted to wait until the report was published before asking someone to address the subject. I would like to thank Georgina sincerely for agreeing to write what has become the closing piece in this volume. It is a near impossible task to say something meaningful about a 3,000-page report in a couple of thousand words, and to do so in a meaningful way and with appropriate sensitivity. Not only that, but shortly after the first draft of the article was submitted, the report itself became an evolving news story and one which needed to be revisited by Georgina to take account of subsequent developments.

The accounts you will read in this book run the gamut of human experience over some 1,500 years. There are articles that will make you laugh; others will make you cry; others still will make you recoil in horror at what you have just read; more will simply render you silent, alone with your thoughts. There is humanity here, certainly, but also a great deal of inhumanity. There are parts of our past that we simply cannot allow to be forgotten. But there are also parts of our present that we need to attend to as a matter of priority so that future readers of similar collections will not have cause to shake their heads in dismay at how we have cared for those who are currently preparing to birth the next generation.

★★★★★★

I am grateful to all who have provided images for this volume, and to those who have given us permission to use these images. Every effort has been made to gain relevant copyright clearance.

Sincere thanks, too, to Ronan Colgan and his team at Wordwell, for seeing this volume through to print with their customary courtesy and efficiency.

Finally, my deepest thanks to my family, and my close friends, for their love, encouragement and support, and that listening ear, especially when it was needed most.

Since this volume went to press, I learned with great sadness of the death of campaigner, and widely revered custodian, of Traveller heritage, history and culture, Michael McDonagh who, with his wife, Nell, has been a contributor to previous volumes in this series. Even in the midst of illness, Michael had once again intended to contribute to the chapter on Pregnancy and Birth among the Travelling Community, but, sadly, was too unwell at the time of interview to proceed. I would like to dedicate this volume to his memory.

Salvador Ryan
Friday 30 July 2021

1

A 180-million-to-one Birth in 657AD?

Denis Casey

An *ócaire* (small farmer) in Laraghbryan, just outside modern Maynooth, got something more than he bargained for in 657AD. In late summer or early autumn the previous year, he brought a cow to a bull. A fairly standard procedure, but dangerous nonetheless, for neither bull nor owner was liable for injury done while cows were in heat. She was probably born in the same year as the Irish erroneously thought the Venerable Bede had been (654AD), and it might be said (somewhat unromantically) that the operation was a success. Nothing pointed to what was to come.

The Pregnancy

Now in her third year, and in-calf, the cow grazed in woodland or among the heather and furze of the uplands, and in the autumn fed on harvest stubble after the corn was cut high in the stem and the straw left standing. And the world continued to turn as normal. Life grew within her; it ebbed away from the king of Leinster. Winter came, and she grazed in the lowlands in an enclosed field set aside not far from the farmer's homestead – for, as Bede noted, the Irish did not save hay owing to the mildness of the climate and the availability of grass all year round. Her diet during the darker months was supplemented from the forest with fresh-cut holly and ivy. Meanwhile, the king of Connacht was chopped down and ascetic churchmen like Suibne of Iona and Ultán of Ardbraccan breathed their last, while a Merovingian child not much older than the cow, who would later become king Dagobert II of Austrasia (a kingdom covering parts of modern France, Belgium, the

I

Netherlands and Germany), was exiled to Ireland, perhaps to Slane in neighbouring County Meath.

657AD rolled around and then, as now, the excitement of *lulgachus Beltaine* (May calving) began. Birth is a moment fraught with danger. Mother and child are uniquely vulnerable, and early medieval Irish law recognised this in an oblique way for humans, stating that the oath of a woman – although normally invalid – was incontrovertible if given during childbirth. In imminent danger of death, and the damnation of her soul, should she swear falsely at that moment, her oath became more than simply valid – it could not be counter sworn. Our cow was mercifully free from such eschatological fears, but the farmer worried, nonetheless. So many worries. Both cow and calf could be lost at birth; the cow's protective instinct toward her calf could make her difficult and even dangerous for humans; she might even reject her calf, and if another cow could not be found to nurture it, he might as well take a knife to it, there and then. The 'value of the cow is in her calf' – if she would not nurse, she would not lactate, and her milk, which formed the primary source of most of the fat and protein in the medieval Irish diet, would dry up. If the cow refused to feed her calf, the owner's children starved.

The Birth

All this, and more, was running through the farmer's mind. But a bull calf saw the light and soon stood daintily on all fours like the smiling calf in the near-contemporary *Book of Durrow*, and the farmer breathed a sigh of relief. Perhaps he mumbled a prayer of thanks to St Luke, the evangelist portrayed in Irish gospel books as a winged calf. Or maybe he thanked the Virgin Mary, that 'ever-milking cow' as she was affectionately known. A healthy calf with its mother licking it too, and he could already see the streams of milk filling the pail.

> Oh milk, that best of foods – 'good when fresh, good
> when old, good when thick, good when thin'! Let
> the penitents drink their *ass cen chroith* (skimmed
> milk) for the good of their souls, there'll be good
> fresh milk for the porridge and cream for butter and

> sweet buttermilk for the drinking too, and we'll all be
> shrived as good as any of them when our time
> comes. But before then there'll be cheeses too!
> Delightful fresh curds and even the bitter whey won't
> go to waste. Oh, and we'll heat the fresh milk with a
> pat of butter and make sweet *milsén* and there'll be
> salted hard cheese to take us through the winter, and
> …

All the while he salivated, the cow strained and before long a twin was born. Not as much milk for the farmer's offspring now, perhaps, but two calves was a welcome sight. His *flaith* (lord) had already pledged the clients' firstlings, first-fruits and tithes to the church, in return for religious services, and it was up to the clients to redeem the pledge. And he mused that since this firstling was also a first fruit, might only the first calf of the year go to the church, and he keep the second one?

> Good enough they'd only get one; what would they
> do with it anyway but skin it to make vellum for a
> book before it was even weaned, and then draw
> pictures of calves on the dead calf like that fancy
> book in Durrow? And then they'll begrudge
> themselves the meat on the day of the first fast, or the
> day of the fast? Anyway, they'll have the first as is due,
> and me and mine will have the second, as is only
> right and proper.

He was a little premature in his doubling and halving and hedging. Even more than twos, the Irish loved things that came in threes; a third calf stood before the farmer. Twelve little hooves tapping unsteadily on the ground, and he could hear in the future two of the three sounds of increase: 'the lowing of a cow in milk' and 'the swish of a plough'. Every *ócaire* was expected to have an ox and the third calf might eventually draw a plough, or at least be offered as the bulk of next year's food rent to his *flaith*. Seemed a shame to castrate or kill calves from so prodigious a sire though, and he tried to remember which bull the cow had been brought to; the Donn Cúailnge (Brown Bull of Cooley) had been celebrated for less.

> But by St Luke, she's not finished yet – a fourth beast!
> Perhaps my days as an *ócaire* are drawing to a close?
> *Ferr fer a chiniud* (a man is better than his birth), as the
> law says, and an *ócaire* of sound husbandry can
> become a *bóaire* (strong farmer). Wouldn't that be
> swell! An honour price of five séts and the right to
> make a contract to that much, and half a plough
> team, and … and why stop there? With clients of my
> own I could become a 'man of withdrawal' and leave
> the peasant grades, and maybe not me or my boy, but
> a grandson could yet be an *aire déso* (lord of vassalry).

Whether they became vellum, or oxen, or breeding bulls, the quadruplets sired dreams for his own progeny to the third generation. But within a decade, our *ócaire* lay dead from a plague that ripped through Ireland, along with his dreams for his descendants – just so many more victims of the 'great mortality' of 664AD.

From Fame to Immortality

Even today, the chances of quadruplet calves all being born alive is 1 in 11 million and the chances of all being born alive and the same sex is 1 in 180 million. To be recorded in the vellum of the annals is a measure of fame, doubly so since they were then being written in Iona (now western Scotland). The quadruplets rightly achieved celebrity status, but all glory is fleeting and, if the calves of Laraghbryan became famous, then those of the monastery of Durrow, 70km due west, achieved immortality. Vellum has a curious property known as hygroscopy that makes it curl and flatten depending on humidity, and to the reader it seems that the calf is still lowing across the half-door of the centuries – a warning and an exhortation – *quod tu es, ego fui; quod ego sum, tu eris* (what you are, I was; what I am, you will be)!

Further Reading:

This piece was written as an imaginative reconstruction of the events surrounding the report from the year 657 in the *Annals of Ulster* that *Orta est uacca i lLathrugh Briuin que .iiii. uitulos peperit* (There was a cow in Láthair Briúin which gave birth to four calves).

Fergus Kelly, *A Guide to Early Irish Law* (Dublin, 1988).

Fergus Kelly, *Early Irish Farming: A Study based Mainly on the Law-Texts of the 7th and 8th Centuries AD* (Dublin, 1997).

Seán Mac Airt and Gearóid Mac Niocaill (eds and trans.), *The Annals of Ulster (to A.D. 1131). Part 1: Text and Translation* (Dublin, 1983).

Kuno Meyer (ed. and trans.), *The Triads of Ireland* (London, 1906).

Donnchadh Ó Corráin, 'Ireland *c.* 800: Aspects of Society', in Dáibhí Ó Cróinín (ed.), *A New History of Ireland 1: Prehistoric and Early Ireland* (Oxford, 2005), 549–608.

2

Bullaun Stones and Birthing Saints in Medieval Ireland

Meredith D. Cutrer

> For a mother is a venerable treasure, a mother is a
> goodly treasure, the mother of saints and bishops and
> righteous men, an increase of the Kingdom of
> Heaven, a propagation on earth.
>
> The Law of Adomnán (*c.* seventh century)

Giving birth to a saint in medieval Ireland was often a dramatic affair. In Irish hagiography, a Christian literary genre of sacred biography that was well established by the time the first Lives of Irish Saints were written in the seventh century, the birth of a saint was frequently accompanied by marvels intended to accentuate the saint's exceptional status from infancy. Hagiographical texts, usually called *Lives*, relate accounts of women pregnant with saints experiencing extraordinary signs marking their holy children's births, including miraculous visions, painless births, and angelic visitations.

While much of what hagiography narrates is fictitious, an attentive reader can glean some factual details from among otherwise embellished or invented episodes. Many Irish *Lives* were written hundreds of years after the deaths of their subjects. The *Life of Colmán*, which tells of Saint Colmán Elo (d. 611), abbot of Lynally, County Offaly, provides one such example where fact and fiction coalesce to construct a memorable birth tale. The *Life* assumes its audience's familiarity with what appears to be an actual medieval Irish birthing tradition wherein women in labour grasped a wooden pole that had been fixed firmly in the ground, presumably to assist mothers in giving birth in an upright position. Saint Colmán's birth, however, featured a remarkable twist. The dead wooden pole, which his mother clutched during delivery, came to life and grew into a magnificent tree that the author notes is still part of the landscape when he or she writes centuries later. The tree served as a miraculous testament to the child's sanctity. Such stories that invest the author's contemporary environment with sacral significance, rooted in Ireland's Christian past, are commonplace in medieval Irish hagiography, and the act of sacralisation is regularly mediated through women's bodies during childbirth. Through childbearing, women enjoyed an appreciable role in creating and shaping the sacred landscape of medieval Ireland.

Ireland's rich hagiographical tradition features numerous accounts of miraculous births that offer explanations for landmarks, both natural and constructed, that were contemporaneous with their medieval authors. Curiously, several of them centre on a mother giving birth on a rock, consequently imbuing it with curative or miraculous properties. Saint Fintán (d. 635), abbot of present-day Taghmon, County Wexford, was born in a house that had been built on a large rock. With time, the house disappeared, but due to Saint Fintán's birth, the rock had been granted an extraordinary attribute. After Saint Fintán had been delivered, snow never again fell on the rock, thus memorialising the sacrality of Saint Fintán's birthplace. His birth altered the landscape forever in popular memory.

Irish mothers delivering saints on rocks, and the resultant miracles, appear in several other medieval *Lives* in episodes that bear some striking similarities to each other. The *Life of Áed macc Bricc* recounts the many deeds and miracles of Saint Áed (d. 589), bishop of Killare, County Westmeath. Early in the narrative, the author relates that, after giving birth to him on a rock, Saint Áed's mother immediately laid him down on that same rock. As a sign of the infant's sanctity, the place where his head rested formed a permanent impression that was still present in the author's day many years later. The cavity left by Saint Áed's head collected rainwater which was believed to have curative properties. Consequently, Saint Áed's hagiographer notes that this stone became a place of pilgrimage for those medieval Irish Christians who needed healing.

In a similar vein, at least two *Lives* indicate that local communities incorporated the rocks on which a saint had been delivered into their church grounds. The *Life of Berach* relays that a church was built on the site of his birth, which included the rock upon which Saint Berach had been born as part of the church complex. Similarly, one version of the *Life of Saint Brigit* (d. 524) recalls how the saint's mother sat with one leg on each side of a rock in order to delay giving birth. In this account of her birth, Saint Brigit's mother delivered her on the rock, and Saint Brigit's head left a permanent impression on it just as it did in Saint Áed's birth story. Rather than being left in situ, as a site associated with healing, as was the case in the narrative of Saint Áed, Saint Brigit's rock was subsequently placed in the sanctuary of a church as an object of veneration.

Characteristics of Saint Berach, Saint Brigit and Saint Áed's births on rocks are combined in the *Life of Declán*. Saint Declán, a reputed early saint and bishop of Ardmore, County Waterford, likewise was delivered on a rock. Immediately, however, Saint Declán's head fell on the stone, which created a cavity in the shape of his head. The author of his *Life* affirmed that this impression was still to be seen at the time his *Life* was composed centuries later, and that the rock had become an object of veneration in the author's community. The rock, named 'the Rock of Declán', was located outside the entrance to the church. As a testament to Saint Declán's holiness, the rainwater collected in this rock's cavity, where Saint Declán's head had been, was believed to cure the diseases and pains of those who sought its healing powers. In the account of Saint Declán, the rock on which he was born was incorporated into the church grounds, as in the stories of Saint Berach and Saint Brigit, but it also became a focal point of healing for those in need, as in the case of Saint Áed's rock.

The motif of women giving birth to saints on rocks continued past the medieval period. The sixteenth-century *Life of Saint Colum Cille*, written in Irish by Manus O'Donnell concerning his ancestor and the founder of Iona, Saint Columba (d. 597), relates that the saint's mother, Eithne, received a vision of a resplendent youth the night before Saint Columba was born. This youth instructed her to go to Lough Akibbon to collect a sizeable, miraculously floating rock that was to be transported to the monastic site of Rath Cnó, County Donegal. Eithne was instructed to give birth to Saint Columba on this specially-designated rock, so she dutifully obeyed. At Saint Columba's delivery, the rock opened up to make room for the baby, leaving a cross-shaped cavity where he lay. This rock remained down through the centuries in Gartan, County Donegal, working miracles for faithful pilgrims. In a remarkable addition to the usual motif, this *Life* also indicates that, directly after giving birth to Saint Columba, Eithne then delivered a blood-red, wonder-working stone called *An Cloch Ruadh* (The Red Stone) which is also found at Gartan. The inclusion of this sacred stone motif in an early modern *Life*, and the rock's continued attraction for modern pilgrims, underscores Irish Christianity's enduring interest in the birth narratives of saints and how they have contributed to the shaping and sacralising of the landscape.

The consecration of a stone through childbirth is an unusual characteristic of Irish hagiography. Childbirth provided one of several explanations for the aetiology of bullaun stones, hollowed-out stones frequently found on early ecclesiastical sites, which feature regularly in later Irish pilgrimage sites and whose function has been the subject of debate. A number of medieval authors, primarily from the eighth to twelfth centuries, used a saint's birth on a rock to ascribe a sacred history to the large number of bullaun stones in the Irish landscape. In so doing, they offered their contemporary communities a tangible connection to a renowned holy figure who usually lived in the distant past.

Bullaun stones, created by a saint's birth, served as a physical reminder of the continual presence and power of a saint to heal long after his or her death. The use of a saint's birth narrative as an explanation for the presence of these stones places the saint's mother as a mediator of this drama, playing a pivotal role in sacralising an otherwise mundane object. These idiosyncratic accounts also reflect a deeper theological understanding of their authors and of the Irish Church. These saints were remembered primarily as founders of their local churches and were venerated as such. In a pivotal moment of the New Testament, Jesus affirmed to Saint Peter, '... upon this rock I will build My Church' (Mt 16:18). This image resonated with the medieval Irish authors. By narrating tales of the birth of their saints on rocks, which were often incorporated into ecclesiastical sites, hagiographers were situating their church founders within ancient Christian tradition and were emphasising the legitimacy of both their saints and the churches they established.

Acknowledgments:
This research was generously funded by the Irish Research Council.

Further Reading:

Charles Plummer (ed. and trans.), *Bethada Náem nÉrenn: Lives of Irish Saints*, Vols 1–2 (Oxford, 1922).

Kuno Meyer (ed. and trans.), *Cáin Adamnáin: An Old-Irish Treatise on the Law of Adamnan* (Oxford, 1905).

Brian Dolan, '"Mysterious Waifs of Time": Some Thoughts on the Functions of Irish Bullaun Stones', *The Journal of the Royal Society of Antiquaries of Ireland*, Vol.142/143 (2012–2013), 42–58.

Pádraig Ó Riain (ed. and trans.), *Four Offaly Saints* (Dublin, 2018).

Manus O'Donnell, *The Life of Colum Cille*, Brian Lacey (ed.) (Dublin, 1998).

Richard Sharpe, *Medieval Irish Saints' Lives* (Oxford, 1991).

Charles Plummer (ed.), *Vitae Sanctorum Hiberniae*, Vols 1–2 (Oxford, 1910).

W.W. Heist (ed.), *Vitae sanctorum Hiberniae ex codice olim Salmanticensi nunc Bruxellensi*. Subsidia Hagiographica 28 (Brussels, 1965).

3

Brigit, Goddess and Saint, and Birth Traditions

Jenny Butler

St Brigit (variously spelled Brigid, Bride, Bríd) is a Christianised Celtic goddess who was a member of the mythical people, the *Tuatha Dé Danann*, and many traditions connected with the saint likely have their provenance long before Christianity arrived in Ireland. It is claimed that the saint lived *c.* 439–524CE and that she was born in Faughart, near Dundalk in County Louth and died at the convent which she founded in Kildare. However, there is insufficient evidence to verify the particulars of the life of St Brigit of Kildare, and it seems the figure of the saint took on many aspects of the goddess that went before. This syncretisation is reflected in legends where pagan and Christian elements are combined, as well as the pre-Christian significance of the Christian shrines and holy wells associated with her. Hagiographies of Brigit include the medieval *Vita Prima Sanctae Brigitae* (*Life of Saint Brigit*) and Cogitosus's seventh-century Latin text, as well as the ninth-century Old Irish biography, *Bethu Brigte*.

Stories in these manuscripts about the saint contain many motifs concerning birth, including one telling of a druid named Maithghean hearing the noise of the chariot which was carrying Brigit's mother named Broicseach and his interpreting the noise to mean that Broicseach was carrying a marvellous baby in her womb. Another story tells of the birth of the saint herself in the druid's household at the very moment Broicseach was bringing milk into the house at sunrise, her liminal position being that she had one foot outside the threshold and the other foot 'neither without nor within'. Stories about St Brigit contain themes of fertility, birth and abundance, the latter especially in connection with milk.

The ninth-century text *Sanas Cormaic* (*Cormac's Glossary*) is attributed to the King-Bishop of Cashel and glossator, Cormac Mac Cuillenáin. In this text, Brigit is described as one of the three daughters of the Irish god, the Dagda. The pagan tripartite goddess symbolism extended into Christian stories about the saint where she is presented as one of three sisters of the same name, each with unique correspondences with poetry, healing and smithcraft. The latter association of metalworking by hand by the 'woman of smithcraft' which in Old Irish is *be ngoibnechtd*, is where the connection with the later medieval St Gobnait comes in, who is a possible manifestation of Brigit.

The strong link between the saint and the goddess is shown in the perseverance of motifs in legends of both the literary and oral tradition, as well as in the material heritage of her shrine in Kildare, where the saint is said to have founded her monastery. This place name comes from *Cill Dara*, meaning 'church of the oak-tree', and the oak is symbolically connected with druids and sacred enclosures in the Celtic tradition. Ancient inscriptions and place names connected to Brigit are widespread in the Irish landscape. Fire imagery abounds in legends about the saint, in particular the perpetual flame said to be kept lighting in her honour. Smithcraft, the above-mentioned attribute or ability connected with both goddess and saint, has obvious associations with fire.

Alongside and related to fire, the goddess is associated with the sun and brightness. Some scholars have described Brigit as a pan-Celtic deity and have suggested variants of names for her in different regions. For example, Brigantia was the tutelary or patron deity of the Brigantes, people who migrated from the Celtic continental areas to the north of England, and whose lineage settled in south-eastern Ireland. Several British rivers are thought to have been named for the goddess, including the Braint in Anglesea and the Brent in Middlesex. In eastern Gaul, modern-day France, the goddess Brigindo is also linked with the epithet *Sul* meaning 'sun'. Other variants of the goddess's name are Briga and Brigh, the latter found in early Irish sources.

Fire features in many miracles of the saint in the early Irish literature, and bonfires, embers and ashes are associated with fertility in popular customs recorded in early modern Ireland and Scotland; much is shared in the Gaelic traditions of both places. So strong is the popularity of

Brigit in Irish tradition that she is known as 'Mary of the Gael', being equated to the Virgin Mary as being the object of mass popular devotions. The saint's feast day falls on 1 February, which is the traditional start of spring and the pastoral year, and the pagan fertility festival of *Imbolc*, connected with new plant growth and animal fecundity. The name *Imbolc* or *Imbolg* may mean 'large bellied', in relation to parturition, and its Old Irish variant, *Oímelg*, means 'lactation', names that themselves reference pregnancy and birth. The figure of Brigit is a protectress of human and animal young. The 'plant of Bríd' is said to be the dandelion, as its milky juice is understood to nourish the lambs in the fields and is one of the first wildflowers to bloom following *Imbolc*.

Eight of the miracles of Brigit recorded by Cogitosus have to do with the agricultural fertility of farm animals and dairy produce, and the magical protection of these is linked to her in miracles of increasing food, multiplying butter or milk, or possessing a larder where supplies never dwindle. Symbolism of fertility and birth infuse the traditions surrounding the saint and her feast day. On the last day of January, it was the custom in some parts of Ireland to create a 'Brigit's Bed' out of rushes or birch twigs, often a large basket placed by the fire which represented a place for the saint to come in and rest as she traversed the countryside. In popular tradition, the saint infuses the land with her blessing on the eve of her feast. In southwestern Ireland on the feast day itself, an effigy made of straw called a *Brídeóg* was placed in the basket and brought door to door and householders were asked to give something, particularly milk, butter and eggs, for the 'biddy' (diminutive name of Brigit) to be eaten at a party, referred to in some places as a 'Biddy Ball' and held in the evening.

There is also a custom of leaving a piece of cloth called a *brat Bhríde* (Brigit's mantle) outdoors from sunset to sunrise on the eve of the feast in the belief that the saint would touch or bless it as she passed by. This cloth, when placed on the head of a young animal like a foal or calf, would ensure the animal's mother would suckle it, which connects the saint once again with babies and lactation. It was used as a charm to ensure a good supply of milk especially for calves, lambs and foals. Indeed, the *brat Bhríde* was held to cure infertility in humans and to help and safeguard women in childbirth.

There is also a connection with the practice of midwifery, and in Scottish popular tradition, particularly in the Hebrides, St Brigit is the midwife to the Virgin Mary. The role of midwife may have an older symbolic connection to the mother-goddess's role as one who brings forth life. St Brigit is associated more generally with the maintenance of good health of the family and homestead. The creation of St Brigit's crosses ties in with this aspect, the cross being hung above the door inside the house and placed by farmers in the byre as a protective charm to ward off spirits, as well as to protect the properties from fire and lightning. These symbolic associations that are combined in Brigit – goddess and saint – of regenerative and life-giving powers, of healing and abundance, as well as with the literal birth process and lactation, make her a key figure in the popular traditions of birth in Ireland.

Further Reading:

Kevin Danaher, *The Year in Ireland: Irish Calendar Customs* (Dublin and Cork, 1972).

Lisa Lawrence, 'Pagan Imagery in the Early Lives of Brigit: A Transformation from Goddess to Saint?', *Proceedings of the Harvard Celtic Colloquium*, 16/17 (1996/1997), 39–54.

Séamas Ó Catháin, 'Hearth-Prayers and Other Traditions of Brigit: Celtic Goddess and Holy Woman', *The Journal of the Royal Society of Antiquaries of Ireland*, 122 (1992), 12–34.

4

Ruina Maxima: Shameful Birth in Early Irish Religious Communities

Elaine Pereira Farrell

The concept of honour was central to the social and legal structures of early Irish society, as it was to other medieval societies. If the honour of an individual and, consequently, of his or her family was offended, an honour-price payment had to be made (*eDIL s.v. díre*). The bearing of children, overall, is portrayed in early Irish primary sources as an honour, a right and an obligation. A fragmentary vernacular legal text, dating from the seventh century, suggests that if a husband intentionally refused to fulfil his duty of procreating with his spouse, it was grounds for divorce, for the retention of the bride-price by his wife (*eDIL s.v. 1 coibche*), and for the payment of additional chattels. Likewise, another vernacular text, and a Hiberno-Latin canon law text, indicates that infertility was equally grounds for divorce.

However, within religious communities, this logic could be reversed and conception turned into the cause of social disgrace for an individual, and potentially for his/her partner. The earliest Irish document that attests to this is the *Penitential of Finnian*. Finnian was most certainly a British ecclesiastic active in Ireland, and his cult was spread in Ireland and Scotland (Finnian of Clonard, d. 549, Annals of Ulster; Finnian of Moville, d. 579, Annals of Ulster; Ninian of Whithorn). He wrote a short book on penance, indicating different sins that could be committed by religious and secular people, and prescribes the necessary actions for them to achieve redemption. Finnian's text was the primary source for two other penitential texts, one written by Columbanus and another by Cummean the Long (d. 662, Annals of Ulster). These two latter texts, in their turn, became sources for a very productive field of penitential literature, both in the insular and the continental worlds.

Within the continental penitential literature, we are presented with the possibility of a man, who in the past had wives and children, becoming an ecclesiastic. In this case, it was expected that he would forthwith live a celibate life by not having intercourse with his former spouse, and very importantly, not having her conceive additional children. Despite this expectation, this literature foresees clerics returning to having sex with their former wives, fornicating with a virgin or committing adultery with another married woman. Equally, they also allow for the possibility of women who have taken religious vows also engaging in sexual activity. Thus, different penances were assigned to them, and sometimes, also to their partners. Depending on what each penitential author deemed to be a serious fault, the length of the penance could increase, including its level of hardship.

Finnian's penitential warned his audience that if a clergyman had sex, it represented ruin for him. However, he presents a variety of levels for this offence. If it was a single event, it was a lesser offence than if the couple had been meeting regularly. If this situation did not become public knowledge to the community, it was less grave. A greater ruin (*ruina maxima*), therefore, would be brought about by a pregnancy. If the sexual partner of a clergyman became pregnant and gave birth, and this became known to their community, it was very serious. It could only be worsened by his killing of his own child. This dual offence of having sex and producing a child, followed by the crime of murder, would cost the cleric the loss of his office and exile from his community for seven years (canons 10–12).

A few canons further on, Finnian turns his attention to female sinners. He rules against a woman using any form of 'magic' to destroy a child she has conceived, and in this case, her penance would last for four and half years in total. Yet, if she otherwise gave birth to the child and permitted her sin to become publicly known, she should do penance for six years. After that period, she could be restored to the altar and proclaimed a virgin, indicating here that the canon is dealing with the possibility of a religious woman committing these offences (canons 20–21). It is interesting to note that the length of penance as regards the number of years would be equal for both the male and female sinner, and by the seventh year, both could be restored to the altar, to their roles and, most importantly, to their community.

These are very dramatic scenarios, and we might question why pregnancy was considered such a great ruin and what would motivate a religious person to kill his/her own offspring in this context. It is intriguing that the fact of allowing a pregnancy to become socially known, incontrovertibly proving that sexual relations had taken place, is considered worse in penitential texts than the crime of committing abortion or infanticide, ultimately classified as a crime of murder.

To understand this, we must consider what chastity represented to these communities. To be a celibate is what set this group of people apart. Ascetical practice and the renunciation of pleasures, be it in the form of sex or food consumption, was what, from the theological point of view, made this group of people spiritually elevated and closer to God. Their sacrifices made their prayers stronger than those of lay people given to bodily pleasures. It was their sanctity that made them capable of operating miracles. These attributes, and powers, are what justified their existence as a social group, made them distinct, and attracted followers and devotees to them.

By ruining their chastity, they were in danger of losing their credibility, status, honour and charisma before the eyes of the lay community who not only relied on their prayers, but also acted as their patrons, or as their lay dependants, depending on their own social status and relationship with the religious community. This is the fear underlying the penitential canons. It is very clear from the Penitential of Finnian that he is confident that sinners would, through repentance and penance, achieve mercy and remission of sins from God. He seems, otherwise, to be more concerned with the worldly implications of the sins that could be committed within his community. To predict and legislate against potential sins was, on the one hand, to prescribe a remedy to cure the soul of the sinner and, on the other, to define mechanisms of accountability towards the community itself. In the case of a clergyman who was exiled, it was considered necessary to isolate him from the community to purify himself elsewhere. This was not only a way of setting an example that might dissuade others from falling into the same temptation, but it was also a means of providing justice to the community that was offended and had its honour stained.

It is important to note that religious people were neither allowed nor obliged to make financial payments to restore the honour of others; in this it was different from the secular context. If, for example, a clergyman had sex with the wife of another man, or a virgin daughter of someone, the family offended would not receive financial retribution as would happen otherwise if the perpetrator was a layman. For that reason, the religious community would need to enforce alternative punishments, such as exile, to demonstrate that they were seriously handling the offence to the social order. Considering that clerics, as opposed to monks and religious women, would usually have greater access to and immersion in the lay community by providing pastoral care, it was even more pertinent to isolate them, than a vowed woman, for a lengthy period.

If we now consider the former wives of clergymen, their situation was very precarious, as they lost their right to oblige their husbands to conceive children with them. By joining the religious ranks, their husbands obtained the right and duty of avoiding their beds. As divorce was not accepted in the penitential literature, and a wife should not be dismissed, these women became bound to the relevant religious community which their husbands had decided to join and, consequently, had their rights restricted. It was even more aggravating for their situation if they flouted the rule of celibacy and conceived children. What, in another context, would have been an honour became a disgrace, and the wife suffered the pressure of either aborting her pregnancy, knowing her husband had murdered her newly born child, or suffering the consequences of raising a child that would, for a lifetime, be a reminder of shame.

Further Reading:

Finnian (sixth century), 'Penitential of Finnian', in Ludwig Bieler (ed.), *The Irish Penitentials with an Appendix by D.A. Binchy* (Dublin, 1975).

Zubin Mistry, 'The Sexual Shame of the Chaste: "Abortion Miracles" in Early Medieval Saints' Lives', *Gender & History*, 25:3 (November 2013), 607–20.

Elaine Pereira Farrell, 'The Penitential of Columbanus: Reception and the Shaping of Christian identity', in Conor Newman, Mark Stansbury and Emmet Marron (eds) *Columbanus and Identity in Early Medieval Europe* (Presses Universitaires de Rennes, in press).

Elaine Pereira Farrell, 'Taboos and Penitence: Christian Conversion and Popular religion in Early Christian Ireland' (PhD thesis, University College Dublin, 2012).

5

Gerald of Wales on Birth and the Irish, the Geraldines, and the Marvels and Monsters of Ireland

Diarmuid Scully

Gerald of Wales (*c.* 1146–1223) wrote the first version of his *Topographia Hibernica* or *Topography of Ireland* in 1187. It was the first full-length book written by a foreigner about Ireland, its natural world, marvels and miracles, and its indigenous people, the Gaelic Irish. Gerald also wrote the first history of the later twelfth-century English invasion of Ireland: the *Expugnatio Hibernica* or *Conquest of Ireland* (1189). He makes his own extended Cambro-Norman family, the Geraldines of South Wales, the heroes of this work. He is proud of their high birth: they are the descendants of the Welsh princess Nesta and the Norman lord Gerald of Windsor.

Gerald has much to say about birth and begetting in his Irish narratives. He writes about the begetting and birth of men and women, birds and animals, human-animal hybrids, and God himself in the person of the incarnate Jesus Christ. These reports are linked by an interest in the wondrous, strange and fateful. Gerald's alternative titles for the *Topographia* and *Expugnatio* are instructive: the *Marvels of Ireland* and the *Prophetic History*.

Ideas about geographical location, and related political and cultural assumptions and imperatives, shape Gerald's treatment of birth in relation to Ireland. Ancient and medieval geographers situated the human race within an *orbis terrarum* or circle of lands stretching westwards from India and Sri Lanka to Ireland. In these exceptionally remote places, almost 'other worlds' at the ends of the Earth, nature produced wonders. The *Topography* depicts Nature playfully occupying herself with aberrations in a hidden Ireland. Gerald says that the marvels of the East are famous;

it is his task to publicise the marvels of the West.

The time was right: conquest had opened up the 'the furthest island of the West'. Gerald dedicates the *Topography* to King Henry II of England (1183–1189), the first English king to add 'the Irish world' to his titles and triumphs. Gerald hails him as 'our Western Alexander'. This was an elegant compliment: in imagined memory, Alexander the Great (356–323 BC) had conquered India and introduced the extraordinary wonders of the East to the wider world.

One of the *Topography*'s most influential stories about the marvels of the West concerns the conception and birth of barnacle geese. They 'first appear as excrescences on fir-logs', gradually acquire feathers and then slip into the water or fly into the air. 'No eggs are laid as is usual as a result of mating. No bird ever sits upon eggs to hatch them and in no corner of the land will you see them breeding or building nests.' Gerald's story featured in later medieval bestiaries and narratives linking the wonders of East and West, including the hugely popular Sir John Mandeville's *Travels*. But his story had intentions beyond entertainment or instruction in natural history (as the bestiaries recognised and repeated). Its essential purpose is to attack the 'obstinate will' of Jews who, to their own destruction, deny Christ's virgin birth, 'in which alone is salvation, that is, from a woman without the cooperation of a man'. Gerald directly addresses the 'unhappy Jew': 'At least consider the evidence of nature. She daily produces and brings forth new creatures without cooperation of any male or female for our instruction and in confirmation of the Faith'.

As Christian Europe expanded, embarked on Crusade and more sharply defined itself against 'the Other', increasing antisemitism in Anglo-Norman England and other powerful kingdoms was matched by growing hostility towards perceived false or backsliding Christians in peripheral lands targeted for colonisation. Gerald was instrumental in promoting the English conquest of Ireland as a civilising mission to remote, stubborn barbarians who were either nominally Christian or actual 'pagans'. To emphasise wilful Irish rejection of Christianity, the *Topography* highlights their neglectful behaviour, violence and deviant sexual practices. It uses stories about conception and birth to indict them.

Gerald contrasts Ireland's natural goodness with the wretched behaviour of the Irish. Located far away from the heat and poisons of the East, the island has a temperate climate and fertile soil supporting a uniquely healthy population. 'No indigenous person born here, who has never left its healthy land and air, ever suffers from any of the three kinds of fevers'. Once, this natural beneficence was universal, but 'as the world began to ... slip into the decrepitude of old age ... the nature of almost all things became corrupted and changed for the worst'. Gerald alludes to traditions about the Ages of the World and the Ages of Man. In its natural goodness, Ireland is a microcosm of the newly created Earth: Eden before the Fall in the infancy and first Age of the World. The rest of Earth, in its sixth and final Age, is troubled by the weaknesses of the very old: little wonder that its inhabitants are often sick.

The physical appearance and natural gifts of the Irish testify to nature's generosity in Ireland. Gerald says that 'when they are born, they are not carefully nursed as is usual. For apart from the nourishment with which they are sustained by their hard parents, they are for the most part abandoned to nature'. Yet this barbarous neglect does not harm them. 'As if to prove what she [Nature] can do by herself she continually shapes and moulds, until she finally forms and finishes them in their full strength with beautiful upright bodies and handsome and well-complexioned faces'. But, paradoxically, Gerald has 'never seen among any other people so many blind by birth, so many lame, so many maimed in body, and so many suffering from some natural defect.' This too is the work of nature and 'seems a just punishment from God'; 'it is not surprising if nature sometimes produces such beings contrary to her ordinary laws when dealing with a people that is adulterous, incestuous, unlawfully conceived and born, outside the law, and shamefully abusing nature herself in spiteful and horrible practices'.

Discussing his own birth in the autobiographical *De Rebus a Se Gestis* (c. 1204), Gerald emphasises that his parents were lawfully married and that he and his brothers were lawfully born. Contrast the Irish in the *Topography*. The natural world itself announces their sexual and other crimes. Wolves in Ireland generally have their young in December: 'a symbol of the evils of treachery and plunder which blossom there before their season'. At the time of Prince John's mission to Ireland (1185), many ravens and owls had their young in December too. 'Perhaps they foretold the occurrence of some new and premature evil'. And new evil appears in sexual form in Ireland: 'Only novelty pleases now … Natural love is outworn.' Gerald makes this statement when claiming that a goat at the court of 'Rothericus, king of Connacht … had bestial intercourse with a certain woman to whom he was entrusted'. His purpose is to discredit Ruaidrí Ua Conchobair (*c.* 1116–1198), whom he identifies as the leader of Irish resistance to English rule. What true Christian king would tolerate such sinfulness?

Gerald twists the knife in a nearby chapter where he describes bestiality as 'a particular vice of that [the Irish] people'. At the time when his uncle Maurice FitzGerald was given Wicklow and its castle (1174), 'an extraordinary man was seen – if indeed it be right to call him a man. He had all the parts of the human body except the extremities which were those of an ox'. This man-ox attended dinner at Maurice's court until the indigenous Irish secretly killed him 'in envy and malice – a fate which he did not deserve', because the colonial 'youths of the castle often taunted them with begetting such beings on cows'. A perverse human variation on Nature causing secret aberrations in hidden places, the characteristic barbarian vice of treachery and the wanderers' envy of the settled (Gerald claims that the Irish reject agriculture and urbanism) all feature in this anecdote.

The hospitality and sympathy of the Cambro-Norman Maurice and his nephew Gerald to the Irish man-ox are implicitly contrasted with the Irishmen's conduct toward him. In the *Expugnatio*, Gerald enlarges on the Geraldines' civilised values and decency. Allied to their military prowess, these attributes make them supremely fit to rule Ireland on behalf of the English Crown.

Gerald quotes Virgil's *Aeneid* on his kinsmen's Roman-like qualities. He chose his author well. Virgil presents the Romans as descendants of the Trojan Aeneas, destined to achieve limitless rule across time and space. Because of their Welsh birth-right, Gerald's kinsmen were also the descendants of Aeneas, via Brutus, the mythical founder of Britain. He derived this belief from Geoffrey of Monmouth's *Historia Regum Britanniae* or *History of the Kings of Britain* (1130s). Gerald believed that it was their destiny to extend Trojan-British power to the furthest land west, to Ireland. And the Geraldines' Norman birth-right counted for him too. Gerald gives this speech to Robert FitzStephen, the first of his kindred to land in Ireland: 'In part we come of Trojan stock by direct line of descent. But we are also partly descended from the men of Gaul [Normans], and in part take our character from them. From the former we get our courage, from the latter our skill in the use of arms'.

The *Expugnatio* is indeed a prophetic history. When FitzStephen landed in Ireland and fought with courage and skill, writes Gerald, 'the celebrated prophesy of Merlin Sylvester was clearly fulfilled: *A knight, sprung of two different peoples, will be the first to break through the walls of Ireland by force of arms'*. But prophesy of another kind may be heard in the words that Gerald gives to Maurice FitzGerald, besieged in Dublin by the forces of Ruaidrí Ua Conchobair and the Men of the Isles. Maurice tells his men not to expect English support when the Irish attack them: 'just as we are English as far as the Irish are concerned, likewise to the English we are Irish, and the inhabitants of this island and the other assail us with an equal degree of hatred'. Another birth is foretold here: a nation in Ireland neither English nor Irish, but caught between both.

Further Reading:

Robert Bartlett, *Gerald of Wales. 1146–1223* (Oxford, 1982).

John O'Meara (trans.), *Gerald of Wales: The History and Topography of Ireland* (Penguin Classics, 1982).

A.B. Scott and F.X. Martin (ed. and trans.), *Expugnatio Hibernica: The Conquest of Ireland by Giraldus Cambrensis* (Dublin, 1978).

Nicholas Vincent, 'Angevin Ireland' in Brendan Smith (ed.), *The Cambridge History of Ireland. Volume 1: 600–1500* (Cambridge, 2018), 185–221.

6

Some Colourful Depictions of Birth from the Lays of Fionn Mac Cumhaill

Síle Ní Mhurchú

Hunting, feasting, raiding and fighting are typical activities associated with Fionn mac Cumhaill and his band of men, the Fianna. Women are rather marginal in this world but the literature and lore of Fionn, or the Finn Cycle as scholars call it, does contain some colourful birth scenes. This article presents a selection of these from the Fionn lays (narrative poems about the Fianna).

The lay beginning *A Lía Thulcha Tuaithe shuas* (O stone above on Tulach Thuaithe), dated to the second half of the twelfth century, relates events from the boyhood of Mac Lughach (also known as Gaoine), one of the warriors of the Fianna. His first show of strength is performed even before his mother recovers from labour:

> An úair tainic a hinbaidh
> is ro dhealaigh re a troimiodhnoibh
> rug sí mac ba caoime bladh
> díar comainm Gaíne glégheal
>
> Tainic fo tri tar a bél
> is amlaidh ro-chúala in sgél
> istig ag triall a bhíadhtha
> in eas alainn aimríadhta
>
> Gabhais in eas 'na laim laích
> mór an obair meic bhig bháith
> an eass ina laim ro lean
> no gur eirigh an inghean

> Gidh bé do innisfeadh thall
> eidir sloghaibh na sáorchlann
> iss é sin gan táidhe amach
> ceidgnimh laimhe mic Lughach

When her time had come, and her heavy pangs had left her, she bore a son of fairest fame whose name was bright Gaoine.

Thrice there came across his mouth – so have I heard the tale – seeking to be fed within, a beautiful untamed weasel.

He seized the weasel in his hero hand (it was great work for a little tender boy): the weasel remained in his hand till the girl arose.

It matters not who should tell it, there amid the freeborn hosts: that, without concealment ..., is the first deed of Mac Lughach's hand.

Stories of early displays of physical prowess are also found in the boyhood deeds of Fionn himself.

Bran and Sgeólang are Fionn's loyal hounds. In the lay beginning *Cairdius Logha ré droing don Fhéin* (The kinship of Lugh and a portion of the Fian), dated to *c.* 1300, we learn that their human mother, Uirne, was transformed by a jealous rival into a dog during her pregnancy as were the twins she was carrying:

> Naisgis Fionn flaith na gcuradh
> Tuirn le deaghtríath Uladh
> ro bhoí ag in righ go rath
> go ttarla táobhtrom torrach.
>
> Bean do bhoi roimpe ag in rígh
> ingean Buidhph ba mór a brigh
> a riocht con ba mor in sgél
> ro chuir sí Uirne aithbhél.

> Assaighthear in rioghan réidh
> i ttigh Feargusa fhinnleith
> go rug sí ba cáomh in clann
> Bran ar áon & Sgeólang.

Fionn, the prince of heroes, bound Tuirn [Uirne] to the good lord of Ulster: she lived with that prosperous king and so became heavy and with child.

The king had a wife before her, the very powerful daughter of Bodhbh: she cast Uirne Sharpmouth into the shape of a hound (a great tale to tell).

The gentle queen is delivered (?) in Fearghus Finnliath's house: she bore both Bran and Sgeólang, a lovely offspring.

Uirne is later made human again, but another account of the birth of Bran and Sgeólang explains that because they were not struck by the wand that transformed their mother, they must remain in their canine form.

The boundary between the animal and the human is ill-defined in the world of the Fianna, something which is illustrated again by an account of the birth of Fionn's son, Oisín, as recounted in the eighteenth-century lay 'Seanchus agus Oileamhain Oisín mhic Fhinn' (The Lore and Rearing of Oisín son of Fionn). Fionn is filled with desire for a hind who later gives birth to a human son:

> Ar fhéachain na haghaidhe ar a háille,
> ghlac áilgheas fir é, mar ba ghnách,
> scéal scannalach le n-insin,
> go ndearnaidh Fionn dhi ionad mná.
>
> ... do rug sí mise an ionad laoigh
> a measg na ccraobh is na ccrann.

> When he saw the beauty of her face, carnal desire, as
> usual, overcame him, a scandalous tale to tell, Fionn
> used her as a woman.

> She bore me instead of a deer-calf among the branches
> and trees.

Oisín drinks the deer's milk and he is raised in the wild, staying apart from human society until he is a grown man.

Another late lay contains what is possibly the strangest birth scene in all of the Finn Cycle. The example is 'Laoi Chab an Dosáin' (The Lay of Cab an Dosáin)[1] in which the hot-headed Conán mac Mórna is punished for his lecherous behaviour during a night spent in an enchanted fortress. The woman Conán is pestering for sex takes on the man's role and states that he will give birth to a child before the night is out. He describes the onset of labour as follows:

> Creidim gur fíor do ráite, a bhean,
> óir tá tosach na bhfáscaí [ag] teacht orm anois,
> mo dhá leathmhás, mo dhá dhubhán,
> mo bhléin tinn is mo dhá leis.

> I believe there is truth in your words, woman,
> for I feel the onset of the pains now,
> my two buttocks, my two kidneys,
> my sore groin and my two thighs.

Conán calls upon Diarmuid Ó Duibhne, another warrior of the Fianna, who is also in the fortress, to act as a midwife to him:

> Ó, a Dhiarmuid mura bhfaighe me fóirint,
> titfidh an tóin as an bhfear maol.

---

[1] The excerpts from 'Laoi Chab an Dosáin' are taken from British Library Egerton 208. I have modernised the spelling and made some silent editorial changes.

> Oh, Diarmuid, if I am not given relief,
> the bottom will fall out of the bald man [Conán
> himself].

The narrator of the lay, Oisín, describes the chaotic scene as Diarmuid pulls Conán's offspring out with a rope:

> Ní chuala riamh torc muice allta
> ag dul chun báis ba mhó scréach
> ná Conán maol ag gairm na ngártha
> is Diarmuid láidir ag tarraingt na téide.

> I never heard a wild boar
> in the throes of death scream more
> than bald Conán calling and shouting
> and Diarmuid pulling the rope.

Cab an Dosáin, the owner of the fortress, and its other inhabitants, rush to greet the new arrival, but all is not as might be expected:

> Ansiúd a d'éirigh Cab an Dosáin
> is an t-iomlán dá raibh san gCéis
> agus fuair siad Diarmuid is an corda cnáibe
> [ag] tarraingt sián Chonáin as a bhfréamh.

> It was then that Cab an Dosáin got up
> and all those who were in Kesh
> and they found Diarmuid with the hemp rope
> pulling Conán's testicles from their roots.

The women of the fortress insist on treating Conán as if he has actually given birth:

> Ó tháinig sé chugainn ar cuairt
> is go rug sé san dúnso mac,
> ní cóir dhúinne a léigint uainn
> gan crios glas uaithne agus brat

> Since he visited us
> and gave birth to a son in this fortress,
> we ought not let him leave us
> without a green girdle and cloak.

Seosamh Watson explains that these garments were believed to protect women and newly-born infants from fairy abduction. It is interesting that this most burlesque of scenes gives us a glimpse of a real postpartum custom.

Further Reading:

Gerard Murphy (ed.), *Duanaire Finn: the Book of the Lays of Fionn*, Parts II and III. Irish Texts Society, vols 28 and 43 (London and Dublin, 1933 and 1953).

Máirtín Ó Briain, 'Oisín's Biography: Conception and Birth', in H.L.C. Tristram (ed.) *Text und Zeittiefe* (Tübingen, 1994), 455–86.

Máirtín Ó Briain, 'The Conception and Death of Fionn Mac Cumhaill's Canine Cousin', in A. Ahlqvist *et al.* (eds) *Celtica Helsingiensia: Proceedings from a Symposium on Celtic Studies* (Helsinki, 1996), 179–202.

Seosamh Watson, 'Laoi Chab an Dosáin: Background to a Late Ossianic ballad', *Eighteenth-Century Ireland/Iris an Dá Chultúr* 5 (1990), 37–44.

7

Togail Bruidne Da Derga: Seeding Fate in Conception and Birth

Chelsey Collins

Togail Bruidne Da Derga (*The Destruction of Da Derga's Hostel*) asks, perhaps more than any other medieval Irish saga, whether we choose our own fate, or whether we are inescapably born into it. After recounting the origins and rise to kingship of Conaire Mór, *Togail Bruidne Da Derga* escalates as Conaire is overwhelmed by traitorous foster-kin and monstrous enemies until he loses both life and kingship in the raid on Da Derga's hostel. Interpretations of the story have differed with regard to Conaire's accountability for his own destruction, with many focusing on the point at which, if at all, Conaire makes his first error. Tomás Ó Cathasaigh, for instance, has questioned whether Conaire should be considered 'an innocent victim of fate' or 'the architect of his own tragic end'. Though others have located the turning point of the story in Conaire's false judgement, sparing his foster-brothers (who later betray him), Ó Cathasaigh places his mistake long before, when Conaire first refuses to address their minor thefts and thus creates an environment in which their crimes grow more serious. More recently, Amy Eichorn-Mulligan has placed Conaire's error even earlier, when Conaire is raised with foster-brothers of inappropriate status. She argues that this fosterage later causes Conaire to ignore the boundaries between them (as his subjects) and himself by the time he pronounces the disastrous judgment as king. Yet, could Conaire's fate have been shaped long before any of these events?

The elegance of *Togail Bruidne Da Derga* is that each tragic event is already set up by the event preceding it. This skilled sequencing is perhaps why it has been possible to find multiple causes for Conaire's downfall, because there may be no *single* tipping point. To answer the larger question of whether Conaire is a victim of fate or his own mistakes, it is useful to follow the trail backwards, taking advantage of the full structure of the story rather than just later consequences. Not only are we provided with a description of Conaire's birth and conception, but also those of his mother, his grandmother and his great-grandmother – a multigenerational breakdown before the current story even begins.

Working backwards from where Eichorn-Mulligan left off, Conaire's fosterage is already filled with disfunction. As she points out, he is fostered inappropriately with those of unequal status, the sons of plunderers, though Eichorn-Mulligan does not investigate the cause of this situation. Although fosterage is an institution regularly employed to secure ties with social equals, Conaire's mother, Mess Búachalla, determines that she and the lowly herdsmen who fostered her will share in the fosterage of Conaire, a king's presumed son; by having his mother's childhood abandonment cause a status imbalance with Conaire's own fosterage, the medieval author hints at how issues of birth can accumulate from one generation to the next. Similarly, her son is named matrilineally after her, Conaire mac Mess Búachalla, rather than for a father. Both of these details invite comparison to texts dealing with illegitimate offspring. In both *Aided Oenfir Aífe* and *Cath Maige Tuired*, sons with ineligible foreign fathers are referred to by their mother's name (and raised by her family). Similarly, in *Immathchor nAilella ocus Airt*, the disputed paternity of two children forces the mother to foster them by herself. Conaire is thus coded in the story in the same way as an illegitimate child, as is his mother. These details leave us to assume already that Conaire has no father who can entitle him to name and fosterage, just as Mess Búachalla has no father or appropriate kin with which to foster Conaire.

Conaire's origins are complicated by his claim to dual paternity, on the one hand through an otherworldly father who sleeps with his mother, and on the other through his assumed father, the king Eterscele, who marries his mother around the same time. Scholars have disputed which should be considered his 'true' father within the story, but Thomas Charles-Edwards has shown convincingly how his complimentary paternities work to place him on the throne even as they work to end his kingship and life through their contradictory obligations. That this uncertainty of fathers is deliberate, rather than a riddle challenging us to recognise one or other father as the true one, is also supported in Conaire's name and fosterage coming from his mother, the only certain parent. Conaire's conception, both of uncertain paternity and ensuing choices of his mother, already sets him up for inappropriate fosterage and its consequences – though both are only made possible by his own mother's origins.

Mess Búachalla is herself an uncertain product of her own father, and her complicated unions are made possible after being twice abandoned by him. Her mother, Étaine, is barren and is only able to conceive a single daughter through the intervention of her mother (and a certain mysterious bowl of porridge), after which Cormac abandons both wife and the daughter. To explain the abandonment, we can return to *Immathchor nAilella ocus Airt* for a very similar scenario, where Ailill's wife conceives twins of unclear paternity, causing Ailill to abandon both children and wife (and then be sued for his share of the fosterage costs). Similarities between the two stories suggest that Cormac may have doubted his role in the conception, opening Mess Búachalla's parentage to similar ambiguity as that of her son. This uncertainty could be why, when Cormac eventually takes his wife back, he still orders 'her' daughter to be killed, leading to Mess Búachalla's second abandonment as his servants mercifully hide her away with Eterscele's herdsmen and have her fostered there. Her abandonment there, and subsequent isolation, result directly in her sexual union with Conaire's otherworldly father, who pronounces Conaire's fate of kingship immediately at conception. At the same time, her ambiguous origin is the *specific* reason cited for Eterscele marrying her, as he too pursues a prophecy in which he must marry a woman lacking origins to conceive a kingly son – a condition which she is able to fulfil by events already set up in her own birth. Even the reason her mother, the younger Étaine, was unable to conceive normally – and even then only able to conceive a girl – is planted in Étaine's own parentage.

Her father Echu and mother the elder Étaine represent the ideal union in *Togail Bruidne Da Derga*, and thus the only unambiguous paternity and maternity of the entire multi-generational sequence. In the same way that the standard of Étaine's perfect beauty contrasts with the increasingly malformed and monstrous characters to follow, so too does the idealised marriage contrast with the fragmenting and uncertain relationships to follow. Even in their initial meeting and flirtation, where they decide to be together, Étaine and Echu take the time to exchange a bride-price and formalise an equal marriage contract. If we compare the birth of Mess Búachalla who, as mentioned above, was abandoned by her father only to be rejected upon his return, to Conaire's birth within one recognised human marriage and one illicit otherworldly visitation, we can see that both present a stark contrast to the simplicity and security of the penultimate union from which they all originate – that of Echu and the elder Étaine. By making their marriage legal, the author ensures that the only ambiguity introduced at this point is Étaine's otherworldly origin, as she is from the *síd* of Brí Léith; and though this does not affect her marriage, her origins clearly affect their offspring and descendants, as they become entrapped in the ensuing prophecy and obligation from her origins.

By combining origins from Ireland and the *síd*, the couple sow the seeds of contradictory worldly and otherworldly obligations for younger Étaine, for Mess Búachalla, and eventually for Conaire – with younger Étaine obligated to bear a son by Cormac but a daughter by her mother's prophecy, Mess Búachalla to bear a kingly son to a human and otherworldly man in the same birth, and Conaire himself to exist and rule constrained by both. By gradually tinging the conceptions within Conaire's lineage with illegality, uncertainty and otherworldly interference, the author cleverly prefigures the issues that will plague – and eventually end – Conaire's life and rule. As to whether Conaire's destruction arrives through his fate or his choices, the value of the story is the combination of both into an inescapable momentum, with Conaire trying to choose correctly between opposing obligations set in motion by his birth and seeded long before it.

Further Reading:

Tomás Ó Cathasaigh, 'Gat and Díberg in Togail Bruidne Da Derga', in Anders Ahlqvist *et al.* (eds), *Commentationes Humanarum Litterarum*

CVII: Celtica Helsingiensia. Proceedings from a Symposium on Celtic Studies (Helsinki, 1996), 203–13.

Thomas M. Charles-Edwards, 'Geis, Prophecy, Omen, and Oath', *Celtica* 23 (1999), 38–59.

Amy C. Eichhorn-Mulligan, 'Togail Bruidne Da Derga and the Politics of Anatomy', *Cambrian Medieval Celtic Studies*, 49 (2005), 1–19.

Ralph O'Connor, *The Destruction of Da Derga's Hostel: Kingship and Narrative Artistry in a Mediaeval Irish Saga* (Oxford, 2013).

8

Pregnancy Cravings in Medieval Ireland

Niamh Wycherley

Trí aithgine in domain: brú mná, uth bó, ness gobann
(Three regenerators of the world: a woman's womb, a
cow's udder, a smith's furnace.)

                    – Old-Irish Triad

Given the lack of modern comforts such as electricity, running hot water and online prenatal yoga classes, we might be forgiven for thinking that the experience of pregnancy in medieval Ireland was dark and scary. The archaeological evidence certainly indicates that lives were often short and brutal, and that childbirth was a particularly dangerous time for women. The early Irish laws and other written sources, however, present a somewhat rosier picture of a more ideal society, in which pregnant women are afforded special care and attention.

One intriguing area for comparison with the modern experience is the acknowledgement in a number of medieval Irish texts, some as early as the seventh or eighth century, that a pregnant woman had specific food cravings and nutritional needs, medically known as 'pica' (a nutritional deficiency or pregnancy food craving). These Irish law texts refer to this as *mír méin* (the longed-for morsel) of the expectant mother. The later legal commentary on a law text called *Bretha Éitgid* (a tract on accidental injury and death) makes interesting comments on pica which offer us insight into the care of pregnant people in early medieval Ireland. The commentary discusses at length how a woman is protected under Irish law. She has reduced legal responsibility for theft of food to satisfy a craving. It is an offence for a man to deny his wife her craving during pregnancy and an offence for the woman to be silent about her craving. Even slaves and servants were protected by the law during pregnancy according to another legal tract on distraint, *Cethairslicht Athgabalae*. It stipulates that a man was expected to provide compensation if he impregnated a slave or servant, rendering her incapacitated for work, for a month before and after birth. The legal provision here rightly prompted one modern scholar to comment that this was a medieval maternity leave of sorts.

A desire for ale during pregnancy is also noted in the law texts. A comment on *Bretha Éitgid* notes that this craving could be prompted by the smell of malt, while another law text tells a tall tale about a baby leaping in the womb at the whiff of ale and not giving up until the woman received a draught. The notion that beer was of benefit to the weak and convalescing is one which persevered into the modern era. In more recent times in Ireland, before the potential detrimental effects of alcohol consumption on a foetus were fully realised, stout was regularly prescribed by doctors during pregnancy as a fortifying tonic.

Pregnancy cravings also make a cameo in the tenth century *Life of St Patrick*. Like all hagiography (literary accounts of saint's lives and deeds), the aim of the story is to demonstrate the virtue and intercessory miraculous power of the saint. We also gain a small insight, however, into the experience of pregnancy in medieval Ireland. In this text, Patrick is credited with turning *lúachair* (rushes) into *foltchép* (chives) in order to satisfy a pregnant woman who claimed that she and her baby would die without this specific plant. Today, chives are recognised as a nutrient-dense food. Many pregnancy books and nutritionists promote the addition of chives into the diet as an added source of a whole host of important vitamins and minerals during pregnancy, including vitamin K, vitamin C, and folate (the natural form of the manufactured supplement folic acid).

Lest we be lured into the notion that women in medieval Ireland were receiving foot massages from adoring lovers, I must be clear that the care afforded pregnant women was neither universal nor selfless. The Irish laws were concerned with paternity and inheritance. There was even provision for a woman to become legally impregnated by another man if her husband was infertile, in order to give him a son and heir.

The intent in these texts was to protect pregnant women from malnutrition but also to protect the unborn child from neglect. Legal commentary on both *Cethairslicht Athgabalae* and *Bretha Éitgid* state that a man could be fined for withholding longed-for foods from a pregnant woman. These texts distinguish between whether the harm was intentional or unintentional and inferences are made about the potential mortal danger to both the child and the mother in the case of not satisfying these cravings. This, perhaps, offers us a small insight into the precarious nature of pregnancy in medieval Ireland. Malnutrition was not the only concern; undernutrition and extreme neglect, to the point of starvation, may have been suffered by some women.

It is difficult to know the extent to which these laws reflect the reality of life in medieval Ireland. They do, however, at a minimum, reflect the ideals and culture of the society and show an understanding within legal circles that pregnant women had distinct needs which should, in theory at least, be recognised. We must appreciate the overall context of early Irish law when interpreting the significance of care during pregnancy. Early Irish law-texts portray a hierarchical and patriarchal society and a legal system which was concerned with rank, status, liability and compensation. This highly sophisticated and elaborate system was in force from at least the seventh century, and perhaps many centuries earlier. It is sometimes referred to as 'Brehon Law', but this term is not appropriate for use until the later Middle Ages and the early modern period, when the term was used to define so-called native Irish law, in contrast to English or Common Law, which was introduced from the twelfth century onwards. In light of concerns in early Irish law over liability and culpability, the preoccupation with the health of the mother is perhaps better understood as concern for the offspring of the father and his extended kin. In a case where a foetus is harmed by depriving the mother, seven times more compensation was due to the father's extended family than to the mother's.

It is perhaps unsurprising that nutritional deficiencies during pregnancy were a concern in medieval Ireland. The famous twelfth century texts on women's medicine, the Trotula, acknowledged the seriousness of pica, prescribing beans cooked in sugar for the pregnant woman who desired clay, chalk or coals. Osteoarchaeological analysis of bones at medieval sites such as Ballyhanna, County Donegal and Portmuck, County Antrim revealed the extent of the physiological stresses endured, caused by a variety of factors including a deficiency in vitamins and minerals and cultural practices during pregnancy and breastfeeding. Even today, despite the easy availability of iron and nutrient rich foodstuffs, many modern Irish women are prescribed iron supplements, for example, during pregnancy.

An issue which binds many women over centuries and continents is the biological privilege, or impediment (depending on your perspective), of the unremitting reproductive cycle. This does not affect all women in the same way. The fundamental physiological processes of conception and pregnancy, however, have not drastically changed over time in Ireland, even allowing for modern medical advancements such as IVF and a significant reduction in maternal and infant fatality. It is for this reason that an exploration of pregnancy in medieval Ireland can be particularly grounding and poignant. A woman pregnant in Ireland today may share in some of the experiences of pregnancy of her medieval forebears, albeit without the hot water, electricity and online yoga!

Further Reading:

Brónagh Ní Chonaill, 'Child-centred Law in Medieval Ireland', in R. Davis and T. Dunne (eds), *The Empty Throne: Childhood and the Crisis of Modernity* (Cambridge, 2008), 1–31.

Fergus Kelly, *Guide to Early Irish Law* (Dublin, 1988).

Donnchadh Ó Corráin, 'Early Medieval Law, *c.* 700–1200', in A. Bourke *et al.* (eds), *The Field Day Anthology of Irish Writing, vol. IV: Irish Women's Writing and Traditions* (Cork, 2002), 6–44.

9

Women's Medicine in Late Medieval Ireland: The *Trotula* Texts

Sharon Arbuthnot

In and around Salerno, in southern Italy, in the twelfth century, texts on conception, pregnancy, childbirth and various other medical and cosmetic issues, primarily of relevance to women, were being composed and compiled. Three of these, each with its own style and focus, were brought together in a single compendium now generally referred to as the *Trotula*. This title recalls the fact that, even in early manuscript witnesses, one of the texts, *De curis mulierum* (On Treatments for Women), attributes sections of the learning contained in it to a woman called Trota. Today, it is generally thought that the reference to Trota acknowledges a Salernitan woman of that name who is known to have contributed to gynaecological medicine and medical writing in the relevant period. That a woman was directly involved in the writing of any part of the *Trotula* itself seems unlikely and, indeed, is never claimed in the text.

Composed originally in Latin, the *Trotula* collection was popular throughout Europe in the twelfth to fifteenth centuries, being translated, adapted and supplemented in vernacular languages which included Hebrew, French, German, Italian, English, Dutch and Irish. Interestingly, some of the vernacular versions of the *Trotula* were clearly aimed at women: several explicitly address a female audience and one English translation encourages women to pass on the knowledge that they have gleaned from the *Trotula* to others who cannot read.

The extant Irish versions of *Trotula* material seem to have been made in the mid-fourteenth century. They survive in two fifteenth-century manuscripts. Parts were published by Winifred Wulff in 1934, but Wulff's editions were not accompanied by translations into English and have only a very rudimentary glossary of terms. Unsurprisingly, then, although the extracts preserved in these manuscripts are of considerable linguistic and cultural interest, the contents of the Irish *Trotula* are not well-known.

When considering what these extracts tell us about the understanding and practice of gynaecology and related matters in Ireland in the fourteenth century and after, it is important always to bear in mind that these texts are translations and adaptations of material which was composed elsewhere – rather than being primarily products of an Irish cultural milieu. There are intriguing inclusions here, nevertheless. For example, a passage on methods to forestall pregnancy is retained. In what seems to be a symbolic transferral of seed, women are advised to place grains of spurge or barley inside the afterbirth of an animal, one grain for every year that they wish to remain protected against pregnancy. This is the kind of advice that might be conveyed directly to the women who had most to gain from it (rather than to medical professionals) and, where the corresponding passage in the standardised Latin text makes use of the third person singular, the Irish version sometimes has phrases containing second person singular forms, such as *mad ail leat in toirrces do tairmesg*, (if *you* wish to prevent pregnancy).

The above suggestion on how to prevent pregnancy is typical of one strand of the material that makes up the *Trotula*. Here, charms and rituals coexist with herbal recipes, logic-based diagnosis and pragmatic solutions to the complications that can arise in the course of conception, pregnancy and childbirth. Listed amongst the possible causes of early miscarriage are horse-riding, falling and jumping. The intervention of a midwife is recommended to turn manually a malpresented foetus. It is recognised that difficulty in conceiving can be owing to fertility issues with either the male or female partner. On the other hand, one of the suggested methods for expelling a dead foetus involves the consumption of a portion of butter or cheese which has been inscribed with the five-word Latin palindrome *sator arepo tenet opera rotas*. Known from so-called 'sator squares', the earliest of which was found in the ruins of Pompeii, this formula was probably not meant to be meaningful and was widely used in the West to invoke protection and cure. Conception, meanwhile, is said in the *Trotula* to be achieved by roasting the testicles of suckling pigs and grinding these into a powder for drinking.

As an alternative to roasting pigs' testicles, the Irish *Trotula* suggests that a child might be conceived by drying and pulverising the reproductive organs of a female hare and consuming these in a drink. Presumably, suckling pigs and hares were relatively easily obtained in Ireland in the Middle Ages should a couple choose to pursue one of these suggestions, but the *Trotula* also alludes to plants, spices and fruits that are not native to the country. Pomegranates can be used to treat swollen legs in the advanced stages of pregnancy. Abdominal swelling can be relieved with a concoction containing cloves and cardamom, amongst other things. Pleasant-smelling substances such as aloe wood can be placed at the genitals to attract the womb, causing it to move downwards in preparation for birth.

It is not entirely clear to what extent Irish people, even those of a certain status, would have had access to such exotic items in the fourteenth century. The texts certainly suggest that the Irish language did not have the vocabulary to deal with them. To denote cardamom and aloe wood, the Latin terms *cartomomum* and *lignum aloes* are simply embedded into the Irish text. When quinces are called for, a longer statement acknowledges more fully the borrowed word and incorporates a spelling of the Latin term which suggests that it may have been heard rather than read: *na h-ubla re n-abar sitonia* (the apples that are called *Cydonia*). The Irish phrase used to mean 'pomegranate', *uball gráinneach*, is a word-for-word translation of Latin *pōmum grānātum* (seeded apple) and never occurs outside medieval Irish medical texts that derive ultimately from Latin.

Given that some of the recipes and remedies mentioned in the *Trotula* rely on natural produce which is not native to Ireland, and given that even the names of certain substances do not seem to have been familiar to those who made the Irish versions, it is likely that some of these treatments were never actually used in Ireland. Nestled alongside the obvious calques and alien-looking Latin borrowings, however, are rare but seemingly genuine Irish terms of relevance to women's medicine. Curiously, a number of these differ from the well-established names for the parts of the body or processes in question. The phrase *fuil místa* (monthly blood), for example, is known from Old Irish onwards as a way of referring to menstruation. Twice, however, the phrase *bláth banda* (womanly bloom), from *bláth* meaning 'flower, blossom', appears in the Irish *Trotula*. The first instance is in a section of text which explains that this is how menstruation is referred to in common language. Similarly, although the placenta or afterbirth is generally known in late medieval Irish medical texts as *slánugad*, the *Trotula* texts employ the term *brat boinne* on no less than four occasions. *Brat boinne* seems to be comprised of *brat* (a cloak; a covering) and an otherwise-unattested noun related to the adjective *boinenn* (female). There is another probable example in a late eleventh- or twelfth-century comic tale entitled *Aislinge Meic Con Glinne* (The Dream of Mac Con Glinne) which had entirely perplexed scholars before the connection was made with the gynaecological phrase.

The Irish *Trotula* texts seem, then, to offer glimpses into a language for discussing gynaecological matters which existed alongside the terms commonly used by medical professionals. It is tempting to think that phrases such as *bláth banda* and *brat boinne* really do represent a less formal register in use amongst the general populace of late medieval Ireland and that these phrases were deliberately selected to ensure that the advice and remedies contained in these texts would be accessed and accepted, especially by the women who might benefit from them and the midwives who might apply them. In time, we may learn more about the people who made the Irish versions of this compendium on women's medicine and about those who read and used them. The first steps in that direction would be to explore further the language of these neglected texts, which ranges from transparent native terms to incongruous borrowings, and to probe their eclectic content, in which mysterious charms and exotic spices are bundled together with simple, practical tips – including the recommendation that, to kickstart the process of birth, carers should induce a fit of sneezing!

Further Reading:

Monica H. Green (ed. and trans.), *The 'Trotula': A Medieval Compendium of Women's Medicine* (Philadelphia, 2001).

Monica H. Green, 'A Handlist of the Latin and Vernacular Manuscripts of the So-Called *Trotula* Texts. Part 2: The Vernacular Translations and Latin Re-Writings', *Scriptorium* 51 (1997), 80–104.

Monica H. Green, 'Women's Medical Practice and Health Care in Medieval Europe', *Signs* 14, 2 (1989), 434–74.

Winifred Wulff, 'A Mediaeval Handbook of Gynaecology and Midwifery', in J. Fraser, P. Grosjean and J.G. O'Keeffe (eds), *Irish Texts*, fasciculus V (London, 1934), i–xxvii, 1–99.

10

Pleading the Belly?
Pregnant Behind Bars in Medieval Ireland

Yvonne Seale

Not all pregnancies are times of peace or excited anticipation – and some are even more chaotic than most. This was certainly the case for a woman called Isabella who, in early fourteenth-century Carlow, found herself pregnant and on trial for her life. This was a time and place marked by conflict, with the Gaelic Irish engaged in ongoing guerrilla warfare and raids against the Anglo-Norman colonists, but also of social interaction between the two groups. While we know almost nothing about Isabella, the brief records relating to her trial show something of what it would have been like to experience pregnancy in a borderland region during the Middle Ages.

On 30 December 1311, two brothers, William and Tayg Octouthy (or Occothy), appeared before the justiciar John Wogan at a judicial session in Carlow. They were charged with a serious crime: the murder of a local man, Geoffrey Le Lang, and the theft of his three heifers, thirteen cows and forty sheep. A jury of eleven (one juror failed to show up) found William and Tayg guilty and declared them to be 'common robbers'. Tayg's property was forfeit; William apparently owned nothing worth seizing. The brothers were then sentenced to hang.

William and Tayg were not the only members of the family to appear before the justiciar at that session. So too did three of their female relations, all on charges related to Le Lang's murder. Baloch Occothy was found guilty of giving shelter to the brothers and was fined forty pence, which was a substantial amount of money at the time. (Just how Baloch was related to William and Tayg is unclear.)

The two other Octouthy women present that day were not as

fortunate as Baloch. Fynyna, their mother, was accused not only of having provided shelter to William and Tayg, but of having had 'art and part in their robberies knowing that they were evil men' – in other words, that she was an accessory to her sons' crimes. A jury of twelve sentenced Fynyna to death by hanging. Meanwhile, unnamed witnesses accused their sister Isabella of having given food and drink to her brothers, and of having 'talked with them, knowing them to be felons'. Although her actions seem to have been no more serious than Baloch's had been, Isabella was sentenced to death.

However, Isabella's fate was to be slightly different from that of her mother Fynyna. The trial record recounts that Isabella was married to 'Thomas de Valle, an Englishman' and that she was 'pregnant of a living child'. Because of her condition, Isabella was to be sent back to jail, where she was to remain until she gave birth to her child. Only then would she hang.

This was not a unique ruling. The long-standing practice of 'pleading the belly' granted at least a temporary stay of execution to women who were (or who claimed to be) pregnant. It was not intended to be a mercy towards the woman, but rather a law in favour of the child. Yet in order for this plea to be put into effect, a woman's pregnant body had to be the focus of particular scrutiny.

From the twelfth century onwards in areas where English common law held sway – as was the case in colonial Carlow – a jury of matrons (*matronae honestae*) was put in charge of assessing whether a convicted woman was indeed pregnant. (The last known use of such a jury in Ireland occurred during a murder trial in Mayo in the early 1840s.) These juries might examine a woman's abdomen or inspect the size of her breasts for the swelling or tenderness which might indicate pregnancy. If the jury of matrons reported that the woman was pregnant with a 'quick' or 'living' foetus – that is, one developed enough for its movements to be detectable – a stay of execution would automatically be granted.

There is no mention in the surviving record of the names of the women who might have been called on to examine Isabella. However, we do know the names of the men on the jury who pronounced her ultimate fate. Intriguingly, three of them – William, Henry, and John – bore the surname de Valle. Were they relatives by marriage of Isabella's?

The de Valle family were minor aristocratic landowners in the Barrow valley, having held a knight's fee in Ardristran from the late 1240s. Might they have pushed for even a temporary reprieve for Isabella with the aim of saving her child, and perhaps mitigating any lingering bad feeling between the de Valles and the Octouthys? Or might bad familial feeling have soured them against agitating for greater leniency? After all, the de Valles were from a colonial background, whereas Isabella was at least partly of Gaelic Irish descent.

We do not know the ending of Isabella's story. The documentary record from medieval Ireland is fragmentary, and even at the time, no one might have thought the final fate of one woman and her child important enough to record. We are left only with questions.

What might Isabella have felt, losing three members of her family in such a short period of time? What must it have been like to anticipate your child's birth and know that it would also seal your own fate? Did Isabella even survive pregnancy and childbirth? Many medieval women did not, even when giving birth in far more pleasant surroundings than a jail, because of pre-eclampsia or postpartum bleeding or sepsis. Medieval women's fear of such misfortune underpinned widespread popular devotion to St Anne, mother of Mary, and to St Margaret of Antioch, both of whose intercession was believed to be particularly helpful for pregnant women. Did Isabella's child survive? Child mortality rates in the pre-modern world were high. A document of 1349 mentions a John and a David, both sons of a Thomas, and members of the extended de Valle family in Carlow. Might one of them have been Isabella's child?

Did Isabella succeed in securing a pardon? Sometimes pregnant women who 'pleaded the belly' and received a stay of execution were later pardoned, though this was uncommon A study of late medieval English legal records undertaken by the historian Sara Butler found that only about 11 percent of cases of 'pleading the belly' ultimately resulted in a pardon. Was it more likely that Isabella was forced to hand over her newborn and make the last, terrible walk to the gallows?

We can answer none of these questions. But the very act of asking them reminds us of all the complex ways in which pregnancy and childbirth intersected with the legal and social structures of later medieval Ireland.

Sources:

The account of Isabella's trial is in the *Calendar of the Justiciary rolls, or, Proceedings in the Court of the Justiciar of Ireland*, vol. 3, 228–31.

Information about the de Valle family is to be found in *Calendar of Ormond Deeds, Vol. 1, 1172-1350* and *Knights' Fees in Counties Wexford, Carlow and Kilkenny, 13th–15th Century*, 66–9.

For Sara Butler's study, see Sara M. Butler, 'Pleading the Belly: A Sparing Plea? Pregnant Convicts and the Courts in Medieval England', in Sara M. Butler and Krista J. Kesselring (eds), *Crossing Borders: Boundaries and the Margins in Medieval and Early Modern Britain* (Leiden, 2018), 131–53.

11

Childbirth, Christening and Churching in Medieval Ireland

Colmán Ó Clabaigh, OSB

As it emerged into the world of Late Antiquity, the Christian Church absorbed many powerful misogynistic attitudes that influenced its perception of sexually mature, pregnant and parturient women. Eve, the first woman, was held culpable for humanity's expulsion from paradise and the pangs of childbirth to which her daughters were heirs were regarded as punishment for her disobedience. Taboos surrounding blood and the effluvia of birth-giving were particularly potent. A text in Trinity College Dublin, MS 667, a late medieval mendicant codex from North Munster, maintained that menstrual blood caused grass to wither, prevented seeds from germinating, induced rabies in dogs and corroded iron and bronze. These reprehensible views echoed across Europe from the Classical period onwards and found expression in numerous preachers' manuals and confessors' handbooks. The *Rationale* of William Durandus (d. 1296), the most influential medieval liturgical commentary, expressed reservations about bringing the bodies of women who had died in childbirth into church lest it be defiled by seepage from their corpses.

There was another, more positive, side to this: the process of childbirth and the period surrounding it was 'women's space' from which men and male authority were excluded. Ideally, as a woman entered labour, she was surrounded by female relatives and friends in the birthing chamber who encouraged her, reciting prayers and charms, singing songs and incantations and creating a mesmeric atmosphere that assisted the birthing process. Talismans and amulets could also play an important role. The magnetic qualities of lodestone and amber, for instance, meant that they were used to 'draw out' the child, and so in 1478, when Dean John Collyn of Waterford bequeathed his lodestone ring to the cathedral there, it may have been for use by women in travail. Likewise, coral, jet and pearls were regarded as beneficial in alleviating birth pangs and staunching post-partum haemorrhage. These materials were often used in *paternoster* beads, brooches and jewellery carried or worn by pregnant women and a number of examples survive from medieval Ireland. The healing and apotropaic properties of such gemstones were listed in medieval encyclopaedias and texts known as lapidaries, many of which circulated in medieval Ireland. A fifteenth-century copy of the *Liber de Lapidibus* of Marbodus of Rennes (d. 1123) survives from the Dominican priory in Limerick and a number of Latin lapidary texts were translated into Irish.

The use of 'birthing girdles' with which the expectant mother was bound and which were released incrementally as labour proceeded was common. Often these belonged to matrons who had successfully given birth and were applied in the hope that their experience would somehow transfer to the woman giving birth. Sometimes birthing girdles consisted of parchment strips or amulets inscribed with prayers and invocations and wrapped around the woman's body. Although none survive from Ireland, the text used for one such amulet has recently been tentatively identified in the *Liber Flavus Fergusiorum*.[1] The most efficacious were those known as 'Our Lady's girdle' and derived from the legend that, during her assumption into heaven, the Virgin Mary's belt fell to earth and was retrieved by the apostle Thomas. By virtue of the Immaculate Conception, she, uniquely, had been spared the pains of childbirth and her girdle was deployed to secure an easy and safe delivery for her less fortunate devotees. Several dozen of these miraculous belts were listed in relic collections all across Europe including the fourteenth-century inventory from Christ Church Cathedral, Dublin.

Certain saints were also invoked for labouring mothers, most notably Saints Catherine of Alexandria and Margaret of Antioch. Margaret's role in the process was due to an incident in her *vita* where, having been swallowed by a dragon, she beat her way out of its belly using a staff topped with a cross. Her *vita* had been translated into Irish by the late

---

[1] Conor McDonough, OP, personal communication.

fourteenth century and was one of the devotional texts included in the early sixteenth-century codex, the *Leabhair Chlainne Suibhne*, compiled for the use of the Donegal noblewoman, Máire Ní Mháille. The colophon promised a blessing on all who read it devoutly and it may have been intended for use in a birthing chamber. The name Margaret derives from the Latin word for a pearl, which was associated with childbirth as demonstrated above.

The role of midwives and matrons was significant in transmitting 'women's knowledge' to their younger charges. The midwife consequently became a person of great power and was often viewed with suspicion by the clergy. Although a diocesan synod in Dublin in 1312 instructed that midwives should be taught how to perform baptism correctly, the *Summa confessorum* of John of Freiburg, a confessor's handbook that enjoyed widespread circulation in Ireland and Europe, condemned midwives for instructing mothers to continue breastfeeding longer than necessary as a form of contraception. An exemplum from the thirteenth-century *Liber exemplorum* may refer to abortion or infanticide, and Anne O'Connor has noted the influence of such medieval preachers' stories on folktales such as 'Petticoat Jane', wherein a midwife is damned for committing infanticide.

Immediately after birth, the infant's father and godparents took it to church to be baptised. This too was a gendered experience. As instructed in the Sarum *Manuale*, the normative liturgical handbook for much of medieval England and Ireland, the priest, meeting the party at the door of the church, or in the porch, enquired the gender of the child and its name. Then followed the 'anointing of the catechumens' (which, in 1182, Archbishop John Cumin of Dublin instructed was to take place at the church door) and then the priest took the child in his arms (the right arm if a boy, the left if a girl), and led the party to the font. For the rest of their lives, they would occupy these positions in church: women on the north side, or left as one faced the altar, men on the south, or right. Godparents were charged with supervising the temporal and spiritual wellbeing of the child and were expected to transmit the Apostles' Creed, the *Pater Noster* and the *Ave Maria* to their godchildren. In some cases, godparents presented silver spoons with handles in the shape of an apostle to the newborn child and one such 'apostle spoon' was recently discovered during excavations in Rothe House, Kilkenny.

The period after childbirth was also an ambivalent time, when women were separated from family and the broader community for between seven to forty days until they were re-integrated through the ceremony of churching. Whereas this ceremony had its roots in notions of ritual impurity articulated in Leviticus 12: 2–8, it was also an occasion on which a woman gave thanks for a safe delivery, before resuming family responsibilities and sexual relations. Although the liturgical texts of the churching ceremony make no reference to notions of impurity, the relevant sermon material for the feast of the Purification of the Blessed Virgin Mary (2 February) does. This includes influential collections such as the *Golden Legend* of James of Voragine and the *Festial* of John Mirk, both of which circulated in medieval Ireland. The new mother was accompanied to the church by female companions and greeted at the church door by the priest, who blessed her, gave her the end of his stole to hold and led her into the church where prayers were recited before an altar, often that of the Virgin Mary. After this the women made an offering and withdrew. Depending on her social status, the ceremony might be followed by a festive celebration. The excesses associated with these led the corporations of Kilkenny and Galway to enact legislation controlling them in the sixteenth century. In Galway, the problem seems to have been the numbers of people who turned up at aldermen's houses after churchings expecting lavish entertainment. Curiously, the clergy were singled out as being amongst the worst offenders.

The intense emotions and the apotropaic ritual practices surrounding childbirth were responses to the high incidence of death in childbirth and high infant mortality. The human reality of this became clear during excavations in an undisturbed medieval cemetery at Ballyhanna, County Donegal in 2003. Among the burials excavated was one of a young female who survived the birth of twins, only for all three to die shortly afterwards. The mother was a very petite young adult, with an estimated stature of only 4 feet, 9 inches. The care with which the three bodies were laid out was particularly poignant. The babies were positioned to the left of the mother; the head of one rested on her chest, while the head of the other was laid on her abdomen. The mother's arms appear to have been deliberately arranged to cradle both infants. It was a stark reminder that Thomas Hobbes' observation about primitive human life being 'solitary, poor, nasty, brutish and short' was particularly true for the daughters of Eve.

Further Reading:

Clodagh Tait, 'Safely delivered: Childbirth, Wet-nursing, Gossip-feasts and Churching in Ireland *c.*1530–1690', *Irish Economic and Social History*, 30 (2003), 1–23.

Caitriona J. McKenzie and Eileen M. Murphy, *Life and Death in Medieval Gaelic Ireland: The Skeletons from Ballyhanna, Co. Donegal* (Dublin, 2018).

12

Heroes, Saints and Birth-omens

Pádraig Ó Macháin

In his old age, the Donegal poet Fearghal Óg Mac an Bhaird (*c.* 1550–1630) lived in destitution, an exile in Louvain. Disillusioned by life's vicissitudes and contemplating his own mortality, he declared that neither of life's two major events should be greeted with emotion: *breith nó oighidh éanuine / ní fáth faoilte ní fáth bróin* (birth should not be celebrated, nor death lamented). While these lines form part of a resolution of the poet's personal difficulties, the idea expressed is particularly arresting as it runs contrary to Irish tradition, a tradition that was well known to the author. On the subject of birth, for example, in an earlier poem he had listed some of the celebratory events associated with the birth of one of the greatest of Ireland's mythological kings, Conn Céadchathach (Conn of the Hundred Battles), as a legendary parallel for the imagined joyous, natural phenomena marking the election of Pilib Ó Raghallaigh to the chieftainship of his family in 1583.

Birth was always celebrated, and male births were seen as particularly propitious in early Ireland. According to the middle-Irish *Triads*, one of the three sicknesses that was better than health was the *seóla mná for mac* (lying-in of a woman with a male child). Even more auspicious were the births of super-heroes or other figures, mythical and historical, distinguished by their regal careers. The birth of the hero is an international theme with echoes in classical and biblical tradition. In Ireland, this theme found recognition in *coimperta* (conception tales), one of the genres of storytelling recognised in the medieval tale-lists. As in the traditions of many other cultures, such births were frequently signalled or facilitated by supernatural participation. Parentage, for instance, was often the work of the gods. Cú Chulainn's father was the great Lugh, and Mongán's was Manannán, the equally famous god of the sea. Portents at the time of birth included thunder storms (in the case of Cormac mac Airt), showers of honey, silver and wheat (Niall Frossach), or the emergence of an array of natural features responding in celebration, as recorded in Fearghal Óg's poem.

In a culture where physical imperfection disqualified one from kingship, a birthmark could nonetheless be auspicious. In the Middle Ages, many notable chieftains of different families had been known by their red birthmarks: the 'Red Hand of Ulster' is probably the most enduring survival of such a feature. The origin of the *ball dearg* (red mark) is found in the *Life of St Patrick* and later derivative sources, and illustrates the malevolent and benevolent power of saints. Patrick is said to have cursed a chieftain, Cárthann Fionn, for a discourtesy. This curse caused Cárthann's wife to miscarry. The saint later relented by blessing the foetus and turning it into a healthy baby bearing a red mark. The saint baptised the child Eochaidh Bailldearg, whose progeny would henceforth be blessed because his father Cárthann had been the first to receive the Faith from Patrick.

The persistence of this theme was demonstrated in the late seventeenth century. In the wake of the Battle of the Boyne, Aodh Ó Domhnaill, chief of the family, returned from Spain to help the Irish cause, capitalising on a distinguished birthmark:

> He bore the nickname of Baldarg, or a red place, or a red spot, upon the account that some of the family foolishly believed that the true earl of Tyrconnell, marked on his body with such a spot, would come from abroad into Ireland, and do there great matters for his country.

Not surprisingly, the secular hero of Irish tradition and his religious counterpart – the saint – had much in common. Prophecy and portents had an important part to play in the birth of both (see 'Bullaun Stones and Birthing Saints in Medieval Ireland' in this volume); mothers, for example, might delay giving birth until the most propitious day by sitting on a stone. An additional factor in the case of saints was that the wonders associated with their births became part of the dossier of miracles that would single them out as holy persons throughout life and after death. During her pregnancy, the mother of St Finnian of Clonard was visited by a flame that entered her mouth and left again in the form of a bird, attracting to it all the birds in Ireland. Similarly, a ball of fire descended on the head of the mother of St Carthage, and at his birth a stream burst forth, from which water the baby was baptised. The birth of Brendan the Navigator was attended by the appearance of purple sheep, a forest fire, angels, white rain and the birth of thirty calves. And the birth and baptism of St Kevin of Glendalough were marked in the following way:

> At the time of Coemgen's birth no pains of labour nor pangs of childbearing came to his mother, as to other women, for innocent, faithful, righteous was the offspring that she bore. And the high King of righteousness, the King of Heaven, sent twelve angels with golden lamps to his baptism. And the angels gave him the name of Coemgen, that is beauteous shining birth.

A highlight of the parallel between secular and religious birth-events in early Irish tradition is the correspondence with biblical narrative. This is at its most obvious in the case of Conchubhar mac Neassa, whose birth was said to have coincided with the birth of Christ, just as his death occurred on the day of the Crucifixion. There are also more subtle parallels, such as that between the apocryphal wonders on the night of Christ's birth and those that occurred at Samhain on the night of the birth of Conn Céadchathach, mentioned by Fearghal Óg in his poem.

The many wonders that happened at the birth of Conn included the marvellous creation of the river Boyne, and of Loughs Neagh, Ree and Leane, and of the five great highways of Ireland. Just as marvellous were other happenings such as the restoration of the power of speech to Fionntán mac Bóchra – who had survived the Deluge – so that he could, at last, recount the antediluvian history of Ireland; and the singing of twenty-seven white birds in chains of gold at Tara, presaging happiness and prosperity during Conn's rule. In a general way, these find echoes in the list of portents at Christ's birth, which include vines fruiting and palm trees blossoming in winter, the emergence of wells and of streams of honey, and the sun shining at midnight.

To the creators of the Christian apocryphon, the realisation of the portents at the birth of Christ must have been obvious. In the case of Conn Céadcathach, one version of his story spells out the consequences of his birth-omens for Ireland. The country would enjoy bounty, prosperity and undisturbed peace, the secular paradise of the rightful king:

> During that time Ireland was never a season without produce, no night without dew nor day without heat. Every wood was green; every river was full to a knee's depth with fish. There was no spear nor knife nor sword: horse-whips and horse-crops were the only weapons there. Ploughing-time was a fortnight per month in spring, and three crops of corn were taken every year. Cuckoos sang perched on the horns of cows.

Further Reading:

James Carney, *Poems on the O'Reillys* (Dublin, 1950).

Breandán Ó Buachalla, *Aisling Ghéar* (Dublin, 1996).

Brian Ó Cuív, 'The Seventeen Wonders of the Night of Christ's birth', *Éigse* 6 (1950), 116–26.

Charles Plummer, *Bethada Náem nÉrenn: Lives of Irish Saints* (Oxford, 1922).

Whitley Stokes, *Lives of Saints from the Book of Lismore* (Oxford 1890).

Joseph Vendryes, *Airne Fíngein* (Dublin, 1953).

13

Contested Legitimacy: Birth, Incest, Power and Land in Sixteenth-century Connaught

Valerie McGowan-Doyle

In November 1583, 'Shamrock' John Burke, recently created baron of Leitrim, was killed during an attack orchestrated by his older half-brother, Ulick, recently created 3rd earl of Clanricard. Several reports of Leitrim's death to officials in London included allegations that he had committed incest with his sister, Mary, then married to Brian O'Rourke. Clanricard went further to claim that a child had been borne of his siblings' incest and that he could produce as witnesses both the midwife who attended the birth and the priest who baptised the infant. Perhaps better known as the Mac an Iarlas, the co-operation of the Burke brothers in rebellion did not preclude long-standing contention between them over inheritance of their father's title and land. Questions of legitimacy in one form or another formed the bedrock of their contention: their place in the family and, in turn, the family's place and power in Connaught during a transitional period of Elizabethan conquest; portrayals of Leitrim; the conflict that led to his death, and Clanricard's defense of his actions, no less than the encapsulation of all these episodes in claims of the birth of a child conceived in incest. Allegations that Leitrim had produced a child borne of incest functioned simultaneously in the legal and symbolic realms. They focused attention on the role that legitimacy played throughout the brothers' dispute over land and power that extended even into the period following Leitrim's death. Incest was also a well-established trope in medieval and early modern literature and drama that fitted the situation perfectly.

Claims and counter-claims to legitimacy and inheritance between the brothers pre-dated their father's death. Born of different mothers, each claimed to be rightful heir – Ulick as the oldest. John challenged Ulick's legitimacy on the grounds that as the 2nd earl had divorced Ulick's mother (on charges of witchcraft), he was the rightful heir. However, Ulick prevailed, and following their father's death in 1582, he was named 3rd earl by Elizabeth I while John received the lesser title of baron of Leitrim. Critical to events as they would unfold, in this arrangement, Clanricard did not receive all of the lands claimed by his father. They were instead divided between the brothers with the clear stipulation that the holdings of each would pass on to their respective heirs upon their deaths, specifying further that Leitrim's holdings would not revert to the earldom when he died. Two further points in the agreement would resurface as significant when Clanricard later sought to legitimise his brother's murder. Firstly, each agreed that in receiving their lands, they would not practise Irish customs or impose Irish exactions on their tenants. Each was also bound to uphold the peace in Connaught. If one of the brothers contravened this, he was to be declared a traitor and, importantly, his land would then go to the other brother, not his heir, thus restoring the earldom as held by the 2nd earl.

Nine months after this agreement was signed, Leitrim was dead. Clanricard was believed guilty, though various accounts attributed contrasting motives. Some, including Mary Burke and the sources used by *Annals of the Four Masters*, asserted that Clanricard killed his brother in order to acquire Leitrim's land, duplicitously arranging a family meeting where the pre-meditated killing would take place. Clanricard and his allies did not deny their role in Leitrim's death, but presented a very different scenario, one that played into the settlement for distribution of titles and land. Maligning Leitrim as living a life of ill-repute and consorting with various women, these reports also highlighted specific ways in which Leitrim had contravened the terms of the settlement, by practising Irish customs and exactions, disrupting the peace in Connaught and harbouring thieves. Clanricard claimed, in fact, that it was in attempting to capture thieves and restore order that his brother was killed incidentally. Legitimising Clanricard's actions further, reports also asserted the danger Leitrim posed to peace in Connaught. It was better he was dead one report concluded; Clanricard would now be able to establish stability in the province. Such a portrait would have been sufficient to brand Leitrim a traitor, returning his lands to his brother under the arrangement. Nonetheless, Clanricard and his allies turned to questions of legitimacy to cement their argument and his inheritance.

In order to secure the acquisition of Leitrim's lands, Clanricard challenged the legitimacy of Leitrim's widow, Johanna O'Carroll, and their sons. Following Leitrim's death, his eldest son, Redmond, was placed in the wardship of Sir Geoffrey Fenton, Irish Secretary of State, giving Fenton control of and income from Leitrim's lands. Clanricard sought a stay on Fenton's guardianship on the grounds he was expecting a pardon from Elizabeth for his brother's death, whereby he would then expect to receive Leitrim's inheritance. He simultaneously requested that Redmond and his mother be barred from receiving Leitrim's lands until Redmond's legitimacy could be investigated. A commission was established to investigate Johanna's counter-claim that her marriage and sons were legitimate. It was undertaken by the bishop's court in Meath; however, Johanna claimed that because of Clanricard's influence a local court would certainly find against her. It was noted further that an earlier investigation into the legitimacy of her marriage had been abandoned upon Leitrim's death. Though the evidence is scant, Johanna's statement suggests that Clanricard may have sought to contest the legitimacy of his brother's marriage and sons even before Leitrim's death. Clanricard was ultimately successful. The marriage between Leitrim and O'Carroll was declared void, their children illegitimate, and Leitrim's lands returned to the earldom's holdings.

Reinforcing questions of legitimacy and illegitimacy, Clanricard also asserted, as noted above, that Leitrim had committed incest with their sister, Mary. Incest has a long history as a near-universal taboo; in the West, this is predicated on biblical prohibitions and explored in law, myth and literature from the Classical era on. It remained a potent, though sensitive topic in the Elizabethan period given the Queen's very personal experiences of incest through both Anne Boleyn's alleged incest with her brother and Henry VIII's use of biblical incest prohibitions to end his marriage to Katherine of Aragon, thus allowing him to marry Elizabeth's mother in the first place. Both a sin and a crime, incest also functioned consistently in medieval allegorical representations of threats to social order – in Geoffrey Chaucer's 'Man of Laws' tale, but even more prominently in John Gower's *Confessio Amantis* and Thomas Malory's *Morte d'Arthur*. It represented lack of self-control and was conflated with tyranny, disorder and poor rule, precisely the portrait of Leitrim that Clanricard and his allies wished to promote. Use of the trope of incest increased in the early modern period, particularly in drama. Though it could and had been used to explore a range of anxieties, here it came to encompass concerns regarding the future of monarchy, dynastic shifts, upward mobility into the nobility (as had only recently occurred with Leitrim) and, significantly, contested power within families. Brother-sister incest, in particular, functioned even more critically in drama as coded discussion of legitimate inheritance. The charge of incest against Leitrim, which only arose after his death, thus occurred at a vulnerable and transitional moment in family power in Connaught, mirroring the very use of this trope in drama, including its reassertion of stable patriarchy on which social and political order depended. Clanricard, though, took the image one step further. No image could have better suited his pursuit of power and land than claims of not only another illegitimate child borne to his brother, but one borne of incest.

Further Reading:

Elizabeth Barnes (ed.), *Incest and the Literary Imagination* (Gainesville, FL, 2002).

Karen Crady Summers, 'Reading Incest: Tyranny, Subversion, and the Preservation of Patriarchy' (unpublished PhD dissertation, University of North Carolina at Greensboro, 2011).

Bernadette Cunningham, *Clanricard and Thomond, 1540–1640: Provincial Politics and Society Transformed* (Dublin, 2012).

Richard A. McCabe, *Incest, Drama and Nature's Law, 1550–1700* (Cambridge, 2008).

14

Caudle Cups and Sweet Bags: The Material Culture of Later-seventeenth-century Childbirth and Lying-in

Clodagh Tait

FIGURE 1: *Two-handled porringer or caudle cup, 1702. Britannia standard silver 3⁹/₁₆in. x 6⁵/₁₆in. x 3¹⁵/₁₆in. (9cm x 16cm x 10cm). Thomas Parr I (active Ireland, 1687–1728, London, England). Museum purchase through the Theresa E. and Harlan E. Moore Charitable Trust Fund. Krannert Art Museum, University of Illinois.*

In early modern Ireland, as elsewhere in Europe, the aftermath of childbirth might be a time for sociability. Mothers who were in a position to do so were usually expected to spend some time 'lying-in', staying at home during this time as much as possible. The duration of lying-in might be set by local custom, perhaps lasting for a month or six weeks. Its end would often be marked by the mother's first venture to religious services at which, depending on the denomination she belonged to, a ceremony of churching might be performed. The period of a month or so after birth was sometimes viewed with a certain amount of worry: as late as the twentieth century, some Irish Catholics expressed concerns that, until they were churched, women and their infants might be susceptible to the interference of supernatural forces.

During the earlier part of lying-in, female friends and neighbours would often visit the new mother, bringing gifts and keeping her company. In Irish towns, the term 'gossip feasts' was sometimes applied to these occasions, the word gossip coming from 'god sibling' and initially applied to the godparents of the child, who might also be among the visitors. Such celebratory visits were occasions for displays of hospitality and good housekeeping. It was expected that all comers would be provided with food and drink, a fact that some of the (male) members of Kilkenny and other corporations complained about in the early seventeenth century. Citing the disruption and expense, they attempted to restrict gossip feasts to the lying-in woman's closest circle.

Certain special items might be used by well-off women during their period of lying-in. Some Irish wills mention the bequest of caudle cups, and some late-seventeenth- and early-eighteenth-century Irish silver caudle cups survive. Caudle was a thick drink containing spices, eggs and wine or ale. It was given to invalids and to women after childbirth and their attendants. Caudle cups thus were sometimes gifted to pregnant women and had female, sociable connotations. They were two-handled, to facilitate being passed around and used by the bed-ridden. Silver versions might be ornamented with family arms or the owner's initials. Among the fantastic array of silver items that Mary Pepys of Dublin (widow of the Lord Chief Justice of Ireland) bequeathed to family members and friends in 1659 was a silver caudle cup 'with the cover' which she asked her niece Mary Blemell to 'give unto Margaret ffowle the wife of Thomas ffowle ... desiring the said Margarett to bee kind unto my said neece Mary.' So not only did Mary Pepys specially select the cup to go to Margaret, it was to be presented in person by Mary Blemell, a very definite example of a caudle cup being used to commemorate and continue female friendship.

Some late-seventeenth-century wills also mention the bequest of childbed linens, special sets of linen towels, sheets and baby and christening items kept ready for use in childbirth and during lying-in. There might be one particularly fancy pair of sheets to place on the bed once the new mother was ready to receive visitors as testimony to her organisation, provident housekeeping and, sometimes, her personal skill, since it seems these sheets were often embroidered. These items were often cherished and passed down over generations. For example, Susanna Carter of Dublin, in 1670, left her children three feather beds and bolsters and a 'trunke of lynnen being sheetes, Tabling, and Child bed Lynnen'. Sir John Hoey of Johnstown, County Kildare, in 1660, left his wife, Jane Parsons, a 'coach, and coach horses, bed, furniture for a bedd, and other necessaries for a Chamber, and one ... Chest of Linen such as she shall choose and her Child bed linen'. Notably, the linen is described as hers, indicating that she had brought it to the marriage.

An especially elaborate array of childbirth-related items was bequeathed to his granddaughter by Samuel Ladyman, Vicar of Clonmel and Archdeacon of Limerick, in 1683. He left:

> One green satin Christening mantle with the broade gold and sylver lace; three hanging sea-green Sweet Baggs, as they are called, Trim'd with Gold and sylver ribbon, and one more wrought with gold; one pinkissine of the same silk with the bags with gold and sylver lace; one suit of fine wrought Child bead Linenn; with mantle, bags, &c, being used by my deare wife with all her children, my desire and will is that they be kept without any alteration (though used as occasion require).

Grace Hutchinson, Samuel's wife, had died in 1663. Five of his children also predeceased him, three in infancy and two in their twenties. His sorrow is commemorated by an epitaph he composed in Clonmel, where he described his wife and children as 'Alive, beloved, by all bewailed, now gonn'.

The Ladyman collection of childbed linen contained not only 'fine wrought' (finely embroidered) sheets, but a christening mantle expensively trimmed or embroidered with gold and silver lace, a pincushion (probably needed for pinning babies into their swaddling), a mantle (maybe a bed shawl or blanket of some kind for the mother) and four elegant and expensive 'sweet bags'. These would have been filled with herbs and powders to keep the linens they were packed with fresh, and to perfume the air of the lying-in chamber which was often deliberately kept warm and stuffy.

That Ladyman attempted to dissuade his granddaughter from altering the items suggests their sentimental value. They may have been made by his wife or gifted to her (perhaps he understood they were also a bit old-fashioned – sweet bags seem to have fallen out of use in about the mid-seventeenth century). He clearly hoped they would serve as a link between his granddaughter, her mother and grandmother, and children yet to be born. Thus, in addition to their practical uses, caudle cups and childbed linens were objects that recollected and inspired emotion; emblems of friendship, kinship, respectability, continuity, loss and love.

Sources and Further Reading:

The wills of Susanna Carter and Mary Pepys are in the collections of the UK National Archives.

'The Extended Parsons Family of Birr and Bellamont and Related Wills 1628–1692'. Available at: http://dprhcp170.doteasy.com/~tonybeck/files/ParsonsOfBirr&BellamontRelatedWills1628-1692.pdf.

Sarah Randles, 'Early Modern Sweet Bags: Objects of Delight'. Available at: https://www.objectsandemotions.org/post/early-modern-sweet-bags-objects-of-delight.

Linda Pollock, 'Childbearing and Female Bonding in Early Modern England', *Social History*, 22 (1997), 286–306.

Clodagh Tait, 'Safely Delivered: Childbirth, Wet-nursing, Gossip-feasts and Churching in Ireland, 1530–1670', *Irish Economic and Social History*, 30 (2003), 1–23.

John Davis White, 'Extracts from original Wills Formerly Preserved in the Consistorial Office, Cashel, but now Removed to the Court of Probate, Waterford', *Journal of the Kilkenny and South-East of Ireland Archaeological Society*, 2 (1859), 317–22.

15

Determining Paternity in Early Modern Ireland

Eamon Darcy

In one Irish poem from the 1650s, bastardy was a convenient way to emphasise how Ireland's social order had been inverted by the recent influx of men of low standing from England. An incredulous Brian Mac Giolla Phádraig admonished the 'wife of Conn' (who represented Ireland) for she now gave her milk to a *bastard* man of no known ancestry. This *bastard* symbolised the newly-arrived Cromwellian upstarts:

> Ábhar deargtha leacan do mhnaoi Chuinn é
> táir is tarcaisne thabhairt dá saorchlainn féin
> grá a hanama is altram a cíoch cruinn caomh
> do thál ar *bhastard* [*note the use of the English loan word*] nach
> feadair cé díobh puinn é.

> The wife of Conn should blush red with disgrace
> to have shown such contempt for her own noble race;
> her love and the milk of her soft round breasts
> to bestow on a bastard whose ancestry nobody knows.

Beyond the rhetorical level, it was a term of abuse that occured regularly across the early modern historical record. In 1705, Edward Synge vehemently denied claims that Church of Ireland clergy denounced Presbyterian marriages as invalid and consequently called their children 'bastards'. While bastardy was socially stigmatised, it is also clear that illegitimate children were part and parcel of early modern society. By the eighteenth and nineteenth centuries, it has been estimated that 2.5 percent of all live births in Ireland were illegitimate but its exact statistical prevalence in the sixteenth and seventeenth centuries is impossible to determine.

Legal and religious codes discouraged sexual intercourse outside of marriage, but also ensured that the needs of mother and child were catered for by either the father or the wider community. In Irish Brehon Law, which was codified from *c.* 600–*c.* 800 and widely practised until the seventeenth century, fathers of illegitimate children had to provide adequate support. If a man impregnated his servant, or another man's wife, or raped somebody, the child's welfare was his responsibility. In urban contexts, different codes emerged out of similar concerns. Galway corporation, for example, passed a decree in 1520 stating that any man who impregnated a woman outside of marriage had to provide for her until another man married her. In Irish Common Law, fathers of illegitimate children were obligated to provide for them, or if they could not, financial support came from the parish coffers. Interestingly and as a side note, in light of the fact that Brehon Law codes accepted that pregnancy could result from rape, Sir Richard Bolton's *Justice of the Peace for Ireland* (1638) claimed that it could not 'for a woman cannot conceive with child, except she do consent'. One wonders whether this affected cases of contested paternity.

In more modern times, the prevalence of DNA testing kits that can be used at home has caused significant and, in some cases, devastating consequences in terms of determining (or revealing) paternity. It underlines society's longstanding fascination with using precise, dare I say 'scientific', procedures for determining paternity. This is nothing new. In contested cases under Irish Brehon Law, paternity was established by precise procedures of careful observation of the child's physical looks, their gestures and their personality. If a woman had slept with two different men around the same time and did not know who the father of her child was, then the child was to be left alone for three years until 'the kin-appearance, kin-voice, and kin-manners come to him … whichever of the two men he takes after … the child is the offspring of the man whom he resembles more'. It is interesting that contemporaries were advised to wait until the child was three. Midwives also played a key role in determining paternity. In seventeenth-century England, one of their key duties was to obtain an oath from women of illegitimate children: 'the child should stick to me as the bark to the tree', they were supposed to declare in the throes of labour. If not, the midwife could withdraw her support. At that exact same time, midwives also had to ascertain the identity of the father by asking the child's mother. If she refused, the midwife, again, could withdraw her support. In Ireland, this appears to have been the case too. In 1688, for example, Ann Whiterly, a Drogheda midwife refused to help Eleanor Wall as she declined to reveal the father's identity (it was suspected that he was a roguish usher from the local grammar school). Such declarations of mothers mid-labour as to the paternity of their child were considered to be of significant evidential value. Thus, when cases came to court, midwives could be asked to testify. Overall, one of the reasons why societies desired to determine fatherhood was so that the men responsible fulfilled their financial obligations, and not the local parish coffers.

One of the more notable examples of determining paternity in early modern Ireland occurred in the 1690s and illustrates how all of these techniques came into play. In 1694, a Church of Ireland minister based in the diocese of Down and Connor, Thomas Ward, was defrocked for adultery. During the proceedings conducted against Ward, it was also alleged that he fathered five illegitimate children. The commission, led by Church of Ireland bishops, William King and Anthony Dopping, first tried to establish whether Ward sired illegitimate children according to local fame, or *fama*. While some in the diocese believed this, others argued that these were rumours circulated by 'idle' or 'scandalous' people. Secondly, the commissioners investigated whether Ward was the father of specific children. In one instance, seventeen witnesses testified that locals widely believed Ward was the father of Ann Wilson's child. Some claimed that Ward gave money to Wilson, thereby inferring his paternity as these payments were allegedly made out of moral obligation. What is interesting in this case is that the mothers of Ward's alleged illegitimate children did not appear before the commission (we do not know whether they were called or refused to appear), leaving the commissioners to rely on second-hand accounts. Thirdly, the commissioners called local midwives who affirmed that they had heard declarations mid-labour that Ward had fathered the (about to be) newborn child. Finally, the commissioners looked at other important factors: the names of the children and their genetic traits. One mother called her daughter Mary Ward to indicate his paternity. Ann Wilson named her child Betty Ward and the witness stated that Elizabeth was 'very like Dean Ward'. Sadly, the commissioners' decision on whether Ward was the father of these children does not survive but they did announce that Ward was guilty of adultery.

In early modern Ireland, it appears that contested paternity cases concerning illegitimate children were an issue for the entire community. From a financial perspective, provisions were made for illegitimate children from the local parish coffers. Understandably, the preference was for fathers of these children to provide support from both a financial and a pastoral point of view. When some denied their paternity or in cases where it could not easily be established, the whole community took part. Who was the father by village reputation? According to the local midwife, who was the father? Who does the child look and act like? Such instances in early modern Ireland, therefore, reveal profound contemporary social beliefs invested in *fama*, reputation and the intergenerational power of kin identity.

Further Reading:

Angela Bourke *et al.* (eds), *The Field Day Anthology of Irish Writing: Irish Women's Writing and Traditions* (5 vols, Cork, 2002), iv, 277–8.

Richard Bolton, *A Justice of the Peace for Ireland* (Dublin, 1638).

Eamon Darcy, *The World of Thomas Ward: Sex and Scandal in late-Seventeenth Century Co. Antrim* (Dublin, 2016).

Fergus Kelly, *A Guide to Early Irish Law* (Dublin, 1988).

16

Who's the Daddy? Determining Cases of Disputed Paternity in the Eighteenth-century Presbyterian Community

Leanne Calvert

Today, it is fairly easy to determine the biological paternity of children. Innovations in DNA testing mean that cases of disputed paternity can be resolved fairly swiftly. This was not the case in eighteenth-century Ireland. In cases where women became pregnant outside of marriage and the man denied responsibility, it was up to the church courts to determine who was telling the truth. How did contemporaries in eighteenth-century Ireland determine paternity? What role did the Presbyterian Church courts play in deciding who was the daddy?

The minutes of the Presbyterian Church courts in Ireland, known as Kirk-Sessions, offer a fascinating insight into how paternity was established. While these courts had no official civil authority, and their rulings were not legally enforceable, many Presbyterian women and men looked to the Kirk-Session to settle disputed paternity cases throughout the eighteenth-century. When a woman appeared before the Church court and named the alleged father of her child, the Kirk-Session launched an investigation into her claims. Kirk-Sessions asked women to provide as many details as possible. Indeed, their questions may appear intrusive to modern day audiences. The Kirk-Sessions were keen to find out not only when couples had sex, but also where and how often. For example, when Jean McCullan appeared before Templepatrick Kirk-Session, County Antrim, in 1704 and named Andrew McKeown as the father of her illegitimate child, she offered the Session intimate details of their trysts. According to Jean, 'ye act was committed on Bellyclare fair day, when Andrew McKeowns mother was abroad, his brother at … work, and his father about the house'. Similar details were revealed by

Margaret McCrea when she confessed to Cahans Kirk-Session, County Monaghan, that she had committed adultery with her neighbour, John Wales. According to Margaret, the pair had sexual intercourse three times: once in the garden, another time in the stable, and the third time in 'her own bed on a Sabbath morning'.

Like the Church courts in Scotland, Irish Kirk-Sessions were concerned with pinning down the exact date that sexual intercourse had taken place. The fixation on a specific date reflected contemporary beliefs about conception. Pregnancy was usually measured from the last date of sexual intercourse. While estimates varied, nine months was generally used to determine paternity. Unsurprisingly, the reliance on fixed dates caused confusion for some men and many disputed paternity when the dates did not match. A common defence was that the birth did not 'come to his time', meaning that the child was born either too early or too late. For example, in October 1719, Robert McAlpine doubted he was the father of Mary Irvine's child because it did 'not come exactly to his time of guilt with her'. Mary agreed to take an oath that she was telling the truth and the Session confirmed that he was the father.

It was much trickier for the Presbyterian Kirk-Sessions when a man completely denied ever having had sexual intercourse with his accuser. Such a case came before Templepatrick Kirk-Session in November 1710 when Margaret Kennedy named Samuel Reid as the father of her illegitimate child. According to Margaret, the pair had sexual intercourse '14 days before May last in [Samuel's] father's house'. She further added that she knew it was definitely Samuel she had sex with because 'he came down from his own bed to her in the night time' and that 'he spake to her at the time'. Samuel was called in and denied that he 'ever had anything to do' with Margaret. His brother Andrew also appeared and cast doubt on Margaret's character, claiming that she had been caught lying in bed with a man named Alexander Agnew 'ten days before April 1709' – suggesting that someone else was the father. Samuel also told the Session that Margaret had been spotted with Alexander 'standing under a hedge and that she was sore weeping' – a fact that the Session thought 'not materiall' given that Alexander was alleged to have been her 'courtier'. The insinuation here was that perhaps Alexander had called off their relationship after finding out she was pregnant.

Unable to come to a clear conclusion, the case slowly disappeared from the minutes. Two years later, however, the case reappeared. This time it was Samuel who sought the advice of the Kirk-Session. After years spent denying paternity, Samuel appeared and confessed that he had indeed had sexual intercourse with Margaret. Asked why he now confessed guilt, Samuel told the Session that he believed God was punishing him for his sin, remarking that Providence had 'crossed him in all his worldly affairs'. Samuel was subsequently rebuked before the congregation and absolved of his sin.

These short snippets from the minutes of the Irish Presbyterian Church courts cast light not only on the intimate sexual activities of women and men in eighteenth-century Ireland, but also reveal much about their understandings of conception and pregnancy. In the absence of medical testing, women had to convince the Church courts that the man they named was the true father of their child. The wider context of their sexual activities, including the dates, places and the number of times sexual intercourse took place, were essential pieces of evidence.

Sources:

Cahans Kirk-Session minutes, 1751–1766 (Public Record Office of Northern Ireland, CR3/25/B/1).

Templepatrick Kirk-Session minutes, 1700–1743 (Public Record Office of Northern Ireland, CR4/12/B/1).

Further Reading:

Andrew Holmes, *The Shaping of Ulster Presbyterian Belief and Practice, 1770–1840* (Oxford, 2006).

Leanne Calvert, '"He Came to her Bed Pretending Courtship": Sex, Courtship and the Making of Marriage in Ulster, 1750–1844', *Irish Historical Studies*, 42:162 (2018), 244–64.

Rosalind Mitchison and Leah Leneman, *Sexuality and Social Control: Scotland, 1660–1780* (Oxford, 1989).

17

Curing a Woman in Childbed: Charms and Magical Healing in Eighteenth-century Templepatrick, County Antrim

Leanne Calvert

Andrew Kelso reports that Quintine McNeibly, Agnes Wright, Mary McCurtny and Mathew McGladries wife were in John Gutries, and can give an account of what was done there by way of charm … [it is reported that] Marion McKim caused a little bannock to be baked by Agnes Wright, and a fire to be made in the place where the sick woman had been delivered of the Child, that when the bread was burn'd in the fire till it was black, she took it and put it into the bed beside the sick woman, and then took of the Earth and ashes, from under where the fire was, and threw it over the bed. The witnesses say they were afraid at this and left the house believing it to be witching or charming … The Session considered of what these evidences relate, and believe it to be properly a charm, and that Marion McKim was the chief adviser and actor of it, and therefore to be dealt with as guilty of a heinous sin and great scandal … Margaret McQuiston … says further that Marion McKim … said she had done it to her own daughter-in-law, when she was in child bed, who was cur'd by it.
– Templepatrick Kirk-Session minutes, 20-23-30 June 1714

In June 1714, the Presbyterian Kirk-Session of Templepatrick, County Antrim initiated an investigation after reports were spread that 'charms' were used by a member of their congregation. According to the case, a woman named Marion McKim had performed a charm in the house of John Gutrie, whose wife was in her sick bed after giving birth. The case roused the excitement of the Kirk-Session who had not yet dealt with 'that sort of scandal' under their watch. The case raises many questions. Who was Marion McKim, why was she in the Gutrie's home, and what exactly was the purpose of the charm she performed? The minutes of her case provide an unrivalled insight into the rituals of childbirth in eighteenth-century Ireland, casting light not only on the mundane, but also the magical.

The case tells us much about the everyday management of childbirth in eighteenth-century Ireland. As was the case elsewhere in Britain and Europe, childbirth in Ireland was also managed primarily by women. The local midwife, women who had experience of childbirth themselves, and close female friends and family members of the labouring woman were usually present at a birth. While men, as husbands, brothers and fathers, were sometimes on hand to offer help and assistance, childbirth remained largely a female-controlled event. Male medical practitioners were generally only granted access to the labouring woman when problems arose with the progress of the delivery. It was not until the latter half of the period that men formally established themselves in the birthing room as male midwives.

The female-centred experience of childbirth is largely borne out in this case from Templepatrick. The minutes tell us that John Gutrie's wife was attended by a group made up almost exclusively of women. In attendance were Agnes Wright, Mary McCurtny and the unnamed wife of Mathew McGladrie. One man was also in attendance – a fellow named Quintine McNeibly. The source does not tell us anything about the relationships between those in attendance, or why they were chosen, but we can safely assume that they were important enough to the Gutries to be invited into their home for the occasion. It is well acknowledged among historians that invitations to attend a birth were a sign of social acceptance, while being excluded from the occasion was sometimes regarded as a social snub.

Following childbirth, new mothers were expected to rest and recuperate for up to thirty days. This was known as the 'lying-in' period. As the name suggests, the lying-in period was designed to offer a new mother time to recover after the labours of childbirth before resuming her usual household duties. In reality, however, the length of time that a woman could retire from her work was dependent on a number of circumstances. Whereas some women had to return to work as quickly as possible for economic reasons, others were unable to resume their duties on account of bad health. For many women, the days following childbirth could be arduous and dangerous. Complications arising from childbirth, such as bleeding and infection, could quickly become fatal. This is likely what was the matter with John Gutrie's wife. As the case notes, she was lying sick in the bed where she had delivered their child – prompting the gathering of those in attendance.

Aside from the management of childbirth, the case also reveals how the magical was employed to aid the recovery of new mothers. Historians in Ireland and Britain have noted that cunning-folk, also known as wise-women and wise-men, performed a range of medical services to people in their communities. Prayers, love potions, chants, fortune-telling and objects imbued with healing powers were part of their repertoire. Folk-medicine that employed healing magic and charms was one such service. It is likely that Marion McKim was acting in this kind of capacity. The case notes that Marion had performed this same charm when her daughter-in-law fell ill after birth and that she had been cured by it. As a woman with previous experience in childbirth, and as someone who practised folk medicine, it is possible that Marion was called to the Gutries' in a professional capacity.

The charm used by Marion to help cure the sick woman also tells us about the Scottish influences on Irish Presbyterian culture and beliefs. Presbyterianism arrived in Ireland in the seventeenth century, brought over by Scottish settlers. Subsequent waves of migration in the centuries thereafter created a strong, Presbyterian foothold in the north-east counties of the island. The province of Ulster became a stronghold of Presbyterianism. Indeed, by the early eighteenth century, Presbyterians accounted for approximately one-third of the province's population.

Bannock is a traditional Scottish unleavened bread made from oat cakes. It is also a food-stuff that is imbued with folk meaning and folklore. In Scotland, special types of bannocks were baked at certain times of the year and to mark important occasions, such as new births, marriages and on New Year's Day. Bannocks were also used in charms for healing, prosperity and protection, and were sometimes burnt to ward off evil spirits. Marion's use of the bannock in the healing charm points to these Scottish influences. Indeed, that this was a custom newly imported from Scotland is also suggested by the uncertainty of the Kirk-Session on how they should proceed. The elders were unsure of the punishment that Marion should undertake. Usually, those who transgressed the rules of the community were expected to undergo public discipline, a method of punishment that required offenders to stand publicly before the congregation on at least two successive Sabbaths. In this case, however, the Kirk-Session noted that, as this was 'the first of that sort of scandal in ye congregation', Marion should instead be rebuked privately by the elders and a warning issued to the congregation afterwards 'against such Scandalous practices'.

While relatively short, the case of Marion McKim reveals a wealth of information about pregnancy and childbirth in eighteenth-century Ireland. Childbirth was an event that brought the community together, and one that sometimes necessitated the services of folk-healers in times of distress. Marion McKim's employment of a charm using bannock bread points to the ongoing exchange of cultural influences between Presbyterians in Ireland and Scotland.

Source:
Templepatrick Kirk-Session minute book, 1700–1743 (Public Record Office of Northern Ireland, CR4/12/B/1).

Further Reading:

Margaret Bennett, *Scottish Customs from the Cradle to the Grave* (Edinburgh, 2012).

James Napier, *Folklore or Superstitious Beliefs in the West of Scotland* (Paisley, 1879).

Andrew Holmes, *The Shaping of Ulster Presbyterian Belief and Practice, 1770–1840* (Oxford, 2006).

Andrew Sneddon, *Witchcraft and Magic in Ireland* (London, 2015).

Leigh Whaley, *Women and the Practice of Medical Care in Early Modern Europe, 1500–1800* (London, 2011).

18

The *Miscellanea Medica* of David McBride (1726–1779): Surgeon and Man-Midwife

Philomena Gorey

David McBride was born in Ballymoney, County Antrim in 1726. He was educated at the local public school and served an apprenticeship to a surgeon in the town. Like many of his contemporaries, he entered the Royal Navy where he served as ships surgeon until 1748. He then studied anatomy at the University of Edinburgh under Alexander Monro, who was the first Professor of Anatomy appointed at the university, renowned for delivering lectures in English, rather than in the customary Latin. Thereafter, McBride attended a course of lectures in midwifery in London under the tuition of William Smellie. Smellie was among a new breed of medical men who saw midwifery as an adjunct to surgery, establishing themselves as experts and the pre-eminent authority on all matters of reproduction and childbirth as obstetric science advanced. He set himself up as a teacher of midwifery where his course of lectures included anatomy, pregnancy, and the varied positions of the foetus during pregnancy, the management of labour with its complications and care of the mother and baby after delivery. Tuition cost three guineas. Smellie combined his lectures with practical demonstrations on what he described as 'machines' – he obtained real bones – that simulated the female pelvis and the foetus. Significantly, his students delivered 'poor women' gratis to gain experience. For this they paid a fee for each delivery and 'six Shillings more to a common Stock, for the support of the poor Women'. Female pupils could also attend lectures and were instructed 'by themselves'. As well as an entry fee, they paid two shillings to attend each labour. Smellie was a proponent of the midwifery forceps and endeavoured to modify and refine their use.

Where previously the stock in trade of male practitioners was perforators and hooks, which they used to perform a craniotomy and extract the dead foetus, the midwifery forceps could deliver a live infant in cases of prolonged or obstructed labour.

McBride settled in Dublin in 1751 where he continued to practise as a man-midwife. Between 1749 and 1760 he kept a journal of his midwifery practice in which he recorded details of 149 of the deliveries he attended. He was not alone in advancing the notion of male practitioners of midwifery in Dublin at this time. Bartholemew Mosse was the most prominent, founding the Dublin Lying-in Hospital, laterally the Rotunda, in 1745. Another contemporary, Fielding Ould, who studied anatomy at Trinity College Dublin and later in Paris, published his *Treatise of Midwifery in Three Parts* in 1742. In it, he accurately described the internal rotation of the foetal skull during labour. He was appointed Master of the Dublin Lying-in Hospital after Mosse's untimely death. Prominent also in the later eighteenth century were Edward Foster, who ran courses of lectures and demonstrations on the theory and practice of midwifery, and William Dease, who was the first President of the Royal College of Surgeons in Ireland, completing his *Observations in midwifery, particularly on the different methods of assisting women in tedious labour* in 1783. Joseph Clarke was the first Master of the Dublin Lying-in Hospital to recognise, document and attempt to combat outbreaks of puerperal fever at the hospital when they occurred there in the 1780s and 1790s.

Of the 149 deliveries recounted in McBride's journal, eighty-five were normal and many of these were delivered by a midwife. For the remaining sixty-four many of the abnormal presentations and obstetric emergencies that we are familiar with today are recorded. The journal is a mix of booked and emergency cases. McBride refers to women by name, implying that his attendance had been pre-booked, possibly by women whose husbands belonged to the trade and artisan classes. The attendance fee at that period was usually a guinea. His reference to 'poor' women confirms evidence that men-midwives attended women not only as charity cases but to gain obstetric experience as well. A pattern of repeat business emerges. Several women were delivered of between five and six children each, at intervals of around eighteen months to two

FIGURE 2: *David McBride 1726–79.*

FIGURE 3: *David McBride's certificate of attendance at lectures and instruction on midwifery by W. Smellie MD, 7 February 1748 (Royal College of Physicians of Ireland, TPCK/6/1/12, f. 2).*

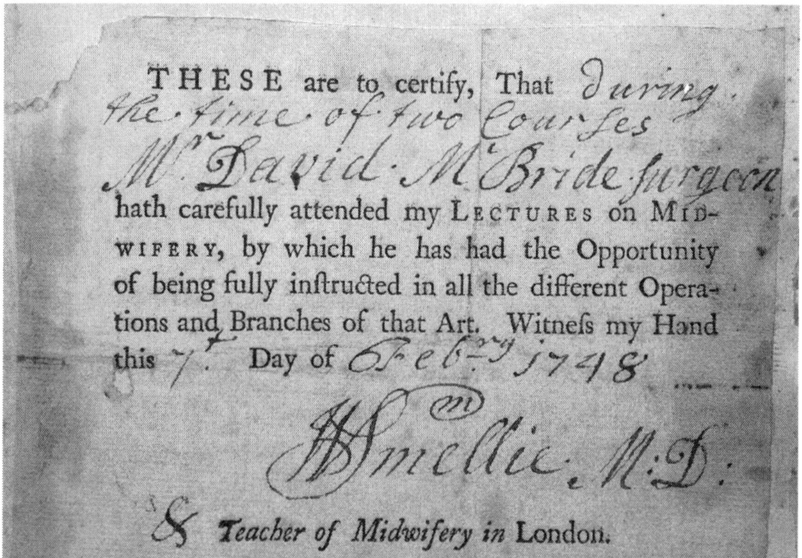

THESE are to certify, That *during the time of two Courses* Mr *David McBride surgeon* hath carefully attended my LECTURES on MID-WIFERY, by which he has had the Opportunity of being fully inſtructed in all the different Operations and Branches of that Art. Witneſs my Hand this 7 Day of *Feby 1748*

Smellie, M:D:

& *Teacher of Midwifery in* London.

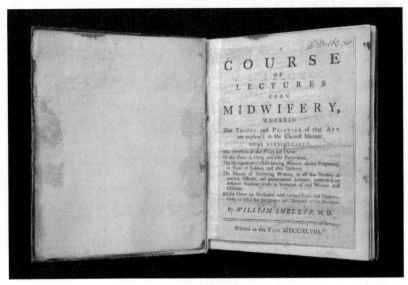

FIGURE 4: *A Course of Lectures upon Midwifery wherein the Theory and Practice of that Art are explain'd in the Clearest Manner, 1748 (Royal College of Physicians of Ireland, TPCK/6/1/12, f. 3).*

years. Geographically, his practice extended from Bolton Street and King Street, north of the River Liffey, and from Dolphin's Barn to Dame Street, south of the river.

By the mid-eighteenth century, male involvement in midwifery in Dublin was well under way. While it is difficult to establish evidence of the use of the midwifery forceps generally, McBride, with the benefit of the best training and experience available at the time, employed them with confidence. Obstructed labour by the head of the foetus was the most common cause of difficulty in labour. The journal illustrates how Mrs Lambert (case 122), a charity case, the 'poor woman in the barracks' (case 23) and Mrs Scott (case 80) were delivered of live babies with the assistance of the forceps. Notwithstanding this, there were cases where McBride was obliged to use a perforator and crotchet to perform a craniotomy to remove the head when the foetus was found to have died in utero (cases 14, 36, 54, 106, 129). There are references to anatomical abnormalities such as a narrow pelvis due to rickets or the 'oblique uterus', described by the Dutch practitioner Hendrik van Daventer, which McBride encountered for the first time when he attended and safely delivered Mrs Wallace (case 77). The journal illustrates McBride's satisfaction in a live birth when it seemed certain the child was already lost (Mrs Craig, case 74). Midwives called McBride when complications of labour arose. A midwife alerted him when Mrs Ball's daughter (case 81) was found to have a knee presentation. He immediately 'upon breaking the membranes got the feet delivered and mother and baby did well'. In December 1752, a midwife attending Mrs Ashmore (case 9) sent for McBride for an arm presentation when she herself was unable to turn the foetus. He 'got to the feet and fixed a noose on them' turned the foetus and delivered a dead child. He attended a 'midwife near Meath St.' whom he knew (case 88) – 'finding little or no pains, and ye os internum open and soft, turned and delivered – did well'.

Obstetric emergencies are described in detail, without a medical term. Mrs Jordan (case 132) presented with placenta praevia which was first recorded as 'unavoidable haemorrhage' in 1775. McBride described it as 'violent flooding in the end of the seventh month … the placenta was growing to the lower part of the uterus.' The infant was safely delivered. Umbilical prolapsed cord was described when he 'found upon breaking of the membranes the cord to come down'. The patient, Mrs Caldwell (case 141) was delivered of a stillborn baby. Eclampsia, a severe complication of pre-eclampsia recognised in 1813, is described in detail when he attended a young woman – Mrs Bryan's daughter (case 147) – who was 'seized with violent convulsions which were preceded by an almost total loss of sight and violent pain in the head'. These 'fits' occurred intermittently for six weeks before McBride was called. He attempted to deliver the baby, the woman's uterus ruptured and she died shortly afterwards. There is little that McBride could have done to save this woman, yet he is obviously upset at the outcome. He concluded:

> I was immensely shocked that I should have
> interfered, and not rather have left her to the pains,
> which I certainly should have done, as there was at
> the time I saw her, no urgent necessity for delivering
> her. But I thought her delivery was the luckiest thing
> that could have happened to her and so it certainly

> would have proved if she had either been left to
> nature, or it could have been done without injury.
> Every labour and abortion should be trusted to the
> natural pains, unless something very urgent requires
> the assistance of the hand.

Many women recovered after difficult and complicated labours. In May 1754, a 'poor woman' in Loftus Lane (case 18) haemorrhaged during labour. McBride delivered a stillborn baby 'by the feet' and the mother recovered after several weeks. Likewise, Mrs Jolly (case 110) had a post-partum haemorrhage with a premature infant and 'did well'. Mrs Kirkpatrick (case 48) was 'seized with a fever in the latter end of the 7th month'. She had a natural labour in November 1755, but developed pain and swelling, possibly a deep vein thrombosis or phlebitis, in her left leg which spread to her thigh and hip. Applications of topical salves, warm fomentations and purges every other day for ten days 'carried off the complaint'.

David McBride's midwifery journal in his *Miscellanea Medica* is a significant contribution to the historiography of midwifery in Dublin in the eighteenth century. His fee-book suggests that he had an extensive practice after 1760, a time when male practitioners began to challenge the midwife's hegemony over normal births. He was a member of the Dublin Philosophical Society which was established in 1756. Through the society, he communicated his many theories on a wide range of experiments, most notably on a treatment for scurvy. In November 1764, the University of Glasgow conferred him with a degree of Doctor of Physic for his experimental work. He established a medical school at his home in Cavendish Row, now Mountjoy Square, where the first course of lectures commenced in 1766. These lectures, published as *A Methodical Introduction to the Theory and Practice of Physic*, were translated into Latin and ran to several editions. He continued to practise midwifery. He was appointed teacher of midwifery at the Dublin Lying-in Hospital in 1774, where he also sat on the Board of Governors. McBride caught an 'accidental cold', which brought on a fever in December 1778, and died on the 28th of that month at the age of 52. He is buried in St Audeon's Church, Cornmarket in Dublin.

Further Reading:

Aquila Smith, 'Illustrious Physicians and Surgeons in Ireland No. III, David McBride M.D.', *Dublin Quarterly Journal of Medical Science* iii, no. 2 (1847), 281–90.

Philomena Gorey, 'Managing Midwifery in Dublin. Practice and Practitioners, 1700–1800', in Margaret H. Preston and Margaret Ó hÓgartaigh (eds), *Gender and Medicine in Ireland 1700–1950* (New York, 2012), 123–37.

Adrian Wilson, *The Making of Man-Midwifery. Childbirth in England 1660–1770* (London, 1995).

Lisa Forman Cody, *Birthing the Nation. Sex, Science and the Conception of Eighteenth-Century Britons* (Oxford, 2005), 152–97.

Jean Donnison, *Midwives and Medical Men. A History of the Struggle for the Control of Childbirth* (London, 1995).

19

The Many Labours of Ellinor Appleyard Hallaran

Clodagh Tait

Ellinor Appleyard, who married Thady Hallaran on 2 June 1763, was from a long-established Limerick family. Her father John Appleyard, a surveyor and estate agent, acquired extensive land in Athlunkard in the 1750s, and she had at least two brothers, Thomas and Edward. Her husband was from middling-sort farming background and had a substantial house at Ballycuneen, County Clare, near Sixmilebridge. The couple went on to have eighteen children, seventeen of them (including one set of twins) born in less than eighteen years between their marriage and March 1781 – meaning that Ellinor would have been pregnant for nearly three-quarters of that period. A final daughter was born four years later.

The main source for Ellinor's life and her many labours is her husband's commonplace book, in which he kept a list of family births and deaths. This volume dated back to Thady's schooldays and also contained passages of information on a variety of other topics such as astronomy, the Irish language and veterinary medicine. Thady's family notes were continued by subsequent writers up until the early twentieth century. Patrick Hogan, whose wife owned the commonplace book, published an edition of the family information from it and further notes on the Hallaran/O'Hallorans in two articles in the *North Munster Antiquarian Journal*. He placed a copy in the National Library of Ireland, but I have not been able to trace whether the original has survived. The copy is a negative photostat and thus is quite difficult to decipher: one of the original pages of the family notes was damaged and sections are illegible. As a result, there seem to be errors in Hogan's published transcription. I have amended it by cross-referencing the legible information with online calendars for the relevant years, but some errors likely remain.

His marriage to Ellinor Appleyard was Thady Hallaran's second. On 26 June 1758, then aged 31, he had married his first cousin, 19-year-old Mary Canny. That September he recorded the sad outcome of his wife's first pregnancy: 'Mary Hallaran miscarried, ten weeks gone.' On 16 August 1759, Mary gave birth to their son Matthew. She died six months later. Thady recorded Matthew's birth surprisingly comprehensively:

> 1759, Aug. 16th Matthew Hallaran was born halfe an
> hour past five in ye afternoon a Thursday 16 hours
> labour baptised Sunday August ye 20th [*sic* 19th?].
> Gossops [godparents]: Matthew Canny, John Hallaran,
> Mrs Edward Hickie.

Thady showed a similar level of interest when it came to recording the births of his other children. His notes allow us some small but significant glimpses of women's experiences of pregnancy and birth in the eighteenth century, as well as hinting at aspects of belief and community life. Unusually for a document of this type, he generally named the midwives in attendance and, in several cases, he also noted the length of the labour as 'x hours in labour' or 'x hours sick' (in Hiberno-English as late as the twentieth century when a woman 'got sick' one meaning was that she went into labour). While this information is not all that useful in the absence of some explanation of what Thady understood 'labour' to be (the time from the beginning of contractions or the duration of more active labour?), they do indicate that Ellinor's later labours were shorter than the earlier ones and that she regularly gave birth fairly quickly.

In most cases, the midwives present were Mrs Rowlette or Ann/Nanny Molloy, indicating the lengthy experience that some midwives might draw on and their familiarity with their clients. Notably, the birth of twins in 1766 led to both Molloy and Rowlette being called in. It may not be a coincidence that in two of the cases where a longer than usual interval between births had occurred, the midwives in attendance

TABLE 1: *Table of Ellinor Appleyard's births.*

Date & time	Name	Interval	Labour	Midwife	Other
8 Apr 1764, 00.15am	John	–	24 hours	Mrs Lucy Davis	
4 Mar 1765, 4.15am	Sally	11 months	10 hours	–	'[Year obliterated] 8ber [Oct] 7th died of ye swine pock'
6 Feb 1766, c.9am	Margaret	11 months	–	Mrs Rowlette	'[Date obliterated] died[?] of ye swine pock'.
19 Dec 1766, 6.15 & 7pm	Edward James (twins)	10.5 months	7 hours	Mrs Rowlette Nanny Molloy	Edward d. 27 'of ye month'; James d. 29 July 1768
4 July 1768, 7pm	Thady	18.5 months	–	Mrs Green of Limerick	
24 May 1769, 1am	James II	10.5 months	–	Mrs Rowlette	
12 May 1770, 7am	Ellinor	12 months	–	Nanny Molloy	
4 Jan 1772, 5 pm	Sarah	19.5 months	–	Mrs Barrett of Limerick	
19 Nov 1772, 11 pm	Margaret II	10.5 months	–	Mrs Rowlette	Nurse Patt Torpey
9 Jan 1774, 1am	Bridget	14 months	1 hour	Ann Molloy	Nurse Patt Torpey d. 6 May 1774
27 Jan 1775, 4.30pm	Mary Ann	12 months	1 hour	Ann Molloy	
1 Feb 1776, midnight	Edward II	12 months	–	Nanny Molloy	Nurse Moore
20 Apr 1777, 6pm	Sophia	14.5 months	6 hours	Mrs Rowlette	d. 5 Sept 1777
15 Apr 1778, 6.30pm	Thomas	12 months	6 hours	Mrs Rowlette	
30 Nov 1779, 0.30am	Andrew	19.5 months	'not long'	Nanny Molloy	d. 7 Dec
16 Mar 1781, 4.30am	Sophia II	15.5 months	2 hours	Mrs Rowlette	
28 July 1785, 2.30am	Lucretia	52 months	1.5 hours	–	'Betty McMahon alias Ned Hallaran's wife nurse'

came from Limerick – Mrs Green in 1768 and Mrs Barrett in 1772. These women may have had specialist training and may have been summoned in circumstances where Ellinor had experienced a period of ill health or complications arising from the previous birth.

The rate of births sustained by Ellinor Hallaran indicates that she is unlikely to have nursed her children for very long, if at all. Where no other contraceptive measures are being used, women who breastfeed are generally slower to conceive than women who do not, usually showing gaps of eighteen months or more between births. Excluding the final gap of over four years, Ellinor's pattern of births shows intervals of between 10.5 and 19.5 months, the median being twelve months. Wet-nurses were commonly used by families of the Hallarans' status in this period, and given evidence of very low intervals between births, it seems likely that wet-nurses cared for many of their children. In four cases a 'nurse' is mentioned in the commonplace book, though it is not clear whether these women assisted at or after the birth or acted as wet-nurses for the infants.

Seven of the children died in infancy or early childhood. Two, Sally and Margaret I, died of 'swine pock' (chickenpox), possibly at about the same time, but the dates are obliterated in both cases (and were not included in Hogan's transcript). No cause of death is given in the other cases.

Several of the deceased children's names were subsequently reused. This practice was common and was a means of commemorating deceased loved ones and perpetuating family names. Other aspects of naming practices are also indicated. Children were named after Thady and Ellinor themselves, and four sons shared names with their godfathers: John was named for John Hallaran, Thady's brother; Rev James Hallaran, another brother, parish priest of Newmarket-on-Fergus, acted as godfather to both of the children called James, and Edward Appleyard, Ellinor's brother, was Edward II's godfather. There were usually three godparents in total. Other godparents were chosen from close and extended family, and as the older children grew up, they might stand as godparents to their siblings. The choice of godparents also indicates wider social networks in the local area and in Limerick. Generally, Elinor and Thady's children were baptised quite soon after birth, reflecting Catholic concerns for the souls of the unbaptised. The officiating clergy are usually named. Ellinor, who would not yet have been churched, is unlikely to have attended most of these ceremonies, which probably took place in the local Catholic parish church. Only the baptism of the twins, Edward and James, who may have been considered weak, was designated 'private'. Edward died a few days later, but James later went on to be 'fully baptised'.

As well as noting the birthdates of his children, in most cases Thady noted the phase of the moon at the time. For example, Sarah was born 'five hours before the new moon' and Andrew on the '1st day of the last quarter of the moon'. The specificity may indicate that Thady was using almanacs, which included calendars indicating the phases of the moon. He may have been able to work out this information himself, since the commonplace book also contains instructions on how 'To find the moon's Age' and 'To find the moon's Southings' (the point at which the moon passed the meridian). It is unclear, however, whether he made these observations merely out of interest, or whether he intended them to be used for other purposes, such as astrology. By the early eighteenth century, interest in natal astrology (casting of horoscopes based on place, date and time of birth) had declined, but many still perceived the movements of the heavenly bodies to have some effect on human and animal health.

Thady Hallaran died in 1798. The commonplace book reveals no clue as to when or where Ellinor died. And though some of their descendants reused it to note the births of their own children, even the lengthiest entries usually record only the conventional details of name, place, date and godparents. The labour of pregnancy, birthing and midwifery, and everyday beliefs and practices surrounding birth and infant-rearing again slip out of view.

Sources and Further Reading:

National Library of Ireland Ms. 5317, Photostat copy of the commonplace book of Thady O'Halloran of Ballycuneen, County Clare.

Patrick Hogan, 'Extracts from the Common Place Book or "Diary" of Thady O'Halloran of Ballycuneen, Bunratty, Co. Clare, 1727–1798',

North Munster Antiquarian Journal, 7:3 (1956), 9–17.

Rosemary Raughter, 'A time of Trial being Near at Hand: Pregnancy, Childbirth and Parenting in the Spiritual Journal of Elizabeth Bennis, 1749–79', in Elaine Farrell (ed.), *'She said she was in the Family Way': Pregnancy and Infancy in Modern Ireland* (London, 2012).

Clodagh Tait, 'Safely Delivered: Childbirth, Wet-nursing, Gossip-feasts and Churching in Ireland, 1530–1670', *Irish Economic and Social History*, 30 (2003), 1–23.

Clodagh Tait, 'Kindred without End: Wet-nursing, Fosterage and Emotion in Ireland, *c.* 1550–1720', *Irish Economic and Social History*, 47:1 (2020), 10–35.

20

Aristocratic Experiences of Childbirth

Terence Dooley

James FitzGerald (1722–1773), 1st duke of Leinster, once wrote to his beloved wife Emily (1731–1814): 'Children and the fruit of the womb are an heritage and gift that cometh of the Lord, … Happy is the man that hath his quiver full of them'. According to this declaration, James must have been a very happy man for he and his wife had nineteen children born between 1748 and 1773. Their voluminous surviving correspondence provides ample evidence of the love they possessed for each other, but also numerous sidelights into Emily's aristocratic experience of childbirth.

When the time came for Emily's lying-in, she moved from the grand Palladian surroundings of Carton House, their country residence in Maynooth, to the family's equally splendid townhouse, Leinster House in Dublin, where the occasion of giving aristocratic birth would generate more news and guarantee more visitors. When labour began, she was diligently attended in the birth chamber by 'the doctor', as she termed her specialist accoucheur, and servants, while in an outer room waited a nurse to bathe and clothe the child and a wet nurse employed to suckle the baby. (Emily believed that breast feeding was dangerous for her eyes, a notion that has some medical foundation, and as she suffered all her life from inflammation of the eyes this possibly explains her disinclination to suckle.) It was also customary for the older siblings to wait in the outer chamber; William (b. 1749, later 2nd duke of Leinster) recalled births as occasions to look forward to because the children were given 'this delicious caudle', a spice wine especially prepared for the occasion.

Following the birth, Emily entered into the traditional month's

FIGURE 5 (above left): *Portrait of James FitzGerald, 1st Duke of Leinster, by Allan Ramsay (1763); oil on canvas (courtesy of the Mallaghan family).*

FIGURE 6 (above right): *Portrait of Emily, 1st Duchess of Leinster, by Allan Ramsay (1774); oil on canvas (courtesy of the Mallaghan family).*

FIGURE 7 (left): *Hermione, 5th Duchess of Leinster.*

FIGURE 8: *Hermione, 5th Duchess of Leinster, and two of her sons, Maurice (standing) and Desmond.*

confinement when she slept and rested, had respite from her daily social chores and was entertained as opposed to having to entertain. For example, in 1761, after the birth of her fourth son, Henry, she wrote to James: 'Lord Powerscourt lounges away some part of every evening here. If he comes early, we make him read *Tom Jones* to us, which diverts the boys.' At the end of the month, she was 'churched', a ceremony in which she was given a blessing in thanksgiving for her survival of childbirth. Afterwards, Emily could return to her daily routine.

In her cycle of life, Emily repeated this ritual most every year or every second year from the age of seventeen to forty-seven, during which time she gave birth to twenty-one children (including two fathered by the children's tutor, William Ogilvie, whom she controversially married after James's death.) Given the many dangers and complications which often attended childbirth at the time, Emily was fortunate. If she complained about the physical pain of delivery, it is not recorded. In fact, on the contrary, she wrote on 1 May 1755, after the birth of a daughter, Caroline: 'I have been up twice and find myself very strong notwithstanding I had so tedious a labour, which generally weakens people vastly.' Unfortunately, Caroline died within four weeks of birth. Emily wrote to James:

> I was not too much affected by the death of our poor little child, which I have now quite got the better of, though I was much more grieved at first than I cou'd have thought it possible to have been for an infant that I cou'd know nothing of. It really convinces me there is a great deal more in what is call'd nature or instinct than I even imagin'd before, for what else but such an impulse cou'd make one feel so much for a poor little thing that does but just exist, as one may say … As for you, it is impossible you cou'd be concerned about it anymore than on my account.

Caroline was her sixth child. She had already lost another daughter, also named Caroline, aged 4, to a childhood illness the previous year. Her letter on Caroline's death should not be read as an ambivalent response to a terrible loss, but rather seen in terms of her youthful emotional confusion, and, indeed, Georgian acceptance of children's deaths as part of God's will. In 1803, as a much older and emotionally mature lady of 72, and on the anniversary of the death of her most famous son, Lord Edward FitzGerald, the United Irish leader who died of wounds in 1798, she wrote to her daughter Lucy: 'the loss of my child is always one of those melancholy thoughts that return almost as often as at first and depress my spirits often …'

While Emily was the 1st duchess to reside at Carton, Hermione (1864–1895), wife of Gerald (1851–1893), 5th duke, was the last. She, too, experienced the loss of a child, but within contrasting circumstances of a difficult marriage. According to Anita Leslie, Hermione Duncombe 'dazzled every London drawing room' with her beauty and vitality. While her beauty survived, her vitality soon dissipated when it was arranged that she would marry Gerald FitzGerald, then styled marquess of Kildare, on 17 January 1884. Unlike Emily, Hermione had to contend with an overbearing husband. She wrote to her sister:

> If I had less vitality and less energy, I should not mind things

so much, I should not be so rebellious, nor restless, nor so irritable. I have nothing on which to expend my energy, no object or aim in life, no great interest … I may not choose my occupations – I thought this winter I would work hard at my modelling – but here is a fresh apple of discord. It is not an occupation K[ildare] approves of. Therefore, I may not go upstairs to my painting room till (under his direction) I have performed my household duties, written my letters and *practiced for one hour on the organ*) within his hearing … And fault is found with me for anything and everything I do.

Unfortunately, we have no record of Gerald's side of the story.

Unlike Emily, who weathered the storm of the death of her infant daughter, with the emotional support offered by her husband, Hermione plunged into despair after the stillbirth of her first child, a daughter, in 1885. She later recalled her experience in a letter to her best friend, Lady Evelyn De Vesci:

After my first little baby was born – the one that died – I don't know if I fancied it or if it is true but a great large fly kept on flying around the ceiling and all that night its wings kept on beating 'the baby won't live, the baby won't live' and now it is the legions of black dogs keep on saying it's all of no use & perhaps it isn't.

In the late-Victorian era, when even the most private letters adhered to strict formalities, this was a remarkably frank disclosure relating to a socially taboo subject, for at the time few accepted and less understood the medical condition of postpartum depression. Indeed, it is only since the mid-1990s that medical research has advanced in this area and studies have shown that up to 40 percent of women will show some depressive symptoms within weeks of birth, ranging from milder 'baby blues' to more severe depressive episodes, often accompanied by hallucination (postpartum psychosis.) Moreover, Michael W. O'Hara's seminal study, *Postpartum depression: Causes and Consequences* (1995), has contended that women with previous histories of depression – as Hermione undoubtedly had – are more likely to develop postpartum depression.

In 1892, the year Hermione's last child, Edward, by her affair with Hugo Charteris, then styled Lord Elcho, was born, Charlotte Perkins Gillman's published her influential short story 'The yellow wallpaper' in *The New England Magazine*. Now regarded as a classic in feminist literature, it tells the story of a young woman recuperating in a country house from a 'temporary nervous depression – a slight hysterical tendency' after the birth of a child. Her physician husband's chauvinistic treatment of her reflected Victorian mores of women's roles rather than any understanding of a medical condition. Thus, his wife and Hermione had much in common, not least of all in finding their intellectually-starved selves trapped in oppressive marriages. In contrast to both, Emily seems to have escaped any signs of postpartum depression and lived a much more fulfilled life in an emotionally supportive and intellectually democratic marriage.

Further Reading:

Terence Dooley, *The Decline and Fall of the Dukes of Leinster: Love, War, Debt and Marriage, 1872–1948* (Dublin, 2014).

Brian Fitzgerald (ed.), *Correspondence of Emily, Duchess of Leinster, 1731–1894* (vol. i, Dublin, 1949).

M.W. O'Hara, *Postpartum Depression: Causes and Consequences* (New York, 1995).

21

The Ladies in the Straw

Olivia Martin

County Sligo doctor Hugh MacDermot married his Roscommon cousin Elizabeth O'Conor on 16 July 1793. The first of their (at least) eleven children was born eleven months later. In December 1811, as Elizabeth neared the end of one of her latter pregnancies, Hugh wrote to her brother, Owen, that as she was so near being confined, his wife would neither wish to be seen nor to venture from her home to visit anyone. This was not unique to this mother-to-be, or to Ireland. Amanda Vickery states that 'genteel' women left their homes less often and received fewer visitors during pregnancies. Visibility of the pregnant shape, as well as health issues and ease of movement, may have factored in the prerequisite for confinement. There is little reference within their correspondence regarding how Elizabeth felt physically during pregnancy, but Vickery records a list of ailments suffered by several English sources during a similar timeline and at varying stages of the prenatal period. In a further letter, Hugh protested that Elizabeth was 'such a Coward' when she refused to allow him to desert her to attend to a distant patient even for a single day. Hugh MacDermot, on the cusp of the eighteenth and nineteenth centuries, had multiple functions as husband, father and doctor, and in the latter role, delivered his own children. He had received his initial medical training in Paris and would undoubtedly have had knowledge of birth control measures of the late eighteenth century, but like many of his Catholic medical cohorts, he may not have approved of their use. In an undated letter, he writes of a relative who was delighted to be pregnant, commenting that if Elizabeth was to discover she was herself expecting, she would be 'miserable', as,

Hugh implied, 'we cannot reconcile our minds to the Will of God'.

There was no effective pain relief available to women during labour before the mid nineteenth century. The practice of drinking caudle to induce labour was usual in England, and Clodagh Tait shows elsewhere in this volume that it is feasible that the spiced drink would have been in use for a similar purpose in Ireland. Mortality rates of mothers during and after childbirth varied between eight per thousand in the later eighteenth century, and five or six in the early nineteenth century. Many women approached childbirth with trepidation, but with resignation to their fate. They, and their families, prayed for the safe delivery of both mother and child, so it is understandable that Elizabeth MacDermot would rely on the presence of her doctor husband to see her safely through the births. Physicians of this era knew little more on childbirth than what Hippocratic texts taught, which, from a medical perspective, was still basic and threatening. Like Elizabeth, many women survived multiple pregnancies and child-bearing, but the number did not lessen the perception of danger for a woman approaching another confinement. While none of the surviving correspondence by any of the mothers within my research describes the childbirth itself, the silence does not indicate that the subject was not discussed, or fear or joy expressed.

In 1813, Hugh wrote of his need to journey to Dublin where he had pressing business, but that he could not as Elizabeth was nearing the end of possibly her final pregnancy. Text books recommended the monitoring of constipation, mild exercise and stable nourishment, and occasionally, bloodletting. Hugh acknowledged that Elizabeth's fear of being alone during the latter part of her pregnancy might cause her to go into premature labour, which, he admitted, she might not survive without his medical support. His frustration at his inability to leave his Sligo home to conduct business in Dublin is palpable: he wrote: 'She still holds out, to my great annoyance', but concluded, 'God send her and me a safe and speedy Deliverance.' There was a common belief that the state of mind of a mother had an impact on the wellbeing of her child, even to the extent of generating deformity.

As a doctor, Hugh MacDermot was often called upon by the extended family for medical assistance and advice. After the birth of one of his brother-in-law's children, Hugh expressed regret at not being there when 'Mrs O'Conor's Indisposition' occurred. In the days and weeks following parturition, many dangers persisted for the mother, including infection and haemorrhaging. Hugh advised that 'Swellings in one of the lower Extremities are not uncommon after lying in'. Husbands frequently wrote to medical practitioners describing in detail symptoms experienced by their wives and seeking advice. Hugh was convinced that the swelling was not dropsical, as it was hard. If it were, he counselled, it would be soft and 'would fail on prefsure'. Jane O'Conor had been attended by another doctor and Hugh did not wish to interfere, but they could, if they wished, loosen the bandage, but not remove it. In an undated letter from Longford to his wife, Hugh revealed that Jane was again ill and in dread of a miscarriage.

Anxiously awaiting the birth of his first child in 1808, Reverend Edwin Stock wrote from his Crossmolina home in north Mayo, to his brother in Dublin, that his English-born wife Louisa 'has been grumbling for this past week'. Edwin's father, Bishop Joseph Stock, reported that the family were all 'in great trepidation for her, she is so large & unwieldy'. Louisa had already been two days 'in pain' and likely to remain so for a further few. For the birth of their second child, two years later, the couple were residing temporarily in Bath, where Edwin was taking the spa waters, and they remained there for her confinement. As the arrival of the baby drew near, another brother visited and reported to Bishop Stock that Edwin 'is in more pain, however, than his wife'. Louisa survived a 'dangerous miscarriage' later that same year. Prior to her own marriage, Edwin's oldest sister, Catherine, was in attendance when their younger sister, Maria Palmer, gave birth in 1807. Their father wrote of the welcome news, declaring his gratitude to 'heaven' and was 'earnest in prayer for the health & happiness of [his son-in-law] Henry's family'. Within a year, Maria had given birth once more and was 'recovering daily from the weaknefs & fever consequent on her lying-in'. Months later, the bishop again wrote about his daughter, but on this occasion stated that 'Dear Maria gains strength apace, & her new born son Joseph is quite a beauty'. When his daughters Catherine and Emma gave birth, he wrote his letters of congratulation 'to the ladies in the straw'. The phrase, not unique to Ireland, refers to the accepted six-week lying-in period after childbirth, during which mothers kept warm, recovered their strength and rested. He later directed his son to send both mothers the sum of five guineas each, as a present from their father on 'their happy delivery'.

Further Reading:

Ciara Breathnach and Brian Gurrin, 'Maternal Mortality, Dublin, 1864–1902', *Social History of Medicine*, 31:1 (2017), 79–105.

For the rural Ireland context see Ciara Breathnach, 'Handywomen and Birthing in Rural Ireland, 1851–1955', *Gender and History*, 28:1 (April 2016), 34–56.

Clare Hanson, *A Cultural History of Pregnancy: Pregnancy, Medicine, and Culture, 1750–2000* (New York, 2004).

Angus McLaren, *A History of Contraception: From Antiquity to the Present Day* (Oxford, 1992).

Linda Pollock, *A Lasting Relationship: Parents and Children over Three Centuries* (London, 1987).

Clodagh Tait, 'Safely Delivered: Childbirth, Wet-nursing, Gossip-feasts and Churching in Ireland *c.* 1530–1690', *Irish Economic and Social History*, 30 (2003), 1–23.

Amanda Vickery, *The Gentleman's Daughter: Women's Lives in Georgian England* (New Haven, 1988).

22

A Mother's Advice to her Pregnant Daughter, 1813

Angela Byrne

In 1813, Martha Wilmot wrote a series of letters to her pregnant daughter, Martha 'Matty' Bradford. Matty was 38 when she announced that she was expecting her first child. Martha the elder's letters brim with undisguised love, affection, concern, advice and support, but her daughter's replies have not been located, if they have survived.

Martha (c. 1742–1830) was one of the Moores of Inishannon, County Cork, and married Captain Edward Wilmot of Oxmaston, with whom she had nine children. Matty (1775–1873), a traveller, diarist and editor, was born in Glanmire, County Cork, where she and her eight siblings were raised. The Wilmots had a comfortable, middling-sort lifestyle. They employed a modest number of servants and regularly travelled around Ireland, Britain and continental Europe. Most of the family relocated to various English towns and cities in the 1810s: Martha, her husband and their unmarried daughter Alicia lived in Clifton, near Bristol from about 1810 and, from 1812, Matty lived with her husband, Reverend William Bradford in Storrington, Sussex. Their marriage was a long and happy one, and produced three children: Catherine Daschkaw (1813–1882), Blanche Elizabeth (born 1814), and Wilmot Henry (1815–1914).

The letters, now part of the Royal Irish Academy's collections, show Martha's experience of the progress of her daughter's pregnancy from its announcement in May 1813, to the preparations for the anticipated birth in October. The expectant mother was fearful and apprehensive following the deaths of a number of her friends during childbirth. Martha's letters hint at her daughter's worried state, even in the early stages of the pregnancy. She wrote on 15 May 1813:

we have received the wished-for delightful intelligence [...]
Keep up your spirits – never fear – you are just the little
creature that will, please God, get through the whole affair
as we all wish, and better you cannot desire. My dearest
Matty, let me beseech you to banish all fears or drooping
thoughts on the subject – put your confidence and entire
trust in God, and look forward with cheerfulness to the
hope of being a happy mother, as I make no doubt you will,
Please God. [...] Set about your works and little
preparations, and interest yourself in them. Walk, but not too
much at a time. Mary Ann took castor oil [*as a laxative*] with
great success. I remember taking a mixture of syrup of
March Mallows [*wild mallow*], sweet oil [*olive oil*], and
magnesia but the Castor Oil did agree so well with Mary
Ann, that I should almost recommend it to you whenever
you want it. Divert yourself, keep your mind in a constant
state of cheerfulness, and banish all apprehension; for, with
God's blessing my darling, you need have none.

The 'Mary Ann' referred to was the wife of Matty's brother Edward;
they lived in London, and her recent safe delivery was hailed by the
older woman as cause for optimism.

Six weeks later, Martha wrote again, this time to try to persuade
Matty to spend the period of her confinement in their house at Clifton.
She emphasises the emotional and physical supports available there and
implies that Matty would be remiss to rely on a maidservant to provide
adequate care for a newborn. Martha rounds out her argument by
unleashing a guilt tactic, stating that she would release Alicia from her
caring responsibilities, to allow her to travel to Storrington to help with
the infant. It is difficult not to find, between the lines, an implied request
that Matty not leave her ageing parents in the position of having to
manage without Alicia. Finally, the emphasis on the family network is
characteristic of the Wilmots, who maintained very close ties over the
generations, and shared responsibilities for the education of nieces,
nephews and grandchildren, for example:

[…] what think you of coming here, […] about the latter end of next September, or beginning of October? Your father's heart is greatly set upon this much, much wished-for plan succeeding, to say nothing of my own warmly affectionate wishes for it, and of your sister's. Here, my best dear Matty, you could be attended by the same person, so successful with Mary Ann. Here you would have your sister's care, and help in the little preparations necessary for the Bee. Here would your poor old Mammy do all she could to serve and please you. Here is good air, pleasant walks and right good assistance of all kinds –Your dear father's extreme anxiety to get you here is indeed very great and he has spoken to me ten times since yesterday evening to write, and will not be at ease till your answer arrives. We are all well aware of the inconveniences that must attend your leaving Home; but then my dear Matty, so many conveniences in being here, during the time of your confinement, outweigh, I really think, the inconveniences […] You like your maidservant, why not bring her to attend on you here to work for you and to take care of your room – would she be fit, do you think, to take charge of the Bee? (I mean, after a nurse tender's charge is over, as I conclude and hope you mean to perform the task of giving the Babe the nourishment designed by Providence yourself.) Alicia leaving home would be a most dire necessity, still, if you will not come, you shall have her.

In August 1813, Martha wrote that she had made for 'The Bee' six cambric muslin wrappers and two petticoats, and that Alicia had made six night-caps from the leftover bits of cambric. This is the last letter in the collection from this period in the women's lives and it closes with a line that continues to radiate warmth and affection over 200 years later: 'most dear little darling Matty, adieu and be assured of the love of your daddy and mammy'. They continued their tender correspondence until Martha's death at the age of 88.

Catherine Daschkaw Bradford was born in Clifton in October 1813

– Matty deferred to her parents' wishes that she deliver her baby in their house. While Martha showered Matty with love, affection and attention during the pregnancy, the middle name Matty bestowed on the infant shows that the new mother may have been missing a dear departed friend. Princess Ekaterina Romanovna Dashkova played a key role in Matty's life, with the Irish woman living at her rural Russian palace for over five years in 1803–8, and later translating and publishing an edition of the princess's memoirs in 1840. Sadly, Matty did not manage to fulfil the promise she made on leaving Russia in late 1808, to return again to her devoted friend. Dashkova died in 1810, broken-hearted at her friend's absence. Matty named her much longed-for first child in memory of this dearest of friends, the woman who referred to herself as Matty's 'Russian mother'.

Note: Spelling and punctuation have been modernised in the quotations above. Explanatory interpolations are italicised in square brackets.

Sources and Further Reading:

Wilmot Papers, Royal Irish Academy MS 12M18: Letters from Martha Wilmot Sr to her daughter M. Bradford.

Angela Byrne, 'Princess Dashkova and the Wilmot Sisters' in Bernadette Cunningham and Siobhán Fitzpatrick (eds) *Treasures of the Royal Irish Academy Library* (Dublin, 2009), 248–55.

Ekaterina Romanovna Dashkova, *Memoirs of the Princess Daschkaw, Lady of Honour to Catherine II, Empress of all the Russias, Written by Herself, Comprising Letters of the Empress, and Other Correspondence*, Martha Bradford [*née* Wilmot] (ed. and trans.) (2 vols, London, 1840).

23

Albert Grant, the Victorian Fraudster, Born in Poverty in Dublin's Slums

Patrick Comerford

When Abraham Zachariah Gotheimer was born on 18 November 1831, his parents were living in abject poverty in a lane off Fleet Street, Dublin. Yet he grew up to become one of the richest men in England, a public benefactor, a Conservative MP, an Italian baron – and one of the greatest political and banking fraudsters of the Victorian era.

How did this poor-born babe from inner city Dublin become so wealthy and such a fraud?

Throughout much of the nineteenth century, as Albert Grant, he was engaged in banking and business frauds on a global scale. Although the scale of his frauds was extraordinary in his day, he was born into conditions of stark poverty and the respectable politician he defeated by bribery and buying votes was also born in Dublin.

Abraham's father, Berton Gottheimer, was born Dov Behr ben Moshe in 1796 in Pozna, then in Prussia and now in Poland. In his teens, he was a Jewish refugee, first living in Liverpool. Abraham's mother, Julia Zachariah, was born in Portsmouth, the daughter of Jewish refugees from Germany. The couple moved to Dublin by 1829, where Berton eked out a precarious living as a poor pedlar.

When Julia gave birth to Abraham in a lane off Fleet Street in Dublin, the family was so poor they had to beg their neighbours to provide swaddling clothes for the baby.

The child was circumcised by Alexander Lazarus Benmohel, president of the synagogue in Stafford Street (now Wolfe Tone Street), Dublin, and his 'sandak' or godfather was Joseph Wolfe Cohen, also from Pozna and a later president of the synagogue in Dublin. Abraham began his working life in Dublin as a humble clerk and then worked for a retailer who sold imported French musical boxes, clock parts and other pieces. The family moved to London, where Berton became a partner in a business importing fancy goods and a commission agent.

But Abraham soon denied his humble origins in the slums of Dublin, his lowly birth and his refugee parents. He claimed he was educated in London and Paris, and by 1851, he was working as a merchant's clerk and then a travelling salesman of fine wines. He was baptised into the Church of England and changed his name to Albert Grant before marrying Emily Isabella Robinson in 1856. Emily was the daughter of Skeffington Robinson from Antrim, a slave-owning sugar planter in Dominica.

As Albert Grant, he was admitted as a freeman of the city of London, and by 1858, he had established himself as a banker and discount agent in Lombard Street. He set up the Mercantile Discount Company in 1859. Concerns were aired about the large salaries and beneficial financial guarantees Grant paid himself and his partners.

When the company failed in 1861 with liabilities of £1.5 million, Grant escaped any personal loss. He was soon financing railway schemes in Yorkshire, Essex and Wales, and in 1863, he set up Crédit Foncier and Mobilier of England to launch ventures for which he found investors by using directories and targeting financially naïve groups, including Anglican clergy and widows.

Soon Grant had built an opulent house at Cooper's Hill near Egham, Surrey, designed in the Gothic revival style by F & H Francis in 1865. He was selected that year as the Conservative candidate in Kidderminster, standing against the sitting Liberal MP, Dublin-born Colonel Luke White (1829–1888) of Luttrellstown Castle. White was a Junior Lord of the Treasury and had previously been MP for County Clare (1859–60) and County Longford (1861–2). During the campaign, Grant was denounced as 'a fraudulent adventurer', but he was elected and held the seat for three years.

Victor Emmanuel II of Italy gave Grant the hereditary title of baron in May 1868. Supposedly this was in recognition of Grant's role in raising finances to build the Galleria Vittorio Emanuele in Milan, one of the largest and earliest fashionable shopping centres in Europe. However, even then, it was alleged that Grant had bought the title. Later, when he was made a Commander of the Portuguese Order of Christ, it was alleged once again that he had bought the honour.

Each of the companies Grant set up in 1864–72 collapsed amid controversy and allegations of fraud. Crédit Foncier fell in July 1868 when Grant left the company, amidst allegations that large commissions had been improperly pocketed by the directors. As the scandals gathered steam, he decided not to contest the general election that year, and Thomas Lea regained Kidderminster for the Liberals.

Between 1871 and 1874, Grant floated many British and foreign companies, including the Belgian Public Works, Cadiz Waterworks, Central Uruguay Railway, Labuan Coal Company, Imperial Bank of China, Imperial Land Company of Marseilles, Lima Railways, Odessa Waterworks and Russian Copper Company. Most of these ventures later proved to be fraudulent.

Grant financed the construction of the North Wales Narrow Gauge Railways (Moel Tryfan Undertaking) in 1872. By then, he was immensely wealthy and that year, he bought Horstead Hall, near Norwich. A year later, he acquired a large slum area south of Kensington Gardens and built Kensington House, a ninety-room Italianate palace, at a cost of almost £350,000.

When a general election was called in early 1874, Grant stood again as the Conservative candidate in Kidderminster and was returned with a majority of 111. This was the only modern British election when a party has been defeated despite winning an absolute majority of the popular vote. The Liberals, with 1,281,159 votes, received 242 seats, while the Conservatives with 1,091,708 votes, received 350 seats. The Conservatives were a minority party in Ireland, Scotland and Wales, but still formed a majority, mainly because so many English seats were not contested.

Grant boosted his public image that year when he presented Leicester Square to the people of London on 3 July 1874. The square, then known as Leicester Fields, had long been in a dilapidated state and had become a dumping ground for dead cats and dogs. Grant bought out the rights of the many, individual owners, planted an ornamental garden, erected a statue of Shakespeare and busts of Isaac Newton, William Hogarth, Joshua Reynolds and John Hunter, and transferred ownership of the site to the Metropolitan Board of Works at a personal cost of £28,000. On the plinth of Shakespeare's statue, he is described as 'Albert Grant, Esq, MP' and not as Baron Albert Grant.

Meanwhile, however, Grant and his election agents were accused of bribery and of buying votes with drinks and food. His declared election expenses were only £300, but he had spent over £1,200 during the campaign. In a ruling in July 1874, Grant was unseated and ordered to pay costs.

Grant was constantly pursued by creditors from 1876 and was declared bankrupt in 1877. He tried to put a railway company in Wales that he had helped finance into receivership over a loan of £7,000, although he had made a clear profit of £8,800 from the project. The company appealed and secured a ruling that it was not liable for the debt and Grant lost the £7,000. He was also involved in the fraudulent sale of shares in an exhausted silver mine in Utah after making a profit of £200,000 from the flotation.

He stood again in Kidderminster in 1880, but was defeated by the Liberal candidate, John Brinton. Brinton's first wife, who died in 1863, Ann Oldham, was from Dublin; his second wife, Mary Chaytor, was from Limerick.

Grant became the model for the corrupt Augustus Melmotte in Anthony Trollope's *The Way We Live Now*. The large house he had built in Kensington was demolished in 1883, the site sold and the marble staircase bought by Madame Tussaud's. His last bank failed with liabilities of £800,000 and he was back in the bankruptcy court in 1885.

Once one of the richest men in Britain, Grant spent his last years in poverty, and another order was made against him just days before he died in Bognor on 30 August 1899 at the age of 67. As his coffin was carried to his grave, a rainstorm began and half the mourners decided to stay inside the church. The burial rites at his graveside were very brief.

Further Reading:

Louis Hyman, *The Jews of Ireland* (Shannon, 1972).

Paul H. Emden, *Money Powers of Europe in the Nineteenth and Twentieth Centuries* (London, 1937).

Thomas Secombe, 'Grant, Albert', *DNB*, 1901 Supplement, Vol 2, 338–9.

24

Fertility Control, Abortifacients and Emmenagogues

Cara Delay

The Belfast Newsletter reported on an intriguing criminal case from Monaghan in 1829, where a boy gave 15-year-old local girl Bridget 'certain deleterious mixtures ... for the purpose of procuring abortion'. Although worthy of a mention in the press, this case was far from rare in nineteenth- and twentieth-century Ireland, when dozens of newspapers reported similar incidents even as numerous criminal court cases, north and south, featured illegal abortion as a troubling crime.

Illegal abortions featuring 'backstreet butchers' may be more well known in popular culture, but in Irish history, women more commonly tried to induce miscarriage by consuming 'deleterious mixtures'. These substances, called abortifacients or emmenagogues (items used to bring on menstruation), could be consumed orally in tinctures, potions or pills. Before the industrial age, they consisted mostly of naturally occurring substances. Plants and herbs known to induce miscarriage included quinine, myrrh, pennyroyal, ergot, savin and juniper. In 1862, a coroner from Monaghan dealt with the death of a domestic servant, Rose, who consumed a large amount of savin to abort a foetus. Indeed, Rose's sister admitted that Rose had taken the same drugs successfully to end a pregnancy six years earlier without ill effects.

Juniper, another reported abortifacient, is a primary component of gin, and drinking gin or bathing in gin was thought to bring on abortion, according to oral histories from Northern Ireland. A 17-year-old girl and her boyfriend, in a 1930 Belfast case, attempted to induce miscarriage through tincture of iron, and lead consumption was a method used in early twentieth-century Belfast as well.

How did women know about these methods? Recipes for solutions that cause abortion may have been available in medical guides or household manuals, but were also passed around by word of mouth. Family members, including mothers and grandmothers, local nurses, handywomen and neighbours all helped other women control their fertility via consumed substances, and indeed engaged in conversations about what methods might work best.

The language describing abortion, however, could be vague. According to Blasket Island tradition, 'mothers would sometimes give a drink to their daughters ... to ensure they had no further children. They used to give them woad and cypress to drink'. Whether this account describes an emmenagogue or a contraceptive tincture is unclear. In the popular mind, however, such distinctions didn't matter much. Before the mid-twentieth century, most people did not discriminate between contraception and abortion before quickening, which is foetal movement, usually occurring in the fourth or fifth month of pregnancy. Through the first few decades of the twentieth century, most people assumed that abortion was neither a crime nor immoral as long as it was self-induced and it happened before quickening.

When Irish women and their partners talked about terminating pregnancies, they often explained their medical issue as one of stopped or blocked menstruation. One Dublin man involved in an abortion case in the 1940s said, 'my fiancée has missed two periods & that we ... were anxious to know what is wrong'. These women and men followed a long tradition of viewing abortion not as the murder of a foetus but as restoring menstruation and thus bringing a woman back to health. A woman could go to a healer/midwife or talk to her friends and neighbours and complain of irregular periods. She could claim that she needed a substance or potion to 'make her courses right again' or bring on menstruation. What she may really have been looking for is something to procure abortion, and this reality may have been understood by all involved. As one Irish woman wrote in the 1930s: 'I got caught and had I not taken *four* doses of a certain drug I would be "off" again'.

We don't know much about whether or not these herbal mixtures actually worked. The strength of such tonics varies, depending on how they are prepared. Some women took too little to have any effect or, conversely, consumed too much and poisoned themselves, resulting in serious illness or even death. Yet because some women described numerous successful abortions via drugs, it is likely that some abortifacients were effective. Ergot is used to induce labor or expel placentas after birth today, and pennyroyal is still considered dangerous for pregnant women.

Although Irish women were aware of the dangers of consuming too much of a particular drug, they persisted in attempting self-abortions, and by the late nineteenth and early twentieth centuries they had more options. Capitalism and commercialisation led to the production and marketing of manufactured emmenagogues, known as 'female pills' in the nineteenth century. These products were advertised widely, giving more women information about drug-induced miscarriages.

Despite the fact that Ireland's 1927 Report of the Committee on Evil Literature sought to prohibit any advertisements for drugs featuring 'the prevention or removal of irregularities in menstruation, or to drugs, medicines, appliances, treatment, or methods, for procuring abortion or miscarriage or preventing conception', newspapers and medical publications contained dozens of such ads and had done so for decades. *The Irish Times*, in the early twentieth century, featured advertisements for Towle's Pills, which eventually would become evidence in several abortion trials. Dr Hooper's Female Pills were advertised for the better part of a century. One advertisement stated that Dr Hooper's Pills were 'the best medicine ever discovered for young women, when afflicted with what is commonly called the irregularities', meaning that they could serve to restore normal

Beecham's Pills advertisement in Munster Express, *19 March 1892*

menstruation in cases of amenorrhea. Advertisements billed Beecham's Pills, another British product available in Ireland, as a cure-all for lots of things, including 'restor[ing] females to complete health. They promptly remove any obstruction or irregularity of the system'. Female pills contained a variety of substances, some potentially effective and some not. Traditional abortifacients including pennyroyal, aloes, myrhh and quinine were present in some pills as well.

By the twentieth century, despite the growth of illegal instrumental abortions, women continued to consume emmenagogues. Many initially attempted to abort pregnancies through 'deleterious mixtures', seeking more invasive procedures only if abortifacients failed.

In 2012, the year that the Savita Halapannavar case brought abortion to the forefront of the Irish public's attention, the abortion rights organisation *Choice Ireland* claimed that there was an extensive 'abortion pill black market' thriving in Ireland during the economic crisis, when it became more financially feasible for women to attempt to buy pills than travel to Britain for a surgical abortion. The Irish Medicines Board, in 2009, reportedly confiscated over 1,200 abortion pills that were purchased online and imported into Ireland.

Even today, then, many women prefer to consume abortifacients in private rather than select an instrumental abortion. The history of abortion reflects significant legislative changes and transformations in terms of popular attitudes, particularly in the twentieth century. It also, however, forms a larger story of continuity across time and space, one in which women have chosen 'deleterious mixtures' to regulate their fertility in difficult circumstances.

Further Reading:

Cara Delay, 'Pills, Potions, and Purgatives: Women and Abortion Methods in Ireland, 1900–1950', *Women's History Review*, 28:3 (2019), 479–99.

Anne O'Connor, 'Abortion: Myths and Realities from the Irish Folk Tradition', in Ailbhe Smyth (ed.) *The Abortion Papers: Ireland* (Dublin, 1992), 57–65.

John Riddle, *Eve's Herbs: A History of Contraception and Abortion in the West* (Harvard, 1997).

25

The Birth of an Heir to a Landed Estate

Ciarán Reilly

In September 1849, there was widespread mourning in Dingle, County Kerry upon the death of the curate Fr John Halpin. Lamenting the demise of the priest, a vast crowd gathered to pay their respects, but were soon outraged to find that a crowd were assembled on a nearby hill where a bonfire had been lit. Almost at once the crowd dispersed from the wake, thinking that the bonfire had been lit in celebration of Halpin's death. However, on reaching the hill, it was discovered that the bonfire had been prepared to celebrate the birth of a child. The lighting of a bonfire to celebrate the birth of child was a long-held tradition in rural areas and, despite the ravages of the Famine, was observed by local communities. However, on this occasion, the people were asked to quench the flames out of respect for the deceased priest and those mourning his loss. This simple tradition to signify new life was usually only celebrated by family and friends, such as was witnessed in Dingle, but occasionally the birth of a child was also cause for much wider public celebration.

The birth of an heir to a landed estate was often cause for celebration amongst the tenantry, allowing them to display their deference to their landlord. On most occasions, the presentation of an address to the young heir and his family preceded the festivities. The address took a standard form, and concluded by wishing that the heir would enjoy health and live to inherit and enjoy his estates. In 1839, at Lisnaskea, County Fermanagh, cannons were fired from Crom Castle to announce the birth of the heir of the Crichton estates. Two years later, the birth of an heir to the Carter estates in Kilcullen, County Kildare coincided with that of Queen Victoria's which created the occasion for double celebrations for the inhabitants of the village. Music and dancing were a central part of the festivities, with travelling fiddlers and pipers employed to entertain the crowds. In 1843, when the village of Colebrooke, County Fermanagh was 'illuminated' with bonfires following the birth of an heir to A.B. Brooke, the Maguiresbridge Amateur Band paraded through the village playing 'popular airs'. In County Monaghan, Kelly's String Band performed for 150 tenants (presumably those of the large farmer class) on the Rossmore estate, in 1852, to celebrate the birth of an heir. On this occasion, the celebrations were more formal with tenants invited to a dinner in the Western Arms Hotel in Monaghan town to celebrate the 'long awaited' birth.

There was often competition amongst tenants as to who could organise the best display, be it a bonfire or another form of illumination. In Kenmare, County Kerry, in 1845, when the grandson of Lord Lansdowne was born, bonfires 'on a brilliant scale, surmounted with tar-barrels' made 'the whole sky around Kenmare luminous'. Likewise, when a Fitzwilliam heir was born, Chinese lanterns lit every house in Carnew, County Wicklow, while the village band played tunes throughout the evening.

Occasionally, the newborn child also made an appearance at these celebrations. In 1860, the tenants of Lord Carew of Castleboro in County Wexford organised a *fête champêtre* (an outdoor garden party) to celebrate the birth of an heir. On this occasion, a nurse carried the newborn child through the air for all to see. A band brought from Dublin for the occasion played on the lawn near a large tent which had been erected for the guests. An address presented to Lord Carew on the occasion by tenants hoped that the young heir would 'tread in the footsteps of his noble parents'.

Very often the land agent was at the centre of the celebrations and received the well wishes of the tenantry. When an heir to the marquis of Downshire was born in 1871, celebrations took place at Hillsborough, County Down, the family's seat, but also at Blessington, County Wicklow and Edenderry, King's County (Offaly) where they owned extensive estates. In Blessington, the birth was celebrated by lighting a bonfire in front of the agent's house. However, the changing political landscape in Ireland meant that a generation later, when an heir to the Downshire estates was born in 1895, there was no such public display in Blessington or Edenderry. Remarkably, memories could be short lived. In 1851, a public dinner was held in Hague's Hotel in Strokestown, County Roscommon to celebrate the birth of an heir to the Pakenham Mahon estates. No expense was spared on this occasion as about 80 of the strong farmers of the estate sat for dinner. However, during the course of the speeches, no mention was made of the fact that the child's grandfather had been assassinated in the town less than four years earlier.

For the majority of tenants, celebrations of this nature broke the mundane nature of ordinary life, and in some instances offered them a chance to engage with estate officials other than on the dreaded 'Gale' or rent day. In Listowel, County Kerry in 1866, we are told that whiskey, ale and porter flowed to welcome an heir to the earl of Listowel's estate. What was remarkable about these affairs was that they were organised at relatively short notice. Perhaps the largest celebration to welcome the news of the birth of an heir occurred at the Ossory estates in Queen's County (Laois) in 1848 during the Famine. When news filtered through in late August of the birth of the young Fitzpatrick in London on 29 July, every village on the Ossory estates celebrated 'getting up on a magnificent scale, bonfires, illuminations and merry making'. Pipers and fiddlers were hired for the occasion and bonfires were lit in every direction. The largest bonfire on the night was to be seen at a place called Garron Hill (Skirte) where George Vandaleur Steele, described as a 'highly respectable tenant', had gone to great lengths to show his affection for the newborn child. With J.R. Price, the land agent, Steele catered for over 100 men who had been employed locally on drainage works who were treated to tea and coffee, while a crowd, estimated to have been in excess of 1,000 people, enjoyed the musical proceedings which continued long into the night as 'lads and lasses joined gaily in the merry dance'. Prior to the birth of the child, Fitzpatrick gave instructions that men and women on his estate should be entertained on the birth of his heir. Remarkably, the following year, there were further celebrations to mark the first birthday of the heir. The child in question was Sir Bernard Edward Barnaby Fitzpatrick (1848–1937), 2nd Baron Castletown. Fitzpatrick led a colourful life as a landlord, soldier, sportsman and adventurer, amongst other things. As a landlord, Fitzpatrick was said to have enjoyed very cordial relations with his tenantry, which began in 1848 when they celebrated his birth so enthusiastically.

Sources:
Waterford News, 19 October 1860.
Northern Standard, 14 January 1843.
Dublin Evening Post, 31 August 1848.

26

Baptism Registers as a Source for Social History 1: Birth, Naming and Godparenthood in Nineteenth-century Cloyne

Clodagh Tait

In 2015, the National Library of Ireland made their microfilm collection of Catholic Parish Registers available online. The earliest surviving documents date from the 1670s, and their numbers and geographical range steadily increase for the eighteenth and nineteenth centuries. The database has rightly been hailed as a significant source for genealogy and family history. However, the Catholic registers and other surviving records of births, marriages and deaths for dissenting communities and the Church of Ireland (unfortunately, large portions of the Anglican records were destroyed in 1922) can also be a hugely important resource to help us understand the social and cultural history of the eighteenth and nineteenth centuries.

This paper draws on the Catholic registers for the parish of Cloyne in east Cork and aims to highlight some ways in which even fragmented runs of baptism records can be used to provide glimpses of communities. Volumes of marriage registers are also available for Cloyne. However, the Catholic clergy, unlike their Protestant counterparts, tended not to record burials, making it difficult to use them for purposes like estimating infant mortality rates. The Catholic Church was increasingly insistent on the proper keeping of records, but official injunctions were interpreted differently in different dioceses. Rev. John Scanlan started his new baptism register in 1803 with the comment 'The Baptisms for the preceding years since the Commencement of his Administration are also in his possession since the year 1787 tho' not collected in one volume as now directed by the Rt Rev'd Dr. Coppinger in consequence of an apostolical [papal] injunction to that purpose.'

The baptism records are somewhat fragmented: there are volumes for Oct 1803–July 1812, Jan 1821–Dec 1831, and July 1833–1878. The format used by different writers can vary, but the information recorded is fairly consistent: usually you'll see the date of the ceremony, the names of the child, their father and mother, and two sponsors or godparents. Townland or street of residence might also be supplied. Comments were added in some cases, usually to identify illegitimate births (for which, see the next chapter, Part 2). The Cloyne documents are in English with the occasional Latin remark, despite the fact that this was a district that was still partially Irish-speaking in the period in question.

Certain other difficulties with the format of parish registers can impede their use as a source. Stillbirths, or infants dying before baptism, were unlikely to be recorded, since the souls of the unbaptised were understood to be excluded from Christian community in death, and were destined for Limbo. The later registers even designate a few baptisms as 'conditional', probably mostly cases where it was not clear whether the infant was already dead when the sacrament was administered (the dead could not be baptised retrospectively). There was a cillín, an unconsecrated burial place for unbaptised infants, outside of Cloyne town and others elsewhere in the parish, so infants and others buried in such locations might never have come to the attention of the clergy at all. Lay baptism was recognised within all Irish Christian traditions, and midwives often received instruction from parish priests on the correct formula for emergency baptism if a newborn was in danger of death. During a visitation of Cloyne in 1785, Bishop McKenna noted that the three midwives in Cloyne 'know the form of Babtism'. During his 1818 visitation, Bishop Coppinger personally lectured one of the two midwives, who are named as Mary Broderick and Abigail Higgins. While the clergy were keen that those subjected to conditional or emergency baptism should be presented afterwards for the full rite, some families may not have bothered to avail of this. Thus, though infants were probably baptised fairly soon after birth, the registers do not capture all births in a parish.

However, counting baptisms can give us some rough figures for births, understanding that an unknowable but probably quite consistent proportion may be missing, and some crude ideas of changes in birth rates over time can be derived from them. They also highlight the workload of the clergy. For example, John Scanlon, in his 1803–11 register, conveniently recorded the numbers he baptised each year:

TABLE 2: *Numbers of baptisms by year, beginning 1 October, ending 30*

1803–4	1804–5	1805–6	1806–7	1807–8	1808–9	1809–10	1810–11
254	236	251	264	253	277	261	277

The impact of the demographic disaster of the Famine years and their aftermath are clear in the Cloyne registers. Counting numbers of baptisms at ten-year intervals draws attention to a marked rise in baptisms just prior to the Famine, followed by a significant decline in 1851 that is sustained in 1861. In the last year represented in the digitised records, 1878, 136 baptisms took place.

TABLE 3: *Baptism rates at ten-year intervals, 1810/11–1861*

1810–11	1821	1831	1841	1851	1861
277	242	243	326	165	168

The registers allow us to consider other issues as well, such as naming practices. In the past as in the present, families chose names for a variety of reasons. In the sixteenth and seventeenth centuries, children were often given the names of their godparents, especially if the godparent was rich or influential: the gift of a name solidified the connection with a patron. Protestant infants would be given biblical names or 'hortatory' names that spoke of faith and virtue; Catholics were given names from the calendar of saints that did the same, as well as creating a symbolic link with another kind of patron. In nineteenth-century Cloyne, family traditions of naming seem to have been strongly influential. People reused the names of family members, signifying continuity, respect and love for their kin. This generally meant that many people got the same names and the stock of names from which parents drew was extremely small. To take 1821 as an example, the top six names account for more than half of all baptisms, and the same names recur year after year. In this context, innovations in naming stand out very starkly: it was surprising to come across a Lancelot, born in 1823, a Rosinda, also born in 1823, a Letitia, born in 1826, and an Emma Maria, born in 1831.

TABLE 4: *1821: Numbers of uses of individual names (nineteen other names appear once or twice)*

John	29	Norry/Hanora	7
Mary	22	Edmund	7
William	21	David	7
Michael	18	Patt	7
Margaret	18	Tom/Thomas	7
Ellen	16	Biddy/Bridget	6
James	11	Eliza	6
Cate/Catherine	8	Daniel	4
Johanna	8	Tim	3

Name recycling can cause difficulties for historians, making it tricky to distinguish between people who shared surnames and between generations of families. However, as noted, though the register is in English, many of those recorded would have been Irish speakers – some of the Johns were probably usually Seán, for example. Furthermore, we should note that Irish communities had their own systems of nicknames and 'local names' that distinguished individuals with similar names from one another. Registers only record a person's 'official' name.

Another element of both Catholic marriage and baptism records that also hints at family connections and emotional bonds are marriage witnesses and godparents. For example, the records relating to John Wilkinson and Mary Mansfield, who married in February 1820, give us the names and dates of baptism of their six children, but also mention the people they had chosen to be present at these events. Their marriage witnesses were John Mansfield and Mrs Foley. John Mansfield was also godfather to their first child, while a P. Mansfield appears on another occasion: it's likely they were Mary's siblings or close relations. Other sponsors are Ellen Ahern, John Aherne, Catherine McCarthy, James Ronayne, Nancy Donovan, Benjeman Knowles, Margaret Fenton, William Harding and Norry Staunton, allowing us to map some of the couple's friendly relationships. This seems to have been a 'mixed' marriage: the baptism entries note John Wilkinson being 'received' into the church in 1828 and notably none of the godparents share his surname – his Protestant relations may have been excluded from sponsoring Catholic children. Several other receptions of adults into the Catholic Church were recorded in the baptism register during this period.

The surviving parish registers, however partial the information they contain and however humble and local their subjects, are a vital source for the study of communities in the past. The scant words that commemorate the births of a Lancelot and a Rosinda and lots and lots of Johns can address big themes, like belief, population change, kinship and friendship.

Further Reading:

National Library of Ireland, Cloyne Parish Registers. Available at: https://registers.nli.ie/parishes/0035.

Brian Gurrin, *Pre-census Sources for Irish Demography* (Dublin, 2002).

Veerendra Leve, '"It's not Really a Nickname, it's a Method": Local Names, State Intimates, and Kinship Register in the Irish *Gaeltacht*', *Journal of Linguistic Anthropology*, 19:1 (2009), 101–16.

Cormac Ó Gráda, 'Liam or Jason? What's in a Name?', *History Ireland* 21:2 (1999).

Clodagh Tait, 'Spiritual Bonds, Social Bonds: Baptism in Ireland, *c*. 1530–1690', *Social and Cultural History* 2 (2005), 301–27.

Clodagh Tait, 'Namesakes and Nicknames: Naming Practices in Early Modern Ireland, 1540–1700', *Continuity and Change*, 21:2 (2006), 313–40.

27

Baptism Registers as a Source for Social History 2: Births Outside Marriage in Nineteenth-century Cloyne

Clodagh Tait

One area where parish registers have proved to be especially useful in Ireland and Britain is in the investigation of births outside marriage. As the Catholic clergy increasingly explicitly identified these births in their registers with the description 'illegitimate' or 'bastard', it can be possible to roughly tally proportions of illegitimate births and changes over time. For example, the Cloyne registers kept by Rev. Kearns and his associates in the 1820s reveal some interesting information.

TABLE 5: *Baptisms with descriptor 'illegitimate', 1821–31*

1821	1822	1823	1824	1825	1826	1827	1828	1829	1830	1831
10 (of 242)	8	7	10	12	4	5	6	9	6	9 (of 243)

They indicate an illegitimacy ratio among Cloyne Catholics that is roughly in line with the national average for the time of about 2.5–3. But we can also read between the lines in certain ways that tell us about changing policies in the Catholic Church, differing attitudes towards illegitimacy, and also give us tiny glimpses of the experiences of mothers and fathers caught in a situation where their child was labelled as morally and legally distinct, and whose birth was likely to bring judgment and disgrace.

There is clear evidence of a policy shift regarding the recording of so-called illegitimate births in the mid-1820s. In the first part of the decade, the entries are haphazard, often lacking the father's name or noting just one sponsor, or none at all. From 1826, names of two parents and two sponsors are almost always supplied: this may have been in line with a contemporary drive to make men responsible for the upkeep of the children they fathered.

We tend to imagine the classic mother of an illegitimate child of this period as a put-upon, friendless woman, her reputation blighted by her circumstances. However, there is only one case in 1821–31 of a foundling, or abandoned child, in the registers, that of John Rail 'mother and father unknown', baptised in June 1831. If illegitimate maternity was insupportably shameful, one might expect a higher rate of concealment of pregnancy and abandonment (though infanticide is invisible in the Catholic registers, and the Church of Ireland vestry in the town may have had jurisdiction over foundlings). And it is clear that parents of illegitimate children had friends: people acted as sponsors after all, their surnames often indicating family connections to one of the parents. Interestingly, in a couple of cases, the sponsors of illegitimate children are named elsewhere as mothers of illegitimate children. For example, the baptism of Ellen, daughter of Ellen Ahern is recorded in 1821, and in 1824, an Ellen Ahern was sponsor to the child of Denis Keeffe and Johanna Coghlan; Mary Wool had an illegitimate son James with John Hanning in 1826, and in 1828, we spot her sponsoring the child of John Shea and Betty Daly. It may be that, as posited elsewhere, parts of the parish were home to groups of marginalised individuals or families, whose reputations were already so compromised that illegitimate parenthood could do little to worsen their standing in the community. But beyond this, as Paul Gray has pointed out, the Commissioners for Inquiring into the Conditions of the Poorer Classes in Ireland, reporting in the 1830s, found a mixed picture of attitudes to illegitimacy, with informants from many parishes suggesting that illegitimate maternity was not necessarily considered that shameful, especially in poorer regions, or if the women concerned behaved well otherwise.

Some Cloyne parents presented more than one illegitimate child for baptism. The name Mary McCarthy appears five times in conjunction with illegitimate births (possibly two Mary McCarthys were involved). Biddy Clark had John in 1821, Margaret in 1823, Mary in 1827, and Biddy in 1829. James Falvey is named as the father of three of the four children, and may have fathered the other as well. This is clearly an established partnership – perhaps marriage was impossible as one of them was married or separated.

In some cases, there were retrospective efforts to regularise the situation of illegitimate parents. Daniel Desmond and Mary Grogan married four months after baptising an illegitimate son in 1829. On 5 July of the same year, John Mullaney and Margaret Beckler baptised their daughter Ellen, and they married eight days later, having obtained a dispensation for consanguinity 'in the 3rd and 3rd degrees' (second cousins). This suggests that, as has been found in Britain, illegitimate pregnancies were sometimes the result of aborted or delayed marriage arrangements in cultures where a certain amount of pre-marital sexual activity was tolerated among those who intended to wed.

Occasionally women who had illegitimate children turn up subsequently marrying men who were not the children's fathers. For example, Mary Bryan had a child called John with John Walsh in February 1825: two months later a John Walsh was a witness to the marriage of a Mary Brien to David Connell. Perhaps John had reached a financial settlement with Mary that had allowed her to marry. The indications here suggest, again as found elsewhere in the Irish and British Isles, that individual circumstances also had an impact on how such births were viewed: experiences of 'illegitimate' children and the prospects of parents might vary widely, often according to considerations of class and circumstances that are largely invisible in our sources.

The terminology used to indicate illegitimacy is also worth noting. In the 1820s, Kearns consistently used the term 'illegitimate'. His eventual successor, John Russell, preferred to use the word 'bastard'. A similar shift in terminology can be noted in the neighbouring parish of Aghada, from illegitimate in the 1830s to bastard in the 1850s (with one use of 'spurious'): in both places there was a switch back to illegitimate by the 1870s. It is unclear whether both terms were considered equally pejorative – were clerics more inclined to stigmatise birth outside marriage by the mid-nineteenth century and did the switch back to 'illegitimate' indicate a change for the worse in its connotations? Kate Gibson suggests that 'bastard' was a particularly loaded term in England by the eighteenth century, and more likely to be applied to the lower classes. Also, to what extent did the attitudes of local clerics change in this period and how did this serve to shape people's experiences of illegitimate parenthood and views of illegitimate children at a local level? By the 1870s, in neighbouring Midleton parish, usually only one female godparent would be named in most cases of illegitimacy, a policy that must have arisen out of a more hardline view of such baptisms as anomalous and problematic. Midleton had a disproportionate number of illegitimate births to very poor parents housed in the workhouse (opened in 1841) – some parents of illegitimate infants baptised there were from Cloyne and Aghada parishes – and this also may have influenced their treatment.

The last year of the digitised Cloyne parish registers is 1878, when four of the 136 children baptised were noted as illegitimate. Hints in the register again may indicate broader attitudinal changes. The fathers are becoming harder to identify; part of a process whereby moral and financial responsibility for illegitimate births was being shifted back primarily to the mother. In one case, John Walsh was named as the father of Catherine, daughter of Mary Duhig née McCarthy (was she a widow or separated?), but a note in the margin reads 'The abovementioned John Walsh came to the celebrant to deny the alleged paternity'. In the case of Mary, daughter of Ellen Keeffe, no father is named, but in the margin is 'The mother says that Edmond Kennefick Ballycronin is the father'. It seems Mary's word was no longer enough to have Edmond's name recorded officially. In the other two cases, fathers are named. One is noted to be Protestant, and inter-faith relationships are evident in cases of post-Famine illegitimacy in other east Cork registers too. (Could increasing antipathy to 'mixed' marriages have been a factor in some of these?)

This is another brief snapshot of a particular area. However, it is hoped that further use of the parish registers will continue to throw light on the identity and experiences of 'illegitimate' children and their parents in the eighteenth and nineteenth centuries. The expected digitisation of the surviving Church of Ireland parish registers will also allow for the creation of fuller studies of particular communities like Cloyne.

Further Reading:

National Library of Ireland, Cloyne Parish Registers. Available at: https://registers.nli.ie/parishes/0035.

Leanne Calvert, '"He came to her bed pretending courtship": Sex, Courtship and the Making of Marriage in Ulster, 1750–1844', *Irish Historical Studies*, 42 (2018), 244–64.

Kate Gibson, 'The Language of Exclusion: "Bastard" in Early Modern England', in Naomi Pullin and Kathryn Woods (eds), *Negotiating Exclusion in Early Modern England, 1560–1880* (London, 2021).

W.P. Gray, 'A Social History of Illegitimacy in Ireland from the Late Eighteenth to the Early Twentieth Century' (unpublished PhD thesis, QUB, 2000). Available at: https://pureadmin.qub.ac.uk/ws/portalfiles/portal/189497376/Gray_A_social_6660026X.pdf.

Alysa Levene *et al.* (eds), *Illegitimacy in Britain, 1700–1920* (Basingstoke, 2005).

Maria Luddy and Mary O'Dowd, *Marriage in Ireland, 1660–1925* (Cambridge, 2020).

28

Foundling Births in
Nineteenth-century Cavan

Brendan Scott

On 1 March 1883, a lay person baptised a baby named Frederick in a private ceremony in the parish of Drumgoon. The baptism was recorded in the Drumgoon Roman Catholic baptismal register as a 'private baptism', which had taken place because the infant was 'in danger of death'. What is unusual about this record is that Frederick had no surname and no parents were listed in the register. Instead, it was noted that young Frederick was a 'foundling'. The term 'foundling' is a term applied to an infant which is abandoned by one, or both, of its parents, normally shortly after its birth, only to be discovered by a third party, and this short essay will investigate such births in nineteenth-century Cavan.

Parish clergy were, in theory, required to keep a note of all baptisms, marriages and burials in their respective parishes during their tenures there. But, in reality, this did not always occur, particularly prior to the nineteenth century in the Roman Catholic Church. By their nature, these registers can be uneven, with not all registers beginning at the same time or being kept to the same standard (not all parishes recorded burials for instance), and civil registration of births was not introduced until 1864.

The Roman Catholic baptismal records for County Cavan (as opposed to the diocese of Kilmore which also takes in parts of counties Fermanagh, Leitrim, Sligo and Meath) on the Roots Ireland website is comprised of thirty-two parishes, some of which go as far back as the 1750s, with the amount of baptisms from 1800–1900 totalling 145,843. The Church of Ireland is represented on Roots Ireland with 27 parishes, and 26,333 baptisms, Methodism with nine parishes (five of which include baptisms) and 887 baptisms, and Presbyterianism with eleven parishes and 2,694 baptisms. This is a total of 175,757 baptisms recorded in Cavan from 1800–1900. Of this number, 68 births were registered as 'foundlings'.

As we have seen in Frederick's case, the fear of a newborn infant dying before he or she received the sacrament of baptism was a very real one in the nineteenth century, a time of high rates of child mortality, and four of these foundlings were baptised by laypeople, in a practice known as 'private baptism', permissible when there is a danger of death. These fears were often well justified and one of these children, named George, who was baptised in the Church of Ireland parish of Drumgoon on 2 April 1826, died five days later on 7 April.

The issue of naming could be a vexatious one – what surname to give these abandoned and nameless children? Oftentimes, it seems that the child's assigned surname was linked to where he/she had been found. A child described as an 'illegitimate foundling' baptised in 1791 in the Church of Ireland parish of Kilmore, for example, was called John Stable, and it seems logical to assume that this is where he was found. There are numerous examples of landmarks or placenames being assigned as a foundling's surname, and they include Catherine Woods, Mary Bogs, John Weeds, Thomas Groves, Catherine Hawthorne, Mary Rock, James Rock and Simon Fields. Two other notable examples are Patrick Kennypottle, who was found on the banks of the Kinnypottle River in Cavan town, and John Drung, so named after the parish in which he was found (Drung & Larah). Another child named Thomas Frost was baptised in Kingscourt on 28 January 1839, and it is likely that his surname referred to the prevailing weather conditions upon his discovery. None of these names appear in the civil registrations for those baptisms following 1864, when the civil registrations were introduced, and it must be assumed that the children were adopted and registered under the name of their adoptive parents or were sent to the orphanage in Cavan which was opened in the 1860s. It is also possible that many of these births were not registered, as there is recorded in the civil registers, in 1867, the death of a boy from Virginia whose name was noted as 'Patrick Mischance', who was most likely a foundling. No record of his birth exists, perhaps unsurprisingly, as it has been estimated that 20–30 percent of births in the nineteenth century were never registered with the local registrar.

Of the sixty-eight foundlings baptised in Cavan during this time period, only twelve were baptised as Catholics. A law dating back to the 1770s stated that in the case of foundlings, when the parents' religion could not be ascertained, the children be baptised into the Church of England. So to baptise these children as Catholics was against the law – possibly why the lay person who had baptised Frederick in Drumgoon was not named and why the reason for the baptism ('in danger of death') was noted in the register. A case was reported in the *Anglo-Celt* newspaper in 1859 of a foundling discovered in Crosserlough, which prior to it being brought to Cavan Workhouse (we do not know the child's gender) had been baptised a Catholic, much to the annoyance of the Board of Guardians. This child's baptism is not recorded in the parish register. It is also possible that members of the Church of Ireland community were regarded as wealthier than their Catholic neighbours, and on occasion, it seems that these children were left in a location where a member of the Church of Ireland would be more likely to find them. In the Church of Ireland register for the parish of Drumgoon, for example, is an entry noting the baptism of a girl named Mary who was left at the gates of the Church of Ireland glebe house on the night of 15 January 1847. This was not always the case, however, and although slightly outside our self-imposed time parameters, a girl named Magdalen Garry in Cavan parish was baptised a Catholic in 1908, according to the wishes of the parents (or one of them at least), who left a note to that effect with the child. Another girl, baptised as Mary Duff in Cavan parish in 1909 had, as one of her sponsors, the Reverend Mother Joseph McGuire, and it seems likely that Mary was reared in the orphanage in Cavan town. When Mary married in 1936, the section of the civil registration which would list her father was left blank.

Although the parentage of most abandoned children was unknown, officially at least, there were likely to have been suspicions, at least in some cases. Although the parents of Catherine Hawthorne, baptised in Cavan parish in 1831, were not named, a note on the baptismal record stated that the parents' identity was indeed known. But the entry recording the baptism of Anne Gibbs of Edenticlare, in 1815, actually goes one step further and lists the parents, James Gibbs and Mary Martin, along with a note that Anne was a foundling. There is no record of a marriage between them, and it is possible that Anne was illegitimate and that her parents gave her over for adoption.

Another case involved the baptism, at the age of one year and three months, of a toddler named William Byers. William was baptised in Annagh Church of Ireland parish on 21 December 1844. In what was an unusual case, his birth father's surname was listed but a note from the minister stated that William, aged one year and three months at the time of his baptism, was, although a foundling, 'in [the] presence of Elizabeth Sheridan and James Walsh, painter'. There is no marriage record for either Sheridan or Walsh between 1830 and 1850, but it is possible that Sheridan was the child's mother, had been abandoned by Byers, the father of the child, and later took up with Walsh, at which point the Church of Ireland minister in Annagh made some effort to regularise the situation by baptising the child. It is also possible of course that neither Sheridan nor Walsh were William's natural parents but that they were bringing him up.

It can be easy to forget the human heartbreak, sorrow and regret which is behind every story mentioned in this short essay. Women (and their children) were the greatest victims in the examples recounted here – pregnant, unmarried and often abandoned by their child's father in what was an unforgiving society. This short essay merely skims the surface of this topic, and much more work needs to be done on it if we are to truly understand this complicated aspect of society in nineteenth-century Ireland.

Acknowledgments:
My thanks to Monsignor Liam Kelly, Mary Sullivan and Concepta McGovern of Cavan Genealogy for their assistance.

Further Reading:
Sean Connolly, 'Illegitimacy and Pre-Nuptial Pregnancy in Ireland before 1864: The Evidence of Some Catholic Parish Registers', *Irish Economic and Social History*, 6 (1979), 5–23.
Roots Ireland. Available at: www.rootsireland.ie.

29

Welcome (Little) Stranger!: Childbirth on the Victorian Goldfields

Katrina Dernelley

In 1869, the world's largest alluvial gold nugget – the *Welcome Stranger* – was unearthed on the central Victorian goldfields, just as the gold rushes were ending and a new period of settlement had begun in colonised Victoria. Over the course of nearly two decades, hundreds of thousands of migrants travelled from around the world in their attempt to strike it lucky and consequently, thousands of babies – often known colloquially as 'Little Strangers' – were born on the central Victorian goldfields.

This article focuses on the story of one woman, Mary Ellen Boyce McMillan (1830–1898), an Irish Protestant from Kircubbin, County Down. Mary Ellen sailed to the central Victorian gold rushes on the *Marion Moore* in 1853 with her husband Hamilton McMillan (1830–1912) of Greyabbey, County Down and their infant daughter Letitia, named for Hamilton's deceased first wife. The *Marion Moore* was bringing families to Victoria, including Hamilton's brother John (1833–1913) and his wife Mary Regan McMillan (1834–1921). Among their fellow passengers were 106 married couples and 150 children under the age of 14 (including sixteen infants). Another eleven babies were born on the journey out.[1]

Mary Ellen and Hamilton had seven children on the central Victorian goldfields: Hamilton (1854) and James (1860) on the Forest Creek diggings (Chewton); William (1856) and Nathaniel (1858) in Taradale; and Robert (1863), Thomas (1867) and John (1872) back in Chewton

---

[1] The *Marian Moore* left Liverpool on 15 November 1852 arriving in Melbourne on 15 February 1853.

FIGURE 9: *A mother holding her baby while helping in the search for gold.*
S. T. Gill (1818–80), Zealous gold diggers, Castlemaine 1852 (1872), H141536 (by kind permission of the State Library of Victoria)

FIGURE 10: *The Forest Creek (Chewton) diggings where Mary Ellen McMillan raised her family. Richard Daintree (1832–78), photographer: Argus Flat, Forest Creek (Chewton), looking towards the south-east, the Mount Alexander Hotel on far right (c. 1858) (by kind permission of the State Library of Victoria).*

where the family settled on the Melbourne Road. Unusually, not one of their children died in childbirth or infancy. The child mortality rate was high on the goldfields, and the history of childbirth on the goldfields has typically been written from the archival records produced when childbirth went wrong. Mary Ellen, however, gave birth to seven healthy babies, raising eight goldfields children.

Midwives advertised their services in the goldfields papers. For example, Irishwoman Mrs Dagge repeatedly promoted herself as a 'Midwife and Nurse Tenderer (*possessing diploma*) Late of the Lying-In Hospital Dublin' (*Kyneton Observer*, 1 January 1858). Midwives, however, were also commonly represented in colonial papers as uneducated and incompetent, and were often held directly responsible for the deaths of both mother and child in childbirth on the diggings. Most women were attended in childbirth by a relative, friend or neighbour, guided only by their own experience. Mary Ellen was most likely attended at first by her mother-in-law, Agnes McLeod (McMillan) McCance (1809–1896) of Grey Abbey, County Down, who arrived Chewton in 1854 with her husband and children.

Mary Ellen's mother, Elizabeth Boyd Boyce, later sailed out as an assisted migrant on the *Ebba Brahe* in 1857, bringing seven of Mary Ellen's younger siblings after her husband Robert (Mary Ellen's father) died in 1854. When Mary Ellen gave birth on the diggings, she was not alone, but rather surrounded by family, guided by both a mother and a mother-in-law who had themselves given birth to large families, nine and eleven children respectively. Additionally, Mary Ellen's sister-in-law lived close-by and she also delivered seven healthy children: the two young Irishwomen often experienced confinement and childbirth together.

On the goldfields, women typically gave birth in their canvas-tent or bark-hut home. Seasonal conditions in central Victoria ranged from temperatures over 40° celsius (104° fahrenheit) in summer, to below zero in winter: frosty, foggy and constantly damp. Even (or especially) in canvas or bark homes, every surface of the home had to be scrubbed and monitored constantly in a battle against the extremes of weather, the mud in winter and the dust in summer, often knee-deep. Irishwoman Martha Holmes Clendinning awoke after her first night's sleep on the diggings, both herself and her bedclothes thickly covered with dust. Then in wet weather, homes flooded, belongings were destroyed and bark floor coverings decomposed, becoming rotten and mouldy.

Clean water was scarce, for both consumption and cleaning. Despite the best attempts of officials to reserve water for drinking purposes, it ran out, dried up or became contaminated, leading to frequent epidemics of disease. Most water was little more than a chalky slurry; undrinkable, filthy with goldfields sludge and decomposing vegetation. Families found that where gold was most abundant, conditions meant that the water was in the worst condition.

For at least her first goldfields babies, Mary Ellen almost certainly gave birth on a rude canvas stretcher held up by saplings driven into the ground, surrounded by furniture constructed from packing boxes. Ventilation was provided by flaps cut into the tent walls, propped open with small branches. Tents were lined, but still cold, wet and damp in winter, hot and oppressive in summer. Mothers then had to protect their children from the multitude of infections that spread rampantly though the goldfields. In 1861 alone, colonial children died of diseases including measles, scarlet fever, whooping cough, dysentery and syphilis. The goldfields themselves provided dangers – mine shafts and the ever-present viscous sludge – as well as fears of the Australian bush.

The records do no show whether Mary Ellen and Hamilton had their *Eureka!* moment, but in birthing and raising all their children into adulthood on the diggings, the family had indeed 'struck it lucky'.

Sources and Further Reading:

'Victoria', *Shipping Gazette and Sydney General Trade List*, 26 February 1853.

Recollections of Ballarat: Lady's Life at the Diggings Fifty Year Ago by M. J. C., State Library Victoria (SLV), MS 10102, Box 4820.

'Diary of Mrs Allen, 1852', *Goldfields diaries and papers of the Allen family*, SLV, MS 16091, Box 4864/5.

Janine Callanan, 'Giving Birth in the Bush: Colonial Women of Victoria and the challenges of childbirth, 1850–1880', *Provenance: The Journal of the Public Record Office Victoria*, 17 (2019), 8–21.

Clare Wright, *The Forgotten Rebels of Eureka* (Melbourne, 2013).

Madonna Grehan, 'Heroes or Villains? Midwives, Nurses and Maternity Care in Mid-nineteenth Century Australia', *Traffic*, 11 (2009).

Desley Beechey, 'Eureka! Women and Birthing on the Ballarat Goldfields in the 1850s' (Master of Midwifery thesis, Australian Catholic University, 2003).

David Fitzpatrick (ed.), *Oceans of Consolation: Personal Accounts of Irish Migration to Australia* (Carlton, 1995).

Henry Brown, *Victoria as I found it: During Five years of Adventure, in Melbourne, etc* (London, 1862).

Kim Torney, 'From "Babes in the Wood" to "Bush Lost Babies": The Development of an Australian Image' (unpublished PhD thesis, University of Melbourne, 2002).

Peter Pierce, *A Country of Lost Children* (Cambridge, 1999).

30

Irish Immigrants and the Experimental Age of American Gynaecology

Joe Regan

James Marion Sims (1813–1883), a South Carolina native, became the nineteenth century's leading authority on female reproductive health after spending several years in Alabama conducting experiments on enslaved women in his backyard hospital during the 1840s. Maintaining Black women's reproductive health was a significant concern for enslavers. After five years of experimentation, Sims was able to repair the enslaved women's obstetrical fistulae. An obstetric fistula is a chronic condition caused by childbirth, where an abnormal opening between the bladder and vagina causes incontinence. Despite years of failed experiments, Sims believed that it was 'God who had called me to this good work, and inspired me with new views for its accomplishment'. Sims's messianic self-belief blinded him to the suffering of his enslaved patients or any associated ethical implications. These experiments allowed him to gain in-depth knowledge of female anatomy. However, his research's trial-and-error process exploited the bodies of three young slave women: Anarcha, Betsey and Lucy, and many other women whose names are absent from the historical record. Although he was not the first physician to experiment with different treatments or surgeries, Sims was the first to publicise his methods and instruments effectively. Sims was internationally praised and rewarded for his surgical discoveries; he is credited with the invention of the Sims Speculum and the Sims Position, and he patented the use of silver sutures (as opposed to lead, silk or catguts, which habitually caused infections).

In 1853, following his work in Alabama, Sims moved to New York City. In 1855, he helped found the Woman's Hospital, a charitable research institution for treating women's reproductive disorders. It was the first women's hospital in the country and it helped transform the field of women's reproductive health in the US, forming the basis of modern gynaecological science. In March 1855, James Marion Sims approached Dr Thomas Addis Emmet (1826–1919), the grandson of the exiled United Irishmen leader, Thomas Addis Emmet (1764–1827). From 1850–3, Emmet had served as the 'Resident Physician in the Emigrant Refuge Hospital', on New York City's Wards Island. During this time, Emmet attended to 'eleven thousand miscellaneous cases, including all the eruptive fevers among adults and children', stating 'I got also some surgical experience and served my time in the obstetrical department, where from five to ten women a day were delivered'. By 1851, 175,735 Irish-born people were living in New York City, comprising nearly 28 percent of the city's population. In 1855, Sims informed Emmet how he was 'organizing a hospital for the treatment of the diseases of women' and asked him to go to the hospital at '83 Madison Avenue to-morrow morning … I will show you something you have never seen before'.

At the hospital, Emmet was introduced by Sims to Mary Smith, a recently landed 'immigrant from the west coast of Ireland, and her condition was deplorable'. As a homeless and sick immigrant woman with severe gynecological ailments, Smith sought treatment in the charity ward of the newly opened Woman's Hospital. Smith was the first patient to be entered into the admittance records for the hospital. Her case provides a window on childbirth experiences and the incidence of vesicovaginal fistulas among the hundreds of Irish women who received treatment at the hospital during its first decade of operations. Smith developed her reproductive and gynaecological conditions in Ireland. She had first given birth at the age of 21, and her labour and delivery were extremely difficult. By the time she arrived at the hospital, she was alone. Her earlier delivery complications had caused Smith to develop the worst case of obstetrical fistula that Sims had ever seen. Emmet recalled that Smith 'was a most offensive and loathsome object'. Indeed, this was the first time he saw 'the application of Sims' speculum and the knee-chest position used'.

While performing their examination on Smith, Sims and Emmet noticed a strange mass in her upper vaginal area:

A grayish mass projected into the vagina which seemed to me to be an immense stone. But as Dr. Sims investigated the case, he found that she had a vesico-vaginal fistula, which appeared to extend from one side of the pelvis to the other. The bladder was filled with a wooden float from a seine-net, which was about the size of a goose-egg. This had been introduced by the local medical attendant before she left home, to prevent hernia of the bladder, which otherwise would have become filled with intestines and protruded through the fistula and out through the labia. The float had become encrusted with a thick deposit and was thoroughly saturated with phosphatic urine. After a remarkable display of patience and dexterity, Dr. Sims finally succeeded in removing it. It was done, however, amid her screams from intense suffering, for it was before the general use of anesthetics.

As he had during the 1840s with his enslaved experimental patients, Sims operated on Smith numerous times without anesthesia in front of onlookers. Emmet recalled that anaesthesia was not used at the hospital 'except for special cases such as ovariotomies, until about the close of our Civil War'. Deborah Kuhn McGregor notes that throughout Sims's medical career, he 'maintained a classbound prescription for the use of anesthesia with an unspoken premise that those women in the wealthy tier were by far the most vulnerable to pain'. For many impoverished immigrant women, their inferior social status did not allow them to decline questionable treatments. In Smith's case, Sims and Emmet performed over 30 surgeries on her over the next six years. Smith was allowed to work in the hospital performing menial labour, just as Sims's enslaved patients had in Alabama.

Sims operated upon Smith, recalled Emmet, 'a great many times without apparently gaining anything'. When the American Civil War erupted, Sims, an avid supporter of the Confederate cause, left the US to travel to Europe and demonstrate his surgical techniques. In August 1861, he began the first part of his European tour in Ireland. Sims gave a demonstration in the Rotunda Hospital in Dublin, recalling how he was 'glad of an opportunity to see many cases in the Rotunda Hospital ... All were anxious to see me perform my operations'. While in Ireland, Sims dined with 'some of the leading men of the day', such as Issac Butt, William Wilde and the Earl of Carlisle, the Lord Lieutenant of Ireland. His numerous publications and travels brought him considerable fame. In 1863, Sims treated Empress Eugénie, wife of the French Emperor, Napoleon III. While on tour, Sims left his junior colleague, Emmet, as Surgeon-in-Chief at the New York Woman's Hospital. Emmet continued to operate on Mary Smith until the early 1860s. These surgeries gained for Smith 'her retentive power, so that she was enabled to discharge her duties as nurse for six or seven years'. However, Smith later turned to Sims for further surgery to remove stones in her bladder, much to Emmet's regret. Sims botched the operation and ruined Emmet's previous surgical work. Smith was left 'incurable'. Sims abandoned Smith's treatment and left her in worse physical condition than when he had initially met her, to become 'a common street beggar'.

Mary Smith was one of the numerous Irish women who received treatment at New York Women's Hospital while Sims operated there. Sims was only one of many physicians experimenting on vulnerable women. As patients, these Irish women helped American physicians in developing standardised surgical techniques to treat other women. However, these physicians often prioritised the professional advancement of developing new surgeries over patients' wellbeing. Sims could not have achieved success as the nineteenth century's foremost gynaecological surgeon without the institution of slavery and the availability of Irish immigrant patients. The foundations of modern American gynaecology rest on the broken bodies of these enslaved and immigrant women.

Further Reading:

Deborah Kuhn McGregor, *From Midwives to Medicine: The Birth of American Gynecology* (London, 1998).

Deirdre Cooper Owns, *Medical Bondage: Race, Gender, and the Origins of American Gynecology* (Athens, GA., 2017).

James Marion Sims, *The Story of My Life* (New York, 1884).

Thomas Addis Emmet, *Incidents of My Life: Professional – Literary – Social with Services in the Cause of Ireland* (New York, 1911).

Thomas Addis Emmet, *Reminiscences of the Founders of The Woman's Hospital Association* (New York, 1893).

31

'None of her Children ever Lived': Stories of Birth and Loss from Irish Pensioners of the American Civil War

Damian Shiels

On 18 May 1871, Chicago attorney J.W. Boyden sat down to pen a letter for illiterate Irish emigrant Jane Murphy. 'She is in my office today', he began, 'debilitated by having borne 13 children, by prolapsus uteri, and by a 6-inch tumour on back of her neck; and in tears, having walked four miles, from her shanty home on the open prairie, to see about her pension'. The 57-year-old Monaghan native had left her dying husband's side in order to make the journey. At most 16 when they had married in 1830, Jane had spent the larger part of three decades moving from one pregnancy to the next. Her prolapsed uterus was testament to the physical toll repeated childbirths had taken on her body. 'I have given birth to thirteen children', Jane explained, before going on to reveal the fate of each of them in turn. As was the case for many other emigrant women, not all had lived to accompany her to America. 'Peter, my 8th', she remembered, 'was born and died in Ireland in 1846'.

Jane Murphy's voice and the story of her children have survived because of an event that, at first glance, would seem to have little to do with Ireland, or with the subject of birth – the American Civil War. Jane's association with that bloody struggle came via her seventh child, Michael. He had been among the *c.* 250,000 ethnic Irishmen who marched off to fight for the Union between 1861 and 1865, and he was one of those who never came home. As a dependent of a deceased veteran, Jane was entitled to apply for a pension from the United States government. Hers is one of the thousands of Irish applications that are today preserved in Washington DC's National Archives. Though they have lain largely untouched by Irish historians, it is a source that almost certainly represents the most detailed record of the lives of ordinary nineteenth-century Irish families to be found anywhere in the world.

Childbirth is a theme that occurs again and again in these files. Children were frequently referenced in the detailed statements that mothers and widows provided as they sought to prove their pension eligibility. Those who were unable to obtain a marriage certificate would often substitute baptism records to demonstrate relationships. When baptism records couldn't be found, applicants called on the women who had nursed them through labour – invariably close relatives or members of the local Irish community – to provide affidavits. Offering up specific details about birthdates and birthplaces was encouraged, given that there was a $2 monthly supplement available to widows for each minor child. Taken together, this evidence provides glimpses into the story of childbirth among the diaspora and the harsh realities of life on the margins in Irish America.

Given the availability of the minor child supplement, many pension agents were prompted to ask Irish women and their friends if a marriage had produced offspring. As with Jane Murphy, their responses often laid bare the all too frequent loss of newborns. Some had experienced this heartbreak before they even finished their journey to America. Famine-era emigrants James and Mary Carey celebrated the birth of their first child before they left Old Parish, County Waterford to cross the Atlantic, but by the time they reached their new home in Albany they were alone again. Their son had 'died on the passage out'. Despite its prevalence, the loss of a child was something to which Irish emigrants never became inured. When asked in 1862 if her ten-year marriage had led to any children, Catherine Eagan's response evokes something of the deep sadness she must have felt, as 'none of her children ever lived to be baptised'. Such testimony serves as a reminder of the individual emotional traumas that underpinned high infant mortality rates. They can also offer insight into the coping responses employed by bereaved parents. In 1858, Sarah McMullen and her husband celebrated the birth of a daughter, having previously lost their first-born girl. They decided to call their new baby Margaret, the same name they had given to her deceased elder sibling. Sarah explained that they did so 'in memory of the first child'. The couple lost three of their four children in infancy, tragedies that may well have contributed to the ultimate disintegration of their marriage.

Many ordinary Irish emigrants in mid–nineteenth century America lived a precarious existence, often just one setback away from a potentially catastrophic change in circumstances. This was an environment that added considerably to the already substantial risks inherent in pregnancy and childbirth. The experience of Limerick emigrant Hanora Hayes is a case in point. When Hanora became pregnant in 1861, she had already given birth to a number of children. But this time circumstances were different. Her husband John, struggling for work in their home of Rochester, New York, made the fateful decision to join the army. Although he must have hoped the move would secure their economic stability, the erratic nature of military pay consigned his wife and children to months without income. They were left to endure the harshest period of the year in 'utter want', with only the intercession of an aunt saving them from the poorhouse. Unable to get either the food or heat she needed, Hanora was left 'very feeble all winter'. By the time she was facing into the final weeks of her pregnancy, she had developed a 'hacking cough'. Hanora finally went into confinement on Holy Thursday 1862, giving birth to healthy twin girls. But her weakened state and the exertion of childbirth meant that now 'there was nothing left of her'. As the Sisters of Mercy came to pray over her each day, her brother rushed to be by her side. Finding her with 'death … pictured in her countenance', there was little left for him to do, but to place the blessed candle in her hand and wait for the end. Hanora Hayes passed away at 3 o'clock on the morning of 26 April 1862. Shortly afterwards, her husband in Virginia received news of a double blow – his wife was dead, and his children had been scattered across a number of institutions and an orphan asylum.

The miserable ordeal of Hanora Hayes is preserved in a letter submitted as part of a pension application. Occasionally, widows and other dependents put such correspondence forward as key supporting evidence to prove their eligibility. The majority of these letters were composed by husbands and sons in service. Most usually dominated by domestic concerns, they provide insight into the relationship dynamics between Irish men, women and children in 1860s America. New babies

– or the prospect of one's imminent arrival – tended to occasion mention.

John Rohan was away with the United States Marine Corps when it came time for his wife to give birth. Though barely literate, the impending due date prompted John to pen a short note home. He expressed his hope that all was well, instructing his wife that 'if a boy call him George and if [a] girl you can take the nam[e] your self'.

Recent emigrant Edward Fitzpatrick from County Laois was in the trenches around Petersburg, Virginia when his wife Catherine sent news that he had become a first-time father in February 1865. The young couple had only wed the previous summer and Edward's excitement was palpable. 'You tell me there is a young son at home there', he wrote back. 'I was very glad to hear of it if the Rebels will only lett me home safe to see him I would like to be home to see him'. Though he tried to fill Catherine in on other goings-on, he soon returned to the subject that was most occupying his mind. 'What ever you do take care of the boy till I ones [*sic*] gett home till I see him'. When he finished his letter, he couldn't resist adding a postscript: 'Rite as soone as you gett this and lett me [k]now how the boy is a getting a long'.

While the widows and dependent pension files offer what are often unique insights into the sometimes hard and unforgiving lives of ordinary nineteenth-century Irish people, those insights only came to be recorded due to a profound loss. All those who applied did so because of the death of a husband, son, brother or father. Just a couple of years after she had received Edward's excited letter from Petersburg, Virginia, Catherine Fitzpatrick bundled it up with a number of others and made her way to the office of her pension agent. There she parted with them permanently, submitting them to the Federal government as proof of the couple's relationship. Perhaps when she did so she brought along her young boy, Michael Edward, who had been born on 8 February 1865. Less than five months after his birth, typhoid fever had taken his father, who – despite his deepest wishes – would never get 'home safe to see him'.

Sources and Further Reading:

Quotations drawn from *Case Files of Approved Pension Applications of Widows and Other Dependents of the Army and Navy*, Record Group 15,

Records of the Department of Veteran Affairs, National Archives and Records Administration (NARA). Specifically, Widow's Certificates WC153520, WC86170, WC25637, WC130536, WC132012, Navy WC9859, WC142303.

Damian Shiels, *The Forgotten Irish: Irish Emigrant Experiences in America* (Dublin, 2016).

Damian Shiels, 'Widows' and Dependent Parents' American Civil War Pension Files: A New Source for the Irish Emigrant Experience', in Ciarán Reilly (ed.) *The Famine Irish: Emigration and the Great Hunger* (Dublin, 2016), 85–97.

32

Six Boys from Ballaghadereen with the Same Parents ... but who was Born the Legitimate Heir?

Patrick Comerford

In 1869, six Irish brothers arrived as boarders at Downside Abbey, the Benedictine-run Catholic public school in Somerset, near Bath. Charles, John, William, Arthur, Richard and John French were all born almost a year apart: 1851, 1853, 1854, 1855, 1857 and 1858. Their father, Charles French, the third Lord de Freyne, had died the previous year, and in the style of the aristocracy of the day, each boy was enrolled with the honorific prefix of 'the Honorable' before his given name.

They must have appeared like peas in a pod. But back at their family home in Frenchpark, outside Ballaghadereen, County Roscommon, it was still not clear which of these six boys was the rightful heir to the family title. Who would be the fourth Lord de Freyne?

Charles French was born on 21 October 1851, the eldest son of Charles French and Catherine Maree; John followed on 13 March 1853, and William John French on 21 April 1854. Surely, as the eldest son, Charles should have been enrolled at Downside as Lord de Freyne, successor to his father's title and estates? But the lawyers were at work. It transpired the parents of these six boys had been married not once but twice – to each other. Which was the legitimate marriage and who was born the legitimate heir to the family title?

These questions continued to entertain legal minds into the following decade, and the family title, Baron de Freyne, of Coolavin in County Sligo, remained in a Victorian limbo. The Roll of the House of Lords, which was issued each year, shows blanks against the name of the holder of the de Freyne peerage in 1875 and 1876, indicating the matter was still undecided almost a decade after the boys' father had died. As

FIGURE 11: *All Saints' Church, Grangegorman: Charles French and Catherine Maree were married here for a second time in 1854 (photograph: Patrick Comerford).*

FIGURE 12: *Frenchpark, near Ballaghaderreen, Co. Roscommon: the house was demolished in the 1970s and the rubble was used as infill for a new creamery building.*

the legal wrangles continued, the vast French estates in County Roscommon were administered on behalf of the family by Valentine Blake Dillon, Crown Solicitor for County Sligo.

Dillon's daughter Nannie later married the third of these boys, John French, and he was a brother of the Young Ireland politician John Blake Dillon (1814–1866). But he was also familiar with family disputes over heirs and titles: the succession to the Dillon title of Earl of Roscommon had been challenged twice in the 1790s, twice again in the nineteenth century, and once more with the death of the last earl in 1850. The confusions in the French family tree were as complicated and as twisted as those in the Dillon family tree, and both are extremely difficult to disentangle.

The boys' father, Charles French (1790–1860), 3rd Baron de Freyne of Coolavin, was born into the French family of Frenchpark House, and for many generations, members of the family sat in the Irish House of Commons as MPs for County Roscommon. John French, MP for Roscommon, was about to be given a seat in the Irish House of Lords as Baron Dangar when he died in 1775 before formalities were finalised.

His younger brother, Arthur (1728–1799), also MP for Roscommon, turned down the offer of the same peerage. But eventually a title came into the family when Arthur French (1786–1856), MP for Roscommon (1821–32), was made Baron de Freyne, of Artagh, County Roscommon, in 1839. However, Arthur and his wife Mary McDermott had no children, and when Arthur was widowed, it was obvious the title would die with him. He was given a new but similar title in 1851 as Baron de Freyne, of Coolavin in County Sligo. This time, however, his younger brothers, John, Charles and Fitzstephen French, were named heirs to the title, in the hope that this branch of the French family would always have a titled representative.

When Lord de Freyne died in 1856, the older title, dating from 1839, died out, but the newer title, handed out in 1851, was inherited by his first younger brother, the Rev. John French (1788–1863). He was the Rector of Goresbridge, County Kilkenny, and was more interested in breeding Irish red setters than either his parish or the House of Lords. When he died in 1863, the family title passed to the next surviving brother, Charles French (1790–1868), as the third Lord de Freyne. Charles was happily married with a large family of seven children, six sons and a daughter. It must have seemed there would be no problem of the family estate and the family title having male heirs.

On 13 February 1851, when he was in his sixties, Charles French married a local, illiterate woman, Catherine Maree from Fairymount. She has been described as a 'peasant girl' who was born around 1830 or 1831. He was more than three times her age: she was 20, he was almost

61, and the marriage was performed by a local Catholic priest. Catherine and Charles quickly had three children, one after another: Charles (1851), John (1853) and William John French (1854). By the time William was born on 21 April 1854, it was obvious that Charles and his children were in line to the family title and estates, and the legal validity of the marriage was questioned: Catherine was a Roman Catholic, Charles was a member of the Church of Ireland, and the surviving legacy of the Penal Laws, even in the 1850s, meant a member of the Church of Ireland could only legitimately marry in the Church of Ireland.

Charles and Catherine were quietly married a second time in 1854 in the hope of legitimising their three children and ensuring succession to the title and estates. This second wedding, on 17 May 1854 in All Saints' Church, Grangegorman, Dublin, was performed by the Rev. William Maturin. Charles gave his address as the Albert Hotel, Dominick Street, Dublin, and Catherine gave hers as Anna Villa, North Circular Road, making them residents of the parish. He was 63 and she was 23; he describes himself as a bachelor, she as a spinster, although their third child had been born four weeks earlier. She was illiterate and signed the register with an X.

Charles and Catherine had four more children: Arthur French (1855–1913), Richard Patrick French (1857–1921), Robert French (1858–1920), and Mary Josephine French (1859–1919), who married Valentine Joseph Blake (1842–1912). Lord de Freyne celebrated his 68th birthday on the day his youngest son was born in 1858. He died on 28 October 1868, and in 1869, all six boys arrived as boarders at Downside to be educated as Catholics, despite the confusion of their parents' marriages.

But it was still uncertain which son was going to succeed to the family title. Eventually, lawyers decided the 1851 marriage was invalid and any children born in that marriage were illegitimate. The first three sons continued to use the prefix 'The Hon', reserved for the legitimate children of a peer. But Arthur French, the first son born after the 1854 marriage, succeeded as 4th Baron de Freyne. His mother, the former Catherine Maree, died on 13 November 1900.

Arthur French was known as a cruel landlord. When his tenants refused to pay their rent, he took leading members of the Irish Party to court in 1902, accusing them of incitement. He had the doubtful pleasure of reading his own obituary in *The Times* on 11 September 1913. On 23 September 1913, *The Times* reported: 'Lord de Freyne, whose death was wrongly announced last Thursday week, died yesterday morning at his residence, Frenchpark, Co Roscommon, in his 59th year'.

Arthur's older brothers, excluded by law from inheriting the titles and estates, continued to live as though their parents' first marriage was legitimate: Charles, the eldest son, was MP for County Roscommon (1873–80); John, the second son, was a Resident Magistrate for Kerry, Limerick and Roscommon; all three used the prefix 'the Hon,' asserting the legitimacy of their parents' first marriage. John French died on 23 May 1916, and the family is remembered in a brass plaque in the south porch of the Church of the Holy Name on Beechwood Avenue in Ranelagh, Dublin, where his widow insisted on describing him as the legitimate-born son of a peer, 'The Honble John French'.

Sources and Further Reading:
Burke's Peerage, Debrett's Peerage, various editions, s.v. 'de Freyne'.
Parish Register, All Saints' Church, Grangegorman, Dublin.
The Times (London), 11 September 1913, 23 September 1913.

33

'Bringing about a Slip': Preventing and Coping with Unwanted Pregnancies in Nineteenth-century Ireland

Fionnuala Walsh

In 1868, Thomas Haslam, husband of the well-known Irish suffragist Anna Haslam, published a pamphlet titled 'The Marriage Problem', which aimed to address what Haslam described as one of the 'most urgent social problems of the day': 'how to secure the satisfactions of married life without exposure to the miseries resulting from an excessive number of offspring'. It outlined several family limitation strategies including barrier methods, coitus interruptus and the use of the 'safe period'. The Haslams had no children, but this is commonly believed to be due to them practising abstinence than the effectiveness of his 'safe period' method. Indeed, his understanding of the female reproduction system was flawed, and the use of Haslam's method was more likely to result in pregnancy than not. His pamphlet was produced for private circulation 'amongst Adult Readers only' and the extent of its readership in Ireland is unknown. Marie Stopes took an interest in Haslam's work and engaged in lengthy correspondence with his widow for several years. In these letters, Anna mentions that that she is 'deeply interested in the question [of birth control] and has helped many women'.

There has been limited scholarship on birth control in nineteenth-century Ireland, making it difficult to ascertain to what extent the Haslams were an anomaly in taking an active interest in the subject. Contemporary British sources indicate such practices, together with abortion, were relatively common in the late nineteenth century. In 1914, the Women's Cooperative Guild asked its membership (married working-class women) to provide details of their maternity experiences. The resulting 386 testaments provide fascinating insight into the use of birth control and abortifacients in England in the late-nineteenth and early-twentieth centuries. One woman, for example, decided after birthing seven children in the first decade of her marriage, that if 'there was no natural means of prevention, then of course artificial means must be employed', and she reported that she was subsequently 'able to take pretty good care of myself'. References to attempts to bring about abortions also appear frequently in the letters:

> I confess without shame that when well-meaning
> friends said: 'you cannot afford another baby, take this
> drug', I took their strong concoctions to purge me of
> the little life that might be mine. They failed as such
> things generally do and the third baby came.

Another wrote that she had resorted to drugs 'trying to prevent or bring about a slip'. That woman had eight living children, two still-births and three miscarriages. These letters refer primarily to urban women living in England, but the high emigration from Ireland in this period and the strong links between Ireland and Britain make it likely that knowledge of such practices existed in Ireland and, indeed, there is evidence that some women in Ireland were familiar with similar remedies.

Although abortion was made illegal by the 1861 Offences Against the Person Act, there is evidence from folklore sources and newspaper adverts that non-surgical abortions were utilised by women in Ireland. Anne O'Connor's study of Irish folklore has revealed home remedies such as soaking the feet in hot water and inhaling mixes of urine, boiling water and onion. Herbal remedies derived from juniper or savin were also used. Writing in 1849, Dr William Wilde referred to 'drastic purgatives' administered by 'she-quacks' in rural Ireland. He blamed their use on Irish societal attitudes towards illegitimate births:

> Can we wonder at the ignorant Irish girl wishing to conceal
> her shame by the destruction of her offspring, in a country
> acknowledged to be one of the most moral in Europe, and
> where caste is most certainly lost by circumstance of
> pregnancy before or without marriage.

He suggested that the absence of discussion of abortion was exceptional to Ireland, asserting that 'in other lands boasted to be the most civilised, induced abortion, even among married females, in the upper ranks of life, is spoken of in society without reserve'. There were also commercially available products which were used for a similar purpose as herbal remedies.

Beecham's pills, for example, were advertised in the *Cork Examiner* in 1890, with the description:

> For females of all ages these pills are invaluable as a few doses of them carry off all humours and bring about all that is required. No female should be without them. There is no medicine to be found equal to Beecham's Pills for removing any obstruction or irregularity of the system.

The advert asserted that the pills were sold by retailers everywhere. Despite the opaque phrasing, adult readers would understand that the pills served as abortifacients. Similar products also sold in Ireland included Dr Hooper Female Pills and Widow Welch's Pills. The only statistics for abortion in Ireland are derived from court cases, but these represent a small minority of those who deliberately ended their pregnancies. Cara Delay's work in this volume and elsewhere indicates that women exercised greater agency in these matters than is often acknowledged and that abortion was not viewed in moral terms. Taking pills such as Beecham's was seen as an effort to restore the natural state of the female body; they were also a private act and so one did not need to articulate even to oneself exactly what action the pills were performing. Ideas about pregnancy and 'quickening' also varied in time and culture, placing different meaning on pregnancy loss. Sourcing reliable pills, or a safe surgical abortion, was nevertheless out of reach for many single impoverished women. They were more likely to resort to the desperate measure of infanticide to cope with their unwanted pregnancy. The high number of infanticide cases in nineteenth-century Ireland suggests that premarital and extramarital sexual relationships were not that unusual in this time, despite the disapproval of the Church and State authorities. The use of family limitation practices is also evident in the declining birth rate.

The late nineteenth and early twentieth centuries witnessed a significant decline in the birth rate across most of Europe. In Britain, the number of live births for each married woman fell from six to two from 1860–1940. Ireland also experienced a noticeable decline in the birth rate, falling from 26.2 per 1,000 for the years 1871–81 to 22.8 per 1,000 for 1881–91. As observed by Mary E. Daly, in Britain the falling birth rate reflected fertility control within marriage, but in Ireland it primarily resulted from the declining marriage rate. However, Daly notes that fertility within marriages was also falling in the same period. Demographic research by Cormac Ó Gráda and Timothy Guinnane demonstrates that by 1911, family limitation was practised by certain social groups in Ireland. Those most likely to do so were Protestants, those in non-agricultural occupations and the more prosperous farmers. Families in Belfast and Dublin were smaller than elsewhere in Ireland and Protestants had significantly fewer children than their Catholic neighbours. In the late 1920s and the 1930s, the use of birth control became a subject of significant concern in Ireland. The popularity of works by Marie Stopes and the growing use of contraceptives by married couples in Britain led to anxiety among Irish politicians and churchmen about declining family sizes. This chapter demonstrates, however, that knowledge of such practices was circulating in Ireland several decades earlier. Women in post-Famine Ireland found numerous ways to control their fertility, and in difficult circumstances, they resorted to extreme measures to cope with unwanted pregnancies.

Further Reading:

Cara Delay, 'Pills, Potions and Purgatives: Women and Abortion Methods in Ireland, 1900–1950', *Women's History Review*, 28:3 (2019), 479–99.

Mary E. Daly, 'Marriage, Fertility and Women's Lives in Twentieth Century Ireland (*c.* 1900–*c.* 1970)', *Women's History Review*, 15:4 (2006), 571–85.

Carmel Quinlan, *Genteel Revolutionaries: Anna and Thomas Haslam and the Irish Women's Movement* (Cork, 2002).

Anne O'Connor, 'Abortion: Myths and Realities from Irish Folk Tradition', in Ailbhe Smyth (ed.), *The Abortion Papers Ireland: vol. 1* (Cork, 1992), 57–75.

Margaret Llewelyn Davies (ed.) *No one but a Woman Knows: Stories of Motherhood before the War* (London, 2012).

34

'The Eternal Salvation of the Infant is here at Stake': O'Kane on the Caesarean Operation in 1867

Thomas O'Loughlin

The rubrician is now an extinct religious animal. It evolved in the aftermath of the Reformation and was part lawyer, part theologian, with a little bit of nerd added in. Rubricians concerned themselves with the exact fulfilment of the rules of ritual as laid down by the Catholic Church, working on the assumption that its ritual was nigh on perfect as an expression of God's will, regulated by authority, and they lived on the edge of an intellectual abyss: if these rules were not fulfilled or found wanting, then the entire edifice of Tridentine certainty might begin to crumble. They also had a constant enemy: human beings continually failed to fall in neatly within the perfect system which they policed. The result was the need to find ways to get human beings to conform to the rules or, in special cases, find ways to adapt the rules to suit them. Because of other distractions, Ireland did not produce any eminent rubricians until the latter half of the nineteenth century, but then in the person of James O'Kane (1825–1874), Senior Dean of Maynooth, it produced a master. His *Notes on the Rubrics of the Roman Ritual*, first published in 1867, would be updated and reprinted until the 1950s, and remain on seminary curricula until the early 1960s.

It was well known among rubricians that women, and particularly their association with child-bearing, posed the greatest problems to the priest seeking to exercise his pastoral duties while simultaneously fulfilling the laws laid down in the *Rituale Romanum* of 1614 – and, in this regard, there was no more awkward problem than what was then called 'the Caesarean Operation'. While today the C-Section is a relatively normal occurrence as a work around for difficult births, until the latter half of the nineteenth century it had a very different, and grimmer, meaning. It was then only performed on a woman already dead – usually in the case of a woman having died in giving birth – where there was some hope that even with the mother dead, the foetus might still be alive and able to be extracted by surgery. It was believed that this was exactly what happened in antiquity to the infant Julius Caesar from which the procedure took its name.

The 1614 ritual had legislated for this situation with regard to the baptism of infants:

> If a pregnant mother dies, the foetus must first be carefully removed, and if it is alive it should be baptised; if dead, and if baptism is not possible, it ought not to be buried in holy ground (n. 20).

Upon this, O'Kane had to comment, and while we might think of, say, what colour vestments a priest might wear, as the normal territory of a rubrician, here he was expected to be an expert in obstetrics. His first comment is wise and sensible: 'there must be a certainty of the mother's death before any incision is attempted, otherwise it is evident there would be a risk of taking away or shortening her life; and this is never lawful, not even to procure the baptism of the infant'. But if the mother is dead, then 'there is a strict obligation of doing all that can be done … to give the infant a chance of receiving [baptism]'.

Having dealt with the objection – by an appeal to facts – that the foetus always dies along with the mother, and whether or not keeping the mother's mouth or her abdomen warm helps preserve its life while waiting for someone who could perform the surgery (an open mouth makes no difference, but warmth may help), he proceeds to his main concern: who should perform the operation? Clearly, a surgeon is the ideal but, failing that, a midwife; failing that, a 'female'; and, if none of these, a man. However, a rubrician had argued that it should never be done by a priest, especially a young priest. In reply, another rubrician had softened the opinion to: 'the priest is not bound to perform it'. Here was the *dubium* that O'Kane would exploit.

First, he noted that this prohibition/exception was only discussed by two rubricians – and several state explicitly that 'it is the duty of the parish priest to perform it'. O'Kane, having noted that 'the operation is extremely unsuited to the priestly character', argued that if 'there is no one but the priest … it is hard to see why he might not, and should not, perform it if he can, since the eternal salvation of the infant is here at stake'. If it must be done, and by a priest, he needs instructions; and so O'Kane supplies them:

> 1. The incision should be made on the side that appears most prominent, lengthwise, and not across. It may be made with a razor when there is no surgical instrument.
> 2. It should be about six or seven inches long. Then having been cut through, and the entrails that may be met with set aside, the matrix [= womb] must be opened very gently, so as not to hurt the infant. When the matrix is sufficiently opened, conditional baptism should be administered with tepid water, lest the infant might die on exposure to air. It should then be taken out, and when the membrane in which it has been is removed, it should again be baptized conditionally.

He proceeded then to give instructions on what the priest was to do if there was even the possibility of life – it was to be baptised using the form 'If you are alive …' – and what to do if it was found dead: it cannot be baptised. Here his text is slightly fuzzy in that he repeats the Ritual's prohibition on its burial in holy ground (assuming its death is discovered after extraction), but by narrowing the rubric, he is then able to present a more lenient view: 'if it is found dead in the womb, however, it should not be removed but buried with the mother'.

O'Kane's book was updated by Thomas O'Doherty (1877–1936) in 1922 and almost no change was made to this section; then in 1932, Michael Fallon (?1895–1965) produced a major revision in light of the 1917 Code of Canon Law, which was last reprinted in 1951. He repeats the 1867 text verbatim and expects that the seminarians, for whom this was a textbook, should learn it. He does, however, add this item of factual updating: 'We may observe that the Caesarean operation is, nowadays, regarded as an ordinary operation even when performed on the living patient, and, thanks to the progress of modern surgery, the cases are rare in which, with skilful handling, it is unsuccessful'.

There is a cold factuality of life/death, salvation/damnation here that affronts us – and O'Kane was lenient for his time. Equally, we are shocked by its lack of pastoral wisdom: there is a haunting silence about consulting anyone who loved the dead woman before the priest mutilated the body with a razor! And what is served, but an increase in pain by burial in 'unconsecrated ground'? But, just as frightening is the conviction of certainty, the sense of a complete possession of knowledge by the Church, underpinning the whole treatment. By 1932, surgical progress could be acknowledged, but theological limitation or the notion that the Church ever erred were not to be admitted.

Further Reading:

James O'Kane, *Notes on the Rubrics of the Roman Ritual* (Dublin 1867), 106–10.

Michael J. Fallon, *Notes* ... (Dublin, 1951 [i.e. edition of 1932]), 90–4.

Ananya Mandal, 'Cesarean Section History'. Available at: https://www.news-medical.net/health/Cesarean-Section-History.aspx.

35

Meeting Medics, 'Monsters' and Mothers in Nineteenth-century Scientific Journals

Clodagh Tait

In 1892, W.J. Smyly, Master of the Rotunda Lying-in Hospital in Dublin, read a paper entitled 'On a case of Double Monster' to the Royal Academy of Medicine in Ireland. The mother of what we would term conjoined twins was 27 and had had three children. 'Four feet presented; it was supposed to be twins. Labour occupied 21 hours, and was easily terminated by traction on the legs'. Smyly described the nature of the 'deformity', which was 'different from any that I have seen or read of. The right sides of both heads are fused together, so that a face appears on both aspects, with an occiput [back of the head] and ear on either side of it.' The bodies were fused as far as the umbilicus, 'but the eight extremities are perfect'. He concluded that this was an example of the 'rarest' form of 'double monster' – united by the heads, but with 'bodies separate below'.

In early modern Europe, infants or animals born with visible congenital disorders aroused huge fascination. Called 'monsters' (from the Latin *monstrum*, in one sense meaning a portent), they were understood as wonders or 'prodigies' that could be read as signs of God's will or warning or blamed on transgressive behaviour and distracted times. They might be attributed to sinful or careless actions by women during pregnancy, or to maternal imagination. Traditional advice given to pregnant women preserved in the Irish folklore collections enjoined them to avoid certain activities that might compromise the health of the unborn child – they should avoid graveyards for example, for fear of bearing a child with crooked limbs, and if a hare was spotted, the woman should use charms like tearing a piece of clothing to avoid the birth of an infant with a cleft palate ('hare lip').

By the nineteenth century, while theological explanations for their appearance had waned, so-called monsters were still a matter of morbid public interest, with living and dead individuals often being displayed in collections of curiosities and 'freak shows'. Meanwhile, doctors increasingly sought to formulate scientific interpretations of birth defects and to categorise their different presentations. Medical journals thus provide a useful source for cases of births of conjoined twins like those Smyly described, and of infants with other rare disorders. However, it is unlikely that the physicians would have asked the permission of the patients or their families to analyse their ailments in print. Historians thus find themselves in a somewhat voyeuristic role, troublingly indebted to 'medical paternalism' and the liberties taken by practitioners, and tied to the language they used.

There are reasons for persevering with problematic sources. The cases discussed here were anonymised in the journals and are thus unidentifiable. And they do succeed in giving tiny, but rare glimpses of the experiences of birthing mothers at times of personal and medical crisis. As well as demonstrating changing understandings of anomalous births, they also reveal how nineteenth-century physicians developed their clinical knowledge and participated in professional networks. They also allow us, occasionally, to look behind the veneer of medical professionalism at the dilemmas that might face the doctors themselves.

R. W. O'Donovan of Belturbet, County Cavan, reported a case of conjoined twins in 1851. He had been called to see a 35-year-old mother of three, 'Mrs L—', who was seven months pregnant. She had not been well for a number of weeks, 'her countenance pale and sickly; loss of appetite; frequent vomiting, and she is much emaciated'. Her abdomen was 'enormously enlarged, having the appearance of a twin pregnancy in the ninth month'. He offered some medicines and departed, but was called back that evening 'in consequence of labour setting in rapidly'. The patient's waters had broken, and an infant's legs, 'cold and livid' were hanging down. On doing an internal examination, O'Donovan found two more legs, and 'assisted' the woman's 'few and weak' contractions 'by gradually drawing down the child'. He said 'I ultimately delivered her of a full-grown monster foetus, with two heads and two sets of extremities.'

O'Donovan was taken aback at what he termed the 'horrible appearance' of the stillborn infants. The heads faced one another, 'the line of junction commencing at the lower lip and continuing perfect to the umbilicus'. The upper parts of the twins' bodies were 'well formed and distinct, except for the juncture', but 'the abdominal parietes were deficient at the junction of the funis [umbilical cord], where there existed only a thin diaphanous membrane'. 'The arms of the children embraced each other in the form of a figure of 8.' O'Donovan was somewhat apologetic that he was unable to provide further scientific details, blaming 'the prejudice that exists among the lower orders in this country', for his inability 'to obtain permission to make an anatomical examination of this monster'.

In 1885, Dr Kidd, Master of the Coombe Lying-in hospital, 'showed a double foetal monster, aged about five months', sent from a Dr Leeper in Armagh. No doubt his audience was well-acquainted with grisly show-and-tells, but Kidd still apologised for the state of his exhibit: 'The specimen had been retained *in utero* for some time after its death, and upon delivery was already somewhat lacerated and decomposed.' Despite this, and inexpert preservation, 'the main features of the monstrosity were quite apparent'. The 'specimen' had two bodies joined at the sternum to a single head, 'one of the most common forms of a double monster'.

Some of the remains that were acquired by physicians like Kidd were retained in the medical schools. In his book *On the Theory and Practice of Midwifery* (1842), Fleetwood Churchill, Professor of Midwifery in TCD, mentioned a skeleton in the Royal College of Surgeons, 'the children being joined by the lower part of the sacrum, and I believe they were also born alive'. He noted that in cases of conjoined twins, surgical intervention to 'lessen the bulk' of the children might be necessary to facilitate delivery, even if death was the result. However, he cautioned his 'junior readers' that 'the destruction of a monster after birth (no matter how great the deformity,) is punishable as infanticide'. Clearly there were concerns that their abnormalities might lead to the murder of infants out of fear or pity.

As Sarah Mitchell points out, for nineteenth-century observers, 'double monsters' were just 'one type of monstrosity, along a graded scale with many others'. For example, William Roe, assistant Master of the Coombe, reported 'A Case of Cycolpian Monster' in 1871. The mother was 35, on her fifth pregnancy and 'never ha[d] nursed her children' (the infants may all have died or may have been wet-nursed or artificially fed for health, economic or social reasons – mothers who did not nurse were believed to be more susceptible to gynaecological issues). Roe went into detail about the grim work needed and the dilemmas he and his assistant faced before 'I delivered her of the monster which I now show the Society'. They were concerned that there might be a twin who might be harmed by their interventions, but eventually discovered a second mass in the woman's uterus to be a large fibroid. As well as presenting with cyclopia, a lethal malformation of the skull and brain that causes babies to be born with a single or partially divided eye and other malformations of the head, the infant girl was also suffering from hydrocephaly, with a significant amount of fluid in the skull.

What is striking about these examples and about other (invariably horrific) cases of complicated pregnancies and births reported in medical journals is how the birthing mothers fade into the background. The doctors place themselves at the centre of their accounts. Their gaze focuses minutely on the infants' remains, ignoring maternal physical or emotional pain, and never indicating how the mothers or their communities reacted to or interpreted the deaths and strange appearance of their children. The mother of the 'Cyclopian monster' disappears from Roe's lengthy report as soon as he 'delivered her' (his work, not hers).

However, we do get some indications of the progress of the births themselves (rare enough in this period), and of episodes of illness leading up to them. We also have hints at the short-term fate of some mothers. O'Donovan, for example, vividly portrays Mrs L's weakened state before the birth and notes that afterwards she was given punch and laudanum and rallied well. However, we know nothing of the effects of their experiences on the mothers' subsequent health and fertility. One wonders in particular about the outcome for the woman whose conjoined foetuses were retained *in utero* long enough for them to begin to decompose. Where 'specimens' were obtained, there is no mention of how this was accomplished, though O'Donovan's failure to acquire

Mrs L's conjoined twins indicates that medical authority was not absolute. His horror at their appearance hints momentarily at the distress some doctors felt, and the accounts also indicate other dilemmas that might face them.

These are not easy accounts to read, and they should be used carefully. We can only attempt to make some amends for our morbid curiosity by highlighting the losses that contributed to the advancement of medical knowledge and reflecting on, if partly in imagination, the lived experience of labouring and bereaved mothers.[1]

Further Reading:

A.W. Bates, *Emblematic Monsters: Unnatural Conceptions and Deformed Births in Early Modern Europe* (New York, 2005).

Fleetwood Churchill, *On the Theory and Practice of Midwifery* (London, 1842).

Sarah Mitchell, 'From "Monstrous" to "Abnormal": The Case of Conjoined Twins in the Nineteenth Century', in Waltraud Ernst (ed.), *Histories of the Normal and the Abnormal* (Oxford, 2006).

The Dublin Quarterly Journal of Medical Science / The Dublin Journal of Medical Science, volumes 12, 51, 81, via Bayerische Staatsbibliothek and Google Books.

Transactions of the Royal Academy of Medicine in Ireland, volume 10, via Google Books.

[1] Many thanks to Dr Aoife Breathnach for her helpful comments on a draft of this article.

36

The Death of May Chichester and the End of her Ten-month Marriage

Maeve O'Riordan

Birth and death might be very closely linked for both mother and baby, even amongst the very wealthiest families in the nineteenth century. While elite women had ready access to the best available nutrition and living conditions, and the 'optimum' available maternal healthcare, there was no guarantee of a safe delivery, or that the medical men involved would understand the ailments which might hit during and immediately after labour. Women of the landed classes may have been better off than their contemporaries, but they were still prone to dying in childbirth at rates much higher than we have grown used to. Antibiotics were not available and post-partum infections could prove deadly. In my research on the landed class during the period 1860–1914, a class deeply committed to reproduction, there are numerous examples of wealthy women dying in childbirth, or shortly afterwards. Of twenty landlord marriages, two ended with the death of a mother in childbirth. In both cases, the couples do not appear to have made any effort to limit their pregnancies. Childbirth and the provision of an heir was an essential duty of landlord's wives, and one which could give them a great sense of dynastic pride.

In 1877, Elizabeth Ryan of Inch House, County Tipperary died four days after giving birth to a child who did not survive her. It was her second birth since she married in 1875. Emily Holmes à Court, first wife of Lord Inchiquin died in early January 1868 eleven days after her fourth birth. She was 25, and had given birth in 1863, 1864, 1866 and 1867. Letters from her husband show that she was severely debilitated by this last pregnancy and that she was barely able to walk. A month later, Emily's sister-in-law Mary Holmes à Court (née Anderson, m. 12 April 1877, d. 22 Feb. 1878), died on the day she gave birth to a large healthy boy, eleven months into her marriage; the boy sadly died at the age of 4. Mary had completed her dynastic duty to her husband Charlie in providing him with an heir, but Charlie initially resented his son, saying he had 'robbed him' of his beloved wife. Charlie's father feared that Charlie would 'fall down at the funeral – he shook like an aspen leaf'. Years later, when Lord Inchiquin had remarried and was expecting his first child with his second wife, Baron Heytesbury wrote to him to empathise with all of the mix of emotions that such a birth would bring. Lord Inchiquin eventually had ten children with his second wife, so he was clearly not paralysed by the fear of potentially losing a wife to childbirth for a second time. With such a strong commitment to reproduction, as was demanded by the system of land bequests and marriages operated by the landed class, and a reluctance to limit the number of births, particularly in the first few years of marriage, it is to be expected that most pregnant women would know of someone within their social circle who had died in childbirth, even if they were not personally impacted.

The death of May Clifford née Chichester, an Irish woman who was living in Sydney, Australia since her wedding ten months earlier in February 1881, was recorded by her bereaved husband Charlie. May was born into a Catholic landlord family in County Roscommon. She was one of nine siblings: two brothers and seven sisters. Three sisters became nuns, three married, and one, Christine, remained unmarried. May died on 7 December soon after giving birth to a healthy son. She must have been pregnant for almost the entirety of her married life. No letters survive from May Chichester, but the letters written by her husband to her father and eldest brother after her death suggest that they had a happy marriage. It appears that Charlie did not write to any of May's sisters about her death, but he remained close with the family and was a regular visitor to his sister-in-law Esther Grehan, née Chichester (in whose papers these letters survive) for years to come. Perhaps, as her sisters were then unmarried, he felt that it was inappropriate to share such a harrowing experience with them.

At first, May seemed to be recovering successfully from the birth.

She was allowed out of bed and as far as the sofa (the first step in elite women's post-partum recovery) for the first time on 4 December. Charlie wrote a letter home to tell them of the good news that she had given birth and was recovering well. She was lying on her sofa and was 'apparently getting quite strong' when she first complained of a pain in her side, which quickly got worse. When Charlie returned the following day, the doctors had left word that she was suffering from 'a severe attack of pleurisy' and that he was 'on no account' to leave her. Pleurisy is an inflammation of the double-layered covering of the lungs, which would now be treated with antibiotics, or even surgery if very severe. The only treatments available to the doctors at the time were poultices and pain management. By Thursday, the family doctor had consulted with an 'eminent physician', Dr Jones. Charlie separately assured May's brother that these were the two best doctors in Sydney. Charlie was told that his wife was dangerously ill, but that she might yet pull through. The priest came and gave her Extreme Unction. By 4 a.m. the next morning, she had become delirious, and it was '6 o'clock in the morning of the eve of the Immaculate Conception when her little head lay back on my arm without a struggle'. For Charlie it meant that the 'the happy joyous dream of the last ten months of unalloyed happiness was at an end'. He described May's death as his 'irreparable loss'.

It is clear from these letters that he was attempting as much to comfort his wife's birth family as he was to tell the story of her death. May was presented as being an esoteric character, who was happy despite her pain; she was saint-like and her humanity was arguably removed as her death was sanitised and sanctified. She was 'resigned', 'beautiful' and died without the 'faintest fear or terror … praying for you and her dear little one & repeating the names of Jesus Mary & Joseph until her soul passed into Heaven with scarcely an effort'. He was more graphic in describing her death to her brother, writing that 'they applied scalding hot poultices in rapid succession to her back & side & you could hear her efforts to breath all over the house'. Throughout the letters, their infant son was barely mentioned. At the end of the last letter, Charlie promised that he would travel to mourn with his in-laws, the people 'who really knew what her worth was' as soon as possible. On his doctor's advice, this would not be until the 4 January as the doctor would not allow the baby and his wet nurse to take the voyage before then. Charlie expected to be united with the Chichesters in mid-February, around the time of his first wedding anniversary. These letters between men demonstrate their sense of loss at losing wives, daughters and sisters to childbirth. That loss might be held for years, though it was expected and desired that men would remarry. Childbirth was a fearful time for everyone connected to the mother, even as it was widely accepted as a necessary, and painful, experience for all married women.

Sources:

The letters referenced in this chapter are found in the Grehan Estate Collection at the Boole Library Archives, University College Cork (IE/BL/EP/G/1292) and the Inchiquin Estate Collection at the National Library of Ireland (NLI/MS/45). The death of May Chichester is also discussed in Maeve O'Riordan, *Women of the Irish Country House: 1860–1914* (Liverpool, 2018).

37

Reconstructing a Narrative of Impoverished Motherhood through the Lens of Irish Institutional Records

Judy Bolger

Traces of evidence relating to the life of a young, unmarried woman named Bridget Dempsy appear frequently throughout the surviving institutional records from Counties Tipperary and Limerick during the 1880s. More specifically, the scattered tracks of Dempsy's history of childbirth and infant death offer crucial examples of the way in which birth and death records can assist in the historian's attempt to reconstruct a broader narrative of impoverished motherhood in late-nineteenth-century Ireland. The earliest traceable references to the life of Bridget Dempsy situated her as an unruly 22-year-old facing charges of 'drunkenness' and 'assault' on two separate occasions in 1878. For the latter charge, Bridget, who was then described as a 'housekeeper', was sentenced to 'one month's hard labour' at the Nenagh Gaol, and this record alludes to her daughter Mary-Jane accompanying her mother while she served her time. Bridget completed her jail sentence, but this would not be her last.

Throughout the 1880s, fragmentary records demonstrate that Bridget Dempsy depended on the workhouse frequently and repeatedly when faced with childbearing and childrearing, as many other unmarried mothers from the period did. The evidence relating to Bridget's life can be, at times, confusing and difficult to connect coherently when attempting to piece together her life story. The surviving birth and death records of her children are significant, with many occurring within the Thurles workhouse in County Tipperary. Together with the already mentioned daughter, Mary-Jane, Bridget had at least three more children; two of whom were born in the workhouse – a son, Edward, in 1880, and a daughter, Anne, in 1886. Neither Edward nor Anne survived infancy. For Edward, the only trace of his life is his birth certificate. We can assume his death occurred during infancy as he is not mentioned in any of Bridget's further engagements with the workhouse in the years directly after his birth. Baby Anne's death from 'debility' occurred in the workhouse when she was four weeks old, having never left the institution in her short life. Three weeks after the death of her daughter Anne, Bridget and her 'bastard' daughter, Mary-Jane, left the workhouse.

Almost a year to the date of the death of her daughter Anne, Bridget was readmitted to the Thurles workhouse in February 1887. With her on this occasion was daughter, Mary-Jane, aged 8, and her 7-day-old son, Edward. Anecdotally, the re-naming of her second son Edward further signifies that her first son of the same name died in infancy. Though born outside of the workhouse, the younger Edward Dempsy would face the same fate as his namesake elder brother by dying in the workhouse from 'convultions', three weeks after his admission, thus marking mother Bridget's second experience of infant death within a thirteen-month period. Three weeks later, both Bridget and Mary-Jane left the workhouse, and determining if they ever went back is challenged by the lack of surviving indoor registers for the Thurles workhouse.

While it is difficult to ascertain if Bridget ever returned to the workhouse, or if she had any more children, this snapshot of her use of the institution during her experiences of childbirth and infant loss demonstrates the challenges a woman of her position faced when mothering in poverty. The challenges affecting Bridget's ability to mother are further demonstrated in her lengthy criminal record. Indeed, many of the crimes Bridget was charged with, such as 'drunkenness', 'assault' and even 'riotous behaviour' towards a sergeant, allude to her being the type of woman contemporarily defined as 'deviant' and such behaviour often resulted in her spending time in the Limerick Jail for periods that were concurrent with her pregnancies. Moreover, some of her charges are evidence of the deeply precarious position that many young, unmarried women who found themselves pregnant in nineteenth-century Ireland experienced. With a lack of financial security or familial support, when faced with the social ostracisation that accompanied unmarried motherhood, many pregnant women and new mothers found themselves reliant on institutional care.

For example, in October 1885, just three months prior to giving birth to her daughter Anne in the workhouse, Bridget Dempsy appeared at the Tipperary Petty Sessions having been accused of 'unlawfully [occupying] a room in Barrack Street, Templemore, County Tipperary, her weekly tenancy at 8d a week [...] duly determined by a notice to quit'.[1] Here we can see exactly why Bridget had to rely on the workhouse, as her ability to make weekly rent commitments was presumably a difficult task and such tenancy agreements provided very little security. Her decision to give birth in the workhouse may not have been a decision at all, but rather a necessity, as both her and her daughter Mary-Jane had few housing alternatives.

After the death of her two infants, Bridget appears to have continued with her 'quarrelsome and scandalous' behaviour, and references to her reliance on alcohol emerge in charges for drunkenness in a public place, 'her second offence within a year', in 1888. Some indefinite evidence suggests that she may have married in 1890; however, without any concrete birth records for Bridget, it is difficult to know for certain. Either way, references to Bridget Dempsy fade on the eve of the 1890s and without any death certificate, it is impossible to know how her story ended. Mary-Jane, the daughter that appears to be Dempsy's first child, also seems to elude the records; without any correlating birth or death record, her name only survives when incidentally mentioned with her mother's on the workhouse or gaol registers. With such fragmentary evidence, what significance does Bridget's life hold in our understanding of impoverished motherhood in late-nineteenth-century Ireland?

The paltry evidence that survives for Bridget and her family perhaps reflects the indefinite nature of not only her narrative, but the very difficult challenges most historians face when attempting to reconstruct the lives of those from the past. So many questions remain unanswered when attempting to tell Bridget's story. Yet what does survive provides fleeting snapshots of what a nineteenth-century 'deviant' woman must have endured when faced with unmarried motherhood, homelessness, grief and poverty. A woman such as Bridget, considered a strain on the

---

[1] Petty Sessions Order Books, CSPS1/9139.

welfare regime, her behaviour deemed abhorrent by her society's moral code, survives within the records as an important signifier in our historical understanding of motherhood, institutionalisation and poverty. Piecing her life together, through the fragmentary records in which her name is found, demonstrates how significant is the task of historically reconstructing an individual's life. Evidence of Bridget's experiences of childbirth and infant death shed light on the, often insurmountable, difficulties of unmarried motherhood in modern Ireland.

Further Reading:

Elaine Farrell, '"Poor Prison Flower": Convict Mothers and their Children in Ireland, 1853–1900', *Social History*, 41:2 (2016), 171–91.

Maria Luddy, 'Unmarried mothers in Ireland, 1880–1973', *Women's History Review*, 20:1 (2011), 109–26.

38

Wet Nurse to *na Daoine Maithe*: Nineteenth-century Breastfeeding and the Otherworld

Carolann Madden

Na daoine maithe (the Good People, a common term for fairies in Irish folklore) love liminality and times of transition in the course of human life. They love cross-quarter days, especially Samhain and Bealtaine; they love dusk and dawn; they love infants, newlyweds, birthing and breastfeeding mothers; they love thresholds of all kinds. The 'fourth trimester', or the twelve weeks following birth, is easily recognised as its own great threshold. It makes sense that we would find *them* active in this time. If we look to Arnold van Gennep's theory regarding human rites of passage, the fourth trimester aligns with the transition from the liminal phase of birthing to the reintegration phase. In this phase, the person re-enters the group having undergone a major transition in role and identity. Reintegration is marked by the recognition of the person's new identity, and sometimes a new name. Beyond the assumption of a new role and new name, in this case 'Mother', the fourth trimester is generally a time of transformation, even for those who have given birth before. And something happens between the fairies and mothers in the fourth trimester because this is when mothers are most often 'away'.

There are many examples of Irish folk narratives and statements of belief that navigate the abduction of new mothers at the hands of the fairies. Some of these mothers become changelings, while others are taken with no one left in their place, often to breastfeed in the Otherworld. We can look to Lady Gregory's *Visions and Beliefs in the West of Ireland* (1920) for evidence of this. Gregory was a talented and empathetic collector, and as such, *Visions and Beliefs* offers a valuable early source of folklore collected by a woman. Importantly, many women are represented within its pages, as well. Perhaps this, or Gregory's own potential interest in folklore and motherhood, resulted in the number of discussions regarding birth and motherhood within the collection. Either way, among these discussions are over twenty incidents where mothers are taken after childbirth. Gregory explains in her preface that 'young mothers are taken that they may give the breast to newly born children among the Sidhe, young girls that they may themselves become mothers there'.

One interesting example of the former comes from Mary Sheridan, Gregory's own childhood nurse at Roxborough. Sheridan reveals that she herself was taken to the Otherworld as a wet nurse. She says that 'the mistress' in a long, flowing yellow cloak with a shining broach took her to a 'very grand' and 'very big place' where she was made to 'give the breast to a child'. Sheridan is offered food in this place, which she refuses. Presumably, according to motif C211.1 in the *Motif-Index of Folk-Literature*, it is because she does not break the 'Tabu of eating in fairyland' that she is allowed to return home. In a similar story told by a Mrs Maher, a woman goes to the Otherworld and also acquiesces when asked to suckle a baby. After this, she is simply returned to the road from which she was taken. Both women are allowed to go home after breastfeeding in the Otherworld, whether offered food there or not. Peter Hanrahan, however, tells the story of a woman asked by a 'grand lady' who arrived at her door in a carriage whether she would come with her to breastfeed her child. The woman declines, saying she can't leave her own children, but the lady brings her 'away to a big house' anyway. When they arrive, the new mother refuses to stay and goes back to her own family. The next morning, her cow is dead. It would seem the punishment for refusing to supply milk in the Otherworld is the inability to access it in this one.

Another woman, Mrs Fagan, states it plainly: 'they never can give the breast to a child, but must get a nurse from here', though we never quite learn why. Interestingly, many of the women taken to the Otherworld as wet nurses are also able to return and nurse their own children. In fact, the majority of 'mother abduction' stories in *Visions and Beliefs* revolve around a mother returning temporarily, often under cover of night, to breastfeed and care for her child. Some of these stories

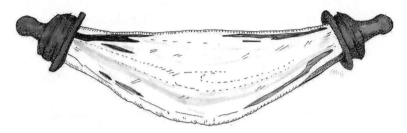

FIGURE 13: *Nineteenth-century feeding bottle, pen-and-ink illustration by Marion McGarry.*

also mention that the child nursed by a mother returning from the Otherworld ends up doing just as well as, or better than, other children. Such is the case of the child in a story from 'A North Galway Woman', who 'grew and throve better than any child around' thanks to her mother returning to breastfeed her. To understand one function of these tales within the wider cultural matrix of nineteenth-century Ireland, we can locate a connecting thread in the contemporary wet nurse.

Combing through the archives of *The Irish Times*, there are myriad ads seeking wet nurses, or wherein new mothers are seeking wet nursing work. Wet nursing had become increasingly popular with the upper classes throughout the nineteenth century, and we can see this reflected in the *weltanschauung* of a few of our tellers. Some women who return and tell of their experience as wet nurses in the Otherworld mention being taken by, or for, its upper classes. At the same time, the prevalence of these narratives and the fact that a number of them make no mention at all of the elite, also presents a recognisable correlation to the lived experience of women across social strata in Ireland. Towards the mid to late nineteenth century, wet nursing in many countries, including Ireland, was expanding from the upper classes to a practice employed by labouring and lower-class families who now had women entering the workforce. In this structure, impoverished women were hired as wet nurses for the children of the labouring class. Wet nurses for upper class families were often not allowed to nurse in their own home, or to take their baby into their employer's home, being forced to leave the child with a dry nurse or carer themselves. Perhaps unsurprisingly, this system occasionally built upon itself, with impoverished women taking on the role of wet nurse for a child whose mother had taken a job as a wet nurse for an elite family. The personal circumstances of the wet nurse varied widely from unmarried mothers, to women whose children did not survive birth or infancy, to married women who had to seek employment outside of the home. Regardless of where a child ended up, we do know that, if not in the care of a wet nurse, frequently these babies struggled to thrive. Due to a combination of contamination, inappropriate foodstuffs and a lack of bottle hygiene, nineteenth-century bottle-feeding led to anything from diarrhoea and dysentery, to around one third of all infant deaths within the first twelve months. Even still, the century saw a steady decline in breastfeeding.

The challenges related to alternative feeding methods in the nineteenth century would start to ease with the advent of accessible food preservation and the ability to better sterilise feeding vessels, though it would take some time for associated practices to become widespread. Since the world of *na daoine maithe* reflects ours so closely, it makes sense that they would be both nervous about the pitfalls and confusion around infant feeding, and would also understand their wet nurse's desire to return home and feed her own child. When viewed through this lens, we can perhaps gain a deeper understanding of what amounts to a preference for breastfeeding in this particular form of 'mother abduction' lore in *Visions and Beliefs*. One interpretation of these stories is that they appear to amplify the importance of breastmilk at a time when breastfeeding itself was on the wane without a suitable substitute. Taken together, the lore suggests a contemporaneous understanding of breastmilk as so valuable that, not only would a mother be taken from her own family for it, but she might also be allowed to leave the Otherworld, if only for a few hours, in order to give it to her own child in this world.

Further Reading:

Sarah-Anne Buckley, '"Found in a 'dying' condition": Nurse-children in Ireland, 1872–1952', in Elaine Farrell (ed.), *'She Said She was in the Family Way': Pregnancy and Infancy in Modern Ireland* (London, 2012).

Valerie A. Fildes, *Breasts, Bottles and Babies: A History of Infant Feeding* (Edinburgh, 1986).

Lady Augusta Gregory, *Visions and Beliefs in the West of Ireland* (London, 1920).

Emily Stevens *et al.*, 'A History of Infant Feeding', *The Journal of Perinatal Education*, 18:2 (Spring, 2009), 32–9.

Stith Thompson, *Motif-Index of Folk-Literature: A Classification of Narrative Elements in Folktales, Ballads, Myths, Fables, Mediaeval Romances, Exempla, Fabliaux, Jest-Books and Local Legends* (Bloomington, IN, 1955).

Arnold van Gennep, *Rites of Passage* (Chicago, 1961).

39

The Mother's Saint

Brendan McConvery, CSsR

In times when medical management of pregnancy and childbirth scarcely existed, and the rate of perinatal mortality of both mothers and babies was high, women sought heavenly protection. The number of Irish children with names like Gerard, Gerardine or Majella is testimony to the popularity of an Italian saint regarded as the protector of pregnant women and their children. Born into a poor peasant family in the village of Muro in the Basilicata region of southern Italy on 6 April 1726, Gerard Majella entered the recently-founded Redemptorist congregation as a brother in 1749. Sickly from birth, he acquired, in his lifetime, a reputation for holiness and great kindness towards the poor. He died from tuberculosis in 1755. Within two years of his death, small printed religious images of him were circulating in the small world where he was known, and his aid was invoked in the everyday needs of rural people – for healing, for a good harvest, to be rid of plagues of rats or mice.

Although obituaries of Gerard were written after his death, the first biography, *The Life of the Servant of God, Gerard Majella, Lay Brother of the Congregation of the Most Holy Redeemer*, appeared in 1811. In the long interval between his death and the introduction of his cause for canonisation in 1843, the legend of Gerard as a holy wonderworker was passed on orally in the relatively small region where he had lived. By the time the cause was opened, most of those who would have known him were dead. It dragged on for almost fifty years. While the evidence for Gerard's holiness of life was clear, much of the evidence for miracles was less so. He was eventually beatified in 1883 and canonised in 1904.

Among the stories of graces received through Gerard's prayers, help received in pregnancy and childbirth are the most numerous. The first case which was documented in the canonical process for his beatification was that of a young mother. While questing for the monastery, Gerard stayed with a family of benefactors called Pirofalo. As he was leaving, one of the daughters noticed that he had dropped his handkerchief. She ran to give it to him, but he said, 'Keep it, it might come in handy someday'. Gerard died shortly afterwards, and the handkerchief was kept in the family as a relic of a holy man. Some years later, the girl was giving birth to her first child. It was a long and difficult labour, but eventually she remembered Brother Gerard's handkerchief. It was brought to her, and the labour concluded shortly afterwards with the birth of a healthy baby. The story spread, and the women of the neighbourhood sent for Gerard's handkerchief when they were close to delivery. In time, it was cut into small pieces, which became much sought-after relics.

The only story about pregnancy that can be traced back with certainty to the life of Gerard is what might today be called 'a new dad' story. It has little of the miraculous. A relative of Gerard's, Alexander Piccolo, lost his young wife and remarried. The new wife was sickly, and Alexander poured out his woes to Gerard. Gerard replied, 'Cheer up, your wife is probably about six weeks pregnant, and you will have a little boy'. To Alexander's delight, Gerard was proved right, and he was determined to call the baby Gerard. While they waited for the birth, Alexander would pat his wife's belly and gently murmur, 'Gerard, Gerard', and feel the baby move in response.

Although widely regarded as patron of expectant mothers, Gerard has never been named so officially, since some Church authorities considered there was something a little indecent in a young celibate male being so concerned with the intimate details of a woman's life!

Devotion to Gerard was widely promoted by the members Gerard's religious family as they spread north of the Alps (from 1787), North America (1832) and further afield. With the approach of his beatification in 1888, the cult of Gerard became more popular. The two Redemptorist churches in Ireland at the time (Limerick and Dundalk) celebrated the beatification with a novena during which the story of Gerard was told over the nine days. Even more significant was his canonisation in 1904. By this time, there were two more Redemptorist churches at Clonard, Belfast and Esker, County Galway.

Evidence of the growing cult of Gerard can be seen in its frequency as a child's name. According to the 1901 census (eighteen years after beatification), there were 227 Gerards in all of Ireland (some were female with Gerard as a second name or, in one case, a religious name). Only a handful were above the age of 20, and most of them were not Catholic. By the 1911 census (seven years after canonisation), the number of Gerards had risen to 1609, a seven-fold increase, and most were Roman Catholic. The name was particularly common where there were Redemptorist churches, although Redemptorist parish missioners were making the story of Gerard more familiar throughout the country. Of the twenty-seven young Gerards in County Antrim in 1901, twenty-six of them were in West Belfast, close to the recently founded Redemptorist monastery in Clonard. By 1911, 178 Antrim babies had been given the name. In 1901, there were eleven little Gerards in County Louth, all in the town of Dundalk: by 1911, there were sixty-nine now scattered throughout the county. Limerick had thirty-five in 1901. Ten years later, there were 197.

It is more difficult to track women's names. Some baby girls were given Gerard as an additional name. A form that became common later, Gerardine (not Geraldine), occurs only three times in the 1901 census, once as a religious name. By 1911, there are fifteen Gerardines. Majella, which became more common later in the twentieth century, first appears in 1911, given to three girls in Belfast, Down and Limerick.

The Redemptorists propagated devotion to Gerard through shrines to the saint in their churches, an annual novena and through St Gerard's League. People were encouraged to apply to join and were sent a small book of prayers with a medal and prayer card. Devotion to Gerard was also passed down from mother to daughter.

Despite the decline in church-going, St Joseph's Redemptorist church, Dundalk draws about 10,000 people daily for the novena each October from the town and the surrounding counties of Down, Armagh, Louth and Meath. Eamon Duffy, emeritus professor of the History of Christianity at Cambridge, grew up in Dundalk and remembers being baffled by the astonishing number of highly pregnant women when he was attending it in the 1950s.

The shrines are also a witness to the continuing devotion to the saint. People are invited to place their prayer intentions in a box. Usually brief, they often record stories of the struggle to conceive, of miscarriage, difficult births, as well as the joy of a healthy child. While the majority are written by women, fathers sometimes include their prayers too. Petitions are sometimes written on pictures of the scan of the expected baby. Most days they receive gifts of flowers, an anonymous 'thank you' for a successful birth.

Further Reading:
Brendan McConvery CSsR, *St. Gerard Majella – Rediscovering A Saint* (Dublin, 2013).

40

The Lisheen/Killeen (an Unconsecrated Burial Site for Stillborn Babies)

Mary M. Burke

Purgatory is an official doctrine of the Catholic Church, but in folk Catholicism 'limbo' accounted for the afterlife of stillborn babies, which the Church dictated could not enter heaven or be buried in consecrated ground due to their unbaptised state (the revised Code of Canon Law relaxed this interdiction in 1983). Archaeological dating suggests that from the Counter-Reformation period on, the bodies of stillborn or premature babies were, as a consequence, buried in isolated parcels of unsanctified ground called 'lisheens' or 'killeens'. *Reilig/reilicín* and *caltra/caltragh* are lesser-used cognates. Such terms are utilised as both place name and map marking, and the latter allows archaeologists to identify them from Ordnance Survey maps. However, such sites are otherwise known only within the local community. Lisheens are prevalent in Ireland's historically poorest and most isolated regions: out of a total of approximately 1,400 children's burial grounds recorded as archaeological sites within the statutory Record of Monuments and Places for the Republic of Ireland, 479 exist in County Galway alone, which gives an average of one lisheen per five square miles. The second-highest occurrence nationwide is Kerry's figure of 260, mostly concentrated on that county's coastline. Lisheens have received little scholarly attention, and were they but more visible – culturally, as well as optically – they would likely be one of the western seaboard's most evident archaeological sites. Moreover, Emer Dennehy claims that when archaeologists have recorded lisheens, they have traditionally done so only when they are associated with more 'prestigious' ancient monuments, a hint that lisheens may be even more numerous than has been suspected.

FIGURE 14: *Lisheen, Blean, 2.3km from Athenry (photo: Lisa Doherty @lisadohertyphotography; with the permission of Michael Hardiman).*

Eileen Murphy adds that even when 'traditional archaeological discourse' has audited such sites, it has 'failed to engage with the trauma of infant and child-loss'. The lisheen/killeen constitutes a currently little-known history of Irish post-natal practice that provides evidence for how traumatic deliveries were intimately memorialised in a period before miscarriage or stillborn births were part of shared social memory. Furthermore, it suggests a repudiation of unyielding Catholic doctrine limiting the use of consecrated burial ground since archaeologists suggest that lisheens were treated as sacred by the families of the dead. The term 'killeen/*cillín*', common outside of Connacht, means 'little church', which indicates that parents of unbaptised babies turned to alternative 'sacred' spaces such as 'pagan'/'fairy' (Iron Age) forts, megalithic tombs, abandoned ecclesiastical sites, graveyard boundaries and isolated natural landmarks such as 'fairy' (hawthorn) bushes. The use of this last site may be the wellspring of what is sometimes jocularly represented in Irish media today as the nonsensical taboo regarding the clearance of 'fairy' bushes for land development. The association with charged sites is clear from the etymology of 'lisheen', the anglicised diminutive of *lios*, a 'fairy' fort. William Wilde's archaeological survey, *Lough Corrib: Its Shores and*

Islands (1872), records only that 'peasant' informants associated the lisheen with the pre-Christian. As an educated, non-Catholic outsider, he may not have been privy to what may well have been the site's most resonant local association. The invisibility of the lisheen (as infant burial site) in print culture is further suggested by the fact that the 'fort' definition of *lios* is the only one provided in many dictionaries of Irish. A notable exception is the second entry for *lisín* in Ó Dónaill's 1977 *Foclóir Gaeilge-Béarla*, a 'cemetery for unbaptised children'. However, Ó Dónaill's entry for '*cillín*' makes no reference to infant burial.

Contemporary archaeological studies note without explanation that the lisheen practice ceased in the 1950s, and I surmise that cessation at that point may be related to Ireland's 1949 Infanticide Act, which seemingly rendered the clandestine burial of infants in any circumstance as inherently suspicious. The Act addressed the anomalous legal status of child murder, rooted in the wider ambivalence regarding the protection of illegitimate babies, who were generally the victims of that crime in post-independence Ireland. However, internees of lisheens were almost always the unbaptised stillborn, though suicides and unidentified foreigners were very occasionally buried therein also. No reference to the burial of aborted, illegitimate, abandoned or murdered infants in lisheens occurs in the (admittedly sparse) relevant literature. Moreover, as a topic that would have come under the euphemism of 'women's problems' (miscarriage or stillbirth), the lisheen custom would not have been openly discussed in mixed gender settings not involving close male relatives; it was tradition for the unbaptised baby to be discreetly buried at dusk by its father. Nevertheless, the culminating implication is that, rather than being illicit in any way, the lisheen custom of the historically less literate, Irish-speaking districts was simply unknown in print culture, urban, educated Ireland. Therefore, the discrete phenomenon of the secret outdoor disposal of an illegitimate newborn by a distressed mother, which usually came to the attention of post-independence Irish authorities and media when infanticide was suspected, was an individual occurrence that was arguably conflated after 1949 with the poorly-understood lisheen custom, which appears to have become less and less known or understood, even in regions where it had once been widely practised as Ireland modernised.

If the lisheen/killeen has been neglected in traditional archaeological studies, then it is merely implied in Irish- and English-language lore concerning the ghosts of unbaptised infants encountered in liminal places. It is also almost non-existent as a major theme in Irish literature in English, with the exception of Mary Leland's 1985 novel, *The Killeen*, in which it is sympathetically depicted as an outlet for unofficial ritual and grief in the spiritually narrow 1930s. Nevertheless, as the obscured history of poor rural Irishwomen has received more attention from scholars and writers in recent decades, the lisheen has, to a minor degree, begun to emerge into public consciousness, especially in contexts that illuminate hidden or controversial contemporaneous issues relating to parturition and pregnancy. For instance, the custom is name-checked in Mommo's powerful closing monologue concerning the poverty-stricken and Church-dominated past in Tom Murphy's seminal drama *Bailegangaire* (1985), one of whose subplots concerns the concealment of an unwanted present-day pregnancy. The play, like Leland's novel, is meant to be understood within the immediate contexts of the Pro-Life Referendum of 1983 and the Kerry Babies trial of 1984. The latter resulted when the unmarried Joanne Hayes buried her stillborn baby on her family's coastal Kerry farm and was, thereby, wrongly suspected in the infanticide of another baby. The sympathetic representations of the obsolete lisheen custom by Murphy and Leland in 1985 seem to aspire to endow Hayes's action with cultural and historical context.

In 2007, Pope Benedict XVI effectively 'demoted' limbo, and the theological conundrum of unbaptised babies buried in lisheens seemingly disappeared. However, the timing of what the media termed limbo's 'closing' is striking in the Irish context, since at about this time, lisheens began to be publicly acknowledged. For instance, at the request of locals, since 1998 a Mass has been celebrated at one such site in Gardenfield, County Galway, and in 2015, participants erected a plaque inscribed with internee names. In short, just as it is about to disappear from living memory and oral culture, the lisheen is finally beginning to fully enter Irish print and commemoration culture.

Further Reading:
Mary Burke, 'Tuam Babies and Kerry Babies: Clandestine Pregnancies

and Child Burial Sites in Tom Murphy's Drama and Mary Leland's *The Killeen*', *Irish University Review*, 49:2 (2019), 245–61.

Deirdre Crombie, 'Children's Burial Grounds in the Barony of Dunmore: A Preliminary Note', *Journal of the Galway Archaeological and Historical Society*, 41 (1987), 149–51.

Emer Dennehy, '*Dorchadas gan Phian*: The History of Ceallúnaigh in County Kerry', *Journal of the Kerry Archaeological and Historical Society*, 2:2 (2003), 5–21.

Nyree Finlay, 'Outside of Life: Traditions of Infant Burial in Ireland from Cillin to Cist', *World Archaeology*, 31:3 (2000), 407–22.

Eileen Murphy, 'Children's Burial Grounds in Ireland (*Cillíní*) and Parental Emotions Toward Infant Death', *International Journal of Historical Archaeology*, 15:3 (2011), 409–28.

41

Some Irish Folk Beliefs of Conception, Pregnancy and Birth

Marion McGarry

In Ireland, great importance was placed on childbearing, and many old folk customs, rituals and superstitions surrounded conception, pregnancy and birth. The general belief was that the whole process could be influenced by, and was susceptible to, preternatural forces. Such beliefs (many of which are likely to be pre-Christian in origin) relate to numerous aspects of Irish rural life including death, marriage, material culture and farming practices. Many of these superstitions and customs were so deep-rooted they persisted until the twentieth century.

Until recently in Ireland, there was a huge importance placed on getting married and having children. If someone did not do both, they were considered lesser members of society and would have felt huge pressure to conform. The idea that one might not have children was a dreadful prospect: an old malevolent curse was to tie knots in a handkerchief at a wedding to stop the newly married couple from conceiving.

If a woman did not have children, for whatever reason, she was called 'barren' and regarded with a mixture of sympathy and suspicion. Ultimately, a cruel form of exclusion was meted out to such women. They were somehow considered harbingers of 'bad luck': it was thought unlucky for a 'barren' woman to see a baby before its Christening, for example. The Otherly status of childless women was thought to make them good herbalists and practitioners of folk medicine, however.

Some folk rituals and remedies were available to enhance fertility: the seed of docks tied to the arm of a woman, for example. Women who were childless – or unable to have children – were encouraged to attend

FIGURE 15: *Iron tongs placed across the cradle, pen-and-ink illustration by Marion McGarry.*

and watch the spectacle of the May Baby, or *Babóg Bealtaine*, a public gathering that occurred on May Day in some parts of the country. A doll made from straw was attached to a pole, and a man and his wife, dressed in straw costume, danced around the doll to a musical accompaniment. They performed a dance that has been described as sexually suggestive. This ritual described by E. Estyn Evans as a 'magical pantomime originally intended to secure the success of the year's crops' is not likely to be of Christian origin. There must have been some deep-rooted fertility aspect attached to it, because the childless women present were encouraged to look on and touch the doll in the belief that it would help them conceive.

Until the twentieth century, many folk beliefs persisted about unborn babies being susceptible to outside influences. If a pregnant woman was injured in some way, then it was believed that that injury would transfer to her child. If a pregnant woman saw a hare, her baby might be born with a disfigurement, so the woman would have to tear a part of her clothing to break the curse. Pregnant women should not be around death: they were not supposed to enter graveyards or attend wakes. Folk medical advice for pregnant women followed a similar line: it was thought that drinking plenty of water during pregnancy would give the baby clear skin. For an easy labour, some advised expectant mothers to eat fish brains. Pregnant women were considered lucky in some ways: a blacksmith would ask a pregnant woman to blow on the bellows in his forge for luck. It was considered unlucky to buy things for the baby before the birth, as it was thought fate was tempted in doing so – this belief remained until very recently in Ireland.

The time of a woman's labour was thought to be a liminal one, when the spirit or Otherworld was closer. The people involved were believed to be more susceptible to these forces at this time, and so they used prayer and ritual to protect themselves as best they could. When labour began, the father had to go and fetch the midwife and someone had to accompany him, as he was believed susceptible to danger from evil forces. Similar beliefs abounded at Irish wakes (also considered a liminal time), where those who had to fetch wake provisions, or break the news of the death to others, had to be accompanied by another for 'protection'.

In his absence, female neighbours and family assisted the woman. During the birth, the chief assistance came from a folk-midwife, usually an older woman, who lived in the locality. Known as a 'handywoman' she was without formal training but had years of practical experience (see Linda-May Ballard's article in this volume). The *brat Bríde*, a cloth left out on St Brigid's Eve and believed to be blessed by the saint as she passed over the land, was considered to have healing powers and was used during childbirth.

No men or children were admitted during the labour or birth, unless a male medical doctor had to intervene. The father would often be told to make himself scarce to work on the farm while the midwife attended the birth. In some parts of County Mayo, a ploughman was summoned in to 'shake' a woman enduring a difficult labour: this has been supposed to relate to his occupation being associated with fertility, as he would symbolically shake seeds on the fields.

The timing of the actual birth was also important: a child born on May Day was considered to be very lucky; indeed, it was the luckiest day of the year to be born. However, a baby born at Whitsuntide was considered cursed to kill someone during their life. A small living thing had to be placed in the hand of the infant (a fly, a worm) and the parent would crush it using the child's hand, fulfilling the prophesy.

The belief was that a child born with a 'caul' (a covering of the cranium) was extremely lucky, as discussed by E. Moore Quinn in the next article. It was believed the child would never drown as long as the mother kept the caul (the caul itself was thought to have magical and curative properties).

After the birth, neighbours and family would visit the newborn and mother, bringing gifts of food or clothes. The time was seen as a risky period for both, until the baby was baptised and the mother 'churched', to protect them from evil. 'Churching' was a religious ritual Roman Catholic mothers had to undergo after giving birth, a fortnight or so after the birth. New mothers could not undertake any household chores, enter a church or take part in any religious sacraments until they partook of the ritual. It was believed unlucky to meet an unchurched woman. It was important that babies were baptised very soon after the birth, and many were baptised without their mothers present simply because they could not attend church.

It was believed that before holding an unbaptised child, one must make the Sign of the Cross over it. It was believed unlucky to take a coal out of the fire in the house containing an unbaptised child. A piece of iron was to be sewn into the baby's clothes and kept there until after baptism. Throughout infanthood, objects and religious artefacts were placed into the cradle to ward off evil, such as the iron tongs placed across the top to prevent faery abduction.

Further Reading:

E. Estyn Evans, *Irish Heritage* (Dundalk, 1958).
Patrick Logan, *Irish Folk Medicine* (Belfast, 1981, 1999).
Seán Ó Suilleabháin, *Irish Folk Custom and Belief* (Cork, 1977).
Lady Jane Wilde, *Quaint Irish Customs and Superstitions* (Cork, 1988).

42

The Caul in Irish Folk Belief and Practice: A Birth-related Example of Continuity and Change

E. Moore Quinn

When it comes to seeking out the customary 'do's and don'ts' of pregnancy, archival sources, especially those preserved in Ireland's National Folklore Collection (NFC) in Dublin, contain an embarrassment of riches. Although, in earlier times, those 'pishrogues' (*piseoga*), as they were often called, were sometimes dismissed as superstitious practices, when coupled with oral tradition, they can be understood as forms of agency in the sense that mothers-to-be attempted to avoid the potential calamities that could befall them and their children.

Irish women, for instance, in order to trick the fairies while they were in their 'condition', donned their husbands' jackets turned inside out. Notwithstanding the fact that creatures of the Otherworld were believed to be tricksters, it was thought that they themselves could be fooled, and if the pregnant one were perceived to be someone other than who she was by virtue of her garments, the rationale was that 'the little people' would not 'sweep her' (or abscond with her) and leave a changeling in her place.

To avoid the appearance of over-confidence in a successful delivery, it was forbidden to rock an empty cradle, a sure sign of bad luck. Another prohibition is preserved in the admonition *Ná dean cró a roimhe na h-arcaibh* (Do not build a sty before the litter comes). These words appear in a slightly altered form in Irish America: 'Never set up the crib before the baby is born'. In addition, expectant mothers were taught to practise patience during the gestation period by acknowledging, 'When time comes, baby comes', or, as the Irish proverb has it, 'The cow won't have the calf till she's ready'.

Other pre-birth taboos were enacted in word and deed. For instance, Irish women who were 'with child' were discouraged from raising their arms above their heads for fear of strangling the baby with the umbilical cord. Although this injunction might seem ludicrous today, it may have stemmed from the more general idea that while they were 'in the family way', expectant mothers should refrain from untoward feats of derring-do.

Stronger constraints forbade the bearers of new life from associating with death. The Irish believed that a corpse could attract the unborn like a magnet. So, too, could things and places that were associated with those who had 'gone the way of truth', i.e. died. Thus, a pregnant woman was cautioned against attending funerals. It was deemed equally unsafe for her to visit cemeteries, for if she turned her ankle on a grave, the misfortune could be visited upon her infant, who might come into the world thereafter with *an cam reilige*, the clubfoot.

In all of these ways, pregnant Irish women resisted becoming victims of unlucky circumstances. Recognising that the time of 'waiting' is a dangerous one, and cognisant of the need to take proper precautions, they attempted to control the uncontrollable until they and their babies were reliably harboured on the other side of birth and delivery. Of course, it is difficult, if not impossible, to predetermine all of the particulars of birth, and wherever babies are born, they emerge from the womb with their own individual stamps of identity, like 'dimpled cheeks', 'full heads of hair', 'concert pianist fingers' and 'grips of iron'.

Arguably, one of the most unique items that emerges with the newborn is the 'caul', also known as the 'veil' or the 'caul cap'. This is the amniotic sac that houses the foetus during gestation. On rare occasions, rather than breaking shortly before birth, it remains intact, which means that the infant arrives as if gift-wrapped, presenting itself in what appears to be a soft transparent balloon. Although the caul can envelop the newborn's entire body, more frequently it encases the face, head, or shoulders. Nevertheless, due to the fact that the phenomenon of being 'born with the caul' occurs in only one in 80,000 births around the globe, it frequently happens that both the object and its owner are imbued with special attributes, powers and labels.

Ireland is no exception. As numerous entries in the Schools Manuscripts Collection of the National Folklore Archives (NFCS) reveal, the caul was hallowed, and so, too, was the baby born with it.

In the Irish language, the caul is referred to as *an brat linbh* (the child's cloak), or more euphemistically, *caipín an tsonais* (the little cap ('capeen') of happiness). It was believed to eliminate birthmarks, heal burns and cure malaria. Thought to bring fame and fortune to its possessor, the caul was said to have the ability to ward off danger, ease one's passage into the next world or even deter a person's premature entrance there. In Limerick, for instance, a fellow who fell from a high tree was thought to have 'had a miraculous escape. His mother believes that he would have been killed but that he was born with a caul and that he is lucky' (NFCS 0527, 41). As this testimonial affirms, the infant of a caul birth was said to possess something unique, the full force of which would become known to the community as time passed.

Cauls were displayed, borrowed, returned and loaned to those who were taking passages on 'coffin ships' during *An Gorta Mór*. They were tucked into prayerbooks and stuffed into the rafters of people's homes. And, throughout the British Isles, these legendary objects were bought and sold, as gleaned from a notice that appeared in the *London Times* in 1835: 'A Child's Caul to be disposed of, a well-known preservative against drowning, &c., price 10 guineas'.

Beck notes that, for those who took to the sea, anything out of the ordinary was deemed to contain a magical force. Thus, it is not surprising that around the islands of Ireland, the caul was coveted by sailors for its talismanic properties. One informant from County Offaly said that the caul served as 'a great keepsake for a captain of a ship as it [was] believed it would save a ship from shipwreck' (NFCS 0803, 35). Another from County Meath disclosed, 'When I was born I had a lucky caul. It was supposed to be lucky to be born with a caul which is considered a sure preservative against drowning and therefore prized by sailors as a protective device to prevent sailors from drowning' (NFCS 0687, 122).

It is interesting to note that, repeatedly, in Ireland's National Folklore Collection, the caul is associated with protection from a watery grave and with good fortune in general. Moreover, ideas about those connections endured, for although the Schools Collection materials

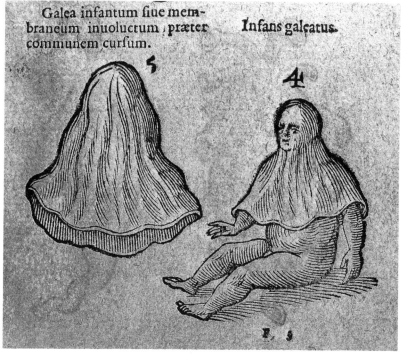

FIGURE 16: *Sixteenth-century illustration of a caul, from* De naturae divinis Characterismis … *by Cornelius Gemma (1575) (Wikipedia Commons; Wellcome Library, London, Wellcome Images, images@wellcome.ac.uk, http://wellcomeimages.org).*

were collected in 1937–8, even as late as the 1970s, members of the Irish medical profession continued to ascribe a seafaring identity to babies born with the caul. A case in point: one of my consultants shared that, upon querying her mother regarding the details of her birth in 1972 at Galway's Regional Hospital (now University College Hospital Galway), her mother explained:

> You were breach birth, and I was struggling after a really long labour, so I didn't see your head before you were whisked away.
> '*Oh, a sailor*', I heard a doctor say during the labour.
> 'I thought I was having a girl', I said.
> 'She has a white lace *cap*', the nurse replied. I was confused

and let it go.

Two hours after the birth my own mother [Annie _____] came to visit.

'The baby has something on her head', I told her.

'Where is it?' [Annie] asked. I told her what the nurse said. She told me it was a 'lucky cap' that meant that the baby will never drown [emphasis added].[1]

In this brief narrative, along with frequently cited words like 'lucky', 'sailor' and 'cap', the caul as a safeguard against drowning is referenced. However, what is equally significant is the mother's final sentence, for it symbolises important behavioural change: 'Later again, the doctor came in and I asked where the cap was. "We couldn't keep those things. They'd go off", she answered, so I never saw it'.

It appears from this account that by the second half of the twentieth century, the earlier practices of deploying the physical caul for multifunctional purposes had been eclipsed by medical discourses about the unlikelihood of its longevity and ability to survive.

Yet, in spite of the fact that the practice of preserving the actual caul is, for all intents and purposes, nonexistent today, beliefs about its efficacy persist. This realisation came to light not too long ago during a collecting conversation with a woman who self-reported that she had been born with the caul. She then revealed that, while taking a boat trip recently, everyone with whom she was traveling had become violently seasick. She, however, had been spared. When she began to ponder why, a likely reason dawned on her. 'All of a sudden', she told me, 'I remembered, "Ahhh! The capeen!"'.

As is clear from this example, Irish folk beliefs regarding persons 'born with the caul' prevail to this day, taking their place among the many suggestions and cautions surrounding the mother-to-be and her child. The folk tradition also confirms that there is still a willingness on the part of the Irish to accept the wisdom that *An rud is annamh is iontach* (the rare thing is valued (wonderful)).

---

[1] Interview conducted by Irish-born Mary Burke, on 25 November 2019 in Concord, Massachusetts, with her Irish-born mother, Catherine Melia Burke. Interview sent via email, 28 November 2019.

Further Reading:

National Folklore Commission, The Schools Collection. Available at: www.duchas.ie

H. Beck, *Folklore of the Sea* (Edison, NJ, 1999).

M.M. Delaney, *Of Irish Ways* (New York, 1973).

L. Flanagan, *The Irish Spirit: Proverbs, Superstitions and Fairy Tales* (New York, 1999).

T.R. Forbes, 'The Social History of the Caul'. *Yale Journal of Medicine*, 25:6 (1953), 495–508.

A.W. Moore, *The Folklore of the Isle of Man* (London, 1891).

S. Ó Catháin, *Irish Life and Lore* (Dublin, 1982).

P. O'Farrell, *Irish Proverbs and Sayings: Gems of Irish Wisdom* (Dublin, 1980).

S. Ó Súilleabháin, *A Handbook of Irish Folklore* (Dublin, 1942).

43

Pregnancy Cravings in Irish Folk Tradition

Pádraig Ó Héalaí

This article is based on the beliefs and customs of a singularly well-documented community – that of the Great Blasket Island in the seventy years or so prior to its evacuation in 1953. During that period, aspects of life on this island have been recorded, not only in the numerous publications of Islanders and visitors, but also, and most relevantly here, in the extensive work of folklore collectors. In large measure, their records are now available in the archives of the National Folklore Collection (NFC) at University College Dublin – and amount to some 17,000 pages of transcripts. Blasket traditions relating to pregnancy and childbirth are by no means *sui generis*, but rather, represent shared customs, beliefs and attitudes prevalent elsewhere in Ireland, and frequently also in the wider European area.

One strand of this tradition relates to an extreme craving for food or other substances, known as *pica*, a phenomenon especially associated with pregnancy. In earlier times in Ireland, Brehon law afforded a woman suffering from it a measure of legal protection in satisfying her cravings and her husband was legally bound to satisfy them as the understanding was that otherwise the child would die (see Niamh Wycherley's article elsewhere in this volume). Later folk belief also strongly urged that the pregnant woman's craving ought to be satisfied, as not doing so was feared to impact negatively on mother or child. An indication of how seriously the obligation to comply with the pregnant woman's desires was viewed, or how fantastically it was imagined, is provided by a story told on the Blaskets of a man whose pregnant wife craved a portion of the calf of his leg, and how he eventually mutilated himself to satisfy her.[1] Leaving aside the fanciful nature of this story, it is quite clear that the cravings of pregnant women were taken very seriously; so much so that it appears some pregnant women sought to take advantage of their situation:

> Faith then, in the old days if you had something nice to eat
> that was not too plentiful, you would be trying to hide it
> from a pregnant woman. If I was roasting meat here and
> she'd get the smell of it, she'd make you out, and you'd have
> to give her a bit of it.[2]

In Irish oral tradition, the pregnant woman's craving was given a sacred association in that it was linked with the apocryphal story in Pseudo-Matthew of the cherry tree bending down to allow the pregnant Virgin Mary to eat its fruit. This story is widely known from the Cherry Tree Ballad, and in Irish tradition, the narrative is used to provide an explanation for why women experience such cravings, while also re-enforcing the traditional requirement to satisfy them. This is a West Kerry variant of the tale:

> Saint Joseph it seems this day got jealous of the Blessed
> Virgin as they were going along and they were passing by a
> tree with fruit on it.
> 'Get some of that fruit for me', says the Blessed Virgin. And
> Saint Joseph said: 'Let the father of the child you are bearing
> get the fruit for you.'
> With that, the tree bent down to the ground and she picked
> the fruit. Since then women bearing children long for fruit.[3]

---

[1] NFC 1202: 244. Permission of the Director, Dr Críostóir Mac Cárthaigh, to reproduce passages from the National Folklore Collection is gratefully acknowledged.

[2] NFC 1202: 244: Ambaiste go gcaithfeá bheith ag ganfhiosaíocht fadó ar bhean trom ar aon rud suaithneach ná beadh flúirseach a bheadh le n-ithe agat. Dá mbeadh feoil á róstadh anso agam, gheobhaidís a bholaith ... agus bheidís chugat agus chaithfeá blúire a thabhairt dóibh.

[3] NFC 1178: 363.

The evidence of folk tradition makes it very clear the requirement to satisfy a pregnant woman's desire for food was taken seriously precisely because an unsatisfied desire was felt to be a threat: 'If you had any novelty at all on the table when a pregnant woman came in, you should force her to have some of it for fear she might have a liking for it.'[4]

Intensely desiring something one does not possess, while another nearby enjoys it, could easily give rise to feelings of envy and begrudgery. A very strong link is made in folk tradition between these feelings and the evil eye – they are believed to have the potential to activate it and occasion its destructive consequences. In light of this, it seems reasonable to assume that fear of the evil eye underlies the pressure people felt to satisfy the pregnant woman's craving. It must be stressed, however, that a fundamental component of the evil eye complex is the notion that an innocent person, someone entirely without malice, could unwittingly cast an evil eye and not even be aware of the damage they had done.

It was traditionally understood that a very close bond existed between the child in the womb and its mother, so that something endured by the mother would affect the child. A manifestation of this belief is provided by the traditional prohibition on throwing an object to, or at, a pregnant woman, as doing so could leave a mark on the child. Similarly, as noted elsewhere in the volume, if a pregnant woman stumbled in a graveyard, the child she was carrying was liable to be born with a clubfoot; or if a pregnant woman encountered a hare, then the child might be born with a cleft palate (hare-lip).

In keeping with the close identification of the child in the womb with its mother, folk tradition also suggests that the effects of the mother's unsatisfied desire could be borne by the child. The actual effect or consequence most frequently spoken of is the child continuously having its tongue sticking out. Peig Sayers, for instance, warns that if a pregnant woman was not offered some of the food on the table in a house she was visiting, this would have an effect on the child when growing up as it would have its tongue out nearly all the time.[5]

---

[4] IFC 702:558: Dá mbeadh aon nuaíocht in aon chor agat ar an mbord nuair a thiocfadh bean go mbeadh leanbh ar iompar aicí isteach, ba cheart duit é thathant uirthi le heagla go mbeadh dúil aici ann.

[5] NFC 910: 185: Bean a bheadh ag iompar linbh … dá dtiocfadh a leithéid iteach i dtigh na gcomharsan agus go mbeadh an bia ar siúl, ba cheart é a thathant uirthi. Mar

Having one's tongue out for something is, of course, a widely used metaphor for greatly desiring something, and in this instance, it is a symbolic way of indicating the child would be longing for the food its mother was denied. Traditional stories assert that the only remedy in this predicament was to allow the child to taste the food its mother craved when she carried him. A story current in Blasket lore illustrates how an unsatisfied desire for food on the part of a child could cause the evil eye, and also how people modified their behaviour to prevent this happening. It tells of a father and son who were visiting a house where churning was in progress, and how, because of the shrewd discernment of the woman of the house (*tuiscint na gile a bheith aici*), she offered the boy some of the buttermilk, saying it would be wrong not to do so: 'because a very small thing could cause a child to develop an evil eye'.[6] There seems to have been a general acceptance that any desire a child (especially a male child) might have with regard to food should be satisfied: 'From six months on they put little bits of food in the child's mouth, but with a male child, nobody would eat anything in the house before first rubbing it on his mouth because *mian mic a shúil*.'[7] The saying *mian mic a shúil* (a child (male) desires what it sees) draws attention to the close link between desire and the eye, and it would easily follow that an unsatisfied desire would lead to a dissatisfied or bad eye.

We can see how integrated these beliefs were with real life from an anecdote concerning a group of Blasket islanders on a shopping expedition to Dingle. When a strong smell of roasting meat emanated from the kitchen of the house they were visiting, one of the group, the husband of a young married woman, was told by a neighbour he should take his wife out of danger. The owner of the house overheard this, and understanding the delicacy of the situation, invited the woman to go into another room.[8]

---

dá gcuirfeadh sí aon nath ann agus ná faigheadh sí é, bheadh a dheascaibh ar an leanbh nuair a saolófaí é, agus nuair a fhásfadh sé suas bheadh a leadhb á shá amach i gcónaí aige.

[6] NFC 1462: 149–155: mar is suarach an rud do leaghfadh súil linbh.

[7] NFC 910: 191: Ó leath bhliain amach bheidís ag cur blúiríocha beaga ina bhéal chuige, ach dá mba leanbh mic é ní bhlaisfeadh éinne aon ghreim sa tigh gan é a chuimilt dá bhéal ar dtúis, mar 'mian mic a shúil'.

[8] NFC 1202: 244–5.

Customs and beliefs associated with pregnancy and childbirth are an attempt to deal with perceived threats to mother and child and reflect anxieties associated with these situations in a traditional community. The evil eye tradition, for instance, offered an explanation, albeit mistaken, of undesirable outcomes in these circumstances. It also afforded a measure of empowerment as tensions occasioned by it could be allayed by well-known preventative and widely-practised remedial measures to counteract perceived threats. Another positive outcome was ensuring pregnant women were well looked after: 'If there was any delicacy in the house the pregnant woman was sure to get it for what lay ahead of her'.[9] The special status of the pregnant woman was highlighted in a number of very practical ways, such as in seating arrangements. When there was only one chair in a house – something not altogether unusual some generations ago – it was always occupied by the man of the house, and the only time he would offer it to any one was when a pregnant woman visited. It was also the case that a nursing mother would never have to yield a chair to anyone and the proverb *Is uaisle banaltra ná banóglach*[10] (a nursing mother has higher social status than a handmaiden), was thus interpreted.

Further Reading:

National Folklore Collection: Index. Section E

Pádraig Ó Héalaí, 'Gnéithe de Bhéaloideas an Linbh ar an mBlascaod', *Léachtaí Cholm Cille*, 22 (1992), 81–122.

Pádraig Ó Héalaí, 'Pregnancy and Childbirth in Blasket Island Tradition', *Women's Studies Review*, 5 (1997), 1–15.

---

[9] IFC 1202: 242: Má bheadh aon chineál nó aon rud maith i dtigh is ag an mbean óg a bheadh ag iompar linbh a bhí sé le fáil i gcóir an chúraim a bhí roimpi.

[10] NFC 1201: 335.

44

Pregnancy and Birth: Traditional Views and Practices

Patricia Lysaght

In different communities around the world, three vital turning points, marking the beginning of human life, a person's passage through life and the end of human life, have always been of importance to the individual and to the community to which the individual belongs. According to Arnold van Gennep's classic work *Les Rites de Passage* (1909, 1960), the ceremonial patterns accompanying the passage of an individual from one social position to another involve rites of separation (*séparation*), transition (*marge*) and incorporation (*aggregation*), though not all three are necessarily of equal importance or receive equal elaboration in every culture. In Irish traditional society these passage rites are discernible in the context of pregnancy and childbirth. A large body of traditional material collected over many decades bears witness to this.

Pregnancy involves a long and complex transition for the woman as she undergoes profound physical changes over an extended period of time in expectation of becoming a mother. At the same time, the foetus is growing and developing in her womb in anticipation of being born and being accepted into society. For both the woman and her unborn child, the gestational period is one of uncertainty on a number of levels. In many communities the perceived influence of various societal, natural and supernatural forces on the welfare of both the pregnant woman and her child, had, in addition to physical and medical considerations, also to be taken into account.

In the Irish traditional worldview, the pregnant woman had responsibility for the well-being of her unborn child. She should, therefore, avoid situations which could adversely affect the life of the child, such as witnessing the birth of animals in case she might suffer a miscarriage. Neither should she be present at a slaughtering, probably for the same reason, but also in order to avoid the risk of blood splatters as this, it was thought, could result in the child being born with a birthmark. Society, too, had responsibility for the welfare of the woman and her unborn child in this sense. Thus, on no account should an object be thrown at her, as this was thought to leave a discernible mark on the corresponding part of the child's body. Even scaring the woman, causing her to put her hand to her face, should be avoided as the hand-touch could be represented on the child's face when born. The mother, however, by taking prescribed preemptive action, such as by touching her hand to her hip, could transfer the defect there, thus leaving the mark on the child where it would not be seen.

While rural women tended to withdraw from heavy farm work during the later stages of pregnancy to avoid injury and the risk of a premature or a stillbirth, it was, nevertheless, almost inevitable that they would have occasion to walk through fields. Here, as discussed elsewhere in this volume, they ran the risk of seeing a hare, a dreaded occurrence as it was thought, probably through the association of ideas, that the child could be born with a cleft lip (hare-lip; *foramine labium*). The pregnant woman was expected to be aware of this danger and also, if it occurred, to counteract it immediately by putting a tear in her cloak, thereby transferring the risk of disfigurement to the clothing. Society, too, owed a duty of care to such a woman in this regard. Thus, if a man carrying a dead hare met a pregnant woman, he should make a tear in the animal's ear in order that her child would be born without blemish.

Traditionally, it was the local 'handywoman' who attended the woman in child-bed, especially in out-of-the-way places in rural Ireland, even after the introduction of the Midwives (Ireland) Act (1918), which specified that a qualified midwife should be present at all births. This was not always practicable, however, especially for island communities such as that on the Great Blasket Island, where, in the early decades of the twentieth century, a local woman, without formal midwifery training, delivered the Island children for more than thirty years.

While the primary role of the midwife was to assist in the safe delivery of the child, her presence was also viewed as a form of protection for the woman and the newborn infant, as after birth, both were thought to be particularly susceptible to fairy abduction. After the midwife's departure, this task fell to the household and to neighbouring women. Referring to this situation on the Great Blasket, the islander, Tomás Ó Criomhthain, remarked that two women stayed with the mother and her newborn child overnight. Provided with food, drink and tobacco during their vigil, they were treated to whiskey in the morning prior to their departure for home.

The keeping of careful watch over the newborn child, especially prior to baptism, and the use of protective measures of various kinds, was part and parcel of post-natal care in traditional society in Ireland until relatively recent times. Substances such as salt – a common household condiment and also used extensively in the preservation of basic foods – was widely used as a form of protection for the infant. Wrapped in a piece of cloth, it was hidden in the child's clothing, especially if the infant was to be taken out-of-doors. Sharp objects, such as a sewing needle secreted in the infant's garments, were also considered to offer protection against the fairies according to B.N. Hedderman, who worked as a formally-trained nurse on the Aran Islands, in the early twentieth century. Iron, too, was regarded as a powerful antidote to the supernatural world, especially if associated with fire. Thus, the iron fire-tongs, the housewife's household instrument par excellence, served to protect the child by being placed across the cradle, if she had to leave the kitchen for any reason.

But fire itself could also be used as a form of protection. Thus, a burnt cinder would be placed in the cradle with the child for this purpose. A red ribbon tied to the infant's clothing was likewise considered protective, as was urine when sprinkled about the room in which the mother and child lay, presumably because of its unpleasant odour.

Baptism, serving to incorporate the child into both the Christian and lay communities, was also regarded as formidable protection in its own right against the fairy world and the evil eye. Then the mother, having concluded her separation and transition phases during pregnancy, birth and confinement, resumed her role in society through her own rite of incorporation – churching. But a stillborn child, or a child dying without baptism, belonged, in traditional thought, neither to the community of the living or the community of the dead.

Sources and Further Reading:

Déirdre D'Auria, 'Nósanna a Bhaineann leis an mBreith in Éirinn' *Béaloideas,* 75 (2007), 48–78.

Alan Dundes (ed.), *The Evil Eye. A Folklore Casebook* (London, 1981).

Arnold,van Gennep, *Les Rites de passage. Etude systematique des rites*, (Paris, 1909).

Arnold, van Gennep, *The Rites of Passage*, (London, 1960).

B.N. Hedderman, *Glimpses of my Life in Aran. Some Experiences of a District Nurse in these Remote Islands off the West Coast of Ireland* (Bristol, London, 1917).

Leslie Matson, *Méiní, the Blasket Nurse* (Cork, Dublin, 1996).

Fionnuala Nic Suibhne, '"On the straw" and other Aspects of Pregnancy and Childbirth from the Oral Tradition of Women in Ulster', *Ulster Folklife*, 38 (1992), 12–24.

Tomás Ó Criomhthain, *Allagar na hInise* (Eagrán nua le Pádraig Ua Maoileoin. Baile Átha Cliath, 1977).

Pádraig Ó Héalaí, 'Gnéithe de Bhéaloideas an Linbh ar an mBlascaod', *Léachtaí Cholm Cille*, 22 (1992), 81–122.

45

Churching the Cow

Clodagh Tait

An almost forgotten ritual these days, churching was commonly undergone by Irish women in the past, usually about a month after giving birth. From the early seventeenth century, the Catholic Church followed the reformed denominations in presenting it as a rite of thanksgiving rather than purification. However, certain elements within the Catholic ceremony retained echoes of older ritual, notably the fact that the woman was met outside the church and led into it by the priest (implying that in her unchurched state she was unworthy or unclean). In popular tradition, the connotation of purification also lingered, and unchurched women were viewed as unlucky and in some way outside the protection of the Church: they were thus particularly vulnerable to being 'taken' by the fairies. In Corca Dhuibhne, west Kerry, according to An Seabhac, 'A woman after childbirth should be watched, or the child should be, for nine days, lest the *púcaí* should take them away. The woman would not be safe until after she was "churched" [coisreactha]'. It was sometimes advised that a new mother should not visit other houses until her churching, as she might bring misfortune or pollution with her – one informant suggested she would cause the house to be 'full of rats', another that 'she would bring in the hunger of the year to you'.

However, the ceremony that receives more attention in the folklore record is 'The Churching of the Cow'. Well into the twentieth century, cows (especially heifers having their first calf) would be formally blessed by their owners after calving in order to protect them from illness and supernatural harm, and to promote the production of milk. A large number of accounts of the rituals used can be found in the Irish Folklore Archive (www.duchas.ie). In Letterfrack, County Galway, 'The cow is churched after calfing. The churching is done as follows. Two people get a red coal in a tongs. They stand one on either side of the cow and pass the coal around the cow three times in the name of the Father Son and Holy Ghost.' In County Mayo, Mary Theresa Tighe described how, after calving, 'people used to put a coal and a tongs over the cow's back and make the sign of the cross three times over her head'. Three oatmeal cakes would be left on the cow's back 'when she was after calving' (the oatcakes may have been ornamented with a cross). In County Galway, the '*Brat Bhríde*', a piece of cloth put out overnight on St Brigid's Eve to be blessed by the saint and kept for healing and protecting animals and people, would be placed on a calving cow.

Often it was specified that a man and a woman should be involved in the ceremony, and objects blessed by the clergy might be used.

> Long ago the people used to tie a red rag around the cow's tail after calfing so that the fairies would not bring the cow and then they would shake holy water on her. Then they would get a lightening blessed candle and a girl would stand on one side of the cow and a man on the other side and the girl would hand the candle under the cow to the man and then the man would bring the candle around the cow so they used to do that to bless the cow.

Blessed candles were usually beeswax and would have been blessed at Mass on Candlemas Day, the feast of the Purification or 'Churching' of the Virgin Mary. Pat Reilly of Edergole, County Cavan described how:

> When a heifer brings forth its first calf a blessed candle is lighted & passed three times around the body of the heifer in name of the Father, Son & Holy Ghost. The candle is then extinguished on the udder of the heifer. The heifer was then milked. This brought luck on the heifer & a blessing on milk.

Elsewhere, a blessed candle or coal would be used to singe the hair on the cow's udder. From Cartron, County Leitrim, Kathleen Taylor reported that the coal used should be 'quinched with the first strug from each of her four tits'. In County Monaghan, 'When a heifer would calve for the first time, a hot coal would be taken out in an old porringer or such vessel and the first dregs from each teat milked down on it. The coal would then be thrown or buried in the "groups" behind the cows.'

Churching cattle was not without hazards. John Waldron of Reask County Mayo told of how an elderly couple went out to perform the rite on a heifer who had just calved, but the animal 'became so infuriated at seeing the fire near her that she broke her tether and rushed from the stable, throwing the old couple and trampling them as she went. They both died in a few months'.

Care was taken about the products of calving and the food and drink taken by cattle soon after birth, and some communities also ceremonially marked the cow's first venture out of the byre. In counties Mayo, Roscommon and Cork, part of the 'cleaning' or afterbirth, or some of the first butter churned from the new milk, might be put in the rafters of the cowshed 'as it is good for bringing butter'. Otherwise, afterbirth might be hidden in a tree or bush where it couldn't be got at by other animals. Cow's beestings might be drunk or cooked as a delicacy (often shared among the neighbours) or used as a cure for backache. 'The cow should be given some of the beestings after calving. The cat should also get some, for luck'. In County Donegal, according to Ellen Breslin, when a cow left the byre for the first time after calving, a fire was lit in the doorway and 'The cow was made walk over this fire. The people thought that this prevented the fairies from interfering with the cow'.

Breslin also described how 'In olden times the people thought the fairies had power over the cows. When a cow was after calving a little bit of blessed candle was tied to her tail. They thought that this prevented the fairies from stealing the butter'. Other items might also be tied to cow or calf before or after calving. Red ribbon or rag is often mentioned (fairies don't like red). In County Sligo, 'A red string was always tied to the cow's tail when her time was up for calving. "That was to ward off the evil eye"'. In Meath, it was feared that if a red ribbon was not used, the calf would die or the fairies would interfere with the cow.[1]

---

[1] For the persistence, among the Travelling Community, of the tradition of tying a piece of red thread to a newborn baby, see Nell McDonagh's interview later in this volume.

Elsewhere a nail was tied to the tail. Calves might have a nick put in their ear or tail or be fed an egg or garlic before they drank milk for the first time. Salt might be placed in the cow's feed or on the calf's back.

In County Waterford, 'Easter water' (water blessed on Holy Saturday) was 'put in first mash of bran given to a cow after calving' and into the churn the first time butter was made with new milk. Elsewhere, a coal or plough coulter might be placed under the churn when the first milk was being churned, or a penny placed in it. A penny or a sliver coin might also be put in the cow's first drink after calving or the first bucket of milk (in Mayo, the coins might afterwards be given to a child to spend).

Ceremonies of blessing or churning cattle after calving, and the other measures to ensure the health of cows and their calves, demonstrate the importance of cattle and milk products to household economies in Ireland (also seen in the folklore of butter-stealing witches, and of May Eve, when butter and, therefore, the profit of the house was seen to be under particular threat). They also highlight the extent to which supernatural beliefs were entwined with and even reinforced by Catholic teaching. Objects traditionally used against fairies and other ill-wishers like red thread, iron tongs and fire were used alongside Christian words, gestures (the sign of the cross), sacramentals (Easter water and blessed candles) and other items that had both Christian and magical properties (salt and the *Brat Bhríde*). Like women, cows needed churching after the ordeal and hazards of birth, and the rituals used were carried out in a similar spirit of thanksgiving and worry, to combat evil influences at this in-between time when threats hovered and the whole household's sustenance and luck might hang in the balance.

Further Reading:

Collections of the Irish Folklore Archive, University College Dublin. Available at: www.duchas.ie.

Déirdre D'Auria, 'Nósanna a Bhaineann leis an mBreith in Éirinn', *Béaloideas* 75 (2007), 48–78.

Fiona Fitzsimons, 'Kindred Lines: Churching', *History Ireland*, 28:1 (2020).

Patricia Lysaght, 'Women, Milk and Magic at the Boundary Festival of

May', in Patricia Lysaght (ed.), *Milk and Milk Products from Medieval to Modern Times* (Edinburgh, 1994).

Clodagh Tait, 'Safely Delivered: Childbirth, Wet-nursing, Gossip-feasts and Churching in Ireland *c.* 1530–1690', *Irish Economic and Social History*, 30 (2006), 1–23.

46

The Birth of Brendan O'Brien: A Son and Heir

Maeve O'Riordan

Mabel O'Brien (née Smyly, 1869–1942) gave birth to Brendan Edward O'Brien on 11 January 1903. He was an eagerly awaited baby, and the fact that he was a boy meant that he solved dynastic questions for his family. He was due to inherit the wealth of his father, the artist Dermod O'Brien, and in turn, as the first-born son of a first-born son, the estate of his grandfather, the landlord Edward O'Brien of Cahermoyle, County Limerick (though that estate was sold before he reached adulthood). Brendan's family were not in urgent need of a male heir. He was his parents' first child, but his father had younger half-brothers from his father's second marriage to Julia Marshall, who could inherit the estate if necessary. Julia, as with so many second wives, knew and accepted that her sons would never achieve the same status as her husband's eldest son, particularly if he himself had a son within marriage. If Mabel never gave birth to sons, then Julia's biological sons and grandsons (as their father's direct male heirs) would inherit the family property rather than Mabel's daughters. The birth of this child changed the line of succession within the family.

The family correspondence surrounding the wedding of his parents, and his mother's pregnancy and labour highlight the undeniable preference among members of the social elite for male children. This preference was not limited to fathers or male relatives; the birth of a son was also touted as an important achievement for the married woman of means. Brendan's family were members of the Irish landed elite. They were one of the many landlord families who were in a state of declining wealth, and they were aware that their time as landlords of vast estates was numbered. Despite the likelihood (and the reality) that Brendan would have no landed estate or country seat to inherit when he came of age, his birth was lauded as significant. His mother, Mabel had not brought vast wealth to the estate, but in giving birth to a son, she had succeeded in securing a direct line of male succession for the family. Her pride, as well as her maternal love, shines through in all of her letters about Brendan.

Brendan's parents were slightly on the older side for heirs of estates and their wives to marry and conceive a first child at this time; he was 37 and she was 33. As with any couple before they embarked on a sexual relationship, the couple did not know if their union would produce a child. Mabel, for her part, dearly hoped that it would and that that child would be a boy. Shortly before their wedding on 8 March 1902, Mabel calculated that the soonest that she could possibly hope to give birth to a son was January 1903. She was right, and gave birth just ten months after the wedding, a day after the expected due date. Before they married, this hoped-for infant was given a pet-name of 'Tommy'. The gender of that pet-name was no accident. In the days before she gave birth, Mabel reported dreaming that she would give birth to quads, and secondly, that her future child would be a girl; neither of these possibilities were favourable and she continued to refer to Tommy by the male pronoun. Six days before she gave birth, she informed her stepmother-in-law, Julia, that all the preparations were made, but that 'Master Tommy sucks his thumb and scratches his head and stays where he is'. It may be that Mabel sought to temper her husband's desire for a son before the birth as he wrote to his father afterwards that they had 'quite made up [their] minds that it was going to be a girl'. He was happy to be in a position to admit that he was 'glad' that it was a boy.

Although Mabel and Dermod enjoyed a demonstratively affectionate relationship, the birth of their child was something which was her experience alone. While the pair shared a bed, he was 'banished to the ground-floor bedroom' a week before the birth. On the day itself, he waited in the drawing room and was not allowed into the room to be shown his child until 45 minutes after the birth. Mabel gave birth with the help of a monthly nurse (a nurse hired to care for mother and baby through birth and the early days postpartum) and a doctor. She also benefitted from the support of her mother, who was with Mabel throughout her labour and sat with her from breakfast time until the doctor came at 4 p.m. Mabel 'never dreamed that she would be allowed to come', but having her mother 'made a lot of difference' and fifteen minutes after he was born, the baby was washed and dressed and by the fire in his grandmother's arms.

Both Mabel and Dermod accepted and expected that the pain of childbirth would be a feature of her married life. Mabel's ability to survive this pain was a source of pride for both of them. Dermod wrote afterwards to his father stressing that it was not mere luck, but Mabel's innate qualities, which made the pregnancy and birth so successful:

> Many thanks for your congratulations which I think on Mabel's part are very well deserved, for she has behaved all through in a most exemplary manner having had none of the worries or hardships to put up with so many women have for months before the birth of a child ... she had not a bad time as such things go I imagine. This was no doubt owing to some extent to her perfect calm & courage having no apprehensions & [perfectly relishing?] that through which she was bound to suffer, that that was the nature of things & had a definite end to be looked forward to. She is now as jolly as possible, eats & sleeps well & enjoys having her boy, whose a great feeder, tugging at her.

Mabel also minimised the pain of childbirth when writing to her husband's family:

> I am quite ready to allow that I have been to tea-parties and even to whist-parties that I have enjoyed more than what my little nurse calls 'the jiminastic' on the 11th, but still it was quite endurable and the time of convalescence and baby-worship that came after has been a time of great luxury & content.

Mabel's post-partum letters are indeed filled with baby worship that would challenge any assumptions about elite women and their emotional connection to their children. She breastfed Brendan and happily included details in her letters of his regurgitating milk all over her dress, stressed the kindness of the nursery servants she hired, and three months later, readily admitted that she, who was deeply religious, did not go to religious services as Brendan was still a 'two-hours baby' and she could not leave him for any length of time. Brendan was weaned at 8 months.

Brendan's parents' emphasis on a male heir demonstrates that the preference for male children, or the requirement for at least one male child, did not decrease with the corresponding decrease in power of the landed class. For Mabel, the act of giving birth to a boy was a moment of pride, as well as an act of love on her part for her husband. In a letter to her mother-in-law in the weeks after giving birth, she wrote; 'you may imagine what a proud moment it was when I showed him his son. I had been thinking of it and looking forward to it for ages and it was quite as good as I had hoped'. In giving birth to a son, Mabel produced a boy who could trace his direct male heritage in *Burke's Landed Gentry* and *Burke's Peerage*, the directories for the leading landed families in Britain and Ireland, through the centuries. He was reputedly descended from the first High King of Ireland, Brian Boru.

While Dermod could see Mabel's side in his son, Mabel stressed the features which he inherited from his father's family; his ears were his paternal grandfather's, his feet his paternal grandmother's and his 'hands are Dermod's own in miniature, they really are absurdly alike down to the long little finger and the turn back of the thumb'. It was not long before Brendan had a sister and later more siblings, all of whom were shown great love, care and affection by their mother who took her parenting role very seriously, but it was this first-born son who showed Mabel that she could produce an heir for her husband's family.

Sources:
The letters referenced in this chapter are found in the Cahermoyle Estate Collection at the National Library of Ireland (NLI/MS/36). The birth of Brendan and his parents' relationship is also discussed in Maeve O'Riordan, *Women of the Irish Country House: 1860–1914* (Liverpool, 2018).

47

'Nóra Mharcais Bhig' and the Unspoken Birth

Marie Whelton

'Nóra Mharcais Bhig' is an Irish-Language short story by Pádraic Ó Conaire which was published in 1909 in *Nóra Mharcuis Bhig agus Sgéalta Eile*. It dramatises the all-too-familiar predicament of an unmarried woman who feels compelled to emigrate from rural Ireland to urban England to wait out her pregnancy and give birth. Ultimately, Nóra is forced to endure the enormous penalty of permanent exile because she does not fully conform to some of the ethical and religious norms espoused by her father and her local community. Remarkably, Ó Conaire manages to tell her story without mentioning the words 'pregnancy' or 'birth' and, while the reader is left in no doubt about the nature of her personal crisis, unanswered questions remain about how Nóra's pregnancy ended, about where she gave birth and about the fate of her child. The story's silence regarding those questions mirrors Nóra's own cautious silence in relation to her situation and it also mirrors the dysfunctional century-and-a-half-long silence in Irish society about birth outside of marriage. Nóra, therefore, powerfully represents a section of Irish society which was, until recently, muted in relation to its experience of birth.

The story skilfully exposes the role gender inequity played in allowing women to bear all the repercussions of not adhering to accepted social rules around marriage. The relationship between Nóra and the young medical student ('mac Sheáin Mhaitiú' – 'the son of Seán Mathew'), with whom she falls in love one summer, is an unequal relationship in that the consequences of the consummation of their relationship are very different for each of them – she is left in turmoil, worrying about 'the shame' she has brought to her family 'because of one sin' (Ó Conaire in Mac Labhraí, 50) and she is condemned to live the rest of her life on the margins of society, while the elusive male seducer (who is not given a proper name by Ó Conaire) shuns his responsibility and leaves unperturbed, without replying to her letters, to fulfil his life-plans. By fleetingly reintroducing an older 'mac Sheáin Mhaitiú' towards the end of the story, Ó Conaire uses contrast to show how the male protagonist has been allowed, by society, to continue to belong in respectable affluent circles where Nóra, and the child he may have fathered, are not spoken about.

The story also discloses the subversive controlling force of societal judgement vocalised by the men who engage in local gossip. Nóra's outward silence is juxtaposed with the revealing, but neglectful, whispers of that local hearsay – there is pity for Nóra and a vague understanding of her fate in the following extract, for example, but no effort to intervene or to help the child to whom she will give birth:

> 'Go bhfóire Dia uirthi,' arsa duine de na buachaillí a bhí
> caite le claí ar phlasóg mhín chaonaigh le hais an bhóthair…
> 'Ach meas tú cén ealaín atá uirthi go bhfuil sí ag
> imeacht?'…
> 'Deirtear gur chuir sí spéis mhór i mac Sheáin Mhaitiú, an
> fear siopa,' arsa seanfhear ina measc.
> 'É siúd a bhí sa gcoláiste mór i nGaillimh?'
> 'An duine céanna.'
> 'Ná creid é. Drochbhuachaill a bhí ann.' (Ó Conaire in Mac
> Labhraí, 48)

> ('May God help her,' said one of the lads who was stretched
> out by a ditch on a smooth patch of moss near the road …
> 'But what, do you think, has come over her to cause her to
> leave?' …
> 'It's said that she had a great interest in mac Sheáin Mhaitiú,
> the shop man,' said an old man amongst them.
> 'He who was in the big college in Galway?'
> 'The same person.'
> 'Don't believe it. He was a bad boy.')

Unsurprisingly in that context, the proud guarding of family reputation within the community is of paramount importance, and it is presented by Ó Conaire as a significant contributing factor to the making of unspeakable births. Nóra's father, in particular, is prepared to put family name before the welfare of his children – all of whom he eventually estranges. Ironically, while Nóra is unable to be open and honest with him about her pregnancy, she does voice her fear of shaming him and damaging his reputation:

> 'Bhí beirt mhac agat,' ar sise leis oíche, 'agus d'imigh siad
> uait. Náirigh an bheirt acu thú. Níl a fhios agat nach
> ndéanfainnse an cleas céanna, mura ligfidh tú dom imeacht
> go toilteanach.' (*ibid.*, 46--7)

> ('You had two sons,' said she to him one night, 'and they left
> you. The two of them shamed you. You don't know but that
> I would do the same, if you don't leave me go willingly.')

Female characters, too, are presented by Ó Conaire as being complicit in prolonging this universal silence. By allowing her daughter to leave, and by presenting her leaving as a positive, Nóra's mother participates in the societal hypocrisy. Even though she is distraught at the prospect of losing Nóra, it is evident in this extract that she feels that the emigration of Nóra would be better than the shame unveiled secrets would bring:

> 'Is í an duine deireanach acu í, a Mharcais,' arsa a bhean,
> 'agus i nDomhnach féin is dona liom scarúint léi i ndeireadh
> mo shaoil, ach,' ar sise agus í beagnach ag caoineadh,
> 'b'fhéidir gurb é lár a leasa é.' (*ibid.*, 47)

> ('She is the last of them, Marcas,' said his wife, 'and indeed it
> is difficult for me to separate from her at the end of my life,
> but,' said she and she almost crying, 'it may be for her own
> welfare.')

Likewise, the lady ('bean uasal'), with whom Nóra finds domestic service employment in London, cruelly obliges her, after a few months, to leave her job. Nóra was made homeless by that unexplained dismissal and the lack of explanation again seems to indicate that the lady heartlessly let Nóra go to save her own reputation because Nóra's unplanned illegitimate pregnancy had become visible:

> D'imigh cúpla mí mar sin, ach sa deireadh dúirt an bhean uasal léi nach raibh sí sásta léi agus go gcaithfeadh sí an áit a fhágáil. B'éigean di sin a dhéanamh. D'fhág sí a raibh aici ina diaidh, agus d'imigh léi. Dídean ná foscadh ní raibh aici don oíche sin ach an bháisteach ag titim anuas uirthi agus na sráideanna crua faoina cosa... (Ó Conaire in Mac Labhraí, 53)

> (A few months passed in that manner, but in the end the lady said to her that she wasn't satisfied with her and that she would have to leave the place. She had to do that. She relinquished all she had and left. She had neither shelter nor cover that night just the rain falling down on top of her and the hard streets underneath her feet ...)

From the moment Nóra decides to leave Ros Dhá Loch, she is essentially abandoned and left to cope alone, and silently, with her first pregnancy, with the birth of her first child and with the grief and traumatic aftermath of losing a child, or of giving a child up for adoption. In fact, within the story, Nóra meets only two truly sympathetic people – a neighbour who initially welcomes her to London and a kind old priest who, having overheard her tormented prayer in an inner city London church, tries to help. All the other characters in the story contribute, in one way or another, to her isolation, with the result that Ó Conaire leaves his reader certain about the extensive nature of the societal exclusion experienced by Nóra.

Ó Conaire's story is a pioneering social commentary on the forces within Irish society which worked together to create the 'unspoken birth'. His three-fold critique: of gender inequity within relationships;

of the collective use of gossip as an instrument of social control; and of the elevation of family reputation over family care, is powerful and effective. Most of all, though, it is his silence about whether Nóra brought her baby to full term, about the actual birth and about whether that baby survived, which masterfully illustrates the cold indifference of a whole society to the frightening plight of an expectant unwed mother and the baby to whom she would give birth.

Further Reading:

Aisling Ní Dhonnchadha, *An Gearrscéal sa Ghaeilge 1898–1940* (Baile Átha Cliath, 1981).

Seán Mac Labhraí (eag.), *Anam na Teanga: Géarscagadh ar Ghlac Gearrscéalta* (Indreabhán, 2012).

Danielle McLaughlin, '"Christian Courtesy for Catholic Girls": Reflections on a Darker Syllabus', *The Irish Times*, 27 October 2018. Available at: https://www.irishtimes.com/culture/books/christian-courtesy-for-catholic-girls-reflections-on-a-darker-syllabus-1.3669124.

Máirín Nic Eoin, *Trén bhFearann Breac: An Díláithriú Cultúir agus Nualitríocht na Gaeilge* (Baile Átha Cliath, 2005).

Lesa Ní Mhunghaile, 'Ó Conaire, Pádraic,' *Dictionary of Irish Biography*. Available at: https://dib.cambridge.org/viewReadPage.do?articleId=a6314&searchClicked=clicked&quickadvsearch=yes.

Samantha Williams, 'The Experience of Pregnancy and Childbirth for Unmarried Mothers in London, 1760–1866', *Women's History Review*, 20:1 (2011), 67–86.

48

'The Mother of the Community': Ada Shillman (1859–1933)[1]

Natalie Wynn

Ada Shillman is one of the few women to receive honourable mention in her own right in the annals of Jewish Dublin. The history of Jewish migration and settlement in Ireland in the late nineteenth and early twentieth centuries – like that of Jewish mass migration in general – is intrinsically gendered. Although one of its distinguishing features is an unusually high proportion of female and child migrants, the story of Jewish migration itself is largely masculine. It is dominated by male struggles and successes at both individual and communal levels, and the communal and social infrastructures that were established, led and developed by men. Women play little more than a supporting role in these narratives. Their traditional image as nurturers of the next generation relegates them to the private sphere of the home, so that the first-generation female immigrant voice is frequently – and, in the Irish case, entirely

FIGURE 17: *Ada in her nurse's uniform, c. 1920 (courtesy of Anne Lapedus Brest).*

[1] With thanks to Anne Lapedus Brest, great-granddaughter of Ada Shillman, for providing me with a family memoir and photos of Ada.

217

– absent from the historical record. In Irish Jewish collective memory, women tend to be celebrated *en masse* for their charitable and philanthropic contributions. At the individual level, their lives are always mediated through the recollections of those who knew them, often with a strong vein of humour that allows for some insight into the personalities involved, but no real understanding of their actual, lived experience. They are fondly remembered as mothers, aunts, grandmothers, family friends; as strong, resilient and widely respected individuals who had a lasting influence on those who knew them, even if they were not always the easiest people to deal with; and idealised as the female immigrant folk-type of *balabosta* (homemaker *par excellence*)-cum-tireless charity-worker.

Ada Shillman was born in Lithuania in 1859, migrated with her husband to Cork in 1882 and relocated with her family to Dublin ten years later. She qualified as a midwife in 1888, delivering hundreds of babies – mostly, but not exclusively, Jewish – over a career spanning almost forty years, and was often referred to as 'mother of the [Jewish] community'.

From 1913, Shillman assisted Dr Bethel Solomons at the Jewish Medical Dispensary which ran twice weekly at 1 Stamer Street, in the heart of Jewish Dublin, under the auspices of the Dublin Hebrew Congregation (DHC). According to the Congregation's Annual Report from 1913, prior to its establishment, the only alternative for poorer members of the community had been a dispensary operated by the Society for Promoting Christianity Among the Jews. Missionary organisations targeted the poorest and most vulnerable members of the Jewish community, often mothers and children, subjecting them to lengthy sermons as they awaited medical attention. Although little headway was made in winning converts, missionaries were an ongoing source of concern and contention among Jewish communities throughout Britain and Ireland, prompting the establishment of a slew of Jewish counter-measures such as the Dublin dispensary. According to the 1913 report, the dispensary treated 318 patients during its first nine-and-a-half months, roughly 10 percent of Dublin's Jewish population, indicating the level of poverty and need that existed within the community at this time. From 1914, at the behest of Solomons, Shillman received an annual grant from the DHC of between five pounds and five guineas for her vital contribution to the dispensary.

The extant records of the Dublin Jewish Board of Guardians (DJBG), dating from the period 1911–14, indicate that Shillman regularly acted as a referee for both men and women applying for financial assistance of various sorts. The DJBG aspired to co-ordinate all of the city's Jewish charitable endeavours, and Shillman's presence in this male-dominated sphere is an indication both of her standing within the Jewish community and of the extent of her service to its members, which had brought her into contact with a broad range of people. Shillman's knowledge of individual circumstances prompted her to charge according to her perception of each family's means. Her surviving record-books show that the better-off were levied up to four times the fees charged to poorer families, while the very poorest paid no fees at all. This was typical of the prevailing spirit of mutual support within immigrant Jewish communities, that is often reflected in the activities of male medical professionals and male-led charities and friendly societies. How these attitudes operated within female spheres and among female medical professionals is very rarely visible to the historian.

In addition to philanthropic work within the Jewish community, Shillman was involved in the founding of St Ultan's Hospital in 1919 by Dr Kathleen Lynn. Reportedly, she raised sufficient funds from Jewish donors to equip an entire floor of the hospital; yet the prevailing narrative of the Irish Jewish contribution to local non-Jewish philanthropy is, again, exclusively male.

On Shillman's death in 1933, Bethel Solomons lamented her loss both as a personal friend and as 'one of the best midwives I have ever met … quite impossible to replace'. It is clear that the full extent of her significance within the Dublin Jewish community has yet to be evaluated. Large families were common at this time, the risk to health was high, and linguistic and cultural differences made access to public services potentially complicated and stressful on all sides. Lara Marks, therefore, emphasises the importance of the Jewish midwife in offering familiarity, support and reassurance to immigrant women at critical moments in their lives. However, according to Linda Fleming, nursing and midwifery had yet to be viewed as respectable and desirable occupations for Jewish women. Paid work carried out within the family home or business was far more commonplace, obscuring the reality of women's work in itself as well as its place within the family economy. Shillman was pioneering in her choice of profession, one that enabled her to be the sole breadwinner for a sizeable family due to her husband's ill-health. That this was an atypical career choice is indicated by the general absence of female medical professionals in traditional renditions of the Irish Jewish success story. Nevertheless, Shillman was not alone. That Myer Joel Wigoder, a deeply pious and observant man, was proud to see his daughter Sarah follow her brothers into the medical profession during the 1910s indicates that Jewish attitudes were changing. Women such as Ada Shillman and Sarah Wigoder may have been unusual for their time, but not entirely unique. They have become representative of the others who have disappeared from the historical record probably because, like Wigoder, they eventually moved on to live out their lives and pursue their careers beyond Irish shores. Recalling these Irish Jewish women is a tentative step towards recovering their untold story and writing it back into communal history.

Sources and Further Reading:

Linda Fleming, 'Jewish Women in Glasgow c. 1880–1950: Gender, Ethnicity and the Immigrant Experience' (unpublished PhD thesis, University of Glasgow, 2005).

Mark Gilfillan, 'Jews in Edinburgh: 1880–1950' (unpublished PhD thesis, University of Ulster, 2012).

Lara Marks, 'Carers and Servers of the Jewish Community: The Marginalized Heritage of Jewish Women in Britain', in Tony Kushner (ed.), The Jewish Heritage in British History: Englishness and Jewishness (London, 1992), 106–27.

Cormac Ó Gráda, Jewish Ireland in the Age of Joyce: A Socioeconomic History (Princeton, 2006).

Ray Rivlin, Jewish Ireland: A Social History of Jews in Modern Ireland (Dublin, 2011).

Myer Joel Wigoder, My Life, Samuel Abel (ed.) and Louis E. Wigoder (trans.) (Leeds, 1935).

Natalie Wynn, 'The History and Internal Politics of Ireland's Jewish Community in Their International Jewish Context (1881–1914)' (unpublished PhD thesis, Trinity College Dublin, 2015).

49

The Handywoman

Linda-May Ballard

The Midwives Act, which was aimed at ensuring that women in childbirth were attended by a practitioner trained in midwifery, was applied to Ireland in 1918. However, it is at least highly likely that for some time after that date, especially in more remote areas, women continued to rely on 'the handywoman' or unofficial midwife. Oral evidence also indicates that at around the turn of the last century, women who were known to practise as handywomen, without any formal training, could register for formal recognition. Some may also have continued to work as unofficial assistants to qualified women. A major qualification for an unofficial midwife was that she had herself given birth, and it is likely that daughters followed their mothers in the role of unofficial midwife. It is difficult to acquire information about a practice that ceased a century ago, but the suggestion is that daughters learned their skills by assisting their mothers as handywomen once they too had experienced childbirth. Sometimes, mothers acted as midwives for their daughters.

A claim frequently made of these handywomen is that they never lost a child, and no doubt some were skilled practitioners, but the high rates of infant mortality prevalent in Ireland make it likely that the preference was to minimise the record in relation to stillbirth or neonatal death. Women, too, were at great risk of dying in childbirth. Nonetheless, there is evidence to suggest that as trained nurses became more involved in the delivery of babies and in early childcare, this was resented by women who preferred to be attended by a neighbour who was familiar to them. There were fears, too, of extra expense for items required by trained nurses, with materials such as talcum powder being viewed by some as an expensive and unnecessary luxury.

Handywomen were also responsible for laying out the dead, and often continued in this role long after they ceased being active as midwives. The liminal nature of their role as gatekeepers who assisted at times of birth and death is reflected in a widespread story of the handywoman taken to assist at the birth of a fairy child. The story usually specifies that a mysterious stranger arrives late at night at the home of the handywoman and takes her to an unknown location. There she delivers a child, but accidently rubs some ointment she is given during the process into one of her eyes. She is taken home after the child is delivered, usually paid and told not to speak again of the incident. The tale often concludes with a subsequent encounter at a fair, where she recognises a man as the mysterious stranger who had called at her home. Frequently, she sees him stealing apples from a stall. When she greets the man, he is furious and asks with which eye she sees him. It is of course the eye to which she has applied the ointment. He stabs at her eye with a finger, seeking to blind her, before vanishing. While there may be no relation between this story and another aspect of local folk tradition, it is worth noting that there are suggestions that amniotic fluid may have been retained to be used as a cure for ailments of the eye.

Women in childbirth and very young children (particularly boys) were at particular risk of abduction by the fairies, of being taken away completely or 'changed'. This tradition no doubt helped to account for maternal and infant mortality and for certain medical conditions. However, methods of seeking to be rid of a changeling included exposure either to the elements or to fire, which may relate to the practice of infanticide. The fact that young boys were dressed in skirts is sometimes cited as protective behaviour to confuse the fairies into thinking that they were girls, although there were also strong practical reasons to dress infant boys in this way.

Particularly within the Catholic tradition, women delivered of babies were required to be 'churched', to undergo a service of purification, before being able to resume their usual household duties. They were subject to dietary restrictions and were not permitted to brush their hair until churching had taken place. As a result, if possible, hair was carefully

brushed and plaited before labour commenced. Sometimes the churching ceremony took place in the church porch, and women were often keen to undergo it as early as possible in order to be able to return to their normal routines.

The idea that an unbaptised child may not be buried in consecrated ground is familiar, as is the idea of killeens or burial places with the unmarked graves of babies. There have also been suggestions that in the cases of stillbirth or neonatal mortality, a sextant in the locality might be approached to arrange a quiet burial in a grave opened for the funeral of an adult. A woman who had to wait some days to be churched after childbirth usually arranged for godparents, who would come as quickly as possible after the birth, to bring the child to church and ensure baptism took place. Even in denominations of the Reformed tradition that do not consider baptism absolutely necessary in all cases to ensure salvation, there was a popular inclination towards believing that an unbaptised child would not thrive.

Such a fundamental aspect of life was often little discussed, or not talked about at all, except possibly among those who had given birth. Certainly, when I began collecting information about traditional practices associated with childbirth, the women with whom I worked were careful to ensure that I had, myself, had a baby before even considering addressing the subject. The handywoman as unofficial midwife has a shadowy place in history, and undoubtedly much about her goes unrecorded and undocumented. For many women who had no other recourse, a sympathetic or skilled handywoman must have offered a measure of comfort at a potentially dangerous time. She operated in an environment in which belief in the supernatural was frequently very strong, and at a time in which poor women in particular had few resources available to them when in labour. While labour and childbirth posed threats to both mother and child, many must have felt grateful for, and reassured by, this help from trusted neighbour women.

Further Reading:

Linda Ballard, '"Just Whatever They Had Handy": Aspects of Childbirth and Early Childcare in Northern Ireland prior to 1948', *Ulster Folklife*, 31 (1985), 59–72.

Linda Ballard, 'Some Photographic Evidence of the Practice of Dressing Boys in Skirts', *Ulster Folklife*, 34 (1988), 41–7.

Linda Ballard, 'A Singular Changeling?', *Folklife: Journal of Ethnological Studies*, 54 (2014), 137–51.

Jacqueline Simpson, 'The Folklore of Infant Deaths: Burials, Ghosts and Changelings', in Gillian Avery and Kimberley Reynolds (eds), *Representations of Childhood Death* (Basingstoke, 2000), 11–28.

50

Maternal Mortality in Limerick City, 1920–38

Eugenie Hanley

Maternal deaths were a sad, yet realistic, part of everyday life in twentieth-century Limerick, and indeed, the rest of Ireland. From 1922, the Irish Free State co-ordinated maternity services to lower maternal mortality rates and introduced new measures including more advanced obstetric care, ante-natal supervision and sulphonamide drugs, which facilitated a decline in maternal deaths by the 1950s. Disparities existed between the level of maternity care in rural and urban areas, including Limerick City and County. Since the sixteenth-century, voluntary maternity hospitals offered poor city women a 'safe' place to give birth. In 1812, two charitable ladies from different religious backgrounds, Miss White (Catholic) and Miss Banks (Protestant), founded the Bedford Row Lying-In Hospital in Limerick City. Limerick Corporation also provided a maternity lying-in at the City Home and Hospital. Outside the city, Croom County Hospital and district hospitals offered limited maternity provision to expectant mothers, alongside the services of local handywomen and district nurses. Bedford Row accepted patients from all denominations and social classes. Paying patients contributed one guinea per week towards maintenance and from the mid-1920s, admissions from outside Limerick City paid a contribution towards their confinement.

During the 1920s, the Department of Local Government and Public Health sought to reform county health services and empowered local authorities to establish maternity and child welfare schemes. The 1915 Notification of Births (Amendment) Act encouraged local authorities to set up maternity and child welfare clinics which would distribute free milk to poor expectant and nursing mothers and children under the age of five and offer a health visitation service. From 1921, Limerick County Council ran a maternity and child welfare scheme in co-ordination with the Bedford Row Maternity Hospital. It was commonplace for Irish mothers to die as a result of childbirth and conditions and accidents linked to pregnancy. Expectant mothers died from puerperal infection, post-natal haemorrhage, toxaemias of pregnancy, thrombosis and abortion. The maternal death rate continued to rise throughout the 1920s; however, Limerick's maternal mortality rates fluctuated. The rates soared during the Civil War (1922–3), possibly due to widespread social unrest, violence, milk shortages and the disruption of local health services. In 1922 alone, Limerick City and County experienced more than double the national maternal mortality rate at 14.29 deaths per 1,000 registered births compared to the national average of 6.29. Indeed, the total number of maternal deaths may have been much higher, given that births were not always notified.

Puerperal sepsis posed a serious threat to new mothers; it accounted for one-third of maternal deaths nationwide. Both urban and rural parts of Limerick experienced outbreaks of puerperal sepsis which often exceeded the national sepsis death rates. Although the Irish government and medical profession blamed untrained midwives for the spread of infection between new mothers, recent research suggests that no direct link existed between maternal deaths and the practices of handywomen. Legislative measures, including the 1918 Midwives (Ireland) and the 1919 Nurses Registration (Ireland) Acts, were passed to regulate midwifery and phase out the practices of handywomen. The Central Midwives Board's new regulations applied to Bedford Row Maternity Hospital, especially the rules related to nurse training. In 1920, the staff doctors taught a six-month course for staff nurses, followed by an examination; staff rules were devised and Miss Laffan was appointed as permanent matron in 1924.

Despite these reforms, hospital births were potentially more dangerous than home births. In 1921, Bedford Row's Visiting Medical Staff reprimanded a staff nurse for failing to notify Dr Massey when a patient was in labour and for failing to report a case of pyrexia, a high temperature (the first symptom of puerperal sepsis) to the matron two days later. Nurse Kennedy, who worked at the hospital for nine months, was consequently banned from night duty. The fact that the nurse was given 'the benefit of the doubt' after questioning suggests a greater leniency afforded to trained nurses in an institutionalised setting compared to women who worked outside the physical and professional boundaries of maternity care.

Maternity hospitals witnessed significant changes in the 1930s: The Irish Hospital Sweepstakes, founded by a group of voluntary Dublin hospitals, offered financial assistance to maternity hospitals. By 1930, the Irish government assumed control over the distribution of the funds. Bedford Row Maternity Hospital welcomed state grants because it had not received Corporation or governmental funding for almost two decades. The Ladies Managing Committee frequently complained about overcrowding and the need for suitable isolation facilities at the hospital. Ante-natal cases were sometimes refused due to shortage of beds, and patients were also discharged early from hospital. In March 1933, their concerns about insufficient isolation beds were justified when an outbreak of septic pneumonia occurred at the hospital, causing five patient deaths. The hospital staff and the Medical Officer of Health temporarily closed the hospital and on 1 April 1933, it reopened after disinfection of the wards. Owing to the lack of isolation facilities, certified cases of pyrexia and puerperal sepsis cases were sent to the fever hospital or the City Home and Hospital. Additionally, patients who required caesarean sections, including primiparous mothers over the age of 35, and cases with specified obstetrical conditions, were transferred to St John's Hospital for treatment.

The Hospitals Trust and Bedford Row engaged in discussions regarding the possibility of opening a new maternity hospital in Limerick. However, the Ladies Managing Committee struggled to find a suitable site for the erection of the new hospital and, by 1936, it became clear that a 200-bed regional maternity hospital was needed to accommodate patients from Limerick and the surrounding counties of Clare and Tipperary. Participating maternity hospitals had to reserve one third of all beds for poor patients. From 1936 onwards, Bedford Row reserved four beds for unmarried mothers. Until then, maternity provision for expectant unmarried mothers was sub-standard and they were segregated in separate institutions from married women because Irish society frowned upon pregnancy outside of wedlock. Under the 1923 Local Government (Temporary Provisions) Act, Limerick Corporation offered maternity provision for unmarried mothers and illegitimate children at the City Home and Hospital. Following confinement, the Board of Health transferred some unmarried mothers to Bessborough Mother and Baby Home in Blackrock, County Cork. By the 1930s, maternity hospitals began to accommodate cases where a difficult or complicated labour was anticipated. Bedford Row accepted emergency maternity cases from the City Home and Hospital. However, hospital admissions were dependent upon patient morality; Bedford Row's 1948 rules for management of the maternity hospital stressed that patients were required to produce a signed 'certificate of good character' by the hospital's subscribers or medical staff before admission.

Expectant mothers' health attracted further interest and was inextricably linked to infant mortality rates during this period. In 1931, Limerick's Medical Superintendent Officer of Health (MSOH) described expectant mothers as 'undernourished', and an ante-natal clinic was set up at the hospital. Ante-natal supervision was of key significance to the early detection of medical conditions and helped to prevent maternal and infant deaths. By 1933, the Ladies Managing Committee agreed that the hospital would oversee the urban district nursing services in Limerick City. Despite these developments, Limerick City and County continued to be characterised by high maternal death rates; for example, in 1935, for every 1,000 births, 7 mothers died in childbirth in Limerick County, compared to 5.46 in Limerick City.

Limerick City experienced high maternal mortality rates throughout the 1920s and 1930s, especially in rural areas where maternity provision was limited. Although the Bedford Row Maternity Hospital provided a suitable place for women to give birth, it cannot be properly appraised without noting both its successes and failures. Funding from the hospital sweepstakes and the centralisation of maternity care heralded the expansion of Limerick's maternity services after decades of stagnation; unmarried mothers had greater access to advanced maternity care and domiciliary births were supervised.

Sources:

The materials discussed in this chapter can be consulted in the Bedford Row Lying-In Hospital Collection, Limerick Special Committee Meeting Minute Books, and Public Health Services Pre-1960: Limerick City Council at www.Limerick.ie.

Mortality rates were taken from the Annual Reports of the General-Registrar for Ireland.

Further Reading:

Lindsey Earner-Byrne, *Mother and Child: Maternity and Child Welfare in Dublin, 1922–60* (Manchester, 2007).

51

The Urban Infant Mortality Penalty:
Lessons from Sligo — 1920–1947

Fióna Gallagher

Newborns in the Ireland of the 1930s faced many health obstacles, including disease, poor nutrition, social inequality and poor housing. Infant mortality rates are one of the key barometers of public health, and in Sligo town by the 1930s, the outlook was not good.

By 1930, Sligo was the eighth largest town in the State, with a population of about 12,000. It had an intractable housing problem, manifested in poor health outcomes for the labouring class, and particularly for their infants. Overcrowding was endemic, existing housing insanitary and there was little prospect of betterment for the vast majority of the poorer classes. Data from the 1926 census show that almost 23 percent of the population lived in dwellings of two rooms or less. Shockingly, 9 percent, or 770 people, lived in dwellings of just one room. In the Free State as a whole, the typical habitation in 1926 consisted of three rooms, with 7.5 percent of all families consisting of six or more persons. Consequently, health and life expectancy suffered. Average life expectancy for both men and women in 1926 was just over 57 years.

In 1920, the infant mortality rate in Sligo Borough was unacceptably high, with a rate of 120 per thousand (p/t) births, second only to Dublin's 143 p/t. Some improvement occurred over the following decade, standing at only 86 p/t in 1928. But by 1932, it had risen sharply again to 124 p/t. This shocking rate drew the indignation of the county medical officer, Dr Michael Kirby in 1936. Addressing a special meeting of Sligo Corporation that October, he stated that Sligo Borough 'has the highest infant mortality rate in any town in the Free State. For every

1,000 children born alive, 124 die before they reach their first birthday … At the moment, a child born in Sligo has only half the chance of living which the Dublin infant might expect'. He went on to stress that a large number of the children in Sligo who did survive their first year, never reached five years of age, and even many of those who did, never became 'citizens of utility', owing to the lack of proper care in childhood. Such realities arose because of 'the ill-health of mothers before the child is born; … domestic incompetence; wilful neglect; a low standard of the sense of duty to infants, and bad housing'.

Dr Kirby was a dedicated public health doctor, serving as county medical officer for almost thirty-five years. His observations on familial and maternal attitudes to infants and health, particularly amongst the poorer class, were drawn from long experience and a desire for education and improvement.

Infant mortality is a widely-used indicator of a population's health status because it is associated with a range of socio-economic factors, including education and the availability of health services. Incidences of high numbers of children dying within the first year of life are generally due to poor infant and maternal nutrition, low birth-weight, poor sanitation and personal hygiene, leading to increased risk of infection and reduced immunity to childhood diseases. Lack of access to medicines and war-rationing were exacerbating factors from 1939–45. Large families also increased the pressure on household resources. Infant mortality was clearly subject to a 'steep socio-economic gradient'. So too was maternal mortality, averaging nationally at 4.75 p/t births in the decade between 1921 and 1931; by 1936, it had fallen marginally to 4.70. In 1941, maternal deaths from all forms of puerperal fever were 4.1 p/t in Sligo Borough, but encouragingly, that rate fell to just 1.65 by 1945.

A cursory look at the death registrations for those children in Sligo who died at under one year old during this period reveals that diphtheria and infantile enteritis were the principal causes of infant death, closely related to the social and housing conditions in which the child lived. Contagious diseases were long the scourge of urban districts until the ready availability of synthetic antibiotics in the early 1950s.

Many of the infant deaths that occurred in the first few months of life were directly attributable to the state of health of the mother during, and immediately after, pregnancy. Notable in the reports of the Sligo medical officer are the attempts to promote and encourage good maternal health – not an easy job given the economic conditions, limited money, multiple pregnancies and exceptionally bad housing. Breast-feeding for the poorer mother was often difficult due to maternal malnourishment, and the substitution of improperly treated cow-milk was frequently the cause of infantile gastro-enteritis. In 1936, there were eight midwives registered for Sligo Borough and about thirty-five in the county at large. The vast majority of deliveries were in the home; a clean and safe delivery was the goal, reducing the risk of sepsis and maternal death, and ultimately, infant death.

A substantial mortality 'penalty' for living in urban areas had developed in Ireland in the late nineteenth century and was consistent right through the 1940s. In 1930, mortality amongst women in the urban areas was 25 percent higher than for their rural cohorts; males in the urban areas showed an excess of 40 percent more than their rural counterparts. By the 1930s, the official public health consensus was that infant mortality, poverty and family welfare were all intimately connected. The lower socio-economic groups exhibited the greatest mortality and morbidity rates. The life expectancy of Sligo's poor remained intractably low in the 1930s, with an average death rate in the town of 13.4 p/t, higher than the Free State average.

Despite the rapid construction of new Corporation houses in Sligo after 1933, infant health continued to display worrying trends. The infant mortality rate (IMR) in the urban area remained significantly higher than that of County Sligo and of the State, right up until 1948. In Sligo town, infant mortality stood at 82 p/t live births in 1937. The average IMR in the eight largest towns in the Free State in 1938, was 88.3 p/t. Throughout the Free State, 5,146 children under five years of age died in 1938. The IMR for infants dying before they were one month old was 28.2 p/t. Following the outbreak of the Second World War, there was an epidemic of infant gastroenteritis, caused primarily by poor hygiene and contaminated milk, and reflected in the infant mortality statistics for Sligo, which climbed from 77 p/t in 1940 to 132 p/t in 1945. Post-war figures remained higher than the State average IMR, with a conspicuous spike in 1947 caused by an outbreak of measles and whooping cough, neither of which 'were treated seriously by parents, yet extracted a heavy toll on infants'.

Between 1932 and March 1948, Sligo corporation erected over 870 state-financed modern houses. It demolished 500 condemned dwellings and re-housed almost 4,000 people – 550 families – representing nearly 45 percent of the then population. A new main sewerage scheme was completed by 1942, discharging all the town's foul waste to a municipal collecting plant, and the number of stinking, insanitary back-garden privies decreased rapidly. Household waste was collected on a weekly basis, rather than thrown in gardens, and new houses had fresh piped water. However, there was continued overcrowding in these larger council houses, as poorer families often leased out the smallest room, to supplement their income.

The urban infant mortality penalty was eventually eliminated by multi-faceted public health interventions, most effectively after 1947, when a stand-alone Department of Health was formed. It is questionable if Sligo's new sanitary council-housing had any immediate effect on the condition of infants' health, but it is undeniable that the massive two-pronged State investment in public housing and public health, between 1930 and 1950, translated itself into improved health for mother, child and citizen.

Sources:

Much of the data is taken from the *Annual Reports of the Department of Local Government and Public Health, 1932–1947*. Sligo statistics are taken from the unpublished reports of the County Medical Officer, 1936–1948. This paper draws on my PhD Thesis, 'Rehousing the Urban Poor in Irish Country Towns, 1880–1947: A case study of Sligo' (Maynooth University, 2016).

Further Reading:

Margaret H. Preston and Margaret Ó hÓgartaigh (eds), *Gender and Medicine in Ireland, 1700–1950* (New York, 2012).

Liam Delaney *et al.*, 'From *Angela's Ashes* to the Celtic Tiger: Early Life Conditions and Adult Health in Ireland', *Journal of Health Economics*, 30 (January, 2011), 1–10.

Lindsey Earner-Byrne, *Mother and Child: Maternity and Child Welfare in Dublin 1922–60* (Manchester, 2007).

Ruth Barrington, *Health, Medicine and Politics in Ireland 1900–1970* (Dublin, 1987).

Catriona Clear, *Women of the House: Women's Household Work in Ireland, 1922–1961* (Dublin, 2000).

52

The Darkest Part of a Dark History? Infanticide in Ireland: A Case Study of Donegal 1870–1950

Megan McAuley and Jennifer Redmond

Infanticide in Ireland has been examined from historical, medical, feminist, folklore, sociological and legal perspectives, predominantly from the seventeenth to the twentieth century. Clíona Rattigan, Elaine Farrell, Moira Maguire, Sandra McAvoy, Louise Ryan, Dympna McLoughlin, Karen Brennan, Pauline Prior and James Kelly, among others, have collectively found significant evidence of infanticide, or to give it its proper definition, the murder of an infant under the age of one year, across the island and throughout the ages. All acknowledge that the criminal nature of this history means documented traces of infanticide may be the tip of the iceberg, and yet the recorded figures are stunning. This chapter examines this 'dark history' in Ireland by analysing cases from Donegal during a time of intense demographic change in Ireland, where high fertility was exceeded by even higher rates of emigration.

Infanticide was predominantly committed by young women, afraid of the shame and consequences of birth outside wedlock. It occurred in rural and urban areas, in families of different socio-economic status and was not only perpetrated by mothers, but also by fathers or members of the wider family. Intense social stigma around sexual activity outside marriage is verified by this crime's frequency in modern Ireland. Before examining case studies that highlight the motivations for and consequences of infanticide, the evidence of this crime on a national scale will be discussed.

Farrell uncovered 4,645 cases of suspected infant murder or concealment of birth cases which came to public attention in Ireland from 1850–1900. The incidence of infanticide is possibly higher, as cases were likely undiscovered. Nobody could report the disappearance of an infant that they did not know existed, a baby's body is small and easy to dispose of, and infant bodies may decompose more quickly.

While some historians argue that infanticide in Irish society existed as a form of 'post-natal family planning', illegitimacy was the principal motivating factor for the crime. Overall, 84 percent of cases analysed in Farrell's study were illegitimate. Social intolerance of illegitimacy was rooted in the values of the middle-class or the post-Famine 'strong' farmer who were politically and economically dominant. The archetypal perpetrator of infanticide was typically, but not exclusively, an unmarried Catholic domestic servant. Farrell established that the average age of a woman arrested for infanticide was 26 years old, contradicting contemporary views that the young made such 'mistakes'. Almost 70 percent of the women in Farrell's study were domestic servants and 82 percent were Catholic.

Following a coroner's inquest on the body of a deceased infant, and if police identified a suspect, a case was forwarded for trial at the local Petty Sessions Court. If the presiding magistrates felt there was sufficient evidence, the case would then be tried by the Crown solicitor at Assizes. Infanticide was not legally defined, however, until the Infanticide Act of 1949. Previously, those accused were tried for murder, which carried the death penalty if found guilty. This was uncommon in infanticide cases: between 1850 and 1900, Farrell found only twenty-nine women sentenced to death, none of whom were executed. Instead, they were transported or sentenced to imprisonment in Ireland. Rattigan saw a similar reluctance to hand down capital sentences in her study of the period from 1900–50, and highlighted the incarceration of some women in Magdalen Asylums. Many perpetrators were found not guilty due to insufficient evidence, or were charged with a lesser crime: concealment of birth. Under the Offences Against the Person Act 1861, this was a misdemeanour that carried a maximum sentence of two years' imprisonment with hard labour.

Perpetrators of infanticide were often regarded as victims of circumstance: seduced, abandoned by family due to illegitimate pregnancy, or a victim of hormones that caused insanity. In a Donegal case in 1900, Justice Madden admitted that he 'always had the feeling that the real culprit in such cases was not in the dock'. This verdict illuminates the silence that existed about fathers in such cases and demonstrates that detecting and prosecuting infanticide was as complex in Donegal as any other county in Ireland.

Counties along the western seaboard, including Donegal, had the lowest reported rates of infanticide between 1865 and 1900. Infanticide, however, might not have been less frequent, but may have been less frequently reported. Women in the rural landscape were perhaps better able to conceal pregnancies and births. Families that condemned illegitimacy and emphasised reputation would have been keen to shield a relative who became pregnant outside marriage and may have aided in eliminating the 'problem'. Furthermore, counties were not uniformly policed, especially in rural areas.

TABLE 6: *Causes of death of unidentified Donegal infanticide victims, 1870–1950 (N=162)*

Cause of death as determined by inquest	Number of cases
Neglect/Want of proper care/Improper attention at birth	48
Unknown/Not ascertained/Insufficient evidence to determine cause of death	31
Haemorrhage/Not tying the umbilical cord	20
Smothering/Suffocation	13
Strangulation	10
Exposure	9
Drowning	9
No evidence of being born alive/Cannot say if born alive	7
Natural causes	5
Cause of death not legible	3
Dead born	2
Violence	1
Undiluted milk	1
Delay in birth	1
Acute diarrhoea	1
More than one distinct potential cause of death	1
Total	162

Source: *Civil Records of Births, Marriages and Deaths, General Register Office, https://civil-records.irishgenealogy.ie/churchrecords/civil-search.jsp (11 Apr 2021).*

Between 1870 and 1950, 350 deaths of unidentified infants were recorded in the following districts: Ballyshannon, Londonderry, Donegal, Dunfanaghy, Glenties, Inishowen, Letterkenny, Milford, Strabane, Stranorlar and Castlederg. Of these cases, 196 were newborns and 104 were not; the remainder (48) could not be identified as infants with certainty. Of the 196 infant deaths, 162 were regarded as suspicious, prompting inquests; 34 were not and no inquest was held.

Findings from the 162 Donegal inquests largely coincide with Farrell's conclusions – the most common causes of death in infanticide cases were suffocation, strangulation, drowning, exposure, poisoning, violent abuse, burning and neglect at birth as a result of starvation or haemorrhage. Under 5 percent of infant deaths in Farrell's study were caused by direct violence, and only one of the Donegal inquests gives a verdict of violence. Violence in infanticide cases, however, was commonly expressed in the press. In 1870, the *Cork Examiner* reported on a Donegal infanticide case where a 'young girl' beat 'the skull of her infant with a mallet'.

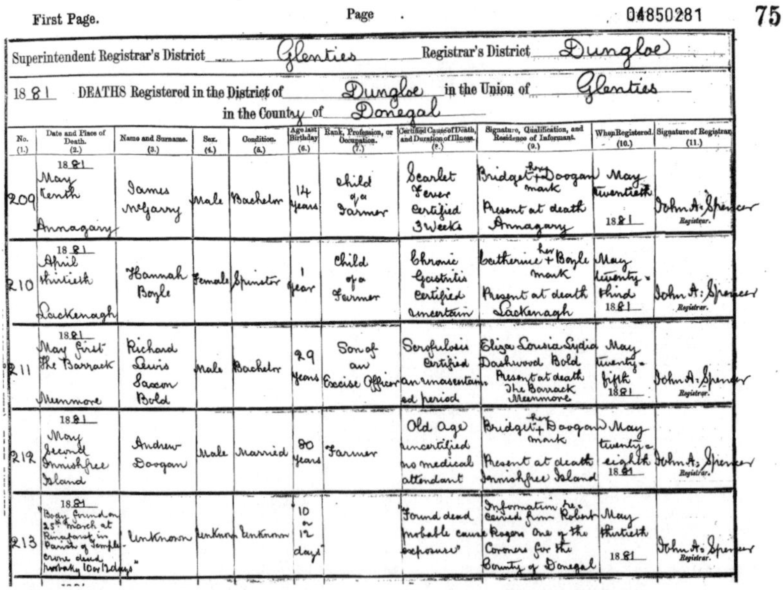
First Page. Page . 04850281 75

Superintendent Registrar's District Glenties Registrar's District Dungloe

1881 DEATHS Registered in the District of Dungloe in the Union of Glenties in the County of Donegal

No. (1.)	Date and Place of Death. (2.)	Name and Surname. (3.)	Sex. (4.)	Condition. (5.)	Age last Birthday (6.)	Rank, Profession, or Occupation. (7.)	Certified Cause of Death, and Duration of Illness. (8.)	Signature, Qualification, and Residence of Informant. (9.)	When Registered. (10.)	Signature of Registrar. (11.)
209	1881 May Tenth Annagary	James McGarry	Male	Bachelor	14 years	Child of a Farmer	Scarlet Fever Certified 3 Weeks	Bridget her + mark Doogan Present at death Annagary	May twentieth 1881	John A. Spencer Registrar.
210	1881 April thirtieth Lackenagh	Hannah Boyle	Female	Spinster	1 year	Child of a Farmer	Chronic Gastritis Certified uncertain	Catherine her + mark Boyle Present at death Lackenagh	May twenty-third 1881	John A. Spencer Registrar.
211	1881 May first The Barrack Meenmore	Richard Lewis Saxon Bold	Male	Bachelor	29 years	Son of an Excise Officer	Scrofulosis Certified an unascertained period	Eliza Lousia Sydia Dashwood Bold Present at death The Barrack Meenmore	May twenty-fifth 1881	John A. Spencer Registrar.
212	1881 May second Innishfree Island	Andrew Doogan	Male	Married	80 years	Farmer	Old age uncertified no medical attendant	Bridget her + mark Doogan Present at death Innishfree Island	May twenty-eighth 1881	John A. Spencer Registrar.
213	1881 "Body found on 25th March at Rinafarst in Parish of Templecrone dead probably 10 or 12 days"	Unknown	Unknown	Unknown	10 or 12 days		"Found dead probable cause exposure"	Information received from Robert Rogers One of the Coroners for the County of Donegal	May thirtieth 1881	John A. Spencer Registrar.

FIGURE 18. *Evidence of an infant found dead from suspected exposure, Glenties, Donegal, 1881. (Source: Civil Records of Births, Marriages, and Deaths, General Register Office, https://civilrecords.irishgenealogy.ie/churchrecords/civil-search.jsp; accessed 11 April 2021).*

Upper- and middle-class women usually did not work and would have had the financial resources to secure a marriage, or to hire assistants to help to kill or conceal the infant. As such, the 'typical' suspect may not be representative of those who committed infanticide, but rather those who were caught, highlighting the dark, hidden nature of the crime. An exception, Edith A., belonged to a well-to-do Church of Ireland family who had a farm of *c.* 92 acres, lived in a large two-storey house and who were described as 'respectable parishioners'. More common examples include that of Jane M., who regretted that 'only for the fear of my brothers the child would be living'. Bridget M.'s 'father had put her out of his house'. Mary C.'s employer Joseph R. was a witness at her trial in 1893 and recounted suspicions of her pregnancy which prompted him to contact the priest and police. Mary's infant was later found buried in a potato field near the house.

Infants were recovered across Donegal: rural fields, bogs, waterways and ditches provided extensive space to conceal the bodies of dead infants, but they also turned up on the streets, yards and privies of urban towns. One Donegal infant was found abandoned on a train track. Other bodies were hidden behind household objects, jammed in bedticks or buried under earthen floors. Rivers were a common location for the disposal of victims because of their accessibility, along with the fact that the water would carry the corpse and would conceal the remains until the perpetrator could distance themselves from the body.

Some women sought to flee as far as possible. Mary G. tried to avoid detection in 1907 by travelling to another part of Donegal and renting a room before she was due to give birth. She gave a false name in her lodgings and told the nurse that she was a married woman whose husband had deserted her. She later attempted to travel to Derry via train to dispose of the infant, but upon the train breaking down, returned home and cast the body into a lake.

Family involvement is revealed in other cases. Bridget L. and her mother Mary M. were both charged with concealment of birth of Bridget's illegitimate infant in 1901. When questioned by police, Mary M. claimed that her daughter 'was not in the family way', maintaining that Bridget was suffering from bile in the stomach and that blood-stained sheets were due to 'coming on' or menstruation. Later, however,

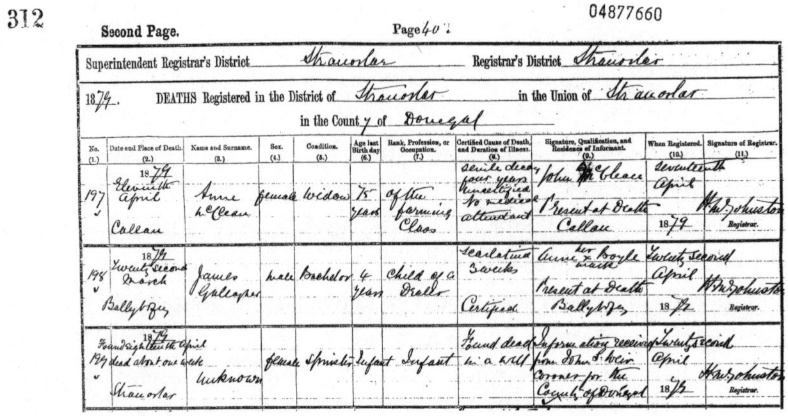

312

04877660

Second Page. Page 40

Superintendent Registrar's District Stranorlar Registrar's District Stranorlar

1879. DEATHS Registered in the District of Stranorlar in the Union of Stranorlar in the County of Donegal

No. (1.)	Date and Place of Death. (2.)	Name and Surname. (3.)	Sex. (4.)	Condition. (5.)	Age last Birth day (6.)	Rank, Profession, or Occupation. (7.)	Certified Cause of Death, and Duration of Illness. (8.)	Signature, Qualification, and Residence of Informant. (9.)	When Registered. (10.)	Signature of Registrar. (11.)
197	1879 Eleventh April Callan	Anne McClean	female	Widow	75 years	of the farming Class	senile decay four years uncertified No medical attendant	John McClean Present at Death Callan	Seventeenth April 1879	W. Johnston Registrar.
198	1879 Twenty second March Ballybofey	James Gallagher	male	Bachelor	4 years	Child of a Dealer	Scarlatina 3 weeks Certified	Anne her x mark Boyle Present at Death Ballybofey	Twenty second April 1879	W. Johnston Registrar.
199	1879 Found eighteenth April dead about one week Stranorlar	Unknown	female	Spinster	Infant	Infant	Found dead in a well	Information received from John S. Weir Coroner for the County of Donegal	Twenty second April 1879	W. Johnston Registrar.

FIGURE 19. *Evidence of an infant which was found dead in a well, Stranorlar, Donegal, 1879 (Source: Civil Records of Births, Marriages, and Deaths, General Register Office, https://civilrecords.irishgenealogy.ie/churchrecords/civil-search.jsp; accessed 11 April 2021).*

an infant body was recovered in a field beside their home, its limbs and head severed. Sarah Jane B.'s mother told police she was present when her daughter gave birth and that she washed the baby and laid it in the crib. The pair later claimed fatal injuries sustained by the infant were caused by the 'cat getting into the cradle'.

Neighbours and family members were often responsible for alerting authorities. In 1899, Ellen M., when questioned about the death of her illegitimate infant, responded: 'someone must be telling you lies about me'. It was the defendant's sister who reported her suspicions to police. In 1893, Cassie M. admitted she entered her neighbour's empty home, uninvited: 'on Monday last I felt a bad smell coming from the house [...] The door was open ... There was no person in the house. I went and lifted the lid off the trunk [...] I felt a bag. [...] When I opened the bag, I saw the appearance of a child in it'.

Fathers also played a role in infant murder cases, although they were involved in just 6 percent of Farrell's case studies. Evidence for Donegal includes Mary G. and her employer Robert M., who were both charged with concealing the birth of their infant daughter in 1902. Mary had been working as a servant in Robert's household for three years and told police he was the father. Mary gave birth in the loft and claimed the baby was stillborn. Robert M. claimed he was unaware of the birth.

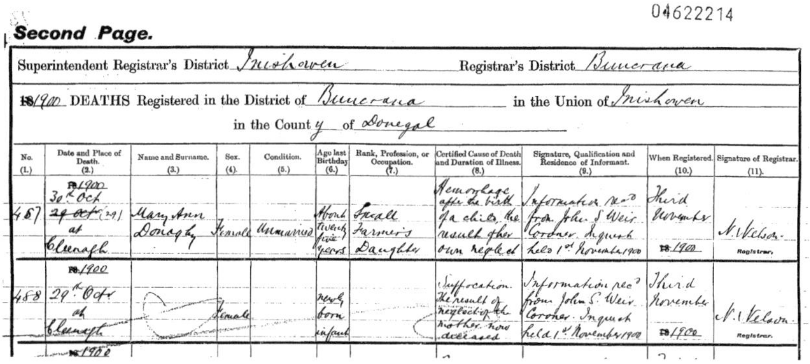
04622214

Second Page.

Superintendent Registrar's District Inishowen Registrar's District Buncrana

1900 DEATHS Registered in the District of Buncrana in the Union of Inishowen in the County of Donegal

No. (1.)	Date and Place of Death. (2.)	Name and Surname. (3.)	Sex. (4).	Condition. (5.)	Age last Birthday (6.)	Rank, Profession, or Occupation. (7.)	Certified Cause of Death and Duration of Illness. (8.)	Signature, Qualification and Residence of Informant. (9.)	When Registered. (10.)	Signature of Registrar. (11).
487	1900 30th Oct ~~29 Oct~~ (29) at Clunagh	Mary Ann Doneghy	Female	Unmarried	About twenty five years	Small Farmer's Daughter	Hemorrhage after the birth of a child, the result of her own neglect	Information rec'd from John S. Weir Coroner. Inquest held 1st November 1900	Third November 1900	N. Nelson Registrar.
488	1900 29th Oct at Clunagh		Female		newly born infant		Suffocation. The result of neglect of the mother now deceased	Information rec'd from John S. Weir Coroner. Inquest held 1st November 1900	Third November 1900	N. Nelson Registrar.

FIGURE 20. *Evidence of an unmarried mother and her infant found dead from suffocation, Inishowen, Donegal, 1900; the mother's cause of death is stated as 'haemorrhage after birth of a child the result of her own neglect' (Source: Civil Records of Births, Marriages, and Deaths, General Register Office, https://civilrecords.irishgenealogy.ie/churchrecords/civil-search.jsp; accessed 11 April 2021).*

It is possible that Mary G. lied, but it is feasible that a sexual relationship developed between them, as was the case among some domestic servants and employers, which may or may not have been exploitative.

Some women who committed infanticide were mentally ill, or perceived as such, in a society where physical trauma was intrinsically linked to mental distress. Edith A. was described by her father as 'mentally defective'. Mary M. was described by the doctor as 'barely normal'. Pregnancy and childbirth were also thought to cause mental anguish and fits of insanity, so women in these cases were not considered accountable for their actions. Mary C. was said to suffer a 'brainstorm' after giving birth and as a result, murdered her infant. Whatever the motivations, this dark part of our dark past illuminates the social mores around birth in Ireland, revealing that the price for straying outside moral norms was paid by innocent infants.

Acknowledgements:

Megan McAuley gratefully acknowledges funding received for her doctoral research from the John and Pat Hume scholarship programme of Maynooth University, the National University of Ireland and the Offaly Historical & Archaeological Society/P&H Egan.

Further Reading:

Elaine Farrell, *'A Most Diabolical Deed': Infanticide and Irish Society, 1850–1900* (Manchester, 2013).

Elaine Farrell, *Infanticide in the Irish Crown Files at Assizes, 1883–1900* (Dublin, 2012).

Clíona Rattigan, *'What Else Could I Do?': Single Mothers and Infanticide, Ireland, 1900–1950* (Dublin, 2011).

53

Concealed Pregnancy, Birth and Infanticide: The Impact of Criminalising Traumatised Women

Sylvia Murphy-Tighe and Joan G. Lalor

Ireland has a chequered history in relation to the treatment of women who experienced an unplanned pregnancy outside of marriage. Those involved centrally in concealing a pregnancy extend beyond the women and family to the Church, State and society, in order to control women's reproductive lives and shame women who did not conform. Mother and Baby Homes, workhouses, county homes and Magdalene Laundries were austere institutions that functioned by incarcerating these women and their children, hiding them from society. The cruelty shown to these women is evidenced in their testimonies and the silencing continues as their voices are yet again sidelined in national commission reports such as the Report by the Commission of Investigation into Mother and Baby Homes and Related Matters (Dept of Children, Equality, Disability and Youth, 2021).

Concealed pregnancy is a complex, multidimensional and temporal process where a woman is aware of her pregnancy and copes by keeping it hidden. The authors of this paper undertook a grounded theory study to explore and understand concealed pregnancy from the perspective of thirty women directly affected; media reports and twenty high-profile cases of public interest drawn from newspaper archives were also included as data.

Concealed pregnancy may lead to a concealed birth which may be unassisted and result in maternal and neonatal death, as in the example of the Ann Lovett Case in Granard, County Longford in 1984. Thankfully infanticide is now a rare occurrence, while judicial records of infanticide trials in the past suggest that many Irish women felt like they had no choice after a concealed pregnancy and an unassisted birth. Readers might be surprised to know that concealment of birth is criminalised in Irish law and remains on the Statute books and is punishable by imprisonment.

Who Conceals a Pregnancy and Why?

Concealed pregnancy crosses many boundaries, social strata and age profiles, and still features in contemporary society worldwide. Women who perceive the pregnancy as a crisis, irrespective of age or occupation, may hide the pregnancy, often paralysed by fear of the future. Some women require protection if they are in a relationship characterised by violence, or if the pregnancy is as a consequence of rape or sexual abuse.

A range of terms are used to describe concealed pregnancy, such as denied, disavowed, negated, cryptic and secret pregnancy. A recent re-conceptualisation of concealed pregnancy identified behaviours such as avoidance, hiding, using a cover story to explain physical changes and staying away from family and friends as mechanisms to keep the pregnancy secret. The duration of concealment may last for months, right up to birth and for some, it can recur. Concealed pregnancy is a frightening experience, which must be fully understood as some women are paralysed by fear and unable to access healthcare, especially if they have also experienced adverse traumatic/abusive experiences in their lives. Therefore, from a theoretical and research perspective, concealed pregnancy/birth must be urgently reappraised and explored from a traumatology perspective, rather than being continually viewed through a predominantly biomedical, pathological or legal lens.

Concealment of Birth, Criminalisation and Societal Opprobrium

The punishment of women by way of a custodial sentence must be re-evaluated in light of research which identifies trauma being closely associated with concealed pregnancy/birth (Murphy Tighe and Lalor, 2020). The legal framework around concealment of birth and infanticide undoubtedly influences societal opinion, while women we interviewed were well aware of the risk of criminalisation which contributed to the fear they felt. Women who experience a concealed pregnancy are sometimes pathologised or demonised and can be subject to surveillance by child protection services in the early months of motherhood, as women are pathologised as having a mental illness, placing their infant at risk.

The use of emotive language and images in media reports involving cases of concealed pregnancy/birth and (if relevant) infanticide are not uncommon. Examining 20 contemporary media reports of cases in Europe, USA and Australia involving concealed pregnancy reveals that many reports are sensationalist and do not examine all the facts (Black, 2015; Murphy Tighe and Lalor, 2016, 2016a) and may not reference the potential cause or health of the woman. It begs the question whether the constitutional right to presume innocence has been undermined, as society is now judge, jury and executioner.

Legal Response to Concealment of Birth and Infanticide

The issue of concealment/denial of pregnancy/birth extends to legal defences in criminal proceedings. Denial has been advanced as a defence in trials where women stand accused of concealment of birth, abandonment or neonaticide. Academics contend that although pathology-based defences may offer individual women a more lenient response from the criminal justice system, they may support stereotypes of irrational women (Black, 2016; Gurevich, 2010). Patriarchal and paternalistic discourses are manifest through professional debates which paint a narrative of deviancy or psychopathology, rather than addressing underlying traumatic and psychosocial reasons for infanticide, such as abuse, poverty or coercive relationships; the simplified discourse is one where women are pathologised or vilified and portrayed as 'mad' or 'bad'.

Highly publicised international cases have seen prosecution teams use telephone or written evidence from women's diaries suggesting they were 'aware' of the pregnancy to undermine any potential defence based on denial. Brooke (2007) reported that a young journalist in the UK arrived in hospital with her dead newborn after an unassisted birth, denying knowledge of pregnancy. Diary extracts read in Court said: 'Please, please help me. I'm scared but trying to block it out … why can't it just go away? Why can't it just go to sleep and leave me alone?'

In another UK case, Ruth Percival a 28-year-old woman gave birth to her baby in a toilet in 2014 and, despite three attempts to charge her, and also her father, insufficient evidence meant infanticide charges were dropped (Parveen, 2016). A baby who dies following a concealed pregnancy/birth does not mean the mother committed a crime. An unassisted birth may result in death, and the neonate may die due to inattention (act of omission) rather than an act of commission. Avoidance as a coping response due to intense fear requires greater examination by researchers and practitioners. The practice of charging women with a criminal offence after a concealed/denied pregnancy with a tragic outcome and later withdrawing charges has been observed in other cases (Ferry, 2014), highlighting scope for a review of the decision making to proceed with such prosecutions. Concealment of birth (COB) is rarely prosecuted in the UK, with only four convictions between 2010 and 2014, while one woman did receive a custodial sentence. Despite the small number of convictions for COB the existence of the law points to societal control over maternal behaviour. There appear to have been no prosecutions against women for infanticide in Ireland since the murder charge against Joanne Hayes was withdrawn in the 1980s. Brennan (2018), a legal academic, noted that Irish criminal law will either be practised according to prevailing social norms, or it will be modified, repealed or replaced to accommodate social expectations about the role of the criminal law and appropriate punishment.

Shifting the Dial on the Conversation in Relation to Concealed Pregnancy and Birth

A narrative of risk has dominated the discourse in relation to concealed pregnancy/birth linking concealed pregnancy with infanticide, which Oberman (2002) says fuels a 'rhetoric of outrage'. A woman who conceals a pregnancy/birth, which results in infanticide, experiences a personal tragedy with lifelong consequences and is highly unlikely to pose a risk to society (Murphy Tighe and Lalor, 2020). Subsequent events may require investigation, but rushing to charge women with concealment of birth has resulted in flawed responses such as charging a woman and her partner when, in fact, a miscarriage has occurred (McLelland, 2015; Gordon, 2016) or when an infant has been stillborn (BBC, 2014). As neonaticide is not a specific crime, charges of concealment of birth and infanticide may be used, leading to a defence of not guilty by reason of insanity or mental disturbance.

Medical, policing and legal responses often follow cases of concealed pregnancy/birth where a rare outcome of infanticide occurs. Infanticide is extremely rare, and yet impacts significantly on the portrayal of women who experience a concealed pregnancy, a more common phenomenon. There is an urgent need for definitions to be clarified or a nomenclature developed to capture a range of experiences/outcomes of concealed/denied pregnancy/birth. Interdisciplinary research is required to progress understanding. In some US States, women convicted of infanticide receive long prison sentences or even the death penalty, while in Europe, Infanticide Laws provide more humane mental health treatment or lenient sentences for women. The voice of women impacted by the experience of concealed/denied pregnancy has rarely been heard until recent times. Listening to these women's experiences is imperative in order that their early life experiences are better understood, in order to shape policy, practice and societal responses. We contend that concealed pregnancy/birth and infanticide are linked and must be urgently reappraised from a traumatology perspective. A legal framework that automatically criminalises women for concealing a birth prevents women from seeking help for themselves and their infant (if born alive). It is time for a more humane and supportive approach that cares for all women and infants regardless of their circumstances and histories and values their lives equally.

Sources and Further Reading:

Karen Brennan, 'Social norms and the law in responding to infanticide', *Legal Studies*, 38 (2018), 480–99.

Lynsey Black, 'The Representations of Offending Women in the Irish Press: A Content Analysis', *Irish Probation Journal*, 12 (2015), 160–78.

Lynsey Black, 'Gendering the Condemned Women and Capital Punishment in Ireland Post-1922' (unpublished PhD thesis, Trinity College Dublin, 2016).

Chris Brooke, 'Bizarre case of the mother, her secret pregnancy and a dead baby in a carrier bag', *Daily Mail*, 3 October 2007. Available at: www.dailymail.co.uk/news/article-485418/Bizarre-case-mother-secret-pregnancy-dead-baby-carrier-bag.html.

Padraig Collins, 'Irish woman held for hiding birth in Australia allowed return home', *Irish Times*, 13 August 2014.

Hannah Corken and Mark Naylor, 'Mum who dumped baby William in her parents' drain jailed for a year', *Grimsby Telegraph*, 2 October 2017. Available at: http://www.grimsbytelegraph.co.uk/news/grimsbynews/mum-who-dumped-baby-william-563985.

Dept. of Children, Equality, Disability, Integration and Youth, *Final Report of the Commission of Investigation into Mother and Baby Homes*. Dublin: Government Publications 2021. Available at: https://www.gov.ie/en/publication/d4b3d-final-report-of-the-commission-of-investigation-into-mother-and-baby-homes/.

Diarmuid Ferriter, *Occasions of Sin: Sex and Society in Modern Ireland* (London, 2009).

Declan Ferry, 'Charges dropped against Irish backpacker accused of concealing birth of baby that died', *Irish Mirror*, 2 October 2014.

Elaine Farrell, *"A most diabolical deed": Infanticide and Irish Society* (Manchester, 2013).

Susan Hatters Friedman *et al.*, 'Characteristics of women who deny or conceal pregnancy', *Psychosomatics*, 48:2 (2007), 117–22.

Susan Hatters Friedman *et al.*, 'Neonaticide: Phenomenology and considerations for prevention', *International Journal of Law and Psychiatry*, 32 (2009), 43–7.

'Gordon A Mother tells of her "living nightmare" after she suffered a miscarriage and was arrested on suspicion of murder', *Daily Mail*, 11 July 2016. Available at: https://www.dailymail.co.uk/news/article-3684133/Mother-tells-living-nightmare-suffered-miscarriage-arrested-police-suspicion-MURDER.html.

Liena Gurevich, 'Patriarchy? Paternalism? Motherhood discourses in trials of crimes against children', *Sociological Perspectives*, 51:3 (2010) 515–39.

IrishLegal.com. 'Concealed pregnancies expert calls for re-examination of 1861 law' 18 Dec. 2018. Available at: https://irishlegal.com/article/concealed-pregnancies-expert-calls-for-re-examination-of-1861-law.

Euan McLelland, 'Mother who suffered a miscarriage at her home when she was 15 weeks pregnant was arrested on suspicion of murder and thrown in the cells for a night', *Daily Mail*, 26 November 2015. Available at: https://www.dailymail.co.uk/news/article-3335382/ Mother-suffered-miscarriage-home-18-weeks-pregnant-arrested-suspicion-murder-thrown-cells-night.html.

Emma Milne, 'Suspicious Perinatal Death and the Law: Criminalising Mothers who do not Conform' (unpublished PhD thesis, University of Essex, 2017).

Sylvia Murphy-Tighe and Joan G. Lalor, 'Regaining Agency and Autonomy: A grounded typology of concealed pregnancy', *Journal of Advanced Nursing*, Mar;75:3 (2019), 603–15.

Sylvia Murphy-Tighe and Joan G. Lalor 'Concealed pregnancy: A concept analysis', *Journal of Advanced Nursing* 72:1 (January 2016), 50–61.

Sylvia Murphy-Tighe and Joan G. Lalor, 'Concealed Pregnancy and newborn abandonment: A contemporary 21st century issue Part 1', *The Practising Midwife*, 19:6 (June 2016), 12–5.

Sylvia Murphy-Tighe and Joan G. Lalor, 'Concealed Pregnancy', in *Myles Textbook for Midwives* (17th ed., Elsevier, 2020).

Michelle Oberman, 'Mothers Who Kill: Coming to Terms With Modern American Infanticide', *American Criminal Law Review*, 143 (2002), 1–110.

Nazia Parveen, 'Prosecutors to re-examine vicarage death of newborn baby', *The Guardian*, 5 October 2016. Available at: https://www.theguardian.com/uk-news/2016/oct/05/prosecutors-to-re-examine-vicarage-death-of-newborn-baby.

Theresa Porter and Helen Gavin, 'Infanticide and Neonaticide: A Review of 40 Years of Research Literature on Incidence and Causes', *Trauma, Violence and Abuse*, 11:3 (2010), 99–112.

Cliona Rattigan, *"What Else Could I Do?": Single Mothers and Irish and Infanticide 1850–1900* (Dublin, 2012).

A.M. Spielvogel and H.C. Hohener, 'Denial of Pregnancy: A Review and Case Reports', *Birth*, 22:4 (Dec. 1995), 220–6.

Margaret Spinelli, 'Infanticide and American Criminal Justice (1980–2018)', *Archives of Women's Mental Health*, 22 (2019), 173–7.

54

Birth on the Battlefield

David Murphy

Since ancient times, women have travelled with armies on campaign, often enduring the harsh conditions and dangers of war. In the past, there was a tendency to dismiss the importance of their presence on campaign, and they have often been discounted by historians as 'camp followers' if not mere prostitutes. Recent research suggests otherwise, and it can be shown that, from the late eighteenth century, increasing numbers of soldiers' wives accompanied the armies in the field. This was particularly true in the case of the Revolutionary and Napoleonic Wars in which Irish soldiers played a prominent role in the British army. Current research would suggest that many thousands of Irish women travelled with their husbands during the Napoleonic Wars, and that they did so in an official capacity, being recorded in the muster rolls of some regiments. While these women may have managed to see Spain, Portugal and Flanders during these campaigns, this was far from travelling on some holiday excursion. The army wives shared the privations of campaign life and there were no special accommodations made for them on the march. If transport was available, they might travel by baggage cart, but otherwise they plodded along behind the regimental columns. In normal times, they were expected to clean and cook for the men and, as only a limited number of wives travelled 'on the strength', they often ended up carrying out these duties for all of the men in their husbands' squads. Due to the poor level of medical services, they also tended the sick and, following a battle, they helped in the evacuation and treatment of the wounded and the dying.

An unusual feature of this service is that these women also travelled with their children and initial indications suggest that, during the

Napoleonic period, two to three children travelled with each army wife. It is perhaps not surprising, given the presence of women with armies in the field, that some of them found themselves pregnant while on campaign. This led to some women giving birth in battlefield conditions that were simply dreadful. A fortunate woman might find herself aided by the regimental surgeon, but many gave birth assisted by their fellow wives and in rudimentary shelter. One of the most notable examples of this phenomenon was the case of Elizabeth McFadden who accompanied her husband during the Waterloo campaign of 1815. Private Peter McMullen, an unemployed weaver from County Down, had enlisted in the 27th Regiment of Foot (Inniskilling Fusiliers) in 1814 at the relatively advanced age of 33. He managed to secure permission for Elizabeth to travel with the regiment and, during the Battle of Waterloo (18 June 1815), she was present on the battlefield despite being 'far advanced in pregnancy'. She rescued at least one wounded solider from the battlefield and was hit in the leg by a musket ball, the leg being fractured. Despite this wound, she later rescued her husband who had been severely wounded. The stresses of the battle and her wound brought on labour, and she gave birth to a baby girl. Her husband ultimately had to have both arms amputated and the couple, and their newborn baby, were evacuated to the York Hospital in Chelsea, via Antwerp. The Duke of York (Frederick Augustus Hanover) heard of their story and visited them in hospital, where he agreed to act as godfather to the baby daughter. She was named Frederica McMullen in his honour, but sadly died a few months later. Thereafter, little is known of Elizabeth's later life, or that of her invalided husband, but one can only imagine that their life after Waterloo was one of extreme difficulty.

Throughout the nineteenth century, we continue to see women not only accompanying armies but also acting as nurses in a more formal capacity. The Crimean War (1853–6) and the American Civil War (1861–5) saw women employed in large numbers in the medical services of the various belligerent nations. By the First World War, the role of women in the armies of all nations became even more formalised. Women served once again in military nursing, but many armies also developed auxiliary women's services. During the early twentieth century, the character of warfare changed rapidly and we can trace changing attitudes towards women in military service. During the course of the Second World War, it was not uncommon for the forces of the various belligerent nations to deploy women in combat roles.

One of the first services to do so was the Special Operations Executive (SOE), which was set up at the direction of Sir Winston Churchill in 1940 and was tasked with carrying out intelligence and sabotage operations in the territory occupied by the Axis powers. Between 1940 and 1945, the SOE would deploy over 3,000 female agents into occupied Europe and also in the Far East, becoming the first such force to use women in this role. Several of these women were Irish and their experiences in the war were often dangerous.

One of the Irish SOE operatives was Mary Katherine Herbert (1903–1983), code name Claudine, who was the only female agent known to have a baby while on service in occupied France. She had excelled at languages at university and had mastered French, German and Arabic. At the outbreak of war, she was working at the British embassy in Warsaw and later worked for the Air Ministry in London before joining the Women's Auxiliary Air Force (WAAF) in 1941. The WAAF was a common starting point for women who later joined SOE, and Mary Herbert joined that organisation in March 1942. The training programme for SOE was intense but, despite being in her late thirties, she thrived and was trained to work as a courier. At the time, her instructors noted that she had a skill for being 'inconspicuous'. In October 1942, she travelled to the south of France from Gibraltar by boat, landing between Marseilles and Toulon. Based in the Bordeaux region, she was to serve with the Scientist network, one of the larger and more successful Resistance operations at this time. In her role as courier, Herbert carried money, false documents and sometimes wireless equipment to the various members of the group. If captured with any of these items in her possession, she would have been subjected to interrogation, torture and eventual execution or death in a concentration camp. On one occasion, while struggling with a heavy wireless set in a suitcase, a German officer gallantly came to her aid and carried the burden to a tram-stop for her.

Against all regulations and standard procedures, Mary Herbert embarked on a love affair with the leader of the Scientist network, Claude de Baissac, and became pregnant. She concealed this fact for some time but, in June 1943, the Scientist network was infiltrated by German intelligence and she had to go into hiding. Claude de Baissac was evacuated from France by light plane and, interestingly, he took his sister, who was also an SOE agent, with him rather than Mary. But it is not certain that he knew that Mary was pregnant. Stranded in occupied France, Mary kept to her cover identity, but was concerned that she might reveal her true identity during the pain of childbirth or under sedation in the labour ward. A fellow operator lodged her in a private nursing home where she had a C-section delivery in December 1943. She named her daughter Claudine.

Thereafter, she wisely cut off all contact with SOE and remained on the run in France. She was arrested by the Gestapo at a compromised safe house in Poitiers in February 1944 and her child was placed in an orphanage. Under interrogation, Mary kept to her cover story, and having a small baby actually proved fortuitous as the German interrogators simply could not believe that an enemy agent would have a baby while deployed in occupied France. Mary was eventually released and embarked on a search for her daughter. On finding Claudine in the care of an order of nuns, she had to persuade them that she was wrongly arrested to secure her release. Mother and child then hid out on a secluded farm until the area was liberated by Allied forces. It was one of the most incredible stories to emerge from within the highly unorthodox SOE during the Second World War and she was awarded the Croix de Guerre by the French government. Mary Herbert later married Claude de Baissac but the couple divorced in 1960. She died in 1983.

Across the world, there is continued debate about the role of women in the military services and whether they should be employed in combat roles. It could be argued that, in an historical sense, women have always been present on campaign and we can see that many even brought their children with them. In some extreme cases, we can see that women even brought their children into the world in the midst of dangerous wartime conditions.

Further Reading:

Marcus Binney, *The Women who Lived for Danger: The Women Agents of SOE in the Second World War* (London, 2012).

Liane Jones, *A Quiet Courage: Women Agents in the French Resistance*

(London, 1990).

Peter Molloy, 'Ireland and the Waterloo Campaign of 1815' (unpublished MA thesis, NUI Maynooth, 2011). Available through the MURAL archive at: http://mural.maynoothuniversity.ie/3099/.

David Murphy, '"I was terribly frightened at times": Irish Men and Women in the French Resistance and F Section of SOE, 1940–45', in Nathalie Genet Rouffiac and David Murphy (eds), *Franco-Irish Military Connections, 1590–1945* (Dublin, 2009), 269–94.

55

Birth in Ireland *c.* 1900–60

Caitriona Clear

'Did you think it would come dressed and all?' an exasperated midwife in the early years of the twentieth century asked a Kilkenny woman who had not one item of clothing ready to put on her newborn baby. In telling this story, Mary Healy reminds us that knitting and sewing small clothes was, from time immemorial, *the* universal preparatory activity of pregnant women. By 1900, however, all European countries were beginning to promote a new kind of ante-natal preparation, one that monitored the health of the poorest mothers-to-be. In Ireland, the Poor Law Unions began, from the 1890s, to employ trained midwives to attend women in their own homes; memoirist, Nurse Hedderman, whose hard work earned the enduring respect of the Aran Islanders, was one of these. The Jubilee and Lady Dudley nurses, founded in 1897 and 1903 respectively, are fondly remembered as tireless apostles of good maternal health in rural areas throughout the country. In the 1920s, district midwife (and novelist) Annie M.P. Smithson was touched to hear little Dublin inner-city children fighting over whose mother's nurse she was. Being told sternly by uniformed figures of authority to value their health must have been a welcome novelty for working-class, labouring and small farming women, even if they could not always act on the advice given.

Although countrywomen in general were better-nourished than townswomen, and therefore better able to withstand the three major childbirth killers – toxaemia of pregnancy, haemorrhage and puerperal sepsis – proximity to doctors and trained midwives improved the chances of survival in the early twentieth century. From 1913–17, the lowest maternal deaths in Ireland were in Belfast and Dublin city (under 4.25 per thousand (p/t) births, when the national average was 5.22). The highest rates were in Counties Monaghan and Tyrone (over 7 p/t). While badly-fed and exhausted women were most at risk from toxaemia and haemorrhage, puerperal sepsis, which was responsible for between a quarter and a third of all maternal deaths, struck randomly. Limerick city, whose notorious lanes rivalled Dublin's tenements for high rates of disease and death, lost the fewest mothers from puerperal sepsis from 1913–17 (0.63 p/t births), while Counties Monaghan and Carlow were the worst hit, at 3.50 and 3.23 respectively.

There was no universal, countrywide provision in independent Ireland for mothers having babies until 1953. Nonetheless, the patchwork of local authority (formerly Poor Law) services, hospital outreach teams and voluntary organisations (including the Lady Dudley nurses) had some impact in the years from 1923, when maternal mortality stood at 5.32 p/t births, to 1945 when it fell to 2.63. This is all the more striking because standards of living – as shown by that infallible indicator infant mortality (see below) – deteriorated for some Irish people in these years. But others were obviously experiencing improvements. The thousands of new local authority houses and flats (with piped water and toilets) built in the 1930s improved not only hygiene, but health during pregnancy, if only by cutting out the twice-or-thrice-daily lifting and carrying of water and waste into the dwelling and out of it. Most babies were born at home until the mid-1950s; Dublin had its renowned maternity hospitals, but elsewhere, institutional birth was a last resort. Mary Healy was upset at having to go into St Joseph's Hospital in Clonmel for the birth of her second child in 1945; her five other children (born from 1943–50) were born at home with the assistance of a trained midwife and, on one occasion, a doctor. Even in Dublin some women chose home births, and the three major hospitals all had domiciliary teams; a mother in the inner city told Olivia Robertson that she only went into the Rotunda hospital for her third, her fifth and her ninth babies. Women made what decisions they could to bring their babies into the world safely. Some women of the Traveller community came all the way from Fermanagh and Tyrone, on horse-drawn transport, to be delivered by the 'lucky hands' of Nora Healy, a trained midwife in Charlestown, County Mayo, in the 1930s.

By 1961 nearly 80 percent of all births were in hospitals or nursing homes, and this change happened in the 1950s. It is not entirely clear whether it was driven by medical interests or by women's own preferences, and while it is tempting to see this change of locale as the cause of improved maternal survival, the decline in mortality was well under way before it. Children's Allowances, introduced in 1944, contributed to mothers' nutrition and resistance to infection by improving family income. The countrywide deployment of Public Health Nurses from 1945, the setting up of the Department of Health in 1947 and the streamlining of existing services established the welfare of mothers and babies as a cornerstone concern of government. Dr Noel Browne's pioneering Mother and Child Scheme in 1950–1 fell foul of the Catholic Church and the medical profession, but Éamon de Valera's much-modified version of it was implemented with little fuss in 1953. Overall, 103 mothers died in childbirth in Ireland in 1951, but ten years later, only twenty-seven women met this fate, an appalling and avoidable tragedy for each woman, an often overwhelming catastrophe for the family left behind.

The deaths of babies between live birth (stillbirths were counted separately) and into their second year had little to do with proximity to medical expertise and everything to do with where and how people lived. The poor sanitation and overcrowding of urban slum living allowed for the spread of gastro-enteritis and other infections lethal for the young and vulnerable. Rurality – however 'primitive' the sanitary arrangements – meant safety. In 1918, Fermanagh, Leitrim, Roscommon and Mayo had an infant mortality of (in ascending order) 37, 45, 48 and 49 p/t births, when the national average was 86. Dublin city and Belfast, in the same year, had infant mortality rates of 149 and 142 respectively. In 1910, Ireland had, proportionately, far fewer babies dying than any other country in north-western Europe (outside of Scandinavia), but independent Ireland did not maintain this advantage, even though nearly all the counties most favourable to infant life before 1922 remained within the Free State/Republic. Rates rose from 66 p/t births in 1923 to 74 in 1941, reaching 83 in 1943. In the same year, wartime Britain with its food shortages, housing disruptions and other privations, had a rate of 50. Dr James Deeny, who was Ireland's Chief Medical Officer in this decade, remarked: 'Very few could appreciate that six hundred little Dublin souls going to heaven every year ... was ... something preventible, something terrible and something to be avoided at all costs.' Deeny instanced Dublin, but he could have been talking about any city or town in the country. And the apathy he described was official, not personal. The contributors to Kevin Kearns's oral histories of the Dublin tenements recall the rapid-onset deaths and the dignified little funerals paid for by the insurance, a payment never defaulted upon because bitter experience taught that it was always going to be needed. By 1961, infant mortality had been reduced to 30.5 p/t births, which seems low, but is not that far behind the lowest rates in 1918.

So, while there were improvements, neither maternal survival nor infant resilience was taken for granted throughout this period, as a thanksgiving entry (one of many such) to the *Irish Messenger of the Sacred Heart* in 1951 shows: 'Thanks to the Sacred Heart for the safe confinement of my wife and the blessing of a fine, healthy baby girl.'

Further Reading:

B.N. Hedderman, *Glimpses of My Life on Aran: Some Experiences of a District Nurse* (Dublin, 1917).

Annie M.P. Smithson, *Myself – and Others* (Dublin, 1944).

Olivia Robertson, *St Malachy's Court* (London, 1946).

John Healy, *Nineteen Acres* (Galway, 1978).

Mary Healy, *For the Poor and for the Gentry: Mary Healy Remembers her Life* (Dublin, 1989).

James Deeny, *To Cure and To Care: Memoirs of a Chief Medical Officer* (Dublin, 1989).

Kevin Kearns, *Dublin Tenement Life: An Oral History* (Dublin, 1994).

Caitriona Clear, *Women of the House: Women's Household Work in Ireland 1921–1961* (Dublin, 2000).

56

Unmarried Mothers: Maternity Care and Ante-natal Care in Britain and Ireland, 1922–60

Lorraine Grimes

Throughout the twentieth century, hundreds of Irish women who became pregnant outside of marriage travelled from Ireland to Britain each year in order to escape the shame and stigma of unmarried motherhood in their local community. Women also feared long-term incarceration in Mother and Baby Homes in Ireland and the high infant mortality rates in these homes. In Britain, unmarried mothers entered institutions similar to those in Ireland; however, there were major differences in terms of maternity care and social assistance in the homes. This article will take a comparative approach, contrasting maternity care and the institutionalisation of unmarried mothers in Ireland and Britain from 1922 to 1960.

In Britain, Anglican and Roman Catholic institutions run by evangelical philanthropic groups and religious congregations offered various standards of care. Some women may have been refused entry to homes based on their religion, class and age, as some homes refused to care for young mothers or those of lower socio-economic status. Access to maternity care and ante-natal care largely depended on the woman's geographical location in the country. Better ante-natal provisions were found in Mother and Child clinics in large towns and cities around Britain. In Birmingham, the 'Birmingham Association for the Unmarried Mother and her Child' carried out ante-natal, as well as practical follow-up, care for unmarried mothers by visiting homes and collecting much needed items such as baby clothes, prams, cots and other necessary items. Quite often assistance from welfare organisations was usually one of a missionary approach and some discriminated against

Irish unmarried mothers. Many welfare organisations made attempts to have Irish unmarried mothers return home and emphasised the economic burden they placed on welfare organisations in Britain.

Many Irish women emigrated during pregnancy in order to avail of better maternity care in Britain than that available to them in Ireland. From the 1940s, the numbers entering hospital for childbirth increased; however, the majority of women still gave birth at home, particularly women in rural Ireland. Unmarried mothers in Ireland were cared for in County Homes or one of the three private Mother and Baby Homes run by Catholic congregations. Some County Homes catered for women in childbirth, but were not necessarily equipped to do so. Those in the private Mother and Baby Homes in Ireland (Bessborough, Castlepollard and Sean Ross Abbey) gave birth in the home without the presence of a doctor, but sometimes had the assistance of a midwife. Oral history testimony from unmarried mothers has revealed a significant lack of adequate maternity care in the homes. In addition, unmarried mothers were more likely to have complications arise in birth such as anaemia (low iron levels) was more common due to poorer diet. Children of unmarried mothers usually had a higher risk of infection leading to significantly higher infant mortality rates. The high infant mortality rates in the institutions in Ireland may have been another reason for migration during pregnancy.

Women resident in Mother and Baby Homes in Britain usually gave birth in hospitals rather than in the institutions, and a doctor visited the Mother and Baby Home once a week, a major difference when compared to the institutions in Ireland. In Britain, women were admitted six weeks before their due date, gave birth in the hospital, then returned to the home until their baby was six weeks old. The exact length of stay varied, as some institutions offered the mother up to six months' confinement after the birth of the baby. The length of stay in the homes in Ireland tended to be much longer. Homes in Britain usually had a one-year *limit*, while in Ireland the *minimum* stay was two years in the private homes unless a fee of £100 was paid to the congregation. The time in the home was to be devoted to 'moral rehabilitation' and 'repentance' for their 'sin'. While the homes had no legal grounds to enforce the two years' confinement, it appears to have been common practice. According to Commission of Investigation into Mother and Baby Homes, one woman entered Bessborough in 1922, aged 20 years, and remained there until her death in 1984 – a period of 62 years. Another entered Bessborough in 1924, aged 21 years, and remained there until her death in 1985 – a period of 60 years.

In Britain, inspection of the homes was compulsory; however, some homes could apply to the local council for an exemption. Inspectors' reports, although regular, were often negative and emphasised the lack of funding in the homes. Visitation from friends or family was often limited and many women revealed a sense of loneliness. Standards in the homes heavily depended on the welfare organisation affiliated with the home and the matron running it. From 1948, there were significant changes in maternity care with the introduction of the National Health Service. Maternity care was free under the NHS; however, women were to pay for their stay in an institution if they had not earned enough credits. The numbers entering Mother and Baby Homes in Britain decreased significantly during the 1950s and 1960s. In the 1960s, the National Council for the Unmarried Mother and her Child issued recommendations setting dietary and accommodation guidelines in an effort to promote a higher standard of care within the institutions. By 1970, the majority of Mother and Baby Home institutions had closed in Britain as more unmarried mothers were keeping and raising their children.

Overall, Irish unmarried mothers travelled to Britain to disguise their pregnancy from their family and community, to avoid long-term committal to a Mother and Baby Home in Ireland and to search for better maternity care. Irish unmarried mothers were subject to discrimination from many welfare workers and were usually encouraged to return home. Some institutions also refused teenage mothers, women of certain religions and those of lower socio-economic status from entering. Women living in rural areas were largely neglected from perinatal care in both Ireland and Britain. Unmarried mothers resident in institutions in Britain usually gave birth in a nearby hospital. For the majority of women in County Homes and Mother and Baby Homes in Ireland, no doctor was present for the birth. The standard of maternity and ante-natal care varied across Britain and Ireland and developed throughout the twentieth century. Mother and Baby Home institutions in twentieth-century Ireland tended to focus more on the religious and rehabilitative aspect, rather than maternity and social care for the unmarried mother and her child.

Further Reading:

Lindsey Earner-Byrne, *Mother and Child: Maternity and Child Welfare in Dublin, 1922–60* (Manchester, 2007).

Paul Michael Garrett, *Social Work and Irish People in Britain: Historical and Contemporary Responses to Irish Children and Families* (Bristol, 2004).

Joan Bourne, *Pregnant and Alone: The Unmarried Mother and her Child* (London, 1971).

Pat Thane and Tanya Evans, *Sinners? Scroungers? Saints? Unmarried Mothers in Twentieth Century England* (Oxford, 2012).

Caitriona Clear, *Women of the House: Women's Household Work in Ireland 1926–1961* (Dublin, 2000).

57

The Material Culture of Domestic Childbirth

Cara Delay

Describing childbirth in the early twentieth century, a Belfast woman remembered that her local midwife made nappies out of old bedsheets, gave labouring women 'a towel to pull on' and rubbed newborn infants with oil. That this occasion took place in the domestic sphere is an important reminder: although childbirth overall would shift to hospitals in the mid-twentieth century, the majority of Irish women, north and south and particularly in rural areas, laboured and birthed in their own homes up to 1950.

What were these experiences like for women in the past? Male partners usually were not present in the birthing room, although some men were tasked with fetching the midwife or keeping the kettle boiling. We could think of labour and birth, then, as feminised occasions that tell us about not only the individual experiences of women, but also women's communities. Narratives of childbirth in nineteenth- and twentieth-century Ireland describe lying-in spaces, the essential roles of midwives and handywomen, and, significantly, the objects related to pregnancy and birth that helped ease women's suffering and created bonds between women in the domestic sphere. The items that were present at birthing scenes – baby clothing, medical tools and things as simple as food and tea – were not only utilitarian but had personal and cultural meaning as well.

Birthing spaces and material culture varied, depending on a woman's economic class: while more well-off women retired to a lying-in chamber not only to give birth but also to rest and recover afterwards, poor women made do with far more humble circumstances. One nurse, describing a maternity case in the rural west in 1905, wrote:

The house was a most wretched one, with practically nothing in it. The patient was lying on a bit of grass on the floor, with no covering except an old skirt and jacket she had on. There was no underclothing, bed or bedclothing. I could not even get a bit of candle to enable me to see her when I went in. It was the most pitiable state of affairs that anyone could imagine, and I shall not forget my experience of that day for some time.

Even women in such desperate conditions, however, made sure to have useful and meaningful things with them during labour and birth. When preparing for the lying-in period, pregnant women carefully collected items they would need. Gathering newspapers and cloths, finding string to tie the umbilical cord and, in some accounts, getting hold of whiskey for pain, were all common practices. Vinegar and cotton wool were obtained to bind breasts if necessary. Spare scraps of cloth, sterilised in boiling water, would later become nappies. In the homes of the poor, crates substituted for cradles or cots, as did cooking pots in some rural areas. In early twentieth-century Cork, mothers frequently placed newborn infants in orange boxes. Midwives and handywomen also wrapped babies in their mothers' petticoats when no other clothing was available.

Pain relief, essential not only to a woman's comfort but also a successful birth, could be managed in several ways. Birth attendants created hot poultices to apply to a labouring woman's abdomen or back. Whiskey eased pain after childbirth and helped a new mother rest. The custom of a woman wearing her husband's coat during labour, called 'couvade', is reported across nineteenth- and early-twentieth-century Ireland and may in fact be what the nurse in the 1905 account described above, who wrote of her patient's 'old skirt and jacket', witnessed. In popular tradition, couvade could cause the husband to take on some of the wife's pain in labour, providing her with some relief and, at least symbolically, sharing the burdens of birth more equitably between men and women.

While many traditions specified what should be present at birth, others clearly cautioned women and their families to avoid certain items.

Some warned that buying clothing for a baby before its birth courted disaster. According to similar beliefs, a pregnant woman could collect clothing for her first baby, but if that infant died, those clothes must not be used in the future or else the next baby would perish as well. In contrast, many items present at birth, and even after, could protect mother and infant. Traditionally, Irish communities considered childbirth to be fraught with danger: not only the very real threat of death, but also abduction by fairy-changelings, who, in legendry, stole away pregnant women and children. Shielding women and infants from these forces required a varied material culture. Important safeguards included both holy water and urine. According to one folklore narrative:

> A little bottle of holy water would then be procured and
> placed under the woman's head and a little bottle of stale
> urine would be stuck into the bed at her feet. The stale
> urine would also be sprinkled around the bed before cock
> crow for the nine nights she lay in confinement.

Also protective, but utilitarian as well, was straw. Nurses in the early twentieth century sometimes found the custom of giving birth on straw evidence of poverty and even ignorance, but straw could be burned after childbirth, a sanitary practice that guarded against infection. In some narratives, the straw used during labour was buried alongside the woman's placenta. Moreover, straw was believed to be lucky, providing additional security for the mother and baby. When burnt, it was doubly protective because fire served as a powerful guard against fairy abduction in traditional beliefs.

Alongside the things that vernacular beliefs recommended, popular religious material culture made its way into the birthing chamber. Several accounts of scapulars being placed on women, to protect and encourage them during childbirth, feature in the nineteenth century, as do charms, amulets and other devotional items. The things present during birth, then, provided not only basic comforts and necessities but also emotional and spiritual support. By bringing certain items into the birthing room, women and their female caregivers demonstrated agency as they attempted to secure the best possible outcome for mothers and babies. They also, by sharing, borrowing and lending birth items with, and to, neighbours, helped create and maintain a sense of female community.

By the mid-twentieth century, the triumph of hospital-based reproductive care transformed the spaces and things associated with childbirth. Comfortable and carefully prepared domestic birthing spaces gave way to more sterile and generic hospital rooms. Still, women's traditions persisted as best they could. In Northern Ireland, some women brought items they had used in home births with them to hospital to labour there; these women demonstrated the importance of their traditions and practices by taking their treasured things into the more regulated space of the hospital.

Commonplace things allow us access to women's private worlds and attest to their desires to manage their reproductive lives and health. Although often hidden from history, these practices, and their persistence across decades, highlight Irish women's remarkable attention to the ordinary as well as their determination to preserve their traditional birth cultures, even in the constantly changing twentieth century.

Further Reading:

Linda-May Ballard, '"Just Whatever They Had Handy": Aspects of Childbirth and Early Childcare in Northern Ireland prior to 1948', *Ulster Folklife*, 31 (1992–3), 59–72.

Anne O'Connor, '"Women's Folklore": Traditions of Childbirth in Ireland', *Béaloideas: The Journal of the Folklore of Ireland Society*, 85 (2017), 264–97.

Pádraig Ó Héalaí, 'Pregnancy and Childbirth in Blasket Island Tradition', *Women's Studies Review*, 5 (1997), 1–15.

Fionnuala Nic Suibhne, '"On the Straw" and Other Aspects of Pregnancy and Childbirth from the Oral Tradition of Women in Ulster', *Ulster Folklife*, 38 (1992), 12–24.

58

Is it a Boy or a Child? Predicting the Sex of Babies – and Chickens – in Irish Folklore

Clodagh Tait

Nowadays, people awaiting the births of their babies often resort to the internet for information, support and advice on a variety of topics. Websites like 'Mumsnet' allow for the discussion of both serious medical issues and rather more lighthearted ones. The question 'How can I predict the sex of my baby' is commonly asked, especially in the early months before ultrasound can provide the 'reveal' to those wishing to get their pink or blue prepared in advance.

A variety of suggestions tend to appear. Some advocate the so-called 'Chinese lunar test', based on your age and the month you get pregnant, or the 'Indian gender predictor', supposedly based on 'Vedic astrology'. Pregnant bodies may provide clues. Girls will 'steal your looks', give you acne or freckles, make the left breast particularly large or make you gain more weight; boys will make your right breast bigger, your urine yellower, your legs hairier and your feet cold. A boy's heartrate will be slower than that of a girl – or *vice versa*. Craving sweet foods betokens a girl, savoury a boy – or the other way around. US websites even advise curious mothers-to-be to urinate on the household cleaner 'Draino', which will fizz blue for a boy or green for a girl (maybe try this when you can still see well enough over your belly to direct your aim accurately). Those not able to access Draino can use baking powder instead – it will fizz for a boy, allegedly. Certain companies sell 'gender prediction tests' that involve testing urine, though with no plausible explanations about how that might actually work nor any proof of their efficacy.

Curiously, predictions based on such signs are sometimes quite ancient. The Greek physician Galen followed even more ancient advice when he suggested that if a pregnant women urinated on both barley and wheat, the wheat would sprout first if she was carrying a boy; the barley for a girl. About 2,400 years ago, Hippocrates was of the opinion that boys developed on the right side of the uterus, girls on the left: pregnancy with a boy would make the mother's right eye brighter, her right breast larger and give her a clear complexion, while girls would make the left eye brighter, the left breast bigger and cause freckles. A succession of medieval and early modern texts continued to offer these tests and to parrot the cultural assumptions about gender and patriarchy on which they were based. For example, the sixteenth-century French physician, Ambrose Paré, explained that the development of boys occurred on the right side of the womb since 'the male infant is more excellent and perfect than the female, maintaining the authority and pre-eminence which God gave him, appointing him as chief and lord over the female'.

One of the most commonly-reported folkloric sex divination techniques involves just looking at the pregnant person. Some say that a high 'bump' indicates a boy, a lower, wider one a girl, and many pregnant women report being accosted by relatives, friends and even complete strangers adamant about the outcome. Another common method is the 'wedding ring test' or 'pendulum dowsing', whereby a ring or needle is hung on a thread or hair and held over the belly, wrist or palm of the pregnant person: it will supposedly move of its own accord, back and forth for a boy, and in a circle for a girl. One self-proclaimed psychic claimed 95 percent accuracy in predicting the sex of babies by dowsing in the *Evening Herald* in February 1983. He also used his powers rather less successfully to assist in the search for the missing racehorse Shergar.

In 1951, Myles Dolan described to Michael J. Murphy how some among 'the old people' in Blacklion, County Cavan, 'could go out and read the planet, and tell you what it was going to be before the birth, a boy or a girl' but 'none of them's able to do it now'. Though he was unsuccessful in garnering further information on how this was done, Murphy followed up on the theme with other informants: he was one of the few collectors willing to press his interlocutors on matters to do with sex and reproduction. For example, Annie McCrea of Teebane,

County Tyrone, reluctantly confessed that scrutiny of the pregnant person's shape for tell-tale signs was well-established by the 1950s. 'If the woman was out in front … they would say she was carrying a girl. If she was broad sideways [towards hips] it would be a boy.'

Informants were far more forthcoming when it came to predicting the sex of animals – and some of the measures suggested sound somewhat familiar. In County Cavan a cow which was 'greatly sprung behind was expected to have a bull calf; a cow which didn't make much of a springing was expected to have a heifer calf'. A 'springing' heifer or cow is in calf, the word in the present day usually referring to heifers, where changes to the size of the udder would be an indication of imminent calving. It is also used in relation to increases in the size of the vulva shortly before calving or the widening and dropping of the pin-bones (pelvic bones). Dolan and Michael Rooney suggested another means of determining the sex of calves before birth.

> You know, a cow before she calves, she puts kays [*Murphy's note* phonetic: slimes] from her, a long time before she calves; they call them kays. Slimes … And they're able to tell be the kay, the cow puts from her … whether it's going to be a bull or a heifer … There's a difference in the kay … A different colour … If it was going to be a bull it would be brown, and if it was to be a heifer, it would be a paler colour.

Michael Leech described how the sex of chickens might be told even before hatching by holding a needle on a thread over the eggs: 'If the needle went round … it would be a hen; for a cock it would go up and down.' Leech interjected 'that's not old though; I don't believe it's really Irish; I think I heard it was Japanese' (the tendency to 'orientalise' divinatory practices is also seen in the online 'Chinese' and 'Indian' gender predictors mentioned earlier). Frank Campbell described a similar procedure 'to determine the sex of a calf or a foal'. A needle was threaded with silk, 'the needle then pierced through a cork with the point protruding: the cork and imbedded needle then suspended over the … back of the animal'. The cork would sway to and fro for a bull, and in a ring for a heifer.

Myles Dolan suggested that the sex of the contents of eggs could be figured out as early as the point of 'setting' them to be hatched. Using a candle in a dark place:

> you can see through the eggs, and you see the space in the eggs, a certain place and where it is, and they can tell whether that's a chicken [hen] or a rooster ... they can set them chickens and have them whatever way they want them.

The practice of candling is internationally known and involves holding a light up to eggs to check their viability. Some poultry rearers still advocate using it also to investigate where the air-cell is located in eggs, and thereby to predict their contents' sex. This is time-consuming and not that accurate; scientists continue to work on developing more effective ways of sexing eggs in order to increase the efficiency of production and reduce the culling of unwanted hatchlings.

Developments in ultrasound technology have, however, made it increasingly easy for sonographers to identify the sex of human, bovine and equine foetuses fairly accurately after a certain point in gestation. Discussions of the ethics of revealing such information in light of concerns about sex-selective abortion were a feature of articles about advances in both human sonography and prenatal tests like amniocentesis in Irish newspapers in the 1980s and 1990s.

Whether it involves urinating on unusual substances, or scrutinising the shape of pregnancy bumps, the folklore of sex divination continues to flourish because it fills gaps in human knowledge and because of its entertainment value. The tools are simple and – unlike for the smallholders of the 1950s, when a heifer calf would have been much more valuable and desirable than a bull – the stakes are usually small. Modern parents might, however, be surprised by the misogynistic roots of some of the very ancient 'old wives' tales still circulating in cyberspace.

Sources and Further Reading:

Collections of the Irish Folklore Archive, University College Dublin. Thomas R. Forbes, 'The Prediction of Sex: Folklore and Science',

Proceedings of the American Philosophical Society, 103:4 (1959), 537–44.

Stephen Hupp and Jeremy Jewell, *Great Myths of Child Development* (Chichester, 2015).

Thomas E. Queensberry, *How to Tell the Sex of an Egg Before Incubation* (Kansas, 1921).

Jonathan Schaffir, *What to Believe When You're Expecting* (Lanham, 2017).

59

Innocence Lost: Perinatal Death in Twentieth-century Ireland

Ciara Henderson

Birth is a momentous and joyous occasion for most families; however, there is a modest number for whom birth is transformational in ways they did not expect. Some babies do not survive birth, and in Ireland every year approximately 350 families will experience the death of a baby during the final months of pregnancy or shortly after birth.

Perinatal death, a statistical term first introduced internationally in 1948, refers to the death of babies in the latter part of pregnancy. The term has evolved since, so that in Ireland it now includes stillbirths (babies born with no signs of life after twenty-four weeks of pregnancy or weighing at least 500 grams) and neonatal deaths (live-born babies who die within twenty-eight days of birth). When looking at historical data relating to perinatal death, it is important to note that there are several definitions that were used over time, in the generation of Irish and international data. Definitions of perinatal death also differ from country to country, with the standard of twenty-eight weeks gestation now used for international reporting. These distinctions may seem negligible in statistical terms, but they carry a definitive impact and can affect medical interventions and even a mother's entitlement to maternity leave. Significantly, the distinction can affect the treatment of human remains, as well as the emotional impact of loss.

The inability to publicly record the existence of a child's life, no matter how brief, can delegitimise a parent's grief. This was compounded in the past, as so many babies never got to leave the hospital or meet their extended families, and in many cases, did not even meet their parents. The bureaucracy around perinatal death registration had a dual consequence. The net effect appeared designed to minimise parental mourning. It also reinforced the idea, in wider society, that perinatal death did not require recognition, and acknowledgement of the death was discouraged. The characterisation of perinatal deaths became one where they were perceived as 'lesser' or inconsequential. What matters gets counted.

In 1995, the Stillbirths Registration Act 1994 was introduced for the first time in Ireland. The Act enabled the registration of stillborn infants born from 1994 and changed the definition of perinatal death from twenty-eight weeks gestation to twenty-four weeks gestation. Crucially, the Act enabled parents to register their infants' births retrospectively, meaning any parent who had a stillbirth any time before 1994 can now register that baby's birth.

There has been a rapid decline in the numbers of families affected by perinatal death since the last century. High infant mortality (which incorporates perinatal mortality) characterised Irish life until the mid-1950s. In nineteenth-century Dublin, three maternity hospitals (the Rotunda Hospital, the Coombe Hospital and Holles St Hospital)[1] catered for an impoverished population with large families, fragmented social welfare, poor nutrition, limited medical care and extreme poverty. Between them, they formed the backbone of what would become the obstetric and midwifery service provision and education for the entire country.

The infant mortality rate around the time of the First World War was higher in Ireland than for soldiers at the front. Maternal and infant health advocates battled against an indifferent public long accustomed to 'nature's way of weeding out the unfit for life', as Ruth Barrington characterises it. In Dublin, which had well developed maternal services, the Maternal Mortality Rate was approximately 0.86 in 1933 versus the national Maternal Mortality Rate (MMR), which was five times this. The MMR dropped 60 percent between 1940 and 1950, which points to the success of hospital childbirth for mothers in the twentieth century. With widespread use of antibiotics from the 1950s, the MMR was

---

[1] The Rotunda Lying-In Hospital was established in 1745; the Coombe Women & Infant Hospital founded in 1826; and the National Maternity Hospital, Holles St, established in 1894.

dramatically reduced, though it remained three times the rate in England.

Despite the significant improvement in reducing maternal mortality between 1940 and 1950, the Infant Mortality Rate (IMR) saw only a marginal reduction; however, with the concerted effort of medics, the rate declined almost 50 percent in the following decade.

With a stable, declining MMR, the obstetrical focus shifted to infant survival rates leading James Deeny, the Chief Medical Advisor, to comment in 1954, that 'one of the greatest triumphs of medicine in this generation has been the reduction in infant mortality'. But as infant mortality declined, perinatal mortality caused concern, and Deeny deemed it a 'matter of serious national importance', worse than deaths from TB and cancer, as 'it cuts off life at the beginning'.

The use of Perinatal Mortality rates from 1953 was an important indicator of both obstetric and infant care used to develop high calibre and safe health service provision. The 1950s data recorded is based on an estimate of Dublin maternity hospitals' perinatal deaths for the early 1950s, estimated at about 3,500 perinatal deaths annually. At this time, approximately 30 percent of births still occurred at home so it is logical to conclude that the figure was, in reality, higher than recorded.

As public health expanded, and hospital consolidation followed, systemic changes happened with the condensing of services into the hospital system. With the extension of maternity services to rural Ireland, the maternity hospital system replaced the social model of childbirth and familial responsibility for both life and death. At first glance, the benefits of medical childbirth seem apparent, with improvements to both maternal and infant mortality rates. The medical model, though, had an impact on parental experiences of perinatal deaths.

Mothers whose infants died were not allowed to see or hold their babies, a practice which continued in some places up to the early 1990s. As late as the mid-1980s, fathers were not typically present in delivery rooms when their wives gave birth. This maternity protocol was not unique to Ireland, and appears similar across Western maternity practice at that time.

Many parents felt isolated, alone, shamed and stigmatised because of the deaths of their babies. There was a strong reticence to discuss or even acknowledge the loss of these infants. Early researchers suggested that hospitals increased the distress of parents as the whole event was veiled in silence. Ostensibly, the idea was that, by ignoring the death, the mother's distress would be minimised – a sort of 'out of sight, out of mind' approach. By the late 1960s, initial research emerged, which highlighted the impact of stillbirth on parents. Gradually, healthcare professionals' understanding of grief following perinatal death improved.

The mid-1970s prompted the first wave of change relating to the care of bereaved parents in hospitals, spearheaded by parents who demanded more humanistic care and social recognition of their grief. In Ireland, parent lobby groups formed in the late 1970s, campaigning for changes in stillbirth legislation and working to raise public awareness of perinatal grief. Today, much is different in the way care is delivered in hospitals, and Irish maternity units now have specialist Bereavement Midwives trained to care for families sensitively.

The 'veiled silence' relating to perinatal death extended outside the hospital, too, and can be linked to the absence of social rituals surrounding the death of a baby, certainly from the 1950s. Part of the difficulty for parents in mid-twentieth-century Ireland was that funerals were not performed for infants. The legacy of this absent social practice is that, still today, many parents seek out the final resting place of their infants.

This lack of socially recognised ritual, and the social solidarity that is an essential part of death rituals, may have limited parents' ability to mourn, leaving them further isolated and feeling their loss was invalidated. In contemporary society, funeral norms are more likely to be followed by bereaved parents. Modern grief theory recognises an ongoing relationship with the dead. This requires a completely different approach to supporting parents and respecting their dynamic relationship with their infant. This relationship does not end with death.

Perinatal death is still predominantly contained within the hospital setting and so, due to its relative invisibility, perinatal loss remains an abstract concept for general society, though painfully personal for parents. Despite shifting social responses to perinatal death over the last seventy years, some things remain similar. Many parents still report feelings of shame and stigma, and continue to feel isolated and silenced.

Raising public awareness of perinatal death can help parents. Encouraging friends, neighbours and professionals to acknowledge a parent's ongoing grief is more difficult. Parents need the warm embrace of their social circles and extended communities. They may need that far beyond the initial days following the death of their baby. Grief changes; it can fade, but it doesn't disappear.

Sources:

Ruth Barrington, *Health, Medicince & Politics in Ireland 1900–1970* (Dublin, 1987).

James Deeny, *The End of an Epidemic: Essays in Irish Public Health 1935–65* (Dublin, 1995).

60

Birth and Death: Changes in Beliefs and Practices Surrounding Stillbirth in Ireland, 1863–1994

Lorraine Grimes

Legal and medical definitions of stillbirth have varied over time and across jurisdictions; however, the World Health Organization currently defines stillbirth as a baby born with no signs of life at or after twenty-eight weeks' gestation. Stillbirths were officially recorded in England and Wales from 1926, and Scotland from 1938, along with most European countries around this time. However, stillbirths were not recorded in Ireland until 1994. Burial customs of stillborn children varied over time and location. The burial of stillborn children in unmarked graves and the silence surrounding stillbirths in Ireland continued until the late twentieth century. This article will focus on cultural attitudes and burial practices surrounding stillbirth and perinatal deaths, incorporating the changing perspective towards stillbirth and infant death in Ireland from the late-nineteenth century to the end of the twentieth century.

Since early Christian Ireland, pagan traditions have been intertwined with Christian beliefs in an attempt to syncretise ideas of Christian baptism, the afterlife and the *sidhe* (fairies). Stillborn children were often buried in special plots called *cillíní*, which were usually near old forts. It was believed that fairies lived in forts and the child was therefore, gone to the fairies. Stillborn children, as well as children of unmarried mothers, criminals, those who died by suicide, strangers whose religion was unknown and women who died in childbirth and were not yet 'churched' were not to be buried on consecrated ground and were buried in *cillíní*. Locations of *cillíní* included abandoned medieval churches and graveyards, ancient monuments, natural landmarks and sea or lakeshores. Sometimes a special plot or 'angel's plot' was located in the back of a graveyard or outside the walls of a graveyard. These *cillíní*, or angel's plots, were used up until the end of the twentieth century in Ireland.

In eighteenth- and nineteenth-century Ireland, stillbirths caused much fear and panic for women, particularly unmarried mothers. Pregnancy outside of marriage was heavily stigmatised for much of the eighteenth, nineteenth and twentieth centuries. There was an assumption that an unmarried mother's claim of stillbirth could be masking infanticide. Unmarried mothers often attempted to conceal their pregnancy and delivered alone, leaving stillbirth difficult to prove. In eighteenth-century England, suspected cases of infanticide, which went before the court, underwent testing on the baby's lungs. It was believed that if the lungs sank in water, the child had never breathed and had been born dead. Many women brought before the courts and charged with infanticide in Ireland were either hanged or sent to a Magdalene asylum.

In the nineteenth century, infants who only lived for a number of hours were not usually issued a birth or death certificate and, therefore, went undocumented. The 1880 Births and Deaths Registration Act made it compulsory to register the death of a child. Stillbirths, however, were not registered. Families from lower socio-economic backgrounds may have passed a perinatal death as a stillbirth, as a stillborn burial was cheaper because it did not involve a funeral service. The compulsory registration and additional costs led to further secrecy surrounding stillbirth and the burial of stillborn children in 'angel's plots' and unmarked graves.

By the early twentieth century, stillborn children in Ireland were usually buried in the family plot, but received no funeral. One woman, 'Mary', recalled burying her baby girl, who lived for thirty-six hours, in 1968. 'She was buried with my father in the family plot'. Stillborn children and young infants were usually buried in the hours of darkness, emphasising the secrecy surrounding stillbirth and neo-natal death. Mary recalled the lack of sympathy: 'There was no thing about it. I don't think my sisters even came. There was no funeral. She was baptised. She deserved a funeral.' There was a lack of understanding from families and the communities in Irish society regarding stillbirth and the loss of a baby. The silence surrounding 'private matters', such as sexual and reproductive health, led to secrecy and stigmatisation with regard to miscarriage, stillbirth and neo-natal death, and contributed to the reluctance to discuss or mark its occurrence. In the early twentieth century, the mother figure was idealised in the construction of national identity in Ireland. The Irish Free State enforced gendered roles, and the position of women as home-makers and mothers was enshrined under Article 41.2 of the 1937 Constitution. Societal and cultural pressures led to the stigmatisation of infertility, captured in the concluding lines from 'The Famine Road', by poet, Eavan Boland:

> Barren, never to know the load
> of his child in you, what is your body
> now if not a famine road?

Self-blame and penance for miscarriage and stillbirth was common, and some women attended Confession after their stillbirth or miscarriage. The ritual of 'churching' was practised in both the Church of Ireland and the Catholic Church after childbirth. Women were also churched after a stillbirth or neonatal death, which further compounded feelings of sinfulness, and which inclined some to regard it as a sin rather than a tragedy.

In 1983, the first support group ISANDS (Irish Stillbirth & Neonatal Death Society) was founded by a group of bereaved parents to support others who had experienced stillbirth or neonatal death. In 1994, the Registration of Stillbirths Act led to the statistical, medical as well as a social recognition of stillborn infants for the first time in Ireland, many decades behind its European counterparts. Stillbirths are now recorded at twenty-four weeks' gestation and after. Infants born prior to twenty-four weeks are regarded as a miscarriage and are, therefore, not registered. In more recent times, unbaptised infants and stillborn children are no longer excluded from consecrated ground and families are now permitted to bury their children in family plots.

Some pagan traditions, Christian beliefs and the workings of the state have all influenced how we perceive stillbirth and neonatal death. Throughout the nineteenth and twentieth centuries, women who experienced infertility were stigmatised and many unmarried mothers were severely punished for having what may have been a stillbirth. Throughout the twentieth century, there were significant changes in practices and beliefs in terms of stillbirth. These changes have led to better recognition of maternal loss and grief surrounding stillbirth in Irish society today.

Sources and Further Reading:

Oral History Interview with Mary (pseudonym) on 27 December 2019.

Anne O'Connor, *The Blessed and the Damned: Sinful Women and Unbaptised Children in Irish Folklore* (Oxford, 2005).

Ciara Breathnach, '"I have Fierce Devotion to the Holy Souls of God's Acre": The Social Memory of the Famine in Tralee, County Kerry', in Salvador Ryan (ed.) *Death and the Irish: A Miscellany* (Dublin, 2016).

Gayle Davis, 'Stillbirth Registration and Perceptions of Infant Death, 1900–60: The Scottish case in national context', *The Economic History Review*, 62:3 (August 2009), 629–54.

Rosanne Cecil (ed.) *The Anthropology of Pregnancy and Loss: Comparative Studies in Miscarriage, Stillbirth and Neonatal death* (Oxford, 1996).

61

The (Out)Law of Foreign Adoption in Ireland: Jane Russell and her Irish Baby

Sonja Tiernan

Hollywood actress and sex symbol Jane Russell made international headlines in 1951 when she adopted an Irish baby. The case exposed a disturbing system of unregulated adoptions of Irish babies abroad, most notably to America. That year, Russell toured Europe on a mission to adopt a son. Russell had already adopted one child and spoke openly about her search for another. Arriving in Frankfurt on 1 November 1951, she met with German welfare agency representatives to explore the possibilities of adopting there. Discovering this was not possible, Russell told *Stars and Stripes* reporter Howard Kennedy about problems that she also encountered with 'the regulations on child adoptions in Italy, France and England and it's just about the same everywhere'. Russell arrived in London the following day for a stage appearance at the Royal Command Film Performance of *Where No Vultures Fly*. While in London, Russell was contacted by an Irish woman, Florrie Kavanagh, who was living there with her husband and three children. Kavanagh had read reports of Russell's search for a child and offered Russell one of her own children for adoption. An agreement was reached and, days later, Russell flew back to America with 15-month-old Tommy Kavanagh.

An adoption law had first been enacted in England in 1926 which enabled the transfer of parental rights from biological to adoptive parents. Russell and Kavanagh ignored the legal processes and an informal deal was struck in a suite at London's plush Savoy Hotel. It may well have been assumed that because Tommy was not English the regulations did not apply. As an Irish baby, Tommy did require a passport to travel to America so that a legal adoption could be finalised there. Once notified of the impending adoption, officials at the Irish Embassy in London acted quickly to issue the required passport.

On the day of Russell's departure from England, media gathered at the airport in the hope of getting a photograph or interview with the Hollywood star. Kavanagh also arrived at the airport to say a final tearful goodbye to her baby. Reporters soon became aware of the future adoption plans and this sparked an international furore. Reports appeared in the pages of British newspapers and news travelled to Ireland before reaching an international audience. Although details of the birth mother's first name differ in various newspapers, and some claim she was originally from Derry while others suggest she hailed from Galway, one fact prevailed: Tommy Kavanagh travelled to America with Jane Russell where she and her husband, Bob Waterfield, initiated a process for legal adoption.

The adoption of an Irish child to a couple in America was by no means the first of its kind. Department of Foreign Affairs (DFA) files show that from January 1950 up until October 1952, there were 330 passports issued to Irish children to enable travel to the United States for this same purpose. The exact number of such adoptions is unknown. In 1996, then archivist at the National Archives of Ireland, Catriona Crowe, made a shocking discovery. While routinely checking a batch of documents submitted for archiving by the DFA, Crowe identified files from the Irish Embassy in Washington relating to 1,500 Irish children sent to the United States for adoption between 1949 and 1957.

The system of foreign adoption of Irish babies was well known in America, as a *New York Times* headline on 18 March 1950 testified. 'Irish orphans fly in, meet new parents' told the story of six children sent from St Patrick's Home in Dublin to New York; perhaps by coincidence they arrived on St Patrick's Day. Not only did such media reports portray Ireland as an impoverished country, where parents were either unable or unwilling to support their birth children, foreign adoption exposed a major contradiction in the Irish legal system. Legal adoption was not introduced in Ireland until 1952. Irish babies were being sent abroad for adoption during a time when Irish people could only adopt a child through an informal and unregulated process.

Ireland was one of the last countries in Western society to introduce legal adoption inspiring an intense campaign on the issue. The Legal Adoption Organisation, established in 1947, was particularly active. In 1948, the group changed its name to the Legal Adoption Society and, among their activities, they placed educational adverts in high-profile publications. Soon, feminist activists and groups joined the campaign. The Joint Committee of Women's Societies and Social Workers (JCWSSW) was central in the drive to introduce legal adoption, and a representative from the Irish Housewives Association (IHA) took a place on their committee for this sole purpose. The issue was tackled head on in the IHA journal, *The Irish Housewife*. In the pages of the 1950 edition, an unnamed social worker described how unregulated adoptions in Ireland mean that nothing prevents 'a child who has been "adopted" and has grown up happily in his adopted home from being suddenly snatched away from it and placed in an entirely unsuitable environment'. The writer and socialist activist, Dorothy Macardle, also took up the cause. Macardle's article 'Chosen Child' appeared in the same issue of the *Irish Housewife* asserting that:

> everywhere experts on child welfare have concluded that institutional life is deleterious to children, retarding them in their powers of expression, emotional response, self-confidence and capacity for adaptation to normal social life. Adoption into suitable homes is recognised as much the happiest solution of the friendless child.

While such well-directed campaigning gained attention for the cause, it was undoubtedly the negative attention brought on by the Russell case that forced the Irish government into action. This case differed because the adoption of Tommy was arranged on foreign soil and British authorities reacted. On 15 November 1951, Col. Marcus Lipton, MP for Brixton, raised the issue in the House of Commons, calling on the Home Secretary to issue a police investigation into the matter. An investigation was launched, and the Kavanaghs were summonsed under the 1950 Adoption Act, UK. The case was heard in April 1952 at Bow Street Court under chief magistrate Sir Laurence Dunne. Jane Russell hired Geoffrey Lawrence as the Kavanaghs' legal counsel and their case was conditionally discharged. Although he showed mercy to the Irish couple, Dunne warned that the adoption laws were in place to ensure that British children were not being sent abroad for sinister reasons. Such pronouncements embarrassed the Irish state due to their lack of any formal legal adoption process and what appeared to be akin to a black-market trade in Irish babies sent for adoption abroad.

On 11 June 1952, the Adoption Bill reached a second stage debate in Dáil Éireann. The Bill was enacted to cover only illegitimate or orphaned children. Minister for Justice, Gerald Boland, acknowledged that this law would 'enable children who do not belong to a family, to secure through adoption the benefits of the family'. Within one year of the Adoption Bill being enacted, over 2,500 adoption orders were officially requested in Ireland.

Russell founded the World Adoption International Fund in 1955 to help place foreign children with adoptive families in America. After his adoption, Tommy was raised by Russell and her husband in America under the family name Waterfield. The tragic life of Tommy's biological mother, Florrie, came to a brutal end. Florrie's body was discovered in her burnt-out council flat in Clapham, London in January 1980 at the age of only 53. It was reported in the *Guardian* that Florrie had been strangled and, in an attempt to hide all traces of the crime, her flat was set on fire.

Further Reading:

Anthony Keating, 'The Legalisation of Adoption in Ireland,' *Studies: An Irish Quarterly Review*, 92:366 (Summer, 2003), 172–82.

Moira J. Maguire, 'Foreign Adoptions and the Evolution of Irish Adoption Policy, 1945–52', *Journal of Social History*, 36:2 (Winter 2002), 387–404.

J.H. Whyte, *Church and State in Modern Ireland 1923–1970* (Dublin, 1971).

62

Giving Birth in Maternity Hospitals: The Case of 1960s Dublin

Deirdre Foley

Dublin's three largest maternity hospitals (the Rotunda Hospital, the Coombe Lying-In Hospital and the National Maternity Hospital, Holles Street) underwent a period of rapid expansion and medicalisation of birth during the 1960s. The new methods applied to patients, their socio-economic profile and the difficulties associated with overcrowding in these hospitals were frequently discussed in clinical reports, newspapers and academic papers by medics working in maternity care in Dublin during this period.

In Dublin from the 1950s onwards, the number of babies born in hospital was increasing. Rising birth rates in the Leinster area, in particular, led to a larger hospital population. As one social worker at the Rotunda hospital noted, another factor in the increased pressure on maternity hospitals in the city was Ireland's somewhat improved economic situation, which resulted in rising numbers of Irish emigrants returning from the United Kingdom to the point that they were 'swelling the waiting list for accommodation'. In 1960, 19.3 percent of all births in Ireland occurred in private maternity homes. This figure had only a small decrease for the decade, sitting at 18 percent in 1970. Conversely, domestic births were in decline, at least in an urban setting. In 1961, 20.3 percent of women in Ireland gave birth at home, with this number decreasing as the decade progressed. By 1966, the National Maternity Hospital reported that its 'District Service', which assisted at some (but not all) domestic births in the hospital's urban catchment area, was near-extinct.

By the mid-sixties, the National Maternity Hospital dealt with more patients than any hospital of any kind in the twenty-six counties, as well

FIGURE 21: *A pram from the 1960s, pen-and-ink illustration by Marion McGarry.*

as the highest number of deliveries and referral cases from different Health Authorities country-wide. A new extension to the hospital opened in 1966 and included, for the first time at Holles Street, 'a waiting room where husbands may await news of their wives' progress and condition'. From 1960, the Coombe Lying-In Hospital also delivered babies in record numbers. The Master of the Coombe, Dr William Gavin, reported that there was, overall, a higher attendance at ante-natal clinics, better ante-natal care, and among patients, an increased willingness to come into hospital in the case of any obstetrical abnormality. In 1963, the Coombe reported that as well as the antenatal clinics held in the hospital twice weekly, the hospital operated one clinic per week in the rapidly expanding suburbs of Ballyfermot and Crumlin. The following year, the Minister for Health, Seán MacEntee, laid the foundation stone for a new premises for the Coombe in Dolphin's Barn, which cost over €1M and opened in 1967. The old portico of the original hospital building in the Liberties was retained and restored by Dublin Corporation as, according to its inscription, 'a memorial to the many mothers who gave birth to future citizens of Ireland in the Coombe Lying-in Hospital and also to the generosity of the staff and friends of the hospital'.

At the Rotunda Hospital, reports from the Social Work Department shed light on the severity of many patients' living conditions. Many of these women appear to have spent much of their married lives in a pregnant state, and the growth of their families was a continuous source of stress. Physical and social problems made it very difficult for them to manage:

> (1) Mother, 39 years, with T.B. history, gravida 21, 12 living children – all the children undernourished, 5 had primary T.B, 1 had cardiac trouble. Chronic financial stress.
> (2) Mother, 35 years, 10 children, last delivered by Section. Husband self-employed tradesman, alcoholic.
> (3) Mother, 39 years … 10 children. Husband had left her, unsupported, on last 4 pregnancies and returned during postnatal periods. Known to a multiplicity of statutory and voluntary agencies. Efforts to effect a legal separation have been fruitless.

In 1965, Dr Mary Martin, head of the Rotunda Hospital Psychiatric Department, reported to the Medical Research Council of Ireland on psychiatric illness in pregnant and post-natal women. Her observations are illuminating in terms of the difficulties faced by many of the Rotunda's less well-off patients and their acute need for specialist psychiatric care. Martin was head of the first psychiatric department attached to a maternity hospital in Ireland, and it appears that her services were invaluable. According to Eleanor Holmes, head social worker at the Rotunda, Martin's appointment 'met a long-felt need'. Visiting these women in their own homes, Dr Martin was struck by how severe the stress was from gross overcrowding. She noted possible precipitating factors to psychiatric illness, such as poor housing conditions and 'an undesired rapid rate of successive pregnancies'. These conditions were also repeatedly outlined by Holmes, for instance, in this report from 1965:

> Many of our patients were found to live in tenement rooms
> with quite inadequate water and sanitary facilities; others, in
> small Corporation houses with relatives. Some families have
> had to split up due to gross over-crowding in these houses.
> Emotional strains have often been great, and many marriages
> have been in danger of floundering due to the unnatural
> family stresses.

The aggrieved situation for mothers with large families led to increased calls for programmes of family planning, but artificial contraception remained illegal for sale under the Criminal Law (Amendment) Act 1935. At the National Maternity Hospital, a programme was introduced whereby some education on the subject was part of the post-natal experience for many. Owing to the hospital's Catholic ethos, the advice given to patients was based almost solely on the safe period or 'rhythm method'. Over 4,000 post-partum in-patients attended lectures run by the family planning clinic in its first year. Two lectures and one clinic were held per week – the majority of patients received information via group instruction and 264 were seen in private. A necessary factor for success in the use of the rhythm method was the need for a co-operative partner. At the National Maternity Hospital, every effort was made to interview husbands as well as wives. Their actual participation rate is unclear, but a follow-up system did exist for defaulters. This, in itself, indicates that participation was low enough to cause concern. Family planning clinics developed at all three maternity hospitals over the 1960s, but the Coombe and the National Maternity Hospital ceased to prescribe the contraceptive pill after the publication of the papal encyclical *Humanae Vitae* in 1968. The encyclical reaffirmed the official ban on artificial methods of contraception for Catholics. The Catholic Archbishop of Dublin, John Charles McQuaid, was *ex-officio* chairman of the board of both the National Maternity Hospital and the Coombe.

At the National Maternity Hospital, Dr Kieran O'Driscoll's 'active management of labour' policy was also in development over the 1960s. By 1973, every woman attending the hospital with their first pregnancy was assured that her baby would be born within twelve hours. The policy had several advantages; in an overcrowded hospital, shorter labour periods allowed each woman, at least in theory, to be provided with a personal nurse; additionally, the policy was seen as reassuring to the patient, as, according to O'Driscoll, 'the mere prospect of prolonged labour is often a cause of serious concern during a first pregnancy'. O'Driscoll's new protocol required artificial rupture of the amniotic sac followed by the administering of oxytocin to speed up labour. By the early 1970s, 55 percent of women giving birth for the first time received oxytocin stimulation. While O'Driscoll's method is still largely followed to this day, the increased medicalisation of labour and birth is not without its critics.

Newer methods for both the discovery and monitoring of pregnancy had yet to arrive in Ireland during the 1960s. Dr John Drumm was one of the first obstetricians in Ireland to use ultrasound equipment to measure foetal growth and to predict date of birth. After training in Britain under the pioneer of ultrasound, Professor Ian Donald, Drumm set up the first dedicated ultrasound unit in Ireland at the Coombe Lying-In Hospital in the early 1970s. Similarly, pregnancy testing kits for home use did not come to the Irish market until the mid-1970s; in 1975, there was only one brand of kit, Predictor, on the market. An *Irish Independent* article by Marianne Heron noted that 'since few women know about it, chemists tend to stock it only on request'.

While the overcrowding experienced in Dublin maternity hospitals was slightly alleviated with building works in the 1960s, many women continued to experience similar problems at home with large families. The 1970s would see new developments such as the increased use of ultrasound not only to measure foetal growth, but also to diagnose abnormalities. Pregnancy testing would soon be brought into the domestic sphere; and as the contraceptive debate rumbled on in Leinster House, statistics speak to the fact that many Catholic women and their partners voted with their conscience prior to a clear legal decision. By the close of the 1970s, married couples had, on average, two babies for every three their parents did. In 1967, about 23 percent of mothers in the National Maternity Hospital were giving birth to their fifth (or more than fifth) child; this fell to 10 percent by 1976. Similarly, at the Coombe, the incidence of high parity was falling rapidly. From the mid-1960s to the mid-1970s, the percentage of mothers giving birth to their eighth or later baby fell from 10 percent to less than 2 percent. By 1981, the average number of children per family was three, in comparison with four in 1971.

Further Reading:

Annual clinical reports of the National Maternity Hospital, Rotunda Hospital and Coombe Lying-In Hospital, 1960–1973.

Tony Farmar, *Holles Street 1894–1994: The National Maternity Hospital – A Centenary History* (Dublin, 1994).

J. K. Feeney, *The Coombe Lying-In Hospital* (Dublin, 1978).

Deirdre Foley, '"Too Many Children?" Family Planning and *Humanae Vitae* in Dublin, 1960–72', *Irish Economic and Social History*, 46:1 (2019) 142–60.

Kieran O'Driscoll *et al.*, 'Active Management of Labour', *British Medical Journal*, 3:5872 (July, 1973), 135–7.

'The Coombe Lying-in (Maternity) Hospital', in Come here to me! Dublin Life and Culture. Available at: https://comeheretome.com/2013/01/07/the-coombe-lying-in-maternity-hospital/.

63

Birth and the Irish:
A Presbyterian Perspective

Laurence Kirkpatrick

As the population of Ireland approaches seven million, fresh challenges face the traditional mainstream churches which are all experiencing a dramatic decline in membership. The focus of this article is the contradiction between rising Irish births and falling Irish religious affiliation, with specific reference to the Presbyterian Church in Ireland (PCI) which is an all-Ireland body.

Although Benjamin Disraeli has been credited as the first to coin the phrase, 'There are three types of lies – lies, damn lies and statistics', the statistics on this subject are telling.[1] The population of Ireland in 2021 is about 6.8 million; 4.9 million in the South and 1.9 million in the North. The birth rate in the South is 13.7 births per 1,000 (p/t) population and the corresponding figure in the North is 12.1 births p/t population (2018 figures). While these birth rates are slowing, the population of the whole island is the fastest growing population in the European Community (2019 Eurostat Report). Impressive as these figures might appear to us, a tempering perspective is added by noting that the cumulative European Community population is over 513 million. The average age of Irish mothers giving birth has risen to 32.9 years, and the number of births to teenage mothers has fallen dramatically by 60 percent in the last ten years. Almost 38 percent of births in Ireland are now outside marriage/civil partnerships. These statistics represent a challenge to all churches.

When the Presbyterian General Assembly was formed in Belfast in 1840, church membership was 650,000, or 12.6 percent of the Irish population. The equivalent figure today is a membership of 198,000, com-

---

[1] Mistakenly attributed to Disraeli by Mark Twain in *Chapters from My Autobiography.*

prising only 2.8 percent of the Irish population. These are sobering figures, especially when it can be added that the rate of decline is accelerating.

Rev. James Wigham was the Presbyterian minister in Ballinasloe in County Galway from 1851 until 1887. The church building still stands in Society Street. Wigham was elected as Presbyterian Moderator in 1885 and is most famous for his 'Presbyterian Map of Ireland', first published in 1885, which still adorns many Irish Presbyterian churches. This map measures 86 x 66cms and depicts the location of every Presbyterian church and mission station in Ireland. It is an ornate document and tangible evidence of Presbyterian self-confidence and belief in its own growing influence and numerical strength. Wigham's key statistical information cites 78,855 families and 102,027 communicants. In truth, PCI was already shrinking prior to Wigham's map; in the preceding twenty years, member families had reduced by 6 percent (from 83,834) and communicants by 20 percent (from 126,207) according to figures published in the 1869 General Assembly Minutes. As a microcosm of the PCI dilemma, Wigham's church in Ballinasloe closed permanently in 2003.

Irish society has changed immeasurably in this new millennium. Perhaps most noticeably, cultural power has drained swiftly away from the churches. Everyday life has rapidly lifted on a rising tide of secularisation, which has largely drowned the former bastions of religion. Social relations are much less formal and Ireland has quickly developed into a more cosmopolitan and multinational society. Nearly one in three Irish families and a quarter of all children under 21 years do not conform to the traditional family model of a married couple in their first marriage (Lunn and Fahey, 2011). Lone parenting and cohabitation are much more prevalent in our society, realities which the churches have been slow to accept. The legal prohibition on divorce was removed in an Irish referendum in 1995, and the churches were united in opposing this move. Likewise, in 2015, the churches opposed the recognition of same-sex relationships, but Ireland became the first country in the world to introduce marriage equality for same-sex couples by a popular vote. In the North, similar legislation was introduced by direct intervention from Westminster in the absence of a functioning Assembly and much to the chagrin of the churches.

Most recently, at the 2018 General Assembly in Belfast, PCI

pronounced against LGBT people, denying them communicant membership or the right to have their children baptised. This refusal to recognise same-sex relationships led to a public schism with the Church of Scotland which had voted to allow gay ministers. An unprecedented critical backlash erupted in the local media. Perhaps most damaging was the decision by Queen's University Belfast to end its working relationship with the PCI Theological College due to the latter's perceived shortcomings in equality and diversity. The Presbyterian Church has responded by suggesting that perhaps the secular university does not want to be associated with a Christian college.

The sacrament of baptism has long been understood in Ireland as marking the admission of a baby into a local church congregation. It is usually administered a few days after birth. The PCI statistics indicate an alarming decline in this area.

TABLE 7: *Presbyterian Church in Ireland Statistics*[2]

Date	Membership	Baptisms
1950	363,112	6,997
1978	358,107	4,494
2000	284,704	2,221
2005	270,753	1,849
2010	237,503	1,501
2015	216,770	1,337
2019	198,788	1,008

Presbyterian baptisms have, like total membership, tumbled steadily downwards; from 7,000 in 1950 to 1,000 today, down by a staggering 86 percent. The fall has been 55 percent since 2000.[3] Presbyterians have always regarded infant baptism as a sign of what God can do for an individual. The baptismal water represents a cleansing agent and the sacrament is a physical enactment of a future invisible spiritual cleansing which takes place when God's Spirit enters an individual at conversion. Presbyterian parents are clearly not finding a welcoming acceptance into their historic church. Parental joy at the birth of a child has too often turned to anger and resentment at an apparent judgemental refusal by the church to provide baptism for that child. Human hurt does not register

---

[2] Figures taken from PCI published statistics.

[3] 2,221 baptisms in 2000 and 1,008 baptisms in 2019, GA Statistics 2000 and 2019.

in cold statistics. In PCI, infant baptism takes place in response to a public profession of personal faith by one or both parents of the child. As fewer parents profess personal faith, so the baptism count falls. A recent PCI report has discussed how individual congregations should ensure that such professions are 'credible'. This 'traffic warden' approach will surely only continue to alienate parents and will surely only serve to further decrease the number of baptisms within PCI. In the past twenty years, PCI membership has dropped by an astonishing 31 percent. This equates to an average reduction of eighty-two people every week since January 2000. If this rate of decline continues, the last Irish Presbyterian will depart Ireland in 2066.

PCI and the other main churches in Ireland are plainly failing to win the argument in presenting their views in an increasingly secular society. Although in theory PCI boasts a democratic structure with representative member voting rights at congregational, presbytery and central levels, it comprises a leviathan of committees and task forces which respond too slowly, and in a Titanic-like way, to contemporary societal challenges. Historic PCI failures to steer Irish society towards prohibition, Sabbatarianism and union with Britain did not prevent the most recent attempts to resist legislative change, in the South and in the North, in relation to abortion or the acceptance of same-sex marriage.

People who perceive themselves to be under threat often retreat noisily to their traditional boundaries and so PCI has adopted an increasingly right-wing theological stance. Recent PCI pronouncements have emphasised the purity of the church and presented current struggles as a conflict between God's ways and the ways of the world. Exclusive claims to Divine insight clash with societal ideals of liberty, choice and equality. PCI will face critical decisions in the very near future. Numerical and financial decline will force difficult decisions on maintenance of infrastructure. Irish Presbyterians must decide whether to actively play their part in a growing modern Irish society or continue to adopt an opt-out mentality which may result in further shrinkage to a point of irrelevance.

Sources:

Pete Lunn, and Tony Fahey, *Households and Family Structures in Ireland* (Dublin, 2011).

64

Uprooting Childbirth: From Home to Hospital Birth in Twentieth-century Ireland

Martina Hynan

To be rooted is perhaps the most important and least recognized need of the human soul.

Simone Weil, philosopher (2002*)*

In 1955, just over 33 percent of all births in Ireland took place in the home. By 1970, home births made up 2.92 percent. In 2019, less than 1 percent of births take place in the home.

Uprooting childbirth from home and relocating it within a hospital setting is a form of displacement that severs birth from its local environment and community. This shift occurred as part of the systemic changes to the healthcare sector during the formative years of the state. This rupture from home to hospital birth belies the complex relationship that the evolving state had with women's bodies. Women's experiences of childbirth are haunted by the spectre of colonialism and postcolonial layers of societal dislocation of birth practices in Ireland. Birth itself is shrouded in patriarchal history and a reading of women's birthing bodies from within the social, cultural and political landscape that carries with it traumatic memories of poverty and institutional authoritarianism.

There are many legislative and policy changes behind the move from home to hospital birth. Three key developments directly affect where a woman can give birth: the regulation of midwifery; the gradual removal of maternity services from local communities and the implementation of the 'active management of labour' (AML) policy. These contributed significantly to the upheaval of childbirth from local communities and placed them firmly within the obstetrically led maternity units and hospitals that dominate the maternity services in Ireland today.

Up to the middle of the twentieth century, most births in Ireland took place in the home, often supported by a local midwife, handywoman or *Bean Ghlúine*. The traditional midwife was firmly rooted in the local community. Her skills were handed down from mother to daughter and other female relatives. Historian, Ciara Breathnach, acknowledges that the role of the traditional midwife survived well into the twentieth century, particularly in rural areas: 'handywomen were deeply embedded in rural communities and difficult to uproot'.

The Midwives (Ireland) Act 1918 outlawed traditional midwifery practices and, with it, not only hastened the eradication of the tacit knowledge of local midwives, but also consigned the role of the midwife to a subordinate one within the burgeoning maternity system in Ireland. Traditional midwives saw their role gradually eroded. This process firmly reinforced the authority of the tripartite relationship of medical professionals, Church and State institutions. This was the beginning of a series of legislative and policy moves that reflected the complex relationship between the midwife, obstetrician and birthing woman working within the obstetrically led institutional model of maternity care that currently persists.

Removing midwifery from local communities has had an enormous impact on the displacement of birth for women and their families, particularly those living in rural Ireland. However, other key regulatory changes supported the increased medicalisation and centralisation of the experience of childbirth. These developments necessitated that both midwife and birthing woman consider the hospital setting as the place where birth should take place. The consequence of these changes has meant that both midwives and pregnant women have been uprooted from local communities and moved from home–place to hospital–space.

The hospital system in Ireland was overhauled following the establishment of a separate Department of Health in 1947, with the chief medical officer, James Deeny, drawing up the new original plan for maternal health which came to be known as the Mother and Child scheme. While more state-sponsored maternity hospitals and units became available alongside private nursing homes, women also retained the option to have a home birth. However, women increasingly gave birth in hospitals within their local area during the 1950s, 1960s and early 1970s.

The centralisation of hospitals took place from the 1970s onwards, which led to the radical reduction of maternity hospitals available. The confluence of government policy and institutional changes led to the closure of maternity units, from 108 in 1973 to just nineteen in 2019.

The 1970 Health Act led to the creation of Comhairle na n-Ospidéal (the Hospital's Council) which oversaw the implementation of the Fitzgerald Report 1968 and the 1976 Discussion Document (Development of Hospital Maternity Services) policies which recommended that women should give birth in obstetric-staffed units. By closing local maternity units, these policies contributed to the seismic shift from home to regional hospital birth, removing the experience of birth from local communities and forcing women to travel longer distances during pregnancy and when in labour. Some areas of the country have been without maternity services for many years. The last maternity unit in County Roscommon closed in 1978, and the last maternity unit in County Clare closed in 1987. Pregnant women living in these counties can have journeys of up to 100km each way for hospital appointments and also have to travel great distances to give birth. This must add a level of stress to an already heightened, and for some, anxious experience.

One further example of a policy that firmly roots birth within the hospital setting is the 'active management of labour' (AML). AML was introduced as early as 1963 by Kieran O'Driscoll, then master of the National Maternity Hospital, Dublin. Central to his vision was the management of the time a woman is in labour. A form of 'obstetric time' has come to dominate the experience of childbirth which involves actively intervening if a woman is perceived to be in labour for too long.

The definition of prolonged labour has changed; in 1963 it was thirty-six hours, in 1968 it was twenty-four hours, and in 1972 it was formally reduced to twelve hours. This method of monitoring a woman's progress during labour is the antithesis of the traditional midwifery practice of 'watchful waiting', which focuses on supporting a woman and allowing her to labour at her own pace in her home-place.

Kieran O'Driscoll, former master of the National Maternity Hospital and main exponent of the AML policy, maintained that its purpose was to enhance the experience of childbirth. However, it seems that the reduction in the length of time that a woman can be in labour has more to do with economics. In 1993, Declan Meagher, former master of the National Maternity Hospital, and Kieran O'Driscoll described the AML policy as 'a prime example of cost effectiveness in contemporary medical practice'. For AML to be cost effective meant closely monitoring the time a woman had to labour, ideally, three births per bed in twenty-four hours. This would mean that a woman has approximately eight hours to labour. 'Obstetric time' is, therefore, of paramount importance for the effective implementation of AML. Not only is AML based on economic factors, but in order for it to be viable, it must take place within the hospital setting; therefore, 'obstetric time' dictates the place where birth happens.

AML is a contentious policy which was questioned by home birth midwife and activist, Philomena Canning, who spoke at the United Nations Committee for the Elimination of Discrimination Against Women (CEDAW), 2017, advocating that the active management of labour is in breach of human rights. The committee recognised that this policy does raise concerns about women's human rights in childbirth in Ireland.

The consequence of the changes outlined here have led to Ireland's current obstetric-led maternity service with a strong emphasis on managing the time a woman has to give birth. To facilitate its policies, birth must therefore take place in maternity hospital settings. However, the centralisation of hospitals, and the dramatic reduction of the number of maternity units available around the country, has meant that women have to travel further distances than in the past during labour and also when in labour, to avail of existing services.

Psychiatrist, Mindy Fullilove uses the term 'root shock' to explore the emotional implications of being forced to move from local environments. She considers how the erasure of place affects our 'emotional ecosystem' and also how people's sense of place is affected when they experience displacement. Perpetually dislodging women during pregnancy, particularly during labour, raises many questions about the implications of this form of disruption for women, their babies and their families. It is time to reimagine the significance of place, of rootedness in relation to childbirth and create a more challenging political landscape. Birthplace, that is the location where the event of birth occurs, is central to the experience of childbirth and should be reinstated.

Further Reading:

Ciara Breathnach, 'Handywomen and Birthing in Rural Ireland, 1851–1955', *Gender & History*, 28:1 (2016) 34–56.

Patricia Kennedy and Jo Murphy-Lawless (ed.), *Between the Lines: Mother and Infant Care in Ireland* (Dublin, 1996).

Jo Murphy-Lawless, *Reading Birth and Death: A History of Obstetric Thinking* (Cork and Bloomington, IN, 1998).

Marie O'Connor, 'Forced Labour: How we manage women in childbirth', *The Irish Times*, 13 August 2001.

Karen E. Till, 'Wounded Cities: Memory-Work and a Place-Based Ethics of Care', *Political Geography*, 31:1 (2011), 3–14.

Simone Weil, *The Need for Roots: Prelude to a Declaration of Duties towards mankind*. (London, 2002).

65

Midwifery and Salutogenesis

Maeve Anne O'Connell

Giving birth is a profound, meaningful, and life-altering event. The impact on women is lifelong and may be intergenerational as birth stories are passed on within families. Memories of birth might be positive and joyful, or traumatic and painful; therefore, women's experiences of childbirth are significant. Birth outcomes have improved vastly with more knowledge about pregnancy, the education of women and the development of the Millennium Development Goals in the twenty-first century, but maternity care standards vary nevertheless. While it is usual for women to survive childbirth now, it is important that women and infants thrive and are supported during this significant life transition.

Traditionally, it has been said 'It takes a village to raise a child', and there is truth in that saying. The social context in which a mother gives birth influences the transition to motherhood. When mothers feel safe, supported and in control, they are more likely to emerge from birth empowered and psychologically intact, prepared to nurture their baby. The changing society in Ireland, mainly since the 1970s, has seen a shift in how women experience becoming a mother. Ireland has seen many cultural and societal changes in this short but important period of time.

Preserving normal physiological processes is an underpinning philosophy of midwifery. However, childbirth in Ireland has been dominated by the technocratic model of care which is widely adopted in the Western world. Through this lens, the human body is seen as a machine which needs to be repaired, in contrast to the holistic model of care which values mind, body and spirit. Thus, Ireland offers a limited choice of models of care. Modern midwifery care aspires to follow the salutogenic model, which focuses on positive psychology, promoting health and well-being as opposed to pathologising pregnancy. The theory of salutogenesis developed by Aaron Antonovsky in 1987 comprises three parameters which comprise the overall sense of coherence: comprehensibility, manageability and meaningfulness.

A definition for the sense of coherence is 'global orientation, a pervasive feeling of confidence that the life events one faces are comprehensible, that one has the resources to cope with the demands of these events, and that these demands are meaningful and worthy of engagement' (Antonovsky, 1987, p. 19).

A person with a strong sense of coherence (SOC) is likely to be assessed as healthy as they are both cognitively and emotionally capable of making sense of and understanding their problems, as well as being able to cope with or face problems. Conversely, those with a weak SOC may not cope as effectively in the face of adversity.

Contemporary pregnancy care has focused on the surveillance of women using various tests, with the aim of avoiding risk in the quest for a certain outcome. There is a heavy reliance on ultrasound, for example, the limitations of which are rarely explained to women. The nature of childbirth is uncertain; therefore, poor outcomes are inevitable, statistically speaking. Women may experience many interventions which they don't need and which may even cause iatrogenic harm (harm which is caused by medical treatment), and they don't feel supported in the decision-making process. While sometimes interventions are required, and can be life-saving, midwives advocate for women and support them in decision-making. Examples of iatrogenic harm may be the overuse of episiotomy, Caesarean births, induction of labour and the augmentation or acceleration of labour to conform with expected labour timelines. It is difficult to quantify exactly what it is that midwives do differently in midwife-led birth settings, but there seems to be tacit midwifery knowledge and recognition of the individual needs of women which results in women expressing increased birth satisfaction in midwife-led settings, with increased psycho-social and emotional support and better clinical outcomes for women randomised to this type of care reported in trials. Women can cope with poor outcomes if they are well supported and, in the case of adverse circumstances, may even perceive a positive experience if they have been in control of decision-making in their care, had a trusting relationship with their maternity team and experienced kind, compassionate care. Women want both a safe and a positive birth experience.

As an example of salutogenesis in practice, a study (Mathias, Davis and Ferguson, 2021) which aimed to explain salutogenic aspects of midwifery care found the following definitions: a predictable caregiver, a predictable system and preparation for an unpredictable experience. Midwives can enhance and support women's internal resilience and create stronger connections to family, community and additional specialist care as required. To support the spiritual and emotional connection with women (meaningfulness), midwives cultivate the mother's autonomy through personalised care which empowers them. If we empower women during childbirth, while also ensuring their safety, we empower them to be confident new mothers. Women in Ireland have realised the need for this deeper connection and a network of doulas has developed in the community in response to this need. Doulas provide emotional and practical support and connection throughout the perinatal period, responding to individual needs, facilitating birth preparation and postnatal support. There is a network of doulas who have undergone training and work under a code of ethics and standards, providing private care.

In Ireland, traditionally, the focus was on having a 'healthy baby', with little consideration for the experience of the woman. The active management of labour was championed by Irish Obstetricians who led the way, globally pioneering the partograph, a timeline for labour. In the 1980s, it was normal to have active management of labour. This was quickly adopted worldwide and birth was increasingly medicalised with a set of interventions which were recommended to speed up labour when it didn't go as expected, according to this timeline using the 'action line'. This partograph has a role in reducing obstructed labour and recognising prolonged labour, and has been endorsed by the World Health Organization for use in active labour. However, it is a complex intervention and there have been concerns in relation to its effective use, with limited evidence of it supporting clinical improved outcomes from a Cochrane Review. In 2018, the World Health Organization finally recognised that the timeline was unrealistic, and every woman does not dilate conveniently at 1cm per hour. Their key recommendation was that women should have a 'good birth'. In *The Lancet* series 'Too much too soon, too little too late', the prevalence of medical interventions was highlighted, when they are sometimes unnecessary, along with the possible adverse effects of the interventions when not explained well to women. The overuse of interventions can cause iatrogenic harm. There may be an associated morbidity. For example, a study of induction of labour in half a million healthy women giving birth in Australia over sixteen years showed that women are being induced more, and at earlier gestations, with more adverse maternal and neonatal outcomes, such as increased episiotomy and postpartum haemorrhage, neonatal birth trauma, resuscitation and respiratory disorders (Dahlen *et al.*, 2021). Furthermore, maternity services rely heavily on medical technologies such as electronic foetal monitoring, which, in more recent times, has been achieved through centralised monitoring systems, despite a lack of evidence of clinical benefit, even in women at risk.

These systems tend to lead to professionals spending less time with women in labour, spending more time completing documentation and an increase in the rate of Caesarean births. In contrast, low-cost, evidence-based simple interventions, which can have a significant impact, are underused, such as a supportive birth partner and midwifery continuity of carer. In 2020, during the COVID-19 pandemic, there was a public health crisis where many countries, including Ireland, struggled to get the balance right between risk mitigation related to the COVID-19 virus, infection control and protecting the birth rights of women and children. The first COVID-19 case occurred in February 2020 and, following the restrictions on society in Ireland – travel ban, closure of all businesses, venues and amenities, and the advice for the general public to stay at home – significant restrictions were imposed on maternity services from March 2020: limiting or prohibition of a companion in labour; visiting restrictions; breastfeeding restrictions, or separation of mothers and babies. Whilst these may have been well meant, since then, women have reported many unfavourable consequences. These have included practices such as limited access to maternity care, suspension of key services and increased interventions. Women attended ultrasound appointments alone, with the result that some faced a diagnosis of a foetal anomaly or even a stillbirth alone.

There was redeployment of midwives from some areas such as the community to COVID-related areas such as test and trace, COVID ICU and vaccinations in response to the crisis, meaning that these maternity services suffered. Reports in the media triggered mass fear among the general public at the time, but even more so among pregnant women who did not know what to expect in terms of the virus, including regarding the level of support they would receive during this significant life event, the perinatal period [pregnancy and up to two years post-partum]. Women had to prepare and adapt to the uncertainty associated with the pandemic and do this with reduced partner support and fewer choices related to birth. The planned schedule of care was reduced for low-risk pregnant women and outreach clinics were returned to the hospital. Key services which were suspended included birthing pools, access to birth reflections and antenatal classes, including breastfeeding. Women reported feeling lonely and isolated and expressed a need for their partners to be with them. Partners felt excluded, anxious and fearful about the process and there were fewer opportunities for infant bonding. There was a policy of one designated parent for infants in neonatal intensive care units (NICUs). The advances of telehealth and video calls were used to assist with care provision, but women expressed frustration with the impracticality of this for midwifery care; it is clear that the presence of a trained midwife is irreplaceable and valued by women and their partners. Women spoke to other women and helped each other out with the transition to motherhood. Some women who became mothers during 2020 subsequently began to campaign for birth rights in the pandemic, particularly in relation to the restrictions on partners, using the hashtags #butnotmaternity and #partnersarenotvisitors. Gradually with the vaccination programme, society began to open up, but restrictions in maternity services largely remained. Where campaigning happened, some units began to open up to partners in some cases, but this was not equitable across all nineteen units in Ireland. These challenges still persist at the time of writing.

In the 1980s, the European Directives transformed Midwifery education, putting parameters on the requirements, activities and competencies. These directives meant that the length of the midwifery programme had to be increased, to meet the requirements, from one year postgraduate to two years. The first direct entry BSc in Midwifery was in

2006 and was four years' duration. The first National Maternity Strategy was published in 2016. This was developed in conjunction with a public consultation, listening to the voices of women and what they wanted. Under this strategy, evidence-based options such as midwifery continuity of care and planned homebirth are recommended as possibilities for normal risk women.

Midwifery has advanced in terms of provision of specialist services such as bereavement services, perinatal mental health and lactation consultants, but there has been limited progress in providing alternatives to the dominant obstetric model of care in Ireland, notwithstanding the recommendation in the strategy. In Ireland in 2021, midwives are striving to provide alternative models of care for women. Homebirth is available under a National Homebirth Scheme, but homebirth remains outside the normal practice with rates less than the US in Ireland. There are two free-standing midwifery-led units and one of these was threatened with closure in 2020 despite positive findings from their evaluation; women had to campaign to keep it open. Many units in Ireland are offering midwife-led antenatal care and DOMINO Schemes where women are cared for by community midwives throughout pregnancy, labour and birth and the first week after the birth of the baby. Cúidiú is a charity run by parents for parents, which provides information and practical support to help guide parents decisions in pregnancy. Similarly, AIMS Ireland – the Association for Improvements in the Maternity Services Ireland – is a consumer-led voluntary group which was formed in 2007 by women following their own experiences. They continue to campaign for the recognition of maternal autonomy and the implementation of evidence-based maternity services, and they provide support for those who have been adversely affected by Irish Maternity Services. Members of AIMS Ireland sit on many local hospital group committees and on many steering groups including for the National Maternity Strategy, Homebirth and Perinatal Mental Health. Childbirth is being reclaimed by women in Ireland with grassroots organisations championing birth rights as human rights ensuring both the safety and positive experience of childbirth in order to prepare competent, confident, new mothers. Shifting towards a more equal balance of power, where women are central to their care and decision-making, is essential in supporting the transition to parenthood.

Further Reading:

Aaron Antonovsky, *Unravelling the Mystery of Health* (San Francisco, 1987).

Hannah G. Dahlen *et al.*, 'Intrapartum Interventions and Outcomes for Women and Children following Induction of Labour at Term in Uncomplicated Pregnancies: A 16-year Population-Based Linked Data Study', *BMJ Open*, 11:6 (2021), e047040.

Raymond De Vries *et al.* (eds), *Birth by Design: Pregnancy, Maternity Care and Midwifery in North America and Europe* (New York, 2002).

Susan Downe (ed.), *Normal Childbirth E-Book: Evidence and Debate* (Elsevier Health Sciences, 2008).

Susan Downe *et al.*, 'What matters to Women during Childbirth: A Systematic Qualitative Review', *PloS one* 13:4 (2018), e0194906.

Gerard Fealy, *A History of Apprenticeship Nurse Training in Ireland* (London, 2012).

Joan Lalor *et al.*, 'Balancing Restrictions and Access to Maternity Care for Women and Birthing Partners during the COVID 19 Pandemic: The Psychosocial Impact of Suboptimal Care', *BJOG: An International Journal of Obstetrics & Gynaecology* 128:11 (2021), 1720–5.

Claudia Meier Magistretti *et al.*, 'Setting the stage for health: Salutogenesis in Midwifery Professional Knowledge in Three European Countries', *International Journal of Qualitative Studies on Health and Well-being*, 11:1 (2016), 33155.

Laura A. Mathias *et al.*, 'Salutogenic Qualities of Midwifery Care: A Best-fit Framework Synthesis', *Women and Birth*, 34:3 (2021) 266–77.

Nancy Medley *et al.*, 'Interventions during Pregnancy to Prevent Preterm Birth: An Overview of Cochrane Systematic Reviews', *Cochrane Database of Systematic Reviews* 11 (2018).

Sunita Panda *et al.*, 'Women's Views and Experiences of Maternity Care during COVID-19 in Ireland: A Qualitative Descriptive Study', *Midwifery* (2021), 103092.

66

It's not Supposed to be Painful

Louise Halpenny

Hypnobirthing is an education in the natural ability of the body to give birth. When I first heard the term, I remembered stage and TV hypnotists and felt wary. But sitting in the room with my partner and four other couples expecting babies, my view of hypnosis and of birth changed profoundly.

It was when our educator, Brenda Campion-O'Toole, a registered midwife with over 20 years' experience, stated, simply, as though it was the most obvious thing in the world, 'It's not supposed to be painful'. A silence followed and, in that moment, a whirlwind of memories and a deep inner knowing filled me. It's not *supposed* to be painful. It's *not supposed* to be *painful*. I knew deep down that this was utterly true.

I later realised that I felt this way due to years of observation of how our animals at home gave birth so easily without obvious pain or distress. It was something I witnessed time and again. But the same event for humans was spoken of as one of the most painful experiences on earth. Women seemed embarrassed by it. It made no sense to me and there was no theory I could find that made the human story of birth make sense.

Brenda explained that the parasympathetic nervous system (PNS) is responsible for our 'rest and digest' functions, causing the arteries to our internal organs to dilate, maximising the delivery of oxygen. Our gut needs plenty of oxygen after a meal so it can contract and digest our food, so our PNS diverts oxygen to the gut by dilating the arteries that feed it. It makes exercising feel more difficult after a meal by constricting the arteries that carry oxygen to the muscles of the arms and legs.

The opposing sympathetic nervous system (SNS), also called the 'fight or flight' response, is activated by adrenaline. It constricts the arteries that go to the internal organs and dilates the arteries that feed the muscles of the arms and legs, so we can run with maximum oxygen supply. The two systems cannot be in control at the same time. If we are threatened by immediate danger, the SNS is triggered so we can physically move our bodies to safety, for our survival.

This must happen, even if we are digesting a meal, and so the SNS always overpowers the PNS, constricting arteries to internal, non-essential organs. When we are stressed, excited, or during exercise, the SNS dominates. As digestion continues, we feel stomach pain where the muscle of the gut is cramping from lack of oxygen as it tries to digest in competition with adrenaline. This is why we are advised not to eat before exercise.

Think about which nervous system the uterus would be controlled by. The 'rest and digest' response-activated PNS or the 'fight or flight' response-activated SNS? For humans, as for all mammals, a calm, safe, birthing environment is one in which the birthing mother feels protected. When the PNS is activated, the arteries of the uterus are maximally dilated facilitating maximum oxygen delivery to the uterus. The muscles of the uterine walls are no different than any other smooth muscle in the body. With maximum oxygen, they contract efficiently, effectively and without pain – they are normal muscle contractions.

Fear, stress, excitement or perceived danger cause adrenaline to be released and activation of the SNS. If these conditions occur in labour, the uterus continues to contract because it is controlled by oxytocin, the love hormone, which is released to birth the baby. We don't have voluntary control of the uterine muscles; in contrast to the arm and leg muscles, which we can stop contracting by choice. The uterus will continue contracting even when its oxygen supply is reduced.

When fear is present, the SNS overpowers the PNS. The adrenaline constricts the arteries that feed oxygen to the uterine muscles. Oxytocin continues to be released so the uterus continues to contract. Uterine contractions are painful when they contract due to oxytocin with reduced oxygen supply due to adrenaline. Adrenaline must be eliminated and the SNS deactivated to allow the uterus to contract with maximum

FIGURE 22: *The birthing mother, like the polar bear depicted here, deeply connects with her Self: hypnobirthing teaches the ability to go deeply within to experience the power of the body and the empowerment of the soul (© Claire Frawley).*

oxygen supply. Then it can work without pain, just as it was designed to in all mammals.

This physiological explanation impacted me deeply in its simplicity. I knew from my medical training that it was true. But it alone wasn't enough to enable a comfortable birth. The fear I had accumulated my whole life about birth, particularly about the medical interventions in birth, had soaked into my subconscious. I couldn't be sure that when I was in labour these fears would not arise, activating my SNS beyond my control. I was afraid. This is where learning about hypnosis was crucial.

I learned that hypnosis is being in the mental state we all reach every day when we are daydreaming or feeling half-asleep when falling asleep. It is this state of mind that a birthing mother needs when giving birth.

And it is beautiful … where the body is free to just be, without the controlling, talkative nature of the mind.

In this daydreaming state, the PNS is in full control and the birthing mother feels so relaxed. The uterus is contracting with maximum oxygen and maximum effect as the baby is nudged a little further down with each contraction. Through hypnobirthing meditation, I learned to release fear and relax completely, falling asleep near the end of my first labour. I felt so peaceful, comfortable and relaxed.

Moving into the hospital environment from home was difficult because, in a foreign place, the body does not feel like being half-awake, half-asleep, the state needed to give birth comfortably. After three hours at the hospital, I heard the midwife murmur about delay. I realised I needed to return to the deep state of relaxation that I had been in at home and did so using hypnobirthing music. About half an hour later, I breathed Matthew down the birth path, his head emerging in what felt like an instant.

The world seemed to stop then. There were only the two of us, suddenly desperate to meet each other. I held his suspended head in my hands and felt it expand like a balloon. In that moment I understood how birthing the baby's head can be comfortable. The skull bones allow significant overlap as they slide over each other at their joints. This smooth elastic movement reduces the size of the head for the instant it passes through the pelvic outlet. It is not the size of a newborn baby's head, into which it grows instantly; it is much smaller. I felt his head expand with my hands and I marvelled. The muscles of my uterus birthed my baby and they did so effortlessly. My only role was to switch off my thinking brain to allow them to carry out their natural function unimpeded by fear, tension or stress.

It was as though I was a witness to this beautiful miracle of birth. I had never known or imagined that giving birth could be so empowering. I felt incredibly empowered by it, as though my body were a living, breathing, superhero, whose costume was cloaked with long hair and soft skin. I was the living essence of claiming control over my body from within while realising that it is, itself, a magnificent creation. I could never have imagined gaining all that from a birth course, but hypnobirthing made it happen and I continue to be so grateful to have found it.

Further Reading:

Birthing with Confidence, with Registered Community Midwife Brenda Campion-O'Toole. Available at: https://www.birthingwithconfidence.ie/.

John E. Hall and Michael E. Hall, *Textbook of Medical Physiology* (14th ed., Amsterdam, 2021).

Marie Mongan, *HypnoBirthing: The Mongan Method* (4th ed., Boca Raton, FL, 2015).

Ruth Ehrhardt, *The Basic Needs of a Woman in Labour* (4th ed., Scarborough, Western Cape, 2011).

Pam England and Rob Horowitz, *Birthing from Within* (Chicago, 1998).

67

'Would You Like it Toasted?': Being a Doula

Michelle Sutton-Ryan

At a recent homebirth, the labouring mom, who was happily floating in the birthing pool set up in the sitting room, in between contractions, told me and the midwife to help ourselves to tea, bread, cheese, fruit, whatever we wanted. We assured her we were grand and that we would get something to eat if we needed to. I asked her if she, herself, wanted anything to eat, and she said, 'Not at the moment'. The midwife picked up a slice of tomato and herb bread to munch on and mom-in-the-pool said, 'Would you like it toasted?', to which we both laughed and said, 'You are the most amazing birthing mother: you're relaxing, breathing beautifully through your contractions and still thinking of us in between! Let us look after you, stop looking after us!'

Being a doula, that is, accompanying a pregnant woman during her pregnancy, labour and birth, is something I became deeply passionate about after the births of my four children. I was genuinely traumatised after my first baby, partly because the hospital staff had not explained or reassured me of what was happening during my labour and birth. Why would they think to? This was all just part of the normal routine of a typical day on the labour ward as a midwife. Why would they explain that contractions/surges only last a minute and some women sleep in between them; that a labouring woman involuntarily producing poo is usually a great sign that the baby's head is well on its way; and that the vocal noises and groans I was making during contractions were perfectly normal during labour. Yet it was what I needed to hear. At the birth confidence workshops that my doula group facilitates, I am the birth sounds woman – I do a range of sounds so that pregnant women can hear that practically any and every sound is wonderful, and actually physically helpful, during labour and birth!

I also found my first birth traumatising because I had never found satisfying answers to my own questions about labour and birth. During the pregnancy of baby number three, I came upon a hypnobirthing course, and the book that accompanied the course had answers I had been looking for: that birth was a natural event, not a medical one; that my body was perfectly designed to birth my baby; that staying relaxed so that I could breathe deeply to give my uterus the oxygen it needed to birth was the most important thing to do during labour. None of this was explained to me on my first two pregnancies. Even the physiology of what happens during birth wasn't clear to me, even after a private antenatal class, numerous hospital and GP appointments and lots of first time mum-to-be reading.

I realised from doing the hypnobirthing course that relaxation is central to the muscles of the uterus being able to work at their most efficient during labour and birth. A relaxed body, I learned, is the product of a relaxed mind. Click. I relax my mind; my body feels relaxed; my body can birth naturally. Why hadn't this been made clear on births one and two?!

So, the next question in my mind was: how do you get a labouring woman to relax? The hypnobirthing book put it simply – what do you do to relax normally? What helps soothe and comfort you? What can another person do to put you at ease? The answers to these questions are as varied and unique as the people answering them: candles; cushions; favorite blanket; favourite music; favourite films; favourite stand-up comedians; favourite pyjamas; favourite book; having a shower; having a massage; having hair brushed; talking to a mum/friend/partner/dog; eating favourite food (*name yours here*)! On my fourth birth, what put me at ease was knowing that a lovely, supportive, kind friend would be present with me. Knowing she would come and meet me at the hospital, accompany me and just be there with me was the greatest support and reassurance to me during my pregnancy. I knew when the time came to give birth, there would be a friend with me, who wanted the best for me. This, I realised, is the best gift for a woman in labour – having someone in your corner, and your corner only.

South African midwife Ruth Ehrhardt has written a book entitled *The Basic Needs of a Woman in Labour*. These basic needs are:

-to feel safe,

-to leave the thinking brain (the neo-cortex) switched off

-silence

-darkness, or low lights

-warmth

-not feeling observed

-no adrenaline

Unfortunately, in a hospital setting, these basic needs are often the opposite to what's provided: nervousness or feeling unsafe being in hospital; lots of questions; instructions; noise and busyness; bright lights; unfamiliar surroundings; being observed; and, because of all these conditions, adrenaline. My experiences at home births as a doula have really made me realise how I was (unknowingly at the time) at a loss, immediately, in the hospital, for my four births. I had to ask my partner to cover my eyes as the lights were hurting and the midwives behind the curtain discussing where my file could be was a distressing, annoying conversation I didn't want to hear during my intense contractions ('Ahem, woman in serious labour here. Can we find the file later?'). Then, after another one of my births, the midwives were so busy and I was freezing; there was no one to get me a blanket; and the tea and toast promised from the kitchen, when it did finally arrive, was cold.

Enter the doula. What can a woman who has already experienced labour and birth do for a labouring, birthing woman?

Just

Be

Present

And see that she has everything she needs and wants.

Being quiet enough to hear and intuit what's needed is a skill. A doula's job ranges from doing nothing, to gently massaging the woman's back/head/feet, to giving the woman a drink of water from a glass with a straw for ease; to preparing snacks; to minding children; to helping dads feel confident in supporting their partners during labour and birth; to simply being a quiet reassuring presence in the vicinity of the labouring woman. A doula is a support, in whatever way the labouring woman needs it. The trick is, can I hear what she needs without asking her all the time? At one homebirth, I placed a cold flannel on the mum's forehead during the final stages (I saw she was sweating and I thought it would cool her) and she said afterwards it really helped. At another birth, I followed the mum's instructions to press her hips firmly with my hands to act as counter-pressure to the pressure of the contraction, and she told me, in between contractions (or 'surges', as hypnobirthing practitioners prefer to term them), that it was helping so much and to please keep doing it. At another birth, any time the labouring mum was offered a drink of water, she took it. She never asked, as she was deeply concentrating on her breathing and staying relaxed in mind and body. She needed water *provided*, not just available. For another labouring mum, I put more lavender drops on her facecloth near her head and she said afterwards it was so lovely and calming to breathe in the refreshing scent. I also offer gentle massage to every labouring mother I work with, which most find really relaxing and soothing. Massage, I learned on the hypnobirthing course, can release floods of endorphins in the labouring woman's body: these endorphins can be much more effective than a muscle-relaxant drug. Additionally, a doula, being familiar with birth, can encourage different positions at different stages of labour and birth. Freedom of movement during labour allows mum to find her most relaxing, comfortable position.

A doula wants to help maintain a relaxed atmosphere, ensuring the labouring mother has nothing to worry about: her other children are being cared for, she has freedom of movement, comfortable surroundings, food and water, nice smells, kind words, affirmations, music, anything that helps give a feeling of safety and security, so that labour and birth can progress naturally. At the last homebirth I attended, the mother went into deep active labour when her little two-year-old daughter was collected by Nana. And, during my second birth, when the midwife suggested I change position from lying on my back, to kneeling and leaning forward on the bed, baby was born within minutes.

A doula does not give medical or clinical advice. A doula gives emotional and practical support. A doula can help birthing couples understand hospital procedures and make them aware of why certain interventions might be offered. The doula wants to make the expectant mother feel safe and at ease so that, as far as possible, nothing interrupts, delays or stops labour and birth. Why does a doula do this? Because she knows the power and importance of a content birth, a birth where the labouring mother feels listened to, respected and deeply cared for. This feeling of empowerment by the mother, and her being honoured during birth, is more than important; it is essential. Every woman has a right to a positive experience of birth. So much of this is dependent on the support she receives during her pregnancy, labour and birth.

On a doula training course I attended, one of the attendees was a midwife. When we were all asked why we chose to come on this course, her answer was profound to me:

> I know all about the physiology of birth, the stages of labour, the complications, the what-ifs, and what to be watching out for. But I don't know enough about how to help a birthing woman herself, how to put her at ease so that she can have the best experience for her. I'm here to learn how to help women feel safe and confident and to trust their bodies.

A well-known doula in the UK, Lilliana Lammers, when asked about the best course to do to become a doula, replied, 'the best way to learn how to be a doula is to BE a doula'. Attending a birth is a sacred privilege. To see a human being born is a most magnificent witnessing. To see a mum content and happy with how it all went, is unquantifiable.

> When a woman births, not only is a baby being born, but so is a mother. How we treat her will affect how she feels about herself as a parent. Be gentle. Be kind. Listen.
> To every mother out there, may your birth be beautiful.
> Ruth Ehrhardt

Further Reading:

Ruth Ehrhardt, *The Basic Needs of a Woman in Labour* (4th ed., Scarborough, Western Cape, 2011).
Wellmama Doulas Ireland: wellmama.ie.

68

An Incarnational Spirituality of Birthing

Bairbre Cahill

I had my theology degree – first class from Heythrop, the Jesuit College in the University of London. Systematic, historical, sacramental theology – all those, and more, had exercised and challenged my mind. Yet it was here, in the carrying, birthing and breastfeeding of our children that I came to truly understand those words, 'This is my body, broken for you. This is my blood, poured out for you'. Here was my Eucharist, my moment of encounter.

It was not the first time that my body had drawn me into a profound and powerful encounter with God. I remember being on an Ignatian silent retreat in my days as a novice with a religious order. Half-way through the retreat, I was aware that I was ovulating. My awareness of the sensations of ovulation opened up for me a very meaningful contemplation on openness, receptivity and fecundity which, in the context of my retreat, brought me to reflect on my openness to the Word of God and the promptings of the Spirit. It was a deeply incarnational/embodied experience. My retreat director, an elderly and much esteemed Jesuit priest, was wonderfully at ease when I came to speak of my experience and, in doing so, I was affirmed in the knowledge that my body could speak to me of God.

The decision some years later to leave religious life and entrust my future to marriage and family life was a continuation rather than a reversal of my journey with God. My mother died when I was 5 years old. My brother died when he was 22 and I was 18, having struggled for two years with a brain tumour. Fear of death, of again losing someone I loved, was a hidden influence in my choice for religious life. It became clear to me that if faith meant anything at all, then it was something to be lived, whatever the risks, in the context and vulnerability of marriage and family.

Above all, it is in labour and birthing that a woman encounters the paschal mystery, has a sense of what passion, cross and tomb feel like from the inside, before the Easter dawning of birth and the joy of lifting a child to her breast. Here is my body, broken for you; here is my blood, poured out for you. It is no wonder that this has become the foundational experience for me to write about the sacramentality of life, the incarnational spirituality of every day.

But it has not always been thus. My mother's generation had to weather the indignity of being 'churched' after the birth of a baby. Though some have tried to dress it up as a 'blessing for the new mother', in reality, churching was about cleansing a woman from sin. Women were in an impossible bind. On the one hand, they were told that their only function in life was to marry and have a family, preferably a large one at that – unless of course they were going to opt for the virgin route of religious life. And yet, fulfilling the role of mother meant engaging in sexual intercourse, involvement in concupiscence, the passing on of original sin – hence the need for cleansing. So, women found themselves hiding in the shadows at the back of churches, waiting for the priest to come and lead them to the altar, blessing them with holy water and restoring them to the community and to the sacraments.

It was a scandalous, demeaning and degrading practice, which disempowered women and left many a scar on women's minds and hearts. Even into the early 1970s, the practice was still going on in places in Ireland.

Churching is not the only thing which robbed women of their power. The over-medicalisation of pregnancy and labour rendered women passive, surrendering their own wisdom to the medical professionals. Rather than a pregnant woman being seen as the fullness of life, she came to be viewed as a patient. I remember being exasperated at my own mother-in-law referring to the time after the birth of my child as 'when you're better'. The rise of the doula, an experienced, non-medical birth companion, and the practice of hypnobirthing in Ireland and elsewhere, have been vital in enabling women to reclaim their bodies, their wisdom and their power. As one hypnobirthing practitioner explained to me:

The class I teach is about how to achieve an undisturbed birth in a very medicalised obstetric-led service. It incorporates the

feelings and emotions of the unborn and gives the couples an
insight into what the baby is feeling and sensing at each stage
of labour. So many women have found it hard to put into
words the joy of birthing unhindered and they explain it as a
spiritual event, empowering and even life changing.

Helping women to be confident in the innate ability of their body to
birth a child has been shown to lead to decreased numbers of caesarean
sections, reduced time in labour, less use of artificial oxytocin to move
labour along, fewer requests for epidurals and greater levels of
breastfeeding.

What is being rediscovered is that birth is holy ground. Women who
are enabled to labour well are deeply in touch with the wisdom and power
of their bodies. I remember on my fourth, sitting at home, with my
normally hyper-busy two-year-old snuggled on my lap, stroking my face,
being my own baby-doula in the early stages of labour. I was deeply aware
of being in a sacred liminal space. Later, I was so in tune with my body
that I was able to tell the midwife, 'After this next contraction, I am going
to want to push', and our son arrived less than forty minutes after we
arrived at the hospital.

Birthing is perhaps the ultimate experience of what it means to be
embodied. As Christians, we speak about incarnation, which means to be
embodied, enfleshed, given form. In pregnancy, we experience what it is
to have another human being develop within us. We feel each kick and
wriggle, each hiccup and stretch – and it is a thing of wonder. Birth, too,
is surreal: how can my body sustain such pressure, such pain, and choose
to do this not just once but, in my case, four times? In breastfeeding, we
provide our child not only with nutrition but also anti-viral, anti-bacterial
and even anti-cancer properties. Our milk changes and adapts to the child's
needs, becoming richer in protein for a hungry baby or increasing the
level of immunity-boosting cells when a baby is sick. In our embodiment
is our sacredness.

Churching was an expression of deeply negative attitudes within the
Catholic Church towards the body, sex, pregnancy and birth and,
consequently, towards women. For more than twenty-five years, I have
written about family life with all its mess and chaos as a place of God's

presence and action. I speak of an incarnational spirituality, one which takes our physical reality as the first place of encounter with God. As Christians, we believe that Jesus was the Word, the Wisdom of God who became like us – God at the heart of our humanity, and our humanity at the heart of God. We speak of his Incarnation, by which we mean that, in him, God's desire to be with us takes form. He developed within the womb of Mary. She laboured him to birth with the pain, the struggle and the sweat of every woman who has laboured. She nurtured him at her breast with milk rich and amazing in its properties. She held him in her arms, ragged and exhausted from her labours and was entitled to say to him, 'This is my body, broken for you; this is my blood, poured out for you'.

Further Reading:

Louise Lewis, '"Churching" women after childbirth made many new mothers feel ostracised'. Available at: https://www.thejournal.ie/readme/churching-women-after-childbirth-dublin-tenement-1913-1061449-Aug2013/.

Patricia Larkin *et al.*, 'Women's preferences for childbirth experiences in the Republic of Ireland: A mixed methods study'. Available at: https://bmcpregnancychildbirth.biomedcentral.com/articles/10.1186/s12884-016-1196-1.

Jan Tritten, 'Midwifery is standing on holy ground'. Available at: https://midwiferytoday.com/mt-articles/editorial-midwifery-standing-holy-ground/.

Serene Therapy and Wellbeing - Bernie Frain, Reflexology & Hypnobirthing. Available at: https://www.facebook.com/Serene-Therapy-and-Wellbeing-Bernie-Frain-Reflexology-Hypnobirthing-1766668403597699.

Ina May Gaskin, 'Birth Matters'. Available at: https://www.youtube.com/watch?v=kHW17Dx8ajY.

Ina May Gaskin *Spiritual Midwifery* (Summerton, TN, 2002).

Mary Letourneau, 'The miracle of breast milk'. Available at: https://www.cvmc.org/blog/womens-health/miracle-breast-milk

Alex Mlynek, '6 magical ways that breastmilk changes to meet your baby's needs'. Available at: https://www.todaysparent.com/baby/ breastfeeding/magical-ways-breastmilk-changes-to-meet-your-babys-needs/.

69

Pregnancy and Birth among the Travelling Community

Salvador Ryan interviews Nell McDonagh

Tell me something about how a girl within the Travelling community might be prepared for the experience of having children? Who was traditionally responsible for looking after this aspect of a young person's education?

It's actually a very strange one, and even now in modern times, it's a conversation that is never really discussed. I mean, when I look back, when I had my first child (and I was an only girl), my mother brought me up to the Coombe, left me at the door of the Coombe, and I hadn't an iota; I had the brain of a 10-year-old, I think. But my mother just left me there and said to me 'Don't let them start you' (I didn't even know what that meant at that time). But there would always be women – like a sister-in-law – or a younger aunt; it would always be someone closer in age to you, that would discuss that. Strangely enough, it wouldn't be an elderly person, because elderly people, whether they be male or female (well, males wouldn't be involved in the topic of conversation at all), and elderly woman wouldn't have that conversation with you, particularly around pregnancy and how you became pregnant. That was always a younger woman, a younger married aunt, someone closer in age to you. But still, it would be a very strange conversation.

I could tell you a story. I have an aunt and she was married at 15, and as soon as she married, they moved to England. And they were there for months and months (she lived quite close to her sister). Now she went from rural Ireland to Manchester. Well one day (the women used to meet every Saturday to go to the park – that was their social part of the week), they were chasing around after each other (they were so young!); they used to play swinging, or chasing, or rounders, or whatever.

So, they were there all day, and on the route home that evening, she said to one of the women, 'Do you know, I feel something jumping in my stomach!' And her sister was there, and her sister said, 'Well, we need to go to the doctor', and she said, 'No, it's not paining me or anything – I think I got it when I was running'. And when they brought her to the doctor, she was six and a half months pregnant. And she didn't even know …

Anything to do with a conversation around sex education was considered not an appropriate subject, whether it be male or female. Now, of course, young women today have much more access to education and have an ability to read up on stuff. Having said that, it's still not a comfortable conversation.

When a couple would announce when they were expecting a child, at what point in the pregnancy would they usually do this? Would they wait for three months to pass, for instance, as many 'country people' (people within the settled community) do?

I would say it's a bit different within the Travelling community because as soon as a young girl finds out she's pregnant, they almost tell it immediately; and I think there's many reasons for that. It's considered such a blessing, and a gift from God to have your own child, and the joy it brings in having a baby. Now, earlier on, when I had babies (particularly my oldest one or two) you would be told by the women, 'Don't tell anybody until you're over three months'. The only time you would tell it prior to that is if the father of the child was either sent to prison, or if he died. You would have to tell as soon as you knew you were pregnant, then, so you wouldn't have people assuming that you were pregnant before you got married, or pregnant after the man had died or had gone to jail. So, as soon as the man was out of the scene, whether he was in prison, or whether he had died unfortunately. Or also if there was the death of an immediate family member, another child in the family, or a very close family member, like a father or mother; you would tell immediately, because sex wouldn't be something that you would be having a conversation about, you'd be seen that you had nothing else on your mind. So if you were pregnant you would announce it immediately so as to let people know that 'I was pregnant prior to this happening'; so as not to let people think that I wasn't grieving for a death.

The announcement was, and is still, very much associated with huge joy and happiness, so you would be very, very pleased to announce it. And when a young girl even gets married now, everybody is almost always waiting for the announcement of the pregnancy, because the gift of a child is so much; it is so revered and so special that, even the young women who think they're modern, and think they know it all now, they would tell immediately because it is seen as a great gift of joy.

Given what you have just said, I am wondering about whether the availability of artificial contraception over the past number of decades has had much impact on Traveller attitudes to pregnancy. Have attitudes changed much?
They have changed. I mean, in my grandmother's time, and in my mother's time, and even in my time, a woman would not have been allowed use contraception. It was totally unheard of when my mother was having children. Now my mother only had five children, but she would have had fourteen pregnancies, but only five of us survived. My grandmother (my father's mother) had five living children, but she had twenty-four pregnancies, and she would've had about seventeen live births, and some of them would have died at two and three, for different reasons. But contraception was something unheard of and it would have been forbidden. Who would ever not want to have children? So contraception wouldn't have been accepted. There are some families associated with having very big families, particularly in the west of Ireland. So, contraception is not a choice. And I know one woman that worked in a project that was run by country people (settled people), but she had nine children and she was still in her early thirties, if even she was in her thirties. So, the woman directing the programme arranged a health day, and so you went to see a doctor. Anyway (and I know it would probably be considered illegal today) the doctor put her on the contraceptive pill because he felt that, at that young age, she was having a baby every ten months – and she wasn't able. So, with all goodness of heart, the doctor prescribed the contraceptive pill. But, in her naivete, she actually thought she was on iron tablets, and she thought it was for her health, so she was religiously taking them. But the husband then

questioned why there was no babies after a two-year break. And she stopped taking it, because if he had found out that she was taking contraception, there would have been uproar. And that was the cause years ago of a lot of domestic violence among Travellers, because if you couldn't give the man a child, and particularly a male child, there was a huge stigma. And it's very much still alive today – and I know that young women mightn't admit it – even if times have changed and thankfully girls in the majority of Travelling families are very much looked up to, but still a man wants a son. Women have to give him sons, to carry on the name. The more sons you had, the stronger it proved to the family, and it gave you a stronger image as a family – 'I have six sons; or I have eight sons; or I have ten sons'. The more boys, the more men you had in your family, the stronger it was perceived. This is why contraception wasn't accepted at all years ago. However, young women do use contraception now, and young women are limiting their families, and young women are of the thinking now: 'I have enough in four or five'. Now four or five in Irish society today is still considered by some people relatively big. But that's small for Travellers. But it's more the woman that favours [contraception] than the man, even still.

If you look back, the amount of women of my grandmother's generation, and my mother's generation, that had babies well into their forties. Those women, I do not believe for a second, had those babies out of choice. My granny had a baby at 46. I know a woman who had one at 54. Those women had babies because you weren't allowed use contraception. And the man just wanted sons; he wanted children. Years ago, women would've took on the family planning method, or whatever; but it would be very much on the thinking of the Catholic Church. It was very much what the Catholic Church said was the right thing to do. And if it went against the teachings of your Catholic faith, it wasn't allowed.

When a woman becomes pregnant, are there things that she is expected to do, or things that she is forbidden from doing? I remember, for instance, hearing you speak before of Travelling women who are expecting a baby not entering cemeteries for burials.

That is very much still practised today. Going into a mortuary or going into a graveyard. That would not be encouraged. Now there are some young Travelling women who, when a close family member dies, will go in. But it would have to be extremely close. Years ago, even when I was having children, you weren't allowed get your hair cut. No way. You could not cut your hair. Hair was a symbol of status among Travellers. And, of course, the more times you were pregnant, the more times you couldn't cut your hair. And if a young woman announces a pregnancy to the Travelling community today, she will not use sunbeds. She won't get her hair coloured. You're not allowed smoke. And because so many Travelling women smoke now, you could almost tell when they are pregnant. And they don't drink alcohol. And you don't fly. And those who have flown would be very much frowned upon. Anything that might damage the potential of delivering a healthy baby …

Now when a young woman announces her first baby – particularly her first baby – she is almost treated like a little queen. She almost wouldn't be allowed walk. You're sat down and everything is done for you. It's almost like the stories of the little monks in Tibet – they don't let their feet touch the ground! It's very similar with a young woman within the Travelling community. This is bringing so much joy to the extended family, that anything that would protect this little baby is so important.

And that's why there is so much sadness around miscarriages. And Travelling women who miscarry early in their pregnancies, they still want to bury the little baby. And I have seen huge funerals, particularly, again, in the west of Ireland. I've been to funerals that would be massive funerals – I mean hundreds of people there! And it would be a little baby that was stillborn, but it was still very much part of that family. And it was part of that community. So, you showed the same respect to that little baby that was stillborn as you would to an adult or an older person. And there's awful sadness.

I've known people that if a little baby has a cot death, or a woman has a miscarriage, and if she was living in a trailer at a halting site, they would move out of the trailer. They would do the same customs as burning the trailer, as if was an older person. It would still bring the same amount of sadness and tragedy.

And when a woman would be asked a few years later how many children had she, would she also count those who had died?

Oh yes, without a shadow of a doubt. 'I had five children, and I had three children that went to heaven', or 'I had three children that God took early'. They're still very much counted. And I remember when I had my youngest girl, I was in hospital with a woman that was a good bit older than me; but she was having her youngest child. And we both were in the Coombe. But I met her the following maybe month, or six weeks, at a wedding in Navan, and I went over, and I said to her, 'How is your baby?' And she suddenly got so emotional, and so upset, that I actually thought the baby had died, or something tragic had happened. She was inconsolable. And, I'll never forget it. So, when she calmed down, I said 'Oh my God, I'm so sorry'. I didn't know what I had done. But why she was so upset was, because she was a woman well into her forties, she had to be sterilised because of the traumatic birth of her last baby. Now the baby survived and was a lovely baby, but because she had to have a hysterectomy, it was the most awfulest news that she could receive. Now she was a woman well into her forties. And she said to me 'I only have seventeen'. And I said to myself, 'Jesus, Mother of God'. Now she had seventeen living children, and she said to me 'I *only* have seventeen'. And I was thinking in my own head, 'I had four, and only that I was looking for another son, I wouldn't have had five'. But she was devastated. She had seventeen babies and she couldn't have any more. And that was the most tragic news that she could receive.

When a Travelling couple are expecting a baby, has it become the practice, as among some in the settled community, to find out whether it is a boy or a girl beforehand?

That's a very new phenomenon among Travellers. And there are a number of young women today who still would come from the family thinking that, regardless of what it is, I'm celebrating this birth, so please don't find out; you don't be flying in the eyes of God. Pray that it's a healthy baby. Having said that, the new thinking among the Travellers today, and the new attitude, is very much as soon as I come to sixteen or twenty weeks, I'm having this gender reveal; I'm having this scan to find out what I'm having. I personally believe still that it's about finding out if they're having a son. If the young women have a couple of girls, they want to know if they're going to be blessed with a boy. They want to find out instantly so they can celebrate extra much. I don't believe it's just for the sake of finding out.

Are there any particular prayers or saints that are prayed to for pregnant women? Or pilgrimages that are taken?
It's very important that young girls get blessed – a pregnancy blessing. Anything that is new that is brought into our world is blessed – whether it is a car, or a van, for example, to bring you luck and happiness. As soon as a girl finds out she is pregnant, she is brought for a pregnancy blessing so that the child will be delivered safely. St Joseph is a huge favourite among Travellers. And St Gerard Majella, the patron saint of pregnant women. And you'll notice, you know, the way we have the red string we put on our children not to be overlooked …

Tell me about that …
All our children, even now, no matter what age they are, we put a red cord around their hand or their feet; I have an 18-year-old granddaughter who thinks she is so glamorous, and she has all the latest fashion, yet she would freak out if she lost her red cord that's tied around her ankle. That red cord means that she won't be overlooked and that she will be blessed. And we do that to all our babies. And even if you have a child, a girl, who has exceptionally long, beautiful hair, you will always see red pinned on her hair, so her hair won't be overlooked. When my youngest grandson, Paddy, only a month old, was born prematurely, he immediately got a piece of red flannel sewed onto his vest. When you look at your baby, your eye is immediately drawn to the red, and you're not overlooking it, and you're blessing it. All young women wear the red, around their wrist, or around their ankle. Some of them are made out of wool. So, after a number of showers, obviously the red wool gets weaker and weaker. And if it breaks off, it has to be replaced immediately. Now they tell you that when it breaks off it's an answer to your prayer; your prayer is answered now. So, replace it immediately. It's pinned onto a child's vest. It's tied round, in ribbon form, a child's ankle, or its wrist, and it's there until it breaks itself. My son is 31 and he still

wears it. My son-in-law wouldn't go for a minute without his red cord.

Are there particular holy wells that are visited by pregnant women?
Travellers have a lot of favourite wells. There's a cure in St Brigid's shrine in Dundalk. So, if you were living in this area, you would go for the blessing. There is a stone – I can't say 'allegedly', because I believe it is – a stone that is shaped in the form of a woman's stomach. And when you find out you're pregnant, the girl will go and put her stomach into the form of the stone to receive a blessing. She will kneel down, and put her stomach into the shape of the stone to receive a blessing.

There is a prayer, that everybody knows off by heart, to St Gerard Majella, that all the Travellers pray. And that's considered almost gospel. They would pray that religiously – and to Our Blessed Lady. You would repeatedly say the three Hail Marys for a safe delivery.

As soon as you announce your pregnancy, you're brought to a priest – and particularly if you know it's a healing priest, a priest that has known cures; you'd bring your daughter, or your daughter-in-law, to this priest to get a pregnancy blessing. And that's done almost immediately. As soon as you find out you're pregnant, you have to have a blessing.

Would most Travellers go to the hospital to have their babies delivered?
Yes, and it's probably a good thing, because the conditions that some Travellers are living in are way below standard as compared to the settled community; and the infant mortality rate among Travellers is far more than among the settled community. So, I think the idea of going to a hospital is probably a very good thing for the safety of the mother and child. However, my grandmother (my father's mother) was known among the Travelling community as a midwife, and she told us stories that she went to the delivery of a first child when she was only 14 years of age. Her mother brought her. So, my granny delivered most of her grandchildren – in the backs of tents, in wagons; underneath wagons. They wouldn't have access to hospitals, nor many women of my mother's generation. My granny was particularly known. So, you'd try to camp near my granny and grandfather when you'd know you were due to deliver a baby, so that my granny could assist at the labour.

And tell me, when it comes to the point of delivering the child in the hospital, are Traveller men usually present for the birth, or not, these days?

There's an odd *ludar* that thinks 'I should be there', but it's very much not the done thing, even in these modern days, because if you were here in the room and you were talking to ten young women now, they will tell you up straight 'What does he know about it? Leave him out! He's only a bother more than he's anything else'. It would always be a family woman member. I was at the delivery of all but my last two grandchildren, and my daughter-in-law's mother went to the delivery of all her four grandchildren. Now there are a few men who go in, but it's not goin' down too well! I mean, how useful are they? Women believe it's more a woman thing, and they're more aware of what's happening. So, it wouldn't be in a disrespectful way to the young men, but they would say 'What does he know about it? He's as valuable as an ashtray on a motorbike!'

And what would happen when the child arrives home? Are there any traditional rituals attached to the homecoming?

Unfortunately, no. In the past, a woman always had to be 'churched'. You'd see Travelling women sitting up on the altar on a chair and there's no babies, and no man, and I found out afterwards that they were being blessed and churched after the delivery. It's kind of like a cleansing process. But young women today, when they come home, would be minded very, very well (now that's not saying every Travelling girl), but they're still very well minded. Something that has caused a lot of distress to Travellers now is … we, or at least women of my generation, would want a baby baptised within a week if we could, but now you have to do baptism courses, and it brings a lot of anger from Travellers towards the Church, because we want our babies baptised. And there are many women out there who, if they had a choice, within a week, their babies would be baptised, whereas there are other women who would wait for a couple of months because they want to plan a party or whatever. But if you speak to any Traveller over the age of 50, or probably even 40, they would tell you, 'No, get the baby baptised as soon as possible for its own strength'.

Nell, you were talking about being 'churched': was it seen as something positive, or not, by Travelling women?

Well, I'm sure the Travellers had a positive thinking behind it. Now there are young Traveller women today who would ask 'What were they insinuating? Were they saying the woman was dirty?' Well, it was very much a ritual. If you miscarried your baby, or if your baby died at birth, you still had to be churched. So, in the past, my mother sent us home from hospital (she was very ill), but on the day that we were born, as soon as the children were considered fit enough to leave the ward, we were sent home with my granny, or maybe an uncle and his wife, and we were sent to get baptised immediately, because the child wouldn't thrive. If a woman miscarried her baby, she had to be churched in order to facilitate her baby not going to Purgatory. It had to be blessed so it wouldn't go to the Souls in Purgatory. So, it was considered a positive thing. I know the young thinking women will say 'What were they insinuating?', but I do believe that Travellers considered it a very positive thing.

And tell me about how names are chosen? Is there still a strong tradition of naming after grandfathers, grandmothers, and so on? How much freedom have a couple in choosing names?

Boys would have to be family names. Now you do hear what they call now 'television names'. Like, 'Why did you call your child "Cody"?' (and I apologise to anyone who has a Cody!). It may be due to an argument in the family. So, if I'm not allowed call it after my father, I'm not going to call it after your father, or anybody in your family, so we're going to go mad and call it Cody. But, in the majority of family names today, [even] in the very modern-thinking young women that are delivering boys, they are definitely family names [that are used]. So, it's either your father, or my father, and the husband. If I have daughters, whilst they may have a family name as a first name, they could also have a second name. My three girls have family names as their first names, but they also are not known by them. They still have the family name legally, and would be baptised using the family name, but they might be called by another name at home. So, it doesn't cause any issue when it's a girl. Or, for example, if my mother's name was 'Winnie', I might call the child

'Whitney' because it begins with a W and could be considered a modern version of the name. So, if they go to school, they won't stand out with all these old-fashioned names. But that doesn't apply to boys.

Nell, I want to ask you about some of the more difficult situations regarding pregnancy and birth. So, for example, let's say a Travelling woman isn't married and gets pregnant; or a Travelling woman gets pregnant as a result of a rape; or there's a Travelling woman who might choose to have an abortion. How are these dealt with in the Travelling community?
They would be dealt with very quietly. It wouldn't be a conversation you would have. And I think that the awful sad thing about that is I know women who have had children out of wedlock, or maybe who have had children with black men (and here it really shows the prejudice), they would really almost be ostracised. If women give birth as a result of an assault, I always find the very tragic thing about cases like that is the child suffers; because it wouldn't be accepted; it's still considered very different. It's still not welcomed with open arms. Those children live very much on the margin of Traveller society. Our community, unfortunately, still has a very negative attitude towards cases like this. For a woman who would become pregnant by choice, without being married, her chances of marrying into the Travelling community would be very slim; and both her and the baby would be kept very much on the edge of society. And if she does marry, the child is still never 100 percent accepted. And I know Travelling women who have had children for men from different parts of Africa, and those children are not accepted. There's a huge amount of discrimination. Not in all, but in 99.9 percent of the family cases. Children that are born as a result of assault or sexual abuse are still considered children that are almost – it's a horrible thing to say – but, almost 'damaged'. You'd imagine that you'd try and protect those children more, and those women more; but no, they're very much kept to the side. There's a lot of exclusion, and ignoring it.

It was very often the case years ago, in the settled community, that if a young girl got pregnant very early, and they weren't married, oftentimes that child would be taken into the family and would be brought up as another sibling of the girl who

had delivered the child. So, years later, the person you thought to be your sister was, actually, your mother. Did that also happen in the Travelling community?
That would be unusual among Travellers, for the simple fact that everybody got married so young, and we lived very much as a community, and there was no secrets. Where this has happened, that child would have been reared as a son or a daughter by the grandmother.

And would it be usual to tell the child at some stage who his or her real parents were?
It would be, because you cannot keep secrets in the Travelling community, by the fact that we live in groups, and everybody knows your business; so it would be a disaster trying to keep it quiet; the first argument you would have, it would be told. So, it would not be something that would be possible.

Given the huge emphasis on having children, and children being a blessing from God, how are instances of abortion treated within the Travelling community? And have attitudes to abortion changed in more recent years?
I don't think attitudes have changed all that much. When you think back to the last abortion referendum, I reckon that 99 percent of Travellers voted against that. However, there has been cases of women, particularly single women, or women who have had affairs, or who have been abused, have had abortions, and these are cases that are unspoken of, and treated with the utmost, almost horror, because babies, regardless of their circumstances, should be considered a blessing, regardless of how they got here. The belief among the majority of Travellers is that there is no room for abortion under any circumstances.

Are there any other aspects of childbirth among the Travelling community that you'd like to comment on, Nell?
There's another thing – and I think it was a lovely thing – what happened around childbirth years ago, and it still happens to this day: very often if a young woman and a young man marry and can't have children, the very common practice was for their sister to have a baby and give you that child to rear as your own. And I know many very young Travellers, under the age of 35, who couldn't have children of

their own, but who reared their sister's children. I can tell you of one case in particular. It was a double wedding – a brother and sister married a brother and sister – and one couple had babies immediately, and one couple couldn't. But the sister said, 'when I have my third child, regardless of whether it is a boy or girl, I'll give it to you'. And she did. And that child now lives in the family unit and calls his mummy and daddy 'Mummy' and 'Daddy', and treats the other woman (who was his birth mother) as his aunt.

I know many young couples who, after you pray, and pray, and do the novenas, and do everything in the hope that you'll have a baby; but, if you can't, after seven or eight or nine year, it wouldn't be unusual for a Traveller woman to get fertility treatment. That's a new one among the Travelling community, but because Travellers are wealthier now, and have more access to money, they can afford fertility treatment. But you wouldn't let six or seven year go by with no babies that you wouldn't be looking for an alternative way to have a child. So, whether it was family members having a child for you, or through fertility treatment …

Any final words?
The most important thing is, regardless of how Travellers have become modernised or moved away from their culture (or think they have moved away from their culture and traditions), the birth of a child is held in such high esteem. Children are … whether you can afford [them] financially or not – I often said, 'My God, how is it they're having children and they can't provide for them?' – but you'll find a way of providing for them some way. They are adored so much that it's almost as if you couldn't have enough of them. And I often said, with the new modern couples that are out there now (or think they are), I'm surprised at something like waiting a couple of year before we have our first baby. No, that's not a discussion in the Travelling community. As soon as you marry, you're looking for a baby. And, well and good, I might have three or four quick children, and then stop, or use contraception; but don't tempt fate, – have a child as soon as you can.

Thank you very much, Nell.

70

Pregnancy Loss: A Silent Loss and Challenging Birth

Daniel Nuzum and Keelin O'Donoghue

The birth of a baby for most people is a happy event, and is as much a social event as it is a familial one. In our current era, where most pregnancies lead to the birth of a healthy baby, it can be easy to forget that it is not always so. Alongside the excitement and celebration that accompanies most births, there is also the ever-present and unwelcome shadow of pregnancy loss and perinatal death. Despite many modern advances in obstetric, midwifery and scientific understandings, up to one in four pregnancies will end in miscarriage, one in every 240 babies born in Ireland will die just before birth (stillbirth), and a smaller number will die shortly after birth (neonatal death). Globally, 2.6 million babies are stillborn annually. The conflation of the high emotion of expectation and pregnancy with the devastatingly low feelings of death and grief leads to an unwelcome and bewildering experience which has a long-lasting impact on parents, families, communities and wider society.

Historical Situation

As a nation, the legacy of how we responded to the loss of a pregnancy or the death of a baby casts a long shadow over the individual, familial and communal experience of perinatal loss. The experience of this shadow continues to be felt today. The loss of a baby was shrouded in an unspoken cloak of silence and invisibility, with little if any opportunity for shared grieving and support. A century ago, infant mortality in Ireland was, on average, one death in every twelve births, with the highest rate being one in six births in Dublin. In the early decades since the establishment of the State, infant mortality was almost double in large urban areas; a situation that continued until the 1960s. In a context of high infant mortality, one simply cannot consider the history of birth without also recognising the reality and pain of loss. An examination of burial registers from this period presents a confronting and stark reality of this particular loss.

Society and Church(es)

In a context where infant mortality was high, the wider cultural and religious backdrop concerning birth, death and salvation (not unique to Ireland) played a significant role in the societal response to pregnancy loss and infant death. The reality for parents was that, in addition to the pain of grief and loss, there was a troubling spiritual/ecclesial shadow of invisibility and uncertainty concerning the very existence and status of infants who died before or shortly after birth. The unfortunate and narrow coupling of baptism of a living baby with salvation led to a devastating and yearning reality for parents faced with a disregarding approach to the life of their baby who died before birth, or more particularly before or without baptism. The most tragic consequence of this was the denial of the usual supportive rituals and rites of passage such as a baptism and a funeral to welcome and to say goodbye to a baby. A baby who died without baptism was denied burial in consecrated ground and, in effect, was disregarded by society. This led to a troubling tableau of burial sites outside consecrated ground, likewise with life-long impact and spiritual pain and uncertainty for parents and families. In a country that was predominately Catholic, concepts like 'Limbo' ran deep in popular Catholic understanding, and this remained the case, to a greater or lesser degree, until formally clarified by Pope Benedict XVI in 2007.

Faced with this harsh backdrop, parents buried their babies under the literal cloak of darkness and secrecy, outwith consecrated burial grounds or church yards and the usual comforts of religious and community support. Ireland is therefore scattered with the tender rebellions of parents who buried their babies in *cillíní*, consecrated not by formal religious ritual, but by the intention, love and deeply felt and innate value of the life of each baby. In these places of burial, there was no public memorial or gravestone, and at best, there were entries in the margins of burial registers; lives not worthy of their own entry or record. There have been many reclamations of these burial grounds in recent years and notable efforts to give them their place of honour in communities.

Civil Recognition

Civil registration of births has been a legal requirement since 1864. However, this only applied to live births and did not include babies who were stillborn. Civil registration of deaths was introduced a year earlier, in 1863, and likewise did not apply to stillbirths. The Central Statistics Office (CSO) did, however, begin to count stillbirths (from twenty-eight weeks) for statistical purposes from 1957. Following much effort and campaigning by bereaved parents and support organisations, it was not until 1995 that the Civil Registration of stillborn babies was enacted in the Stillbirths Registration Act, 1994. Civil registration confers a legal status and acknowledgement, and for parents of babies who were stillborn, this was a watershed moment in the societal acknowledgement of the life and death of their baby. The definition of 'stillbirth' was, and continues to be, 'a child born weighing 500 grammes or more, or having a gestational age of 24 weeks or more who shows no sign of life'. However, with all definitions, the Act excludes earlier pregnancy loss and, in particular, miscarriage. It remains a painful reality that parents who grieve the death of their baby through late miscarriage, who are faced with the birth and burial/cremation of their baby, will receive no legal recognition of their baby's life, with either a birth certificate, death certificate or a stillbirth certificate. The sensitive and challenging reality of complicated and crisis pregnancy also continues to evolve and has caused our society to reflect on the painful realities of abortion and reproductive rights. However, the reality of pregnancy is that ethical complexities are ever-present and rarely manifest in black-and-white terms. For the purposes of this chapter, it is important to acknowledge that this has always been a painful if unspoken burden – another challenging reality when considering 'Birth and the Irish'.

Current Developments

As the definition of stillbirth has evolved globally to include earlier gestations (varying from 20–22 weeks +), a recent study from University College Cork has recommended that the definition used in Ireland be lowered to twenty-two weeks' gestation and 400 grammes. However, the reality is that definitions by their nature will always exclude. This raises the question of how, then, can society recognise and honour those who fall outside any given parameter of civil definition? The experience and practice of parents and families, and indeed faith communities, has contributed much in this regard. It is a comforting and reassuring fact that even if there is no formal civil recognition for early pregnancy loss, the provision of ceremonies of blessing, naming and various other religious and secular rituals have responded meaningfully in recent years to publicly mark and honour these short lives. In addition, all Irish maternity hospitals now hold annual ecumenical Services of Remembrance which include all those who have experienced loss in the maternity services; one such example is www.cumhremembers.ie.

There has also been much development in the overall care of babies and families and their experience of care with the publication and implementation of the first ever *National Standards for Bereavement Care following Pregnancy Loss and Perinatal Death* by the Health Service Executive in 2016.

Breaking the Silence

Bereaved parents often remark, 'How come I never knew this was a possibility until it happened?'. The very inclusion of a chapter such as this gives voice to what, for so many, over many generations, was a silent and unacknowledged grief. Today, those of us who work in maternity services, in whatever capacity, wish to acknowledge the reality of loss alongside the joy of healthy newborn life. It is true to say that we consider our care of bereaved families amongst the most important and rewarding work in a maternity hospital. We will continue to work tirelessly through our research to eliminate all preventable stillbirth and we are proud, at the Pregnancy Loss Research Group at the INFANT Centre at University College Cork, to take our place alongside global colleagues in this regard as researchers.

Pregnancy loss and perinatal death will sadly always be a part of pregnancy and birth. We will not be able to prevent all loss in pregnancy; however, with good care, modern science, compassion and support we can make a difference. Bringing the conversation into the foreground is an important part of that.

Links:

Pregnancy & Infant Loss Ireland. Available at: www.pregnancyand infantloss.ie.

'Miscarriage Information & Resources'. Available at: www.cork miscarriage.com.

71

Birth When Life is Short:
Difficult Decisions and Care

Caoimhe Ní hÉalaithe, Keelin O'Donoghue and Daniel Nuzum

Pregnancy and birth are, for the most part, happy and exciting life experiences. The arrival of a new baby brings joy, hope and dreams for the future. From the moment there is a positive pregnancy test, the baby takes his or her place within the family tapestry. The future of all involved changes irrevocably. Unfortunately, though, for many parents, this time can be shrouded in doubt, uncertainty and grief. It is a sad reality that not all babies will survive, and the diagnosis of a fatal foetal anomaly or life-limiting condition (FFA/LLC) often causes that tapestry of expectation and hope to unravel. The death of a baby disrupts the natural order of birth, life and death, and has long-lasting effects for parents, families and communities as a whole. In their own right, birth and death are two of life's most significant events, and when perinatal death occurs, they fuse inseparably with devastating consequences.

Reality of FFA/LLC Diagnosis in the Past
For decades, those who experienced a perinatal death often simultaneously experienced a 'silent grief'. The impact of miscarriage, stillbirth and foetal anomalies was wholly under-acknowledged by society, and many women and couples weathered the storm bereft and alone. In relation to a FFA/LLC diagnosis, and in particular for those who chose to terminate their pregnancy, many felt their story was swept under a carpet or had to be locked away and kept as a devastating secret, a monumental burden to bear.

Prior to 2013, Irish law stipulated that pregnant women who received antenatal diagnoses of fatal foetal anomalies were not permitted lawful terminations in Irish hospitals. Over a number of decades from the 1960s, parent groups have lobbied for change which was incremental, from the provision of information about termination services overseas and the right to travel for such terminations, to the enacting of The Protection of Life During Pregnancy Act, 2013. This new legal framework allowed for the termination of a pregnancy in Ireland in just three specific circumstances: a 'real and substantial risk' of loss of life from physical illness; a risk of immediate loss of life from physical illness in an emergency, and a 'real and substantial risk' of loss of life from suicide. Women, and their partners or families, when given a diagnosis in pregnancy of an FFA/LLC, had a frightening path ahead of them – did they choose to continue the pregnancy or choose to travel abroad and end the pregnancy? These options were presented to parents by a foetal medicine specialist, and while some obstetricians provided care at this time and afterwards, others felt unable to do so. While parents who continued with their pregnancy were able to receive ongoing care, including perinatal palliative care, this option was not possible for those who chose to terminate a much-wanted pregnancy. Being unable to provide a formal and recognised perinatal palliative care approach for management of all of these pregnancies in Ireland was the cause of much publicised distress. Many obstetricians did, indeed, provide this care before and after termination of pregnancy, but its unrecognised nature led to it receiving little attention.

The Health (Regulation of Termination of Pregnancy) Act 2018 was signed into law in Ireland in December 2018. This legislation now makes provision for termination of pregnancies where an antenatal diagnosis of an FFA/LLC within certain parameters of expected lifespan has been made. Such anomalies are usually diagnosed as part of the routine ultrasound screening in both the first and second trimesters of a pregnancy. It is also possible for anomalies to be seen at routine scans carried out as part of general antenatal care in late pregnancy.

The option of continuing the pregnancy with planned perinatal palliative care for the baby and family, or terminating the pregnancy with perinatal palliative aftercare, is then discussed with the parents by their foetal medicine specialist and obstetrician. Within the decision-making process, parents face a significant challenge related to the degree of certainty of the diagnosis, the expected prognosis and the certainty of death before or shortly after birth, as well as the meaning of the FFA/LLC diagnosis for the parents. For some parents, termination is the correct decision for them and their family at that time. It is rarely what we understand and refer to as a 'choice', but rather a traumatic 'least-worst' option. On the other hand, others may benefit from continuing with their pregnancy to term and delivering their baby. For both scenarios, a perinatal palliative care approach allows for the complete care of a baby to be provided with dignity and care. A perinatal palliative care approach can provide support and guidance to parents who make either decision following an FFA/LLC diagnosis.

Development of Perinatal Palliative Care as a Discipline

Internationally, palliative care currently has two distinct disciplines, namely adult and paediatric. When one thinks of palliative care, a hospice might come to mind or a specialist palliative care team in an acute hospital setting or even end-of-life care in a paediatric unit – but it is not all that common to think of bereavement care delivered in a maternity hospital setting. And, as such, the relatively new concept of perinatal palliative care (PNPC) has not been as readily embraced as it has in other areas of medicine. Numerous medical advances in the last decade or so in antenatal diagnostics, developments in both obstetric and neonatal care, as well as care provision at the margins of viability, have initiated several discussions on decision-making in end-of-life care for a baby and bereavement care for families experiencing perinatal death.

In essence, PNPC is not simply a pathway or protocol of care – but rather a philosophy of highly planned and professional care for a baby and his/her parents following antenatal diagnosis and expected birth with a fatal foetal anomaly or life-limiting condition. Juxtaposed within this environment are medical science, the foremost technology, deep questions of ethics and belief systems, all of which intermingle in ways that affect each individual differently. The aim of this care is to ensure that both baby and parents are looked after physically, emotionally and spiritually from diagnosis through to birth and death.

Albeit that it is off to a slow start, there is a growing evidence base for PNPC and the role of structured care pathways to help healthcare professionals optimise the care they are delivering in such scenarios. PNPC is an active and comprehensive approach to care, from the moment a diagnosis is given, right through the child's birth, life, death and beyond. The fulcrum of this care is the multidisciplinary healthcare team who must embrace the physical, emotional, spiritual and social elements of the bereavement, while focusing on quality-of-life enhancement for the baby and unwavering support for the grieving family. The care that parents receive during this time can shape their entire grieving process. Whether a person of faith, or of no professed faith, perinatal death profoundly challenges our sense of meaning and often provokes polarised viewpoints for people. For some, their faith or philosophical belief structure can be their support throughout their grieving process or even foster a deeper relationship for them; while for others, such loss can shake the very foundations of their belief or faith system.

Current Situation

The provision of the National Standards for Bereavement Care following Pregnancy Loss and Perinatal Death (NSBC) in Ireland in 2016 sought to bring consistency of high-quality care for all who experience pregnancy loss and perinatal death regardless of the circumstances.

In terms of perinatal palliative care, the NSBC were designed to guide care in two circumstances: in the case of antenatally diagnosed FFA/LLC, and the inevitable birth of a pre-term, pre-viable baby. The pathway of care was designed, prior to the 2019 legislation, to enable clinical staff to deliver streamlined, excellent quality and ongoing care to families, as well as to develop advanced care plans in appropriate scenarios. For the first time, the NSBC articulated that ongoing care should also be provided to women who chose to travel abroad for a termination of pregnancy. It was significant that this care pathway was introduced before the enactment of the current legislation for the provision of termination in Ireland. The standards also highlighted the importance of training and the provision of support services for staff involved in the provision of bereavement care.

The NSBC have been updated in 2021 to include care from the time of diagnosis of an FFA/LLC, in addition to covering all areas of pregnancy loss – early and late miscarriage, stillbirth, intrauterine and intrapartum death, as well as terminations of pregnancy. Following on from the NSBC, work was done to devise and implement care pathways specific to each type of pregnancy loss, with step-by-step guidance to aid both healthcare workers and families to develop a personalised, comprehensive and tailored care plan to look after them throughout their bereavement and beyond.

Perinatal palliative care is an approach rather than a 'place', and this care is provided in the place that is most appropriate for each family. For many, this will be in the comfort and familiarity of home, supported by healthcare staff; for others it will be in hospital. While the opportunity to provide this care in Ireland is a step in the right direction, challenges remain for both healthcare professionals and parents. The challenge of prognostication of 'lethality' and expected life span remain challenging – as they do in all palliative care.

The development of comprehensive perinatal palliative care in Ireland has enabled us to provide compassionate and high-quality care to all babies and families when faced with the devastating reality of a limited lifespan. This area is characterised by stigma for some and immense pain and desolation for all. Caring for parents who are faced with heart-rending choices for a much-loved baby, the common desire and wish of both healthcare providers and parents should always be to provide the best care for each baby.

Sources and Further Reading:

Stacey Power, Sarah Meaney and Keelin O'Donoghue, 'The Incidence of Fatal Fetal Anomalies associated with Perinatal Mortality in Ireland', *Prenatal Diagnosis*, 40:5 (April, 2020), 549–56, doi: https://doi.org/10.1002/pd.5642.

Áine Ní Laoire *et al.*, 'Perinatal Palliative Care', in Richard Hain *et al.* (eds), *Oxford Textbook of Palliative Care for Children* (3rd ed., Oxford, 2021).

Health Service Executive, *National Standards for Bereavement Care following Pregnancy Loss and Perinatal Death, Version 2* (2021).

Stacey Power, Sarah Meaney and Keelin O'Donoghue, 'Fetal Medicine Specialist Experiences of Providing a New Service of Termination of Pregnancy for Fatal Fetal Anomaly: A Qualitative Study', *BJOG: An International Journal of Obstetrics and Gynaecology* 128:4 (March, 2021), 676–84, doi: https://doi.org/10.1111/1471-0528.16502.

72

Birth, Miscarriage and Motherhood

Máirín MacCarron

… I had seen birth and death,
but had thought they were different; this birth was
Hard and bitter agony for us, Like Death, our death.
                T.S. Eliot, *Journey of the Magi*

The close relationship between birth and death is perhaps not so surprising to women, many of whom bear physical witness to that narrow line during pregnancy. It is estimated that one in five pregnancies ends in miscarriage, which can occur for a variety of reasons. As the precise cause cannot always be determined, this can lead to elevated levels of anxiety in subsequent pregnancies. The circumstances around miscarriage vary greatly and the grieving process similarly varies: some miscarriages occur so early, one may barely have had time to get used to the idea of being pregnant (if one even knew), while those who suffer repeated losses endure a particularly pointed grief. The experience of grief following miscarriage can also be difficult if the rest of the world is oblivious to the loss or engages with it in an abstract way. Recent attempts to address these concerns by the medical establishment in Ireland recognise that the loss is often no less to the prospective parents than if the baby had been born, even though society does not respond in the same way.

There is also a general, perhaps unconscious, sense that women who experience miscarriage, but have other children, suffer either a transitory loss or perhaps do not suffer the loss at all. They, of course, have the pleasure of a successful pregnancy or pregnancies and the joy that comes with welcoming a child into the world. However, it diminishes the experience of pregnancy to assume that someone, no matter how many children they may already have, does not feel a deep sorrow for the nearly life, the almost birth. Nor do later healthy pregnancies entirely efface the 'hard and bitter agony' of such losses. I know Irish women of different generations with healthy children, and sometimes grandchildren, who speak in hushed tones about other 'disappointments', as though any grief they might feel is somehow less real or less painful.

The deep trauma of miscarriage was experienced by my mother in 1975, when she suffered a miscarriage at fourteen weeks of pregnancy. At that point, she had been married for several years and feared she would never have children. Over the next nine years, she went on to have three of us, though not without incident, as she had a threatened miscarriage while pregnant with me: this prevented her from going to see her mother in Manchester before she died, further binding birth and death together for my mother. Her experience left my mother with a deep anxiety around pregnancy that endured for the rest of her life. This was most apparent when my sister-in-law was pregnant and my mother did not want to talk about it to anyone. On one occasion, about three months before the birth of her first grandchild, one of my friends innocently asked if she was excited about the baby, to which they received a clipped 'Yes' in reply, followed by a swift change of subject; I explained her unusual abruptness afterwards.

At the time of my mother's death, in 2017, she delightedly bore the title of 'Granny Mac' to two adored grandchildren and she was beyond grateful for the many blessings in her life. However, I came face-to-face with the full significance of the miscarriage in her life the summer after she died. We were at the point of organising her memorial card and I knew she had received many such mementoes for deceased family members and friends over the years. I remembered she always kept some in her missal, which remained on a bookshelf in the kitchen at home. She had a traditional Sunday missal but, as she was a lay reader in the local parish, for several years hence she had received a paperback Sunday missal every November containing the full liturgy for the coming church year. I quickly realised that she kept very few memorial cards in this missal: those for her parents were inserted at the liturgical feasts closest to their birthdays and there were a few other small single-ply cards with notes on the reverse that she had received over the years, including a recent one from me. The two that took my breath away were very simple cards with hand-written notes on the back sending her strength and good wishes. In my mother's handwriting, on both, was the year 1975. One was from 'Sr M.O.' who I imagine was a member of the Presentation Sisters community in whose secondary school she taught; the other was addressed to 'Mrs MacCarron' so undoubtedly was from one of her students. Those expressions of sympathy meant so much to my mother that she not only kept them for forty-two years, but every year she transferred them to her new missal. My mother was not a morose person: she lived life to the full and was happy, generous, kind, thoughtful and positive. I like to think that she kept those cards for over four decades to remind her of the kindness and support she had received during a deeply traumatic time in her life, not as a memorial to her private grief. However, the remarkable longevity of those cards speaks to the fundamental significance of the miscarriage in her life.

Birth and death are inextricably bound together, never more so than in the trauma of miscarriage, and the physical experience of pregnancy and miscarriage are borne in a unique way by women. However, despite the large numbers of women who suffer miscarriage – 20 percent of pregnancies ending in this way is a substantial number – there is a silence around the topic in both contemporary society and modern Irish history. Recent studies of topics such as fertility rates, abortion and contraception have revealed much about heretofore undisclosed aspects of Irish society and the lives of Irish women. However, we should not neglect the inherently private turmoil that so many people experience in miscarriage; and remember that, although such pain may be alleviated by successful pregnancies, it is not entirely dissipated.

Further Reading:

Mary Ann Bolger, 'Memorial Cards in Irish Funerary Culture,' in Salvador Ryan (ed.), *Death and the Irish: A Miscellany* (Dublin, 2016).

Caitriona Clear, *Women's Voices in Ireland: Women's Magazines in the 1950s and 60s* (London, 2016).

Mary Daly, 'Marriage, Fertility and Women's Lives in Twentieth-Century Ireland (*c.* 1900–*c.* 1970)', *Women's History Review* 15 (2006), 571–85.

The Miscarriage Association of Ireland. Available at: http://www.miscarriage.ie/.

73

Birth on Screen: How Childbirth is Depicted in Irish Film

Kevin Hargaden

The childbirth scene is a familiar trope in Hollywood movies. The sudden onset of labour, the panicked drive to the hospital, the shots of the sweating mother encouraged to push by the midwife, the hapless, but enthusiastic dad – often the source of comedic relief – struggling to hold it all together, and then the great piercing scream of the newborn heard by the friends and family anxiously waiting outside, bringing the happy episode to a satisfying climax.

This trope is not to be found in Irish cinema. Depictions of childbirth are considerably more ambiguous in Irish films. They are framed, almost without exception, by a combination of looming threats: a society quick to judge mothers, a State apparatus, implemented by the Church, willing to exact punishment for failing to satisfy imagined moral standards, and often a complete absence from the scene of the father figure.

This is most painfully explored in films that deal with the institutional abuse of mothers and children, such as *The Magdalene Sisters*, where childbirth is never actually on screen, but represents the entire frame for the profoundly troubling stories that are told. Peter Mullan's 2002 film focuses on four women, two of whom are consigned to the laundry for giving birth out of wedlock. The second scene of the film introduces us to Rose. Her moral intuition is one of the few persistent lights in a deeply dark movie. She has just given birth, and surrounded by authority figures but with no father in sight, she insists that the baby born to her, and taken from her, is beautiful. Crispina, the other woman who finds herself in the laundry due to childbirth, bears the sharpest tragedy in a

FIGURES 23 AND 24: *Stills from the motion picture* Hush-a-Bye Baby *(1990), produced by Tommy Collins and directed by Margo Harkin (by kind permission of Besom Productions, Northern Ireland).*

film heavy with sorrow. The viewer is left to assume that she gave birth to a boy conceived in rape, perhaps at the hands of a priest. Her sister rears that child. They visit when they can, as they can, by standing by a gate hoping to catch sight of Crispina, who spirals into madness under the torturous conditions of her captivity. *The Magdalene Sisters* relentlessly convicts twentieth-century Ireland of a psychotic fixation on female sexuality, but watching it again in 2020, it testifies to the licence granted to men to abscond from situations they create. Only women give birth; in Irish film, men have turned that fact into a loophole to liberate themselves of all responsibility.

Perhaps the best-loved Irish film dealing with pregnancy and childbirth is Stephen Frears' 1993 adaptation of Roddy Doyle's novel, *The Snapper*. Sharon Curley becomes unexpectedly pregnant at the age of 20, after a drunken encounter with an older man, George Burgess. Burgess is married, an acquaintance of Sharon's father, Dessie. Sharon protects his identity, apparently out of embarrassment and shame born from the circumstances. As the film unfolds, Sharon's trauma from the encounter prompts the viewer to consider whether it is actually rape. *The Snapper* is witty, warm, empathic and fundamentally hopeful, which explains why it is so treasured. But even though it is explicit in its delight at the arrival of Sharon's daughter, and the loving relationship between Dessie and his daughter is the narrative frame of the film, it remains the case that the child's father is a nefarious character; his absence to be welcomed. Sharon gives birth to the child without accompaniment. Waking from her post-labour slumber, she can only laugh as she realises that she has unthinkingly named the girl Georgina. The trauma of conception is overcome by the joy of delivery. The final freeze-frame features the wider Curley clan rushing into the ward to welcome their newest member.

The theme of the absent father takes a very different shape in Margo Harkin's 1990 *Hush-a-Bye-Baby*. Set in Derry, in 1984, against the backdrop of the 'supergrass' trials, 15-year-old Goretti Friel hides her pregnancy while her first love, Ciarán, has been swept up in a wide-reaching internment. Goretti's sincere faith, particularly her devotion to Mary, is a recurring theme through the movie. The question of continuing the pregnancy or pursuing a termination is artfully explored as Goretti cracks eggs into a cake mix she is preparing while a conversation on the radio in the background discusses the 8th amendment to the Irish constitution, which had passed the year before, prohibiting abortion in all cases. In another scene set on a beach, Goretti sits and observes the relentless tide come in and out, and the viewer keenly understands the waves of problems threatening to engulf her. Rejected by Ciarán, when she finally gets to visit him, Goretti attempts and fails to administer a home-made abortion. Social opprobrium of unmarried mothers is everywhere Goretti looks: in the jokes of her friends, the conversation of her family, the literature on her school curriculum. Even as Ciarán repents of his initial reaction and promises to stand by her, the weight of the pregnancy falls entirely on her young shoulders. Having ratcheted the tension to breaking point, secrecy is no longer possible in the final scene when Goretti's labour begins suddenly one Christmas night, at home. The father is not there, but the alienation of the mother runs much more deeply as religion, family and the wider culture are clearly set against her.

But even in lighter fare, the unreliability of the dad is notable. In Shelly Love's 2019 comedy – also set in Derry – *A Bump in the Road*, Bronagh Gallagher plays Pamela, a 44-year-old single mother to a teenager, who finds herself pregnant after a one-night stand with a 24-year-old man from the same neighbourhood. At three critical points in the narrative, Barry, the father, is given opportunities to embrace his parental role and, in each instance, he rejects them. The father of Pamela's first child is similarly feckless, declaring to his daughter at her sixteenth birthday dinner that he 'doesn't like to be tied down'. When push comes to shove, and the baby is to be born, Pamela's daughter, Allegra, who was initially mortified with embarrassment, becomes her chief support. *A Bump in the Road* is set in a drastically changed Derry, where the coercive force of religion has receded, as has the trauma of the Troubles. Men remain fundamentally irresponsible.

Interweaving the themes of pregnancy and religion in modern Irish cinema is surely an expression of the on-going project of processing how the State, the Church and wider society colluded through the twentieth century effectively to criminalise fertility. While an unambiguously positive narrative about pregnancy can be imagined, they are difficult to locate on the Irish screen. Among films that could be discussed at further length we would list *Sinners*, directed by Aisling Walsh in 2002; Richard Standhaven's 1998 adaptation of Deirdre Purcell's novel, *Falling for a Dancer* and, in its own way, Stephen Frears' critically-acclaimed 2013 film *Philomena*. In each of these films – and there are others – the complex entanglement of an oppressive society, a repressive religion and the weakness of men, who paradoxically benefit from an invincible patriarchy, is explored.

The experience of childbirth can be profound, transformative, even numinous. This clichéd truth is cast in a strange new light when we consider that such a scene is rarely depicted in Irish cinema. Film is one of the primary means by which a society comes to understand the stories it tells about itself. The depictions of childbirth in Irish cinema suggest the pains of labour are dwarfed by the alienation and shame commonly inflicted upon women who gave birth outside of the approved strictures. Female friendship is one ever-present consolation. We might anticipate that societal shame and religious repression would loom large in cinematic depictions of childbirth in Ireland. But the recurring theme of the deficiency of men is almost more prominent than such depictions. Unknowingly, perhaps, Irish society is using its films to come to terms with the continuing modes of patriarchy that persist, even in an age of increasing secularity, prosperity and social liberalism.

74

Birth in Prison: A Second Separation

Keith Adams

Despite being associated with a diminishment of life and the absence of hope, prisons have historically always had pregnant women, nursing mothers and young babies within their walls. Pregnancy, the quintessential human experience of life knitting together and hope forming for a future unknown, represents an incongruity within an institution of punishment and reformation. Since 2016, ten women have given birth while in custody in Ireland, with all babies delivered in a nearby maternity hospital. At present, babies can now only be present in prison if they are born to mothers in custody. It was not always so.

In the nineteenth century, while some babies were born behind bars, others would accompany their incarcerated mothers to prison, as responsibility for childcare was the sole domain of the mother. Between 1854 and 1882, the female convict prison, where all women in Ireland who were sentenced to penal servitude of at least three years were sent, admitted 3,740 women and 214 children. In addition, based on annual reports from the time, the historian Elaine Farrell estimates that at least ninety-eight infants were born behind prison walls during this period and stayed in prison with their mothers.

Positively, and humanely, increasing restrictions were imposed on the admission of infants to prison as the nineteenth century progressed. However, pregnant women and new mothers and babies remain a feature of Irish prison life. Ireland has two female prisons: Dublin's Dóchas Centre which opened in 1999, the first new prison for women in almost 200 years, and Limerick female prison. In the first nine months of 2019, twenty-three pregnant women were in custody in Ireland's female prisons, an upward trend from a total of twenty-one pregnant women in both 2017 and 2018. Pregnant women receive maternity care in the prison to which they are committed until the end of the second trimester. At the beginning of the third trimester, any pregnant women in Limerick prison are then transferred to the Dóchas Centre as it has a mother and baby unit for accommodation post-partum. No information is available on official protocols in relation to women in custody giving birth, with most decisions being made at the discretion of the prison governor in relation to birthing partners and temporary release.

Prisons are emotional places. Within the daily rhythms of a modern prison, people – both prisoners and staff – are in a continually heightened emotional state, adjusting to the loss of freedom, navigating an environment where every movement is choreographed and surveilled, becoming accustomed to an environment where tobacco functions as currency and violence is never far from the surface. Each slight, however fleeting or unintentional, demands a response. Any sign of weakness, such as crying in public, is stringently avoided for fear of being seen as an easy target. With every act under scrutiny, and interminable time to reflect, heightened emotion takes a toll on each person within a prison.

When a pregnant woman is incarcerated, the space within a prison to process and account for emotions can be amplified. Lucy Baldwin, a criminologist, argues that the natural process of how maternal emotions and the maternal role are assembled is challenged in prison. Pregnancy, giving birth and the post-partum months are already emotionally heightened times, including struggles with former and emerging identity; senses of fulfilment; fears for the future; worries over money; or, simply, hearts filled with relief after years of disappointment and grief. The opportunity to engage with these anxieties and joys is necessary to allow a woman to process this life-changing and life-affirming event. Experiencing all that in prison is doubly hard.

Naturally, not every pregnancy will carry to term. Enduring the end of new life and the extinguishment of hope within the confines of a prison, separated from family support, can be an excruciating grief to bear, amplified by the slowness of time. Prison, already an emotionally fraught environment, is not an appropriate place for pregnant women or new mothers as emotions, particularly negative emotions, are only further intensified. Coupled with Ireland's female prisons being the most over-crowded prisons within the prison estate, the emotional space to assemble for a new role is not available.

Birth, at its simplest, is a separation. Ruth Carr, a Northern Irish poet, writes in *Body Politic* of, amid the medicalisation of birth, the separation of the two bodies which happens:

> Far beyond the clinical ceiling of this partitioned room
> Beyond the unsolicited stab of pethidine in my thigh
> Beyond the refusal to deliver you into my arms
> Beyond blocked roads and minds,
>
> You came out
> Of my body
> To claim your own
>
> Your voice breaking over every fixed thing
>
> Bearing me on its tide.

Many contemporary women writers have explored the trauma which birth entails. Katharina Walter an academic of literature at Innsbruck University, is helpful in interpreting the symbolism within parturition. The expected injury or scar produced by the separation of mother and child in childbirth acts as 'a constant reminder of our incompleteness and vulnerability as human beings'. The navel, where the umbilical cord transferred the nutrition required for growth and development for nine months, records 'both oneness with the mother in pregnancy and the subsequent separation'.

In Donal Ryan's luminous novel, *All We Shall Know*, Melody Shee is pregnant with a baby – not her husband's – leading to estrangement and social ostracisation when the identity of the real father is revealed. Resolved to give the child up for adoption, Melody's certainty is undermined as she reflects on their connectedness in the stillness of the maternity ward:

> He finished his bottle in the end and he's still now, blinking slowly, his eyes fixed on mine. The warmth of him goes into me and through me. Newborn babies can't see well, they say, but my baby can. He can see right into me, now that he is outside of me. All the sounds of the corridor are muted and faraway, and the traffic outside and the lawnmowers and the singing birds; all things orbit us, our perfect mass. My little eight-pound incarnation of perfect goodness, of love, my little god.

Though Melody's pregnancy was difficult and though adoption promised an escape from her travails, the strength of the bonding between mother and baby shattered her ill-fated attempt to remain disconnected from her new son. Uncertainty often births certainty.

After the first separation and subsequent bonding, new mothers in prison have to endure a second separation. Prison rules allow for a child to remain in the care of his or her mother until the age of twelve months. At this stage, the child is committed to the care of family members or the State while the mother serves out the remainder of her sentence. A visiting regime is established, but little can lessen the heartbreak of this second separation. The second separation occurs as mother and child have bonded, both secure in their mutual vulnerability to each other. For many female prisoners, who have been continually let down and failed by others – family, friends, intimate partners – for their entire life, this baby may be the only person who can see right into them. For the child, the pain of the separation from his mother is untold.

Within contemporary Western societies, birth tends to be framed as transformative for mothers, but the experience of motherhood in prison is disrupted and fractured: firstly, by the emotionally magnified space and secondly, by the second separation. This second separation is often not experienced by mothers outside of prison. If, as prison reformers declare, loss of personal freedom is the punishment, rather than the conditions of the prison, then work is required on how much this second separation constitutes a punishment for mothers and babies.

Sources:

Lucy Baldwin, 'Motherhood disrupted: Reflections of post-prison mothers', *Emotion, Space and Society*, 26 (February, 2018), 49–56.

Ruth Carr, *Body Politic*. Available at: http://www.troublesarchive.com/artforms/poetry/piece/body-politic.

Elaine Farrell, '"Poor prison flowers": Convict mothers and their children in Ireland, 1853–1900', *Social History*, 41:2 (2016), 171–91.

Donal Ryan, *All We Shall Know* (London, 2016).

Katharina Walter, '"Suspended between the Two Worlds": Gestation Metaphors and Representations of Childbirth in Contemporary Irish Women's Poetry', *Estudios Irlandeses*, 5 (2010), 102–12.

75

LGBTQ Surrogacy:
The Making of an Irish Citizen

Patrick Hughes

'The first time I was sure I wanted us to be parents was during the first dance at our wedding'. Adam and Ben had been joined by friends and family to celebrate their wedding in the summer of 2015, just two months after Ireland voted to legalise marriage between two people without distinction as to their sex, the first country in the world to do so by popular vote. 'Just before the wedding, our friends told us they were considering surrogacy. It was a lightbulb moment; that a gay couple we knew could be parents sparked a fire in us'. Within months, Adam and Ben started the research on becoming parents via surrogacy and found Ireland in a legalistic limbo, waiting for the Assisted Human Reproduction Bill (2017), itself subject to much criticism, to pass into law. As commercial (paid-for) surrogacy was not permissible, they looked overseas, finding many online forums arguing for the US as the best location for health and safety outcomes, as well as to guarantee their (and their baby's) rights. 'Surrogacy is not for the faint hearted, not least because it's so complicated', says Adam. 'Three agencies are needed: the first to select an egg donor; second, an IVF clinic for embryo creation; third, a surrogacy agency to find a suitable surrogate'. The bearing of a baby is one thing; ensuring it has appropriate rights quite another.

While the idea that a family could consist of two husbands and their surrogate children seemed practically unimaginable in the Ireland of just twenty years ago, there have been LGBTQ parents as long as there have been families. These parents, our kin, haven't always had the language or space to express their gender or orientation, nor their family and society as reliable places to find acceptance and love. Our queer cousins haven't always been visible, even if they have been hiding in plain sight.

Visibility matters. The thousands of 'comings out' that created a visible groundswell resulting in equal marriage were individual steps towards demystifying sexual and gender identities in Irish society and connecting LGBTQ visibility with human rights. In 2011, then US Secretary of State, Hillary Clinton declared to the UN that 'Gay rights are human rights'. Many voices in a long-active Irish LGBTQ community had made that connection, but Clinton's words gave global legitimacy to gay rights as human rights, a bold speech given her audience. The journey of LGBTQ people and their allies has been from criminal outcasts to marginal group to social acceptability, an onerous process not only globally, but also in an Ireland once knee-deep in religious norms.

The process of visibility continues. 'There's a continual coming out as a gay dad,' says Adam. 'I was at the tills in Mothercare with our son, chatting to a woman in front of me. Suddenly, she said in disbelief, "Oh, is he *yours?*" and you could see her confusion as I suppose people can tell that I'm gay'. While the Referendum widened the pool of who can marry, knowledge about the need for parenting laws is low and slow to enact. There is something of a discourse saying 'Sure, aren't you equal now, since you got marriage'. Adam claims, 'We're not equal and our children aren't equal. We want the same protections and rights as my brother's family, or our neighbour's family'. We need to step through the process of surrogacy to understand how this came to pass.

The Making of an Irish Citizen

While the need to work with a surrogate arises from many different circumstances, same sex male couples have a biological imperative: an egg and a surrogate are needed (not always from the same person). Once Adam and Ben opened the door to parenthood, the initial contact with egg, IVF and surrogacy agencies started a daunting process that, in their case, strengthened their will to be dads. 'Working with each agency is about making the right match,' says Adam. 'The surrogacy agency vetted us and prospective surrogates so thoroughly, they will only recommend a match if they're pretty certain it's spot on. For us, that took nine months and our "match" was so perfect, we'd never swap Kirsty for anything'. Adam and Ben chose a separate egg donor carefully, before travelling to a clinic in

Oregon to provide sperm and arrange the impregnation of the eggs at an IVF clinic. However, it was the surrogate relationship that was paramount: 'Kirsty had a long-established professional career, three kids and a hugely supportive husband, all of whom we got to know.' Things went so well that when Adam and Ben arrived in the US a week before the due date, they found forty of Kirsty and her husband's family and friends surprising them with a baby shower: 'They were so proud to do this for us and their families supported them and us with no embarrassment, only happiness'.

The two couples went together to a pre-natal appointment, to find an induced birth was likely as the baby was in breech position:

> Within 24 hours, the delivery suite was full between ourselves, Kirsty and her husband, and the Consultant and Midwives. Nothing you read prepares you for birth, but we did want to bond with our child via skin-to-skin contact. As Tom was born, he rested on Kirsty until his cord was cut and then he was brought to us. I held him first and then my husband. It was the most emotional moment of our lives.

American hospitals are well-used to surrogacy and two rooms had been prepared side-by-side; little Tom in one, with his fathers, Kirsty and her husband next door. 'We were in and out all the time; Kirsty had offered to breast feed for the first few days'. Within ten days, Tom received his final pre-flight medical sign-off and, with American passport in his fathers' hands, the family were on their way home to Dublin for everyone to meet the new arrival.

Adam and Ben acknowledge that few couples go down this route as it is difficult and expensive. However, they had not gambled on the Irish legislative system being so problematic. In the US state where Tom was born, his birth certificate records Adam and Ben as 'Parent 1' and 'Parent 2'. Adam says: 'This is the root of the problem in Irish law. Kirsty is considered Tom's mother, even though she has no genetic relationship to him as we used an egg donor. She says she loves him like a nephew or godson, but he is not her son. What is even crazier in Irish law is that Kirsty's husband is considered our child's *father*. Under certain circumstances, he could end up having legal or financial responsibility for a child with which he has no relationship.'

Tom's incomplete journey to Irish citizenship relies not only on his fathers' nationality, but their visibility and voice in advocating change to Irish law.

> To obtain Irish citizenship for Tom required one of us to prove paternity and secure the renunciation of rights by Kirsty and her husband. Tom's other father has had to get guardianship. That gives some protections to talk to the school or hospital, but when our son is eighteen, guardianship ends and, by law, you revert to having no technical relationship with your child, with implications for very practical things, like inheritance tax. We are both Tom's dads.

It seems that everyone wants the change, from the Minister to the opposition, but the reality is that the citizenship of a small number of surrogate children is much lower on everyone's list of priorities than health and housing crises. Adam and Ben do want things to move forward when they can: 'We don't receive child support as Tom is considered American, but what really leaves us in a limbo is getting his Irish passport and PPS number'.

Tom's story tells us that human and citizenship rights are always in a state of 'becoming'. The marriage referendum was not an ending but a beginning, calling on us to welcome families of all stripes into our social fabric. While the desire to have children is nothing new, for many would-be LGBTQ parents, the revolution of surrogacy came too late for them to bear and love their children. 'Yes, we did plan our son's life, but that comes from us wanting him so much to be here,' says Adam. 'Surrogate children come from a place of such love. We didn't become parents to fill a void; we did it because we wanted so much to be parents.' In an Ireland much too familiar with social and family wounds, our national healing is progressed by creating a positive legal framework to support families like Adam, Ben and Tom. Their visibility calls us to become attuned to who is invisible now, to those stories erased from our national and international narratives. It asks us how to open our hearts, politics and legislative agendas to those who need a voice.

76

Practising Birth Activism: The Campaign for Mandatory Inquests for Maternal Deaths in Ireland

Martina Hynan

> Ireland has taken a crucial first step in ensuring that families will no longer have to fight their cases at the courts to get answers about the deaths of their loved ones.
>
> Fleur van Leeuwen,
> *International Human Rights Lawyer, 15 November 2019,*
> *Final Event of The Elephant Collective, Birth Activist*
> *Group, The Copper House Gallery, Dublin*

Before 2019, the families of women who died while in the care of Ireland's maternity services had to fight to secure an inquest to learn of the circumstances surrounding her death. Up to this time, investigations into maternal deaths were not mandatory; indeed, there might not even be a robust institutional inquiry, let alone thorough public scrutiny. Obtaining a legal inquiry involved a complex and distressing process, which obliged families at a tragic time to persuade the coroner's office to review the case. Granting an inquest into a mother's death often took many years. Most families could not afford a solicitor and the majority were unaware that an inquest in the case of a maternal death was not automatic. It was as though maternal deaths did not exist in the eyes of the law. This situation needed to change.

In July 2019, the Coroners (Amendment) Act was signed into law by the President, a significant landmark in the history of birth in Ireland, which means that a coroner's inquest into a maternal death is a legal requirement for the first time. Accounts of why women die in our maternity services will now be in the public domain. This has been a hard-won battle from a committed group of community activists working tirelessly to see this legislation through. This is a brief overview of that campaign process and, in particular, how the grassroots birth activist group, The Elephant Collective, contributed to its eventual success.

This new legislation ensures that inquests for all maternal deaths will take place. Mandatory reporting of all maternal deaths, stillbirths, intrapartum deaths and infant deaths are now assured. Coroners have new powers of compellability to command compliance from hospitals surrounding their records and documentation of a maternal death, ensuring it is conducted in a timely fashion. Additionally, and crucially, legal aid for families involved in maternal death inquests will be provided. All of this will help shed much needed light on the circumstances surrounding the deaths of women in the maternity services.

Prior to this, families employed a solicitor to represent them to the coroner's office. Their legal teams had to fight for medical records from the hospitals in question. Between 2008 and 2014, eight families managed to secure inquests, and in all eight cases, verdicts of death by *medical misadventure* were recorded. Medical misadventure is defined as an unintended outcome of an intended medical action, which effectively means that mistakes were made.

The roots of this campaign lie with the battle led by sociologist and activist, Dr Jo Murphy-Lawless who fought for an inquest for Bimbo Onanuga. Bimbo, aged 32, and a refugee from Nigeria, died in the Mater Hospital, having been transferred there, unconscious, from the Rotunda Hospital on 4 March 2010. After almost three years, an inquest was held over four days in 2013. The verdict was medical misadventure.

Up to 2009, when the Maternal Death Enquiry (MDE) was established, there was no central record of maternal deaths in Ireland. From data gathered by the MDE between 2011 and 2013, we learned that there were twenty-seven maternal deaths. Of these twenty-seven, three were granted inquests; all three recorded verdicts of medical misadventure. These deaths were included in the total of eight inquests granted between 2008 and 2014.

It became increasingly evident that mandatory inquests were needed. Dr Murphy-Lawless sought the support of Clare Daly (then TD) for Bimbo Onanuga's campaign. Subsequently, Clare Daly and her team worked to initiate new legislation. Clare Daly introduced her private members' bill to reform the 1962 Coroners Act with the crucial amendment to legislate for compulsory inquests into maternal deaths.

During 2014, a growing number of concerned people coalesced around the need for legislation and vowed to support it. They became the Elephant Collective, which is made up of birth educators, midwives, midwifery students, artists and community activists. The group was determined to raise public awareness of the need for this new legislation, and lobby local and national public representatives. The name for the Elephant Collective was inspired by the fact that when an elephant gives birth, the herd surrounds her and her calf to protect them both. The Collective began by inviting people to knit squares for a commemorative quilt to remember the eight women who had died in our maternity services between 2007 and 2013. The quilt also honours the women who died and whose names we do not know because there were no mandatory inquests.

As the quilt grew, so too did the momentum behind the campaign. Very soon the idea of creating a multimedia art project to encourage the public's knowledge became a reality. In November 2015, the multimedia exhibition *Picking Up the Threads: Remaking the Fabric of Care* was launched in Dublin. At that time, it was comprised of the knitted quilt, painted portraits by Martina Hynan of the eight women who had inspired the campaign and the documentary, *Picking Up the Threads*, by Anne-Mare Green, with details from each of the eight inquests.

Between 2015 and 2019, the exhibition travelled the length and breadth of the country. Each time, members of the Elephant Collective worked with local community groups and activists to create better understanding of maternal deaths and why they were happening, and to garner the much needed support for the new legislation.

In 2016, Clare County Councillor Mary Howard learned of the campaign and within weeks, put forward a motion supporting the legislation before Clare County Council; it was passed unanimously. Spurred on by this decisive action, the Elephant Collective stepped up

FIGURE 25: *The quilt commemorating the eight women who died in our maternity services between 2007 and 2013, and also those whose names we do not know because there were no mandatory inquests.*

its lobbying of county councils nationwide. Within a short space of time, twenty-four county councils lent their support.

While the Elephant Collective's multimedia exhibition was building support for the legislation, Clare Daly (TD) continued to progress her private members' bill through the Dáil (Irish parliament). However, in May 2017, it was blocked by the government, and everyone feared the worst. Clare Daly and her team acted at once to meet with then Minister for Justice, Frances Fitzgerald, and to the relief of the Collective, the Minister announced that the government would draft a separate bill to secure mandatory inquests for maternal deaths. When, in June 2017, Charlie Flanagan took over as Minister for Justice, again there was concern that the promised draft legislation should remain a priority. Clare Daly and her team continued to press for progress on its introduction and to craft a strong series of measures for what was a new government bill.

A significant strength of the campaign was the synergy between Clare Daly and her committed team, and the Elephant Collective. A parallel

FIGURE 26: *Eight women who died in our maternity services between 2007 and 2013, and whose families secured inquests. In all eight cases, verdicts of death by 'medical misadventure' were recorded.*

Top row, L–R: Bimbo Onanuga, d. March 2010; Dhara Kivlehan, d. September 2010; Evelyn Flanagan, d. October 2007; Tania McCabe, d. March 2007.

Bottom row, L–R: Sally Rowlette, d. February 2013; Jennifer Crean, d. February 2009; Savita Halappanavar, d. October 2012; Nora Hyland, d. February 2012.

and critical strength was the Elephant Collective's work with local communities to actively engage with the legislative campaign. Members of the Collective, community groups and families directly affected were present at all stages of debate and corresponded extensively with legislators across the country as well as holding local events. Our goal was reached in July 2019 when the bill completed all its stages in the Dáil and Seanad (Senate).

The Elephant Collective exemplifies a form of social practice in action, supporting creative interventions at grassroots level to draw attention to this critical need. On 15 November 2019, the Elephant Collective hosted its closing event at the Copper House, Gallery, Dublin to thank everyone involved. Clare Daly, now Member of the European

Parliament (MEP), spoke at this event, as did the human rights lawyer Fleur van Leeuwen and Dr Jo Murphy-Lawless.

The Coroners (Amendment) Act 2019 safeguards inquests for all maternal deaths. It places Ireland in full compliance with Article 2 of the European Convention on Human Rights. Now when a woman dies in our maternity services, families are spared the anguish of battling to learn the reasons for the death of their wives, partners and mothers of their children. As Clare Daly expressed it:

> Mandatory inquests for maternal deaths ... will have a triple effect. It will give families the fullest picture about the train of events that led to the death of a loved one. It will give clinicians and the HSE [Health Service Executive] a crucial insight into where the system is failing women. Finally, it will give us, as policymakers and those holding the purse strings, the information to make our services safer.
>
> Clare Daly, TD,
> Committee for Justice and Equality,
> 12 December 2018

Although this is a massive achievement with regard to accountability and scrutiny in cases of maternal death and the first law of its kind internationally, a concerted effort is needed to address the ongoing acute issues affecting maternal healthcare in Ireland. Therefore, we must continue to ask painful, troubling questions of our maternity services.

Further Reading:

Nadine Edwards, Rosemary Mander and Jo Murphy-Lawless (eds), *Untangling the Maternity Crisis* (Abingdon, 2018).

Jo Murphy-Lawless, 'A Brief Glimpse into Hell', *AIMS Journal*, 26:1 (2014).

Lorna Siggins, 'Ireland "failing international obligations" in maternal deaths inquests', *The Irish Times*, 5 February 2017.

77

A Snapshot of Irish Birth Trends over the Last Century

Roy K. Philip

Baby boom is the term coined when an unprecedented increase in fertility rate and birth rate happens in a region or country, out-of-sync with the pre-existing demographic and population trends. Despite the improvements and uptake in birth planning options, there are many other inherent human factors that could still result in a baby boom. In the USA, 'baby boomer' denotes an individual who was born between 1946 and 1964. Baby boomers emerged at the end of the Second World War when birth rates around the world spiked. The baby boomer generation makes up a substantial proportion of the world population, especially in developed countries.

The earliest theory of baby boom in social sciences was proposed by Richard Easterlin in 1966. He suggested that generations entering adulthood under favourable economic conditions, relative to those that prevailed in their childhood, were more inclined to have larger families. Human reproductive behaviour shows significant variations at individual and population levels, and behavioural ecologist B.V. Dawson proposed 'adaptive hypotheses' to explain this variation. Variation in fertility, in both traditional and industrialised populations, reflects a trade-off between reproductive rate and 'parental investment'.

The first baby boom in Ireland occurred during the State of Emergency which existed in the country during the Second World War. Laws on contraception were restrictive in Ireland and the baby boom was more prolonged. The Irish birth rate fell during the 1980s, coinciding with the economic downturn and legalisation of contraception in 1979. The positive change in Irish economic fortune (during the 'Celtic Tiger') in the mid-1990s led to an immediate and substantial upward trend in births. The rate continued to rise until 2008 followed by a steady decline thereafter as per the Central Statistics Office (CSO) of Ireland. When the economic boom crashed, along with a 'property bubble', the baby boom went into reverse (baby bust). Perhaps the tougher economic times, reduction in wages, property bubble, high childcare cost and greater uncertainty had some negative influence on people's decisions about whether to have more children.

Through the mid-1990s, there was another type of lesser-known boom, involving multiple births in Ireland. The number of twins, triplets and quadruplets born in the country increased significantly. Many neonatal intensive care units (NICU) couldn't cope with the steady influx of premature and very low birth weight (VLBW, <1,500 gm birth weight) higher order multiples, often with associated significant neonatal morbidities. This was the result of a surge in the uptake of artificial reproductive techniques including in-vitro fertilisation (IVF), use of ovulation stimulation medications and the lack of legal restrictions on the number of embryos allowed to be replaced during IVF cycles. While the natural twinning rate is approximately 1 in 80, that through IVF could be as high as 1 in 4. Subsequent legislation in this regard, and medical awareness, eased the rapid surge or 'multiple births boom'. However, with the wider availability, uptake and affordability of assisted reproduction techniques, multiple birth frequency remained high. As an example, in 2004, there were 1,849 twins born in Ireland compared to 2,526 in 2013. Triplets in 2004 were 54 and in 2013 there were 87 (CSO).

During the last decade, the Irish birth rate contracted significantly (a reduction of almost one fifth) and it is now the lowest since records began 150 years ago. A recent national survey (2018) in Britain found that 87.0 percent of women and 73.8 percent of men accessed at least one source of contraceptive supplies in the previous year. Socio-economic factors, parental education, accessible health care systems and the perceived cost of fertility regulation, as compared to benefits expected from children, also powerfully influence contraceptive uptake. With termination of pregnancy legalised in Ireland, economic and academic achievements considered as societal priorities, the age of child-bearing rising and child care becoming more expensive, it is probable that the downward trend in the Irish birth rate will prevail. However, compared to many other EU member states, Ireland still has one of the higher birth rates (12.352 births per 1000 in 2020 even with a decline of 2.66 percent from 2019).

Now, with the arrival of COVID-19, is there an impact on Irish birth rates? Will there be an accentuated bust or a mini boom? Following the first report of COVID-19 in the city of Wuhan in the Hubei province of China in December 2019 followed by a World Health Organization (WHO) declared pandemic on 11 March 2020, populations around the world were increasingly homebound. Based on societal and family norms, cultural variations, as well as general economic and political stability, countries and regions have a predicted birth rate which remains at a reasonably steady state. Could this be altered by the widespread COVID-19 mitigation measures, societal impacts and the behavioural responses of couples in relation to fertility decisions? Even though there is no obvious evidence of a widespread COVID-19 baby boom (COVID babies) yet in Ireland (as of November 2020), we will have to wait for a little longer to ascertain the real impact of the summative effects of homebound fertile couples, social isolation, economic concerns and commuting restrictions as part of the COVID-19 lockdowns.

Some interesting and unexpected positive news that has emerged in the midst of the pandemic concerns a significant reduction in premature births, particularly involving VLBW infants during the COVID-19 lockdown. Our report from Limerick in June 2020 was one of the first in the world suggesting such an association, along with an independent Danish study. While an Irish paper published an unprecedented 73 percent reduction in VLBW infants during the COVID-19 lockdown of 2020 compared to the previous twenty years, Danish research reported a 90 percent reduction in extreme prematurity when compared to the preceding five years. Since then, many reports from around the world have reported similar observations. Is this just a cluster of regionalised decline in births of very premature infants during lockdown or a sign of a widespread 'preterm bust'? What could be the reason for this intriguing observation? Perhaps the summative effects of multiple socio-environmental factors operating with maternal behavioural adaptations during lockdown has resulted in the observed reduction in premature births. These modifiable factors include: opportunities to work from home, less work-related stress, less commuting, better maternal nutrition, reduced exposure to common infectious agents, a decline in environmental pollution, better sleep and rest, better partner and family support, uptake of maternal immunisations, economic assistance, avoidance of alcohol, cigarette smoke and street drugs.

Whichever way we look at the trends and outcomes of Irish births over a century, it is mostly positive. From the poverty-stricken and infectious diseases rampant in the early twentieth century, with a high birth rate coupled with a very high infant mortality rate (IMR), Irish mothers, newborn babies and infants are healthier and safer in the early twenty-first century. As per the CSO, the IMR in Ireland, in 1916, was 81.3 per 1,000 (p/t) live births, whereas that in 2014 was 3.7 p/t live births, further decreasing to 2.536 in 2019. The impact of COVID-19 will also hopefully ease off over the coming years; however, it is a certainty that nature will challenge societies, including ours, with new and previously unknown threats, and it is our hope that humanity finds ways to survive and to protect the offspring of the next generation.

Further Reading:

Jan Van Bavel and David S. Reher, 'The Baby Boom and its Causes: What We Know and What We Need to Know', *Population and Development Review*, 39:2 (2013), 257–88.

Central Statistics Office (CSO) Ireland. Available at: https://www.cso.ie/en/releasesandpublications/ep/p-1916/1916irl/bmd/births/.

Roy K. Philip *et al.*, 'Reduction in Preterm births during the COVID-19 Lockdown in Ireland: A "Natural Experiment" Allowing Analysis of Data from the Prior Two Decades', medRxiv (2020), doi: https://doi:10.1101/2020.06.03.20121442.

Gitte Hedermann *et al.*, 'Changes in Premature Birth Rates during the Danish Nationwide COVID-19 Lockdown: A Nationwide Register-based Prevalence Proportion Study', medRxiv (2020), doi: https://doi.org/10.1101/2020.05.22.20109793.

United Nations (UN) – World Population Prospects. Available at: https://www.macrotrends.net/countries/IRL/ireland/birth-rate/Ireland/Birth Rate 1950-2020 www.macrotrends.net.

78

The Mother and Baby Home Report, 2021

Georgina Laragy

The Commission to inquire into Mother and Baby Homes and related matters published its report on 12 January 2021, following five years of work by researchers who examined the relationship between institutionalised state welfare, religious orders' management and social and cultural stigmatisation of single mothers and their children. The public outrage that led to the establishment of the Commission itself grew out of a lack of knowledge and archival evidence around the burial of almost 800 children in a septic tank in Tuam, County Galway. To understand how that happened, pathways into the Mother and Baby Homes, and the outcomes for women and children were incidental almost to the ultimate question: why were babies buried in such an ignominious manner in twentieth-century Ireland? For the women who entered those institutions, there were key moments tracked and traced through the records; their moment of entry into the homes, their departure (exit-pathways), the birth of their children, and the death of their children. Other 'events', including conception and labour, are less traceable through the archive, but the Commission's report does shine a light on these previously difficult to access areas of female experience; however, the report is problematic because the conclusions revealed in the Executive Summary and the experiences of women included in the Confidential Committee are at odds with each other.

It is valuable at this point to outline what the Executive Summary reveals about the experience of giving birth within Mother and Baby Homes. Except where medical reasons justified hospital admission, or where a maternity hospital was close by, the majority of single pregnant women, from the 1930s onwards, gave birth in the Mother and Baby Homes. It is difficult to use the Commission's statistical reports to be clear about the numbers of children born in individual homes; in many cases, particularly in Dublin and Cork in the early years of the system, women gave birth in the city's hospitals such as the Rotunda and Cork district hospital, or a Mother and Baby Home with an attached maternity unit, such as Pelletstown (Dublin) and Bessborough (Cork). In the rurally-located homes, women tended to give birth at the institution itself, such as Sean Ross Abbey (County Tipperary) and Castlepollard (County Westmeath). However, the statistical analysis conflates children's birth with their admissions, so the picture of the homes themselves as sites of birth is not terribly clear. In total, at least 57,000 children between 1922 and 1998 were born or admitted to the Mother and Baby Homes that were sampled as part of the study, but this is not the total number of children born in such institutions. Funding from the Hospitals Trust Fund enabled local authorities and religious orders to 'construct and equip the maternity units and carry out other improvements to mother and baby homes' [59]. Pelletstown and Sean Ross Abbey both had maternity units on site from the 1930s. This was, in part, because 'unmarried mothers were not welcome in county hospitals' [61]. Women in Tuam received the attention of a dispensary doctor and a midwife, and the Commission stated that this was similar to the level of care accessible to Irish women who birthed at home [80]. Later in the Executive Summary, it furthered this point, that the majority of Irish women in the first half of the twentieth century gave birth in their homes, attended by midwives and 'untrained handywomen' [244]. Placing the birthing conditions of the state-funded Mother and Baby Homes in contrast to home births was a deliberate strategy on the part of the Commission, showing that the 'care' offered in the homes was no different to what might be accessed from a woman or girl's own home. This echoes the strategy of the Poor Law Commissioners who created the Irish workhouse system in the 1830s; that the conditions in the Irish workhouse should not be any better than those available in the homes of the poor. In suggesting that the conditions in Mother and Baby Homes, in terms of access to doctors and sterilised medical equipment, was an improvement on a woman's actual home attempts to paint these homes in a positive light. The Commissioners also sought to offer a contrast between the Mother and Baby Homes and the county homes (the twentieth-century term for the Victorian workhouses) to which many pregnant girls and women were sent, with county homes being described as 'ill-equipped and often insanitary' [260]. However, the extent to which the 'care' received in Mother and Baby Homes was preferable to a homebirth with a handywoman is put into sharp relief by the evidence from the Confidential Committee. Mother and Baby Homes were considered preferable to the mother's home, where medical treatment was not available. These homes were considered preferable to maternity hospitals where single women who gave birth were subjected to 'unfriendly comments by fellow-patients and their visitors' [17].

A key point in the Executive Summary is no. 245 which details the evidence of medical care during and after labour. The Commission concluded that there was no evidence that women giving birth in these homes were denied pain relief. This contrasts with evidence revealed in the Confidential Committee. It also concludes that there is evidence of women 'being stitched following birth', suggesting a degree of access to medical treatment unavailable to women who laboured at home. However, while the Confidential Committee reveals instances of stitching, the quality of that stitching and the purpose with which it was conducted is absent from the conclusions in the Executive Summary and it is that qualitative, experiential information that reveals a punitive and traumatic environment in which women laboured. Finally, the Commission did conclude that 'women may have been left without qualified nursing care during the early stages of labour, especially at night' [245]. In the matter of giving birth, 'It appears that there was little kindness shown to them and this was particularly the case when they were giving birth' [16]. Many women had a traumatic experience. The overwhelming majority were first-time mothers, and they were probably uninformed about childbirth. First-time childbirth can be frightening for any woman; it was undoubtedly worse for women whose pregnancy had devastated their normal life and resulted in their removal from home, family and friends. The trauma of childbirth must have been especially difficult for the many women who had no prospect of keeping their child [17].

The section of the Confidential Committee's report which deals with the moment of birth is nineteen pages out of a total of 190 pages; those nineteen pages of evidence amount to less than 1 percent of the entire 2,865-page report. Under the Commission's Terms of Reference, the Confidential Committee was to hear from former residents of the institutions and enable them 'to provide accounts of their experience in these institutions in writing or orally as informally as is possible in the circumstances'. The report that was produced was to be 'of a general nature' (Confidential Committee, p. 5). In June 2021, one of the Commissioners revealed that the evidence heard in the Confidential Committee had not been considered when making conclusions that went into the Executive Summary. This was because the information was not taken in an evidentially robust way and privilege was given to archival and documentary historical evidence rather than oral evidence. The women who spoke with the Confidential Committee were not aware of this at the time. Despite this apparent legal difficulty, the Commission concluded the Confidential Committee's report by stating that 'the depth and honesty of what witnesses revealed to the Committee about what had happened to them having left the mother and baby homes, was startling' (p. 190). While historians, legal scholars and others have questioned the methods by which the evidence heard in the Confidential Committee was taken, largely because it did not provide adequate support to witnesses or adopt recognised professional practices of taking oral historical evidence, the startling contradiction between the testimony of women who gave of their time and their life stories and experiences and the conclusions put forward in the Executive Summary, deserves attention.

The birth of a child in modern times typically produces a number of historical records; chief amongst them is the birth certificate, detailing the name of the child, the date and place of birth, mother's and father's names, the occupation of the father and the informant to the registrar. Other records emerge from the medicalisation of maternity and the ante- and post-natal treatment of women by doctors, midwives and nurses via the GP and hospital systems.

Alongside the official and medical records that a birth produces, the experiences of women in labour are often not accessible to the historian.

The Report of the Confidential Committee of the Mother and Baby Homes Commission of Investigation (MBHCOI) is a new addition to the historical record about how women experienced labour and birth in twentieth-century Ireland. This is a 'general' report arising from the testimony of 304 mothers who gave birth in the homes or hospitals. It is organised according to decade, presumably in the hope that it would demonstrate change over time. The last story included refers to 'kindnesses' shown to a young mother whose baby had died at birth sometime in the 1980s. She had been made to travel to the hospital alone when she went into labour. The individual experiences, that preceded this young woman's experience, detail unimaginable cruelties and while they may not be representative of the birth experiences of the majority of women in modern Ireland, they provide evidence of systemic abuse of single mothers at the hands of nuns, nurses and doctors at a moment in their lives when they were at their most physically and emotionally vulnerable.

The section of the report entitled 'Circumstances of Pregnancy and Admission' reveals that many women who gave birth in the homes had no idea how babies were conceived. Single girls and women, for whom knowledge of sexuality and reproduction was considered evidence of promiscuity, were at a severe disadvantage when it came to giving birth; 'labour and what followed came as a shock'. The education system and their families had not equipped them adequately to protect themselves from an unwanted pregnancy; similarly, there was no education around labour even when a young woman revealed she was pregnant and sought medical care. Some women spoke of how they did not know how or from where their growing, kicking baby might emerge. For some women, they thought the baby would come out of their 'naval'; another girl spoke about how she thought it would come 'out of my backside'. The lack of knowledge about the labour and birth process mirrored quite clearly the lack of sex education that existed for women in twentieth-century Ireland. Considering that many girls and women had become pregnant as a result of rape or sexual abuse, the circumstances in which they gave birth – in the dark, alone and with no information about what to expect in many cases – likely compounded their trauma.

During their labours, women from, and in, the homes included in the study were told that the pain they were experiencing was the 'payment' for the 'pleasure' they had experienced nine months previously. Others were told to focus on a nearby Crucifix to think about the fact that 'Christ suffered on the Cross for you!', but also perhaps to reconsider their own pain in contrast to the pain of crucifixion. A 16-year-old girl who gave birth in the 1960s was told she was 'paying for … [her] … sins'. In many cases, there was no pain relief given, and by framing the natural pain of childbirth as punishment, many women likely did not understand that this was part of a normal birth, for which medical science had developed multiple measures to relieve the pain. This was in contrast to the finding in the Executive Summary.

The tendency to scream during labour was not tolerated; women were forced to remain silent in a variety of ways, through fear, by being 'slapped … across the face' and by being 'hit with a belt'. One 18-year-old was told she was an 'unclean bitch'. For one 20-year-old woman in the 1970s, the gynaecologist treating her told her that they 'wanted me to feel every pain'.

Alongside what women were told during labour, they also overheard their 'carers' discussing their own likely outcome and that of their children. In their presence, doctors and nurses and nuns discussed how women were going to die and that their babies had died; they heard doctors instruct nurses to 'strap her', and one woman heard a nun state: 'now another little piglet born into the world'.

One woman who gave birth in the 1970s believes her size meant she ought to have had a C-section ('I was tiny'); she overheard the doctor say, '… she's an unmarried mother. She can have it this way; she'll remember it and she won't ever do it again'. Appropriate medical care was withheld in this case because of the moral condemnation of the doctor in charge.

Medical practice was infused with religious and moral beliefs during this period, an issue which impacted the medical treatment of all pregnant women. However, without a broader history of childbirth in twentieth-century Ireland and an understanding of the experiences of women of all marital status, it is difficult to understand the interplay between religious and moral condemnation and compromised medical care in the case of single mothers. Nevertheless, women who gave evidence to the Confidential Committee reported lifelong medical problems because, in the aftermath of a damaging labour, doctors and nurses performed necessary medical procedures such as post-natal stitching in a way that caused permanent harm. When one woman became pregnant again later in life, the doctor who treated her then was horrified and remarked that 'maybe someone was trying to prevent you from having sex?' A 17-year-old who gave birth in the 1980s was stitched by a male nurse who remarked to his colleagues, 'she'll be tighter now than she was before'. This occurred while married women were receiving symphysiotomies in hospital settings to facilitate unrestricted pregnancy and to prevent recourse to contraception which contravened Roman Catholic teaching.

As well as compromised medical care of mothers, babies were equally victims of social medical practices. In two cases, witnesses revealed that to ensure no one suspected a pregnancy, babies were induced early.

The individuals caring for women in labour instrumentalised the natural pain of childbirth alongside medical procedures to inflict further punishment and shame on unmarried mothers and to ensure that, where possible, concealment of the pregnancy was maintained.

There has been much discussion about responsibility in the aftermath of the report's publication. The report itself places 'responsibility for that harsh treatment', experienced by women who gave birth outside marriage, at the door of 'the fathers of their children and their own immediate families'. Taoiseach Micheál Martin broadened the scope of responsibility to include 'the State, and … we as a society'. However, if we look solely at the birth process, the harsh treatment of girls and women cannot be laid at the door of the fathers or their parents. In those moments between contractions, as the baby emerged from the birth canal and during post-natal medical treatment, doctors, midwives and nuns had the opportunity to treat with dignity and kindness the women who were giving birth under their 'care'. It was the responsibility of the medical profession to 'do no harm' to their patients, both mothers and children.

It is impossible to summarise an almost 3,000-page report within a short article. In focusing on the testimonies of women who gave birth within this system, while there were 'positive witness accounts' of birth, what shines through is the unanticipated pain and trauma of labour, compounded by ill-treatment and, in some cases, wilful obstetric violence. The role of religious and medical professionals who mistreated and injured women during, and immediately after, they gave birth in Ireland's carceral archipelago still needs to be thoroughly interrogated by scholars. More important, however, is that this report is read far and wide; that these women's experiences be acknowledged by the wider public.

Further Reading:

Government of Ireland (2021), Report of the Confidential Committee of the Mother and Baby Home Commission. Available at: https://www.gov.ie/en/publication/d693a-report-of-the-confidential-committee-to-the-commission-of-investigation-into-mother-and-baby-homes-october-2020/.

Government of Ireland (2014), Report on Symphysiotomy in Ireland 1944–1984: Professor Oonagh Walsh. Available at: https://www.gov.ie/en/publication/8535fb-report-on-symphysiotomy-in-ireland-1944-1984-professor-oonagh-walsh/.

Statement of Taoiseach Micheál Martin on Commission of Investigation into Mother and Baby Homes, 13 January 2021. Available at: https://www.oireachtas.ie/en/debates/debate/dail/2021-01-13/10/.

Statement by the Oral History Network of Ireland on the Role of Oral Testimony in the Commission of Investigation into Mother and Baby Homes, 5 June 2021. Available at: https://oralhistorynetworkireland.ie/statement-re-mother-and-baby-homes-commission-june-2021.

Notes on Contributors

Keith Adams is a social policy advocate at the Jesuit Centre for Faith and Justice in Dublin.

Sharon Arbuthnot is a historical linguist and lexicographer based at the University of Cambridge and at Sabhal Mòr Ostaig, Isle of Skye.

Linda Ballard is a writer and folklorist based in Bangor, Northern Ireland.

Judy Bolger is a PhD researcher in the Department of Modern Irish History at Trinity College Dublin.

Mary Burke is a professor of English at the University of Connecticut.

Jenny Butler is a lecturer in the Study of Religions Department at University College Cork.

Angela Byrne is a historian and research associate at Ulster University.

Bairbre Cahill is a writer and facilitator with a particular interest in the spirituality of everyday life.

Leanne Calvert is a senior lecturer in History at the University of Hertfordshire.

Denis Casey is a medieval historian who teaches at Maynooth University.

Caitriona Clear lectures in history at the National University of Ireland, Galway.

Chelsey Collins is a doctoral researcher in the Department of Early Irish, Maynooth University.

Patrick Comerford is an Anglican priest in the Diocese of Limerick and a former adjunct assistant professor at Trinity College Dublin.

Meredith Cutrer is a DPhil candidate in medieval history at Worcester College, University of Oxford.

Eamon Darcy is a historian of early modern Ireland who teaches at Maynooth University.

Cara Delay is a professor of history at the College of Charleston, South Carolina.

Katrina Dernelley is a PhD candidate in history at La Trobe University, Melbourne, Australia.

Terence Dooley is professor of history at Maynooth University, where he is also director of the Centre for the Study of Historic Irish Houses and Estates.

Elaine Pereira Farrell is a medievalist working as research fellow and grant manager at the School of Nursing and Midwifery, Trinity College Dublin.

Deirdre Foley is a historian with a particular interest in birth control and the legal status of women in twentieth-century Ireland. She is Roy Foster Irish Government Research Fellow at Hertford College, University of Oxford.

Fiona Gallagher is a post doctoral researcher at Dublin City University, where she is conducting an IRC funded study, mapping the extent of the 1832 cholera epidemic in Irish provincial towns

Philomena Gorey is a historian of childbirth and midwifery history in Ireland particularly the regulation of Irish midwives from *c.* 1615 to the Midwives (Ireland) Act 1918.

Lorraine Grimes is a postdoctoral researcher at Maynooth University.

Louise Halpenny works as a medical doctor in Dublin and is in training to provide GP, hypnobirthing, doula and breastfeeding services in her local community.

Eugenie Hanley is a PhD student in history at University College Cork.

Kevin Hargaden is the director and social theologian at the Jesuit Centre for Faith and Justice in Dublin.

Ciara Henderson is a writer and social scientist researching death, bereavement and burial with a specific interest in stillbirth and baby loss in the nineteenth and twentieth centuries.

Patrick Hughes is a writer and YouTuber. He has a specific interest in LGBTQ matters, travel and culture. He is the editor of www.planetpatrick.net.

Martina Hynan is a maternal artist/birth activist based in Ennis, County Clare and a PhD researcher with the Centre for Irish Studies, National University of Ireland Galway.

Laurence Kirkpatrick is a former senior lecturer in the Institute of Theology, Queen's University Belfast.

Joan G. Lalor is a professor of midwifery at Trinity College Dublin and Chair of the EU COST Action DEVOTION CA18211 which is a multidisciplinary pan-European Research Network dedicated to minimising birth trauma and optimising birth experiences.

Georgina Laragy is Dublin Cemeteries Trust Assistant Professor in Public History and Cultural Heritage at Trinity College Dublin.

Patricia Lysaght is *emerita* professor of European ethnology and folklore, University College Dublin.

Máirín MacCarron is a historian and lecturer in digital humanities at University College Cork.

Carolann Madden is a postdoctoral researcher at Maynooth University, and recipient of a Fulbright to the National University of Ireland, Galway for her research on early folklore collecting in the West of Ireland.

Olivia Martin completed a PhD in history at the National University of Ireland, Galway in 2020.

Megan McAuley is a PhD student at the Department of History, Maynooth University.

Brendan McConvery, CSsR, is a Redemptorist priest, author and editor. He taught Scripture for many years at St Patrick's College Maynooth.

Nell McDonagh holds a master's degree from Dublin City University and has an interest in the Traveller community and cultural issues and Traveller history.

Marion McGarry is a lecturer in the Galway Mayo Institute of Technology.

Valerie McGowan-Doyle is professor of history and co-ordinator of the Women's, Gender and Sexuality Studies programme at Lorain County Community College.

David Murphy is lecturer in Military History & Strategic Studies at the Department of History, Maynooth University.
Sylvia Murphy-Tighe is a lecturer in midwifery at the University of Limerick.

Caoimhe Ní hÉalaithe is a doctor working in Cork University Hospital, whose early areas of interest include obstetrics and palliative care.

Síle Ní Mhurchú is a lecturer in the Department of Modern Irish, University College Cork.

Daniel Nuzum is a healthcare chaplain and clinical pastoral education supervisor at Cork University Hospital and lecturer at University College Cork.

Colmán Ó Clabaigh, OSB, is a medieval historian and monk of Glenstal Abbey, County Limerick.

Maeve Anne O'Connell is a senior lecturer in midwifery, in the School of Healthcare Sciences, College of Biomedical and Life Sciences, Cardiff University.

Keelin O'Donoghue is a professor of obstetrics and gynaecology at Cork University Maternity Hospital and University College Cork.

Pádraig Ó Héalaí is a retired senior lecturer at the School of Irish, National University of Ireland, Galway.

Thomas O'Loughlin is a professor emeritus of historical theology at the University of Nottingham.

Pádraig Ó Macháin is professor of modern Irish at University College Cork.

Maeve O'Riordan is a lecturer in women's and cultural history at University College Cork.

Roy K. Philip is a consultant neonatologist at University Maternity Hospital Limerick and Medical School University of Limerick, Ireland. E. Moore Quinn is a professor of anthropology at the College of Charleston, South Carolina.

Jennifer Redmond is an assistant professor in twentieth-century Irish history at the Department of History, Maynooth University.

Joe Regan is a history PhD graduate of the National University of Ireland, Galway.

Ciarán Reilly is a historian of nineteenth- and twentiethcentury Irish history at the Arts & Humanities Institute, Maynooth University.

Salvador Ryan is a professor of ecclesiastical history at St Patrick's College Maynooth.

Brendan Scott is manager of the Irish Family History Foundation and teaches history at Maynooth University.

Diarmuid Scully is a lecturer at the School of History, University College Cork.

Yvonne Seale is an assistant professor of medieval history at the State University of New York at Geneseo.

Damian Shiels is the managing editor of www.irishamericancivilwar.com and the author of two books on the Irish experience of that conflict.

Michelle Sutton-Ryan is a full-time mother of four, and a member of Wellmama Doulas Ireland, with a passion for helping women feeling supported and cared for during pregnancy, labour, birth and parenthood.

Clodagh Tait is a lecturer in the Department of History, Mary Immaculate College, University of Limerick.

Sonja Tiernan is the Eamon Cleary Professor of Irish Studies and co-director of the Centre for Irish & Scottish Studies at the University of Otago, New Zealand.

Fionnuala Walsh is an assistant professor of modern Irish history in the School of History at University College Dublin.

Marie Whelton is a lecturer in Irish language and literature at the Marino Institute of Education, Dublin.

Niamh Wycherley is a lecturer in medieval history in the Department of Early Irish, Maynooth University.

Natalie Wynn is a postdoctoral researcher affiliated to the Herzog Centre for Jewish and Near Eastern Religions and Culture, Trinity College Dublin.